BF 692.2 .P73 2004

Praeger guide to the
psychology of gender

DATE DUE

Praeger Guide
to the
Psychology of Gender

Praeger Guide
to the
Psychology of Gender

Edited by
Michele A. Paludi

 PRAEGER

Westport, Connecticut
London

Library of Congress Cataloging-in-Publication Data

Praeger guide to the psychology of gender / edited by Michele A. Paludi.
   p. cm.
   Includes bibliographical references and index.
   ISBN 0–275–98244–0 (alk. paper)
   1. Sex differences (Psychology)   I. Title: Guide to the psychology of gender.   II.
Paludi, Michele Antoinette.
   BF692.2.P73 2004
   155.3'3—dc22   2004014774

British Library Cataloguing in Publication Data is available.

Library of Congress Catalog Card Number: 2004014774
ISBN: 0–275–98244–0

First published in 2004

Praeger Publishers, 88 Post Road West, Westport, CT 06881
An imprint of Greenwood Publishing Group, Inc.
www.praeger.com

Printed in the United States of America

The paper used in this book complies with the
Permanent Paper Standard issued by the National
Information Standards Organization (Z39.48–1984).

10 9 8 7 6 5 4 3 2 1

In loving memory of
Sue Rosenberg Zalk
for her
advocacy, commitment, and graciousness.
The field of the psychology of gender, and its scholars,
owe a tremendous appreciation to her and her work.

Contents

Acknowledgments

I wish to thank the following family members, friends, and colleagues for their support and encouragement during the preparation of this guide: Rosalie Paludi, Lucille Paludi, Carmen A. Paludi, Jr., Darlene DeFour, Paula Lundberg-Love, and Rudy Nydegger.

I also thank Debbie Carvalko at Greenwood Publishing Group for her dedication to this guide and for being a caring editor. Debbie is most inspiring!

Many thanks to Elizabeth Potenza at Greenwood. I am especially appreciative of her commitment to developing a series on women's psychology for this publishing house.

The dedication and hard work of Karyn Slutsky and Beth Wilson have made this book better. My thanks to them, too.

The contributors to this guide deserve my appreciation for the work they have done to promote gender equity in their research, teaching, and advocacy. I have been honored to be their colleague and friend, and to collaborate with them throughout the years. Some I met while an undergraduate or graduate student; others, as colleagues teaching courses on the psychology of gender and the psychology of women. I've met some for the first time in completing this book. It is a good feeling to see research on the psychology of gender being furthered by the graduate students and junior faculty who contributed chapters to this guide. Each of the contributors to this guide has influenced my own thinking about the psychology of gender. I thank you.

Finally, I wish to acknowledge my parents, Antoinette Peccichio Paludi and Michael Paludi, who taught me to see the "ties that bind, not only the lines that divide." This is your book.

Introduction: *Plus ça change, plus c'est la même chose* (The more things change, the more they stay the same)

Michele A. Paludi, Carmen A. Paludi, Jr., and Darlene C. DeFour

Why Another Book about Gender?

Throughout the preparation of the *Praeger Guide to the Psychology of Gender,* gender issues received prominent attention in national politics, Hollywood and made-for-television movies, and federal legislation. For example:

The fortieth anniversary of the Civil Rights Act was celebrated. Title VII of this act deals with prohibiting discrimination against employees on the basis of sex, race, age, religion, color, or national origin.

The Massachusetts high court ruled that full, equal marriage rights for gay couples are constitutional, and that any civil unions that fall short of marriage would establish an "unconstitutional, inferior, and discriminatory status for same-sex couples."

Federal legislation either passed or introduced included the following:

Women in Trauma Act of 2003

Hate Crimes Prevention Act of 2003

Eating Disorders Awareness, Prevention and Education Act of 2003

Violence against Women Civil Rights Restoration Act of 2003

Runaway, Homeless, and Missing Children Protection Act of 2003.

Movies and television programs dealt with gender issues as well. For example:

Iron Jawed Angels

Matrubhoomi, a Nation without Women

Mona Lisa Smile

Calendar Girls

Normal

Angels in America

The Hours

Frida

Whale Rider

New scholarly books on gender included the following:

Fat Talk: What Girls and Their Parents Say about Dieting, by Mimi Nichter

Women and Men as Friends: Relationships across the Lifespan in the 21st Century, by Michael Monsour

The Spectacle of Violence: Homophobia, Gender, and Knowledge, by Gail Mason

Voicing Chicana Feminisms: Young Women Speak Out on Sexuality and Identity, by Aida Hurtado

Gender, Work, Stress, and Health, edited by Debra Nelson and Ronald Burke

Speaking from the Heart: Gender and the Social Meaning of Emotion, by Stephanie Shields.

2002 was the first year in our history that women earned the majority of research doctorates awarded to U.S. citizens.

By January 2003, twenty-three women had served as governors of nineteen states.

In 2004 the Food and Drug Administration rejected the approval for silicone breast implants, noting the danger to women's health.

Even a cursory glance at the news headlines, movies, books, and legislation related to gender issues in the last few years would lead most of us to ask, "Why another book about gender?" The attention paid to gender makes us believe that equality has been reached; that discrimination is no longer present in economics, politics, the family, and education; and that gender is a central, not a marginal, construct.

While it is true that many gains for women and men have been made in health research, policy making, and educational and occupational attainment, these headlines during the past few years need to be tempered with other statistics that suggest equality between men and women has not been realized, that women and men are not valued equally. For example:

Women's pay gap in 2003 was actually wider than it was twenty years earlier, according to the National Association for Female Executives. Women earn 79.7 cents for every dollar paid to men, versus 80.4 cents in 1983. Women of color earn substantially less than white women.

According to the Department of Justice, approximately 700,000 incidents of intimate partner violence occurred in 2001, with women more likely to be victims than men.

The Equal Employment Opportunity Commission, the federal agency charged with implementing Title VII of the 1964 Civil Rights Act, received 84,442 complaints of workplace discrimination in 2002, 5 percent more than in 2001.

The American Association of University Women reported that 81 percent of students experience some form of sexual harassment during their school lives, with 85 percent of students reporting sexual harassment by their peers and 38 percent by teachers or other school employees.

Women's roles in Hollywood movies were closely tied to their sexuality only: Renée Zellweger's role in *Chicago,* Julianne Moore's character in *Far from Heaven,* Salma Hayek's portrayal of Frida Kahlo in *Frida,* and Diane Lane's character in *Unfaithful.*

According to the U.S. Department of Justice, homicide is the most frequent cause of death of women employees in the workplace.

According to the National Science Foundation, the participation of women in science and engineering higher education continues, but their involvement is not equivalent to their representation among eighteen to thirty year olds in the U.S. population.

Thirty percent of all women are battered at least once in their adult lives; 20 percent have been a victim of childhood sexual abuse; 25 percent have been raped; and 50 percent have been sexually harassed by a teacher, employer, or co-worker (e.g., Golge et al., 2003; Nayak et al., 2003; Paludi & Paludi, 2003; Walker, 1999).

We may be reluctant to believe that discrimination against individuals because of their sex, race, age, sexual orientation, or health status still exists in institutions in most countries. We also may not want to accept the fact that sexual violence is common in all cultures; that women are victims of rape, battering, and sexual harassment each day, despite legislation prohibiting such violence, community policing, workplace policies, counseling, and training programs. Yet this is the reality for most women.

Even students participating in courses on the psychology of gender often initially express disbelief when confronted with these sobering statistics. They believe that discrimination is no longer present in politics, economics, the family, or education. They also claim to have no stereotypes about women and men, and to perceive and treat both sexes equally.

One of the authors of this chapter (Michele Paludi) has frequently used the following riddle on the opening day of her course on the psychology of gender when she hears students voicing such opinions. You may be familiar with the riddle, which was in one of the opening scenes of the movie *Tin Cup*:

> One afternoon, a man and his son go for a drive through the country-side. After an hour or so they get into a terrible car crash. The father dies instantly. The son is taken by a helicopter to the nearest hospital, where a prominent surgeon is called to help save the boy's life. Immediately upon entering the operating room and looking at the boy, the surgeon exclaims, "I can't possibly operate on this boy . . . he's my son."
> How can this be?

Responses to this riddle range from "The father didn't really die—he sustained only minor injuries and could perform the surgery," to "It was the boy's stepfather who died and his biological father was the surgeon," to "The boy's adoptive father is the surgeon and his biological father was with him in the car."

Like many of the characters in the movie *Tin Cup,* students rarely solve this riddle: The surgeon is the boy's mother. Most students, when told the answer to the riddle, are shocked. Some are angry with themselves for not deriving the correct response, especially when they initially stated that they hold no stereotypes about women and men!

The fact that individuals are likely to think of a *man* when they hear the word *surgeon* illustrates how we all hold beliefs, attitudes, and stereotypes that influence our perception of the world around us. Which sex do you associate with "elementary school teacher?" with "model?" with "engineer?" Most individuals still indicate that elementary school teachers are female, models are female, and engineers are male. Individuals also "mark" the occupation if they believe the sex of the person performing this job is "atypical." For example, it is common for individuals to say "*male* model," "*female* doctor," "*male* nurse," and "*female* mathematics professor." Markings are used to alert the listener or reader to something atypical for the occupation: It is held by a person of a sex other than the one with which it is traditionally associated.

Stereotypes refer to individuals' cognitions that typically do not correspond to reality. A stereotype is a "picture in the head," not an accurate mirror of the real world (e.g., Ashmore, 1998; Deaux & Kite, 1993; Doyle & Paludi, 1998).

Stereotypes occur when individuals are classified by others as having something in common because they are members of a particular group or category of people (e.g., African Americans, men, lesbians, Greeks, women). Stereotypes have the following characteristics (e.g., Fiske, 1993; Fiske & Stevens, 1993):

1. Groups that are targeted for stereotypes are easily identified and relatively powerless.

2. There is little agreement between the composite picture of the group and its actual characteristics.

3. This misperception is difficult to modify even though individuals who hold stereotypes have interacted with members of the group who disconfirm the stereotypes.

4. This misperception is the product of a bias in individuals' information-processing mechanisms.

Gender stereotyping is a psychological process which illustrates individuals' structured sets of beliefs about the personal attributes of men and women. For example, when asked to identify what comes to mind when they think of a "typical" woman, people are likely to say "gentle," "talkative," "passive," "tactful," and "emotional." They are likely to use the following words to describe a "typical" man: "confident," "aggressive," "independent," "dominant," "worldly wise," and "unemotional" (see Sigal & Nally, this volume; DeSouza et al., this volume). People cling to gender stereotypes even though they have met and perhaps interacted with individuals who don't conform to their stereotypes (e.g., women who are independent; men who are emotional; women who are not nurturant). In addition to general gender stereotypes about women and men, people also have stereotypes about men and women of various ethnic groups (e.g., African American women are loud, African American males are athletic and violent, Asian American females and males are intelligent) (Niemann et al., 1994). Stereotypes are likely to remain resistant to change when individuals are confronted with statistics about women and men in occupations, in relationships, and in other areas.

An awareness of the contents of gender role stereotypes begins in the preschool years and is rather well-developed by the time children enter first grade (Hughes & Seta, 2003; Murnen et al., 2003; Reid & Paludi, 1993; Sczesny, 2003; see also Marmion & Lundberg-Love, this volume). Parents are among the more important socializing agents for children in shaping values, beliefs, and behaviors related to gender (Heyman & Legare, 2004; see also Marmion & Lundberg-Love, this volume). A classic study by Rubin and his colleagues (1974) illustrates that first-time parents describe their one-day-old babies in gender role stereotypic terms. For example, sons are described by fathers as "firmer, larger featured, better coordinated, more alert, stronger, and hardier" than daughters. These results are more amazing when we note that fathers made these statements during the first twenty-four hours after the birth of the children. Furthermore, children were matched for birth weight, birth length, and neonatal activity ratings.

Rubin and his colleagues, as well as other researchers, find that parents see their children in terms of gender role stereotypic behavior rather the children's actual behaviors. When the child conforms to stereotypes (e.g., girls expressing emotions, boys being aggressive), parents note this behavior; when children do not conform to stereotypic behavior, parents either ignore the behavior or punish the child for engaging in such behavior (Doyle & Paludi, 1998).

Furthermore, knowing the sex of the baby conjures up all kinds of personality characteristics and physical attributes even when these factors are not present in the child (Campenni, 1999; Wood, Desmarais, & Gugula, 2002). Parents communicate their stereotypes to children in numerous ways, such as through play (Campenni, 1999; Renk et al., 2003). Because girls are perceived as more fragile by both mothers and fathers, parents are more likely to interact and talk more with their daughters, while parents of sons are more likely to play more actively with them. In addition, parents encourage sex-appropriate activities by providing children with sex-typed toys. Boys are given building blocks, sports equipment, and model vehicles. Girls, on the other hand, are encouraged to play with dolls, doll houses, and miniature household appliances (Heyman & Legare, 2004).

The media, teachers, and a peer group also help reinforce gender roles for both sexes (see Marmion & Lundberg-Love, this volume). For example, even among six and seven year olds, there is evidence of gender stereotypes in the kinds of occupations children consider for future employment. Girls choose the occupation of nurse, teacher, or flight attendant, while boys choose police officer, truck driver, pilot, or architect. Once set, children's ranges of occupations are difficult to change (Eccles, Wigfield, & Schiefele, 1999). A stereotyped view of the world reinforces many of the common gender role stereotypes and is a factor in prompting young boys' interest in more than twice as many occupations as young girls (Levy, Sadovsky, & Troseth, 2000). Consequently, when girls reach high school, they tend to restrict their occupational aspirations. Many girls focus on jobs that bring less status, less satisfaction, and less money than the jobs that boys think about.

Additional examples of gender stereotypic beliefs held by both sexes across the life span include the following:

Girls and women are more social than boys and men.

Girls and women are more suggestible than boys and men.

Boys and men are visual; girls and women are auditory.

Girls and women have lower self-esteem than boys and men.

Boys are poor at rote learning and simple tasks.

Girls and women lack a motivation to achieve.

Boys and men are more affected by environment; girls and women, more by heredity.

However, as we will discuss in this volume, these stereotypes are not supported by empirical research in the study of gender (see McHugh & Cosgrove, this volume). There are some areas in which there are well-documented differences between the sexes. For example:

Girls have greater verbal ability than boys.

Boys excel in visual–spatial ability.

Boys excel in mathematical ability.

Males are more aggressive than females.

However, it is important to keep in mind the following with respect to these well-documented gender comparisons:

1. We are talking about averages. Thus, on the average, girls have greater verbal ability than boys. But, there are some boys who do better on tests of verbal ability than the average girl. Similarly, on the average, boys excel in visual–spatial ability. However, there are some girls who surpass the average boy on these tests.
2. These gender differences appear to account for approximately 1 percent to 5 percent of the population variance. Thus males and females are more similar than different in these areas.
3. These differences are typically found beginning in adolescence.
4. These differences are not found in studies of race and ethnicity correlates of these behaviors.

As McHugh and Cosgrove state in chapter 8 of this volume, "what we measure for determines what we find. Hence, it is not surprising that often when researchers measure for gender differences, they 'find' them. But these 'findings' of gender difference should not be interpreted as 'objective,' 'true,' or 'universal.' "

When differences are found, they are typically explained not by biology, but by culture and learning (Doyle & Paludi, 1998). In this volume we will use the term *sex difference* only when referring to specifically biologically explained differences (e.g., reproductive differences) and will use the term *gender difference* only when discussing the differences attributable to social, psychological, and cultural aspects (Doyle & Paludi, 1998).

As Ethel Tobach states in chapter 12 of this volume: "Sex is differentiated from gender to elucidate how the similarities and differences between women and men develop, without placing all explanations in biology or culture."

Despite the fact there are a number of self-help books, seminars, and talk shows that are based on the premises that men and women are more different than alike, and that both sexes have to overcome these differences in order to truly enjoy relationships, such a premise is not based on the scientific literature. What the scientific research reveals is that there are more similarities between the sexes than there are differences.

The research also indicates that individuals respond differently to males and females; that they in fact believe in gender differences—what Unger (1979) refers to as "the illusion of gender differences."

Finally, research indicates that men and women respond the way they think people of their sex are supposed to respond, thus engaging in stereotypical behavior, especially in romantic relationships.

Features of the *Praeger Guide to the Psychology of Gender*

Michele Paludi invited researchers, therapists, consultants, and educators to contribute to this volume. Each of the individuals she contacted has published extensively in areas related to the psychology of gender. Some of the contributors are educators; others are therapists; some are management consultants. Graduate students were also included as contributors. The contributors were not provided with any structure to their chapter or suggestions for content except to (1) take a cultural perspective on their work and (2) integrate research and theories for a general audience as well as academicians. Contributors were provided only with a sample chapter title. Thus, they were left to discuss the psychology of gender as they themselves see this field of study and practice.

What emerged from this approach are chapters that are interrelated; contributors highlighted several major themes in the psychology of gender that overlapped all topics, whether it be male and female friendships, romantic relationships, salaries, parental socialization, gendered violence, or interpersonal communication. These overlapping themes are addressed below.

Cultural Socialization of Gender Roles

Margaret Mead wrote the following regarding the socialization of gender roles:

> Many, if not all, of the personality traits which we have called masculine or feminine are as lightly linked to sex as are the clothing, the manners and the form of head-dress that a society at a given period assigns to either sex. . . . The evidence is overwhelming in favor of the strength of social conditioning.

All cultures prescribe certain behaviors, attitudes, and beliefs for girls, boys, women, and men. These prescriptions comprise the *gender norms*. The gender norms taken collectively constitute the *gender roles*. Thus, gender norms are the prescriptive guidelines that form the gender roles.

There are distinct gender norms for each sex. For example, Nancy Felipe Russo (1976) identified a primary gender role for women: the motherhood mandate. She noted that young girls are encouraged to play with dolls, since this is perceived by adults to be an important way for little girls to learn appropriate nurturant behaviors that will assist them in their adult lives as mothers. Thus, having a baby and mothering can be seen as the central feature or gender norm of a woman's life and the core of her identity as an individual, a prominent theme in the movie *Mona Lisa Smile*.

On the other hand, men's gender norms do not focus on the elements of parenting and marriage. Fathering does not carry the same impact for the man's identity as mothering does for the woman's (Doyle, 1995). Brannon (1976) and Doyle (1995) identified the following men's gender norms:

No Sissy Stuff: The stigma of all stereotyped feminine characteristics and qualities, including openness and vulnerability

The Big Wheel: Success, status, and the need to be looked up to

The Sturdy Oak: A manly air of toughness, confidence, and self-reliance

Give 'Em Hell: The aura of aggression, violence, and daring (Brannon, 1976, p. 12).

Doyle (1995) added another male gender norm, the *sexual element.* Sexual conquest is for many men one of the strongest proofs of masculinity.

Many men see themselves as the initiators of sex, whereas most women define themselves in terms of being objects of sexual advances. Thus, sexual conquest is considered to be a gender norm for men, not for women (Doyle & Paludi, 1998).

Not all women and men continuously fulfill all the prescriptive gender norms placed on them. In addition, some gender norms are cultural universals. Shelly Marmion and Paula Lundberg-Love describe in chapter 1 of this volume how children learn gender norms from parents and peer groups across the life span. They discuss parental impact on children's play behavior and children's development of independence and assertiveness. They also review the research on the impact of maternal employment on children's development of gender roles. Marmion and Lundberg-Love emphasize the importance of socialization as the primary means a group uses to teach the young what is expected of them.

These findings are discussed further by Janet Sigal and Maureen Nally in chapter 2 of this volume, on cultural perspectives on gender, including factors affecting the development of gender roles (e.g., degree of modernization of a culture and socialization of children). While we may have a tendency to think that women's and men's relationships are similar the world over, cultural researchers have noted that gender roles vary considerably in different parts of the world. However, most cultures exhibit certain universal patterns of men's and women's relationships, such as division of labor and varying degrees of male dominance.

Sigal and Nally also discuss the role that culture and gender roles play in spousal abuse. In addition they review several immigrant communities, including Asian and Latina communities. Eros DeSouza, John Baldwin, Silvia Koller, and Martha Narvaz continue this discussion in chapter 3, offering a Latin American perspective on the study of gender. DeSouza and his colleagues discuss the problems in defining women only as wives and mothers, which fosters dependency, a major part of patriarchal dominance. Further, men in Latin American communities hold beliefs concerning sexual victimization and believe violence is a form of conflict resolution. DeSouza and his colleagues conclude:

[I]f we are to have a world that values every individual as a human being, we need to develop an interdisciplinary and cross-cultural perspective to address all social inequalities. . . . The progress of women (and men) in Brazil is also tied to the progress of women (and men) in other Latin American countries as well as in North America, because we are part of a global village linked together by interdependent economies, technologies, and societies.

Defining Women and Men When Fulfilling and Not Fulfilling Social and Sexual Scripts

Donna Castañeda and Alyson Burns-Glover continue the discussion of this theme of socialization of gender roles in chapter 4 of this volume by discussing the interface among gender, sexuality, and intimate relationships. They point out that "sexuality . . . is never just a personal act; it is a reflection of many elements that come together to influence behavior." Castañeda and Burns-Glover address cultural diversity in gender and sexual orientation, the sexual double standard, and sexual desire. They also discuss the fact that sexual scripts (i.e., schemas about the ways sexual encounters are to unfold that are used by individuals to guide their own behavior in sexual relationships) are influenced by the socialization of femininity and masculinity.

The impact of gender role socialization on sexual satisfaction is also addressed by Castañeda and Burns-Glover. They conclude:

> For girls the recognition of, and a sense of entitlement to, sexual desire may be difficult in a social and cultural context that, while it highly sexualizes and objectifies women's bodies, allows little room for them to fully articulate, seek, and experience sexual pleasure. In many ways, as women grow and mature, they struggle to come to terms with this contradiction in their own sexual lives.

Rudy Nydegger, in chapter 5 of this volume, on gender and mental health, also discusses this issue of control and autonomy over one's life. He notes that stereotypes abound about women having more mental disorders than men. Nydegger points out, however, that empirical research does not support this stereotype; in fact, "there is little gender difference in overall rate of mental illness, with men having a slightly higher lifetime rate." He also notes that men and women who deviate from cultural gender norms are labeled "crazy" or "bad." Furthermore, women have been socialized to believe it is acceptable to be "emotional," while men have been taught the opposite. Women who are emotionally expressive may be perceived as disturbed. If they are taught and encouraged to express their emotions, and they express feelings of sadness or sorrow, individuals may conclude that women are more readily predisposed to mental illness.

Like Sigal and Nally and DeSouza et al., Nydegger discusses the fact that women's unequal social position and their greater likelihood to experience certain trauma-producing events (e.g., rape) may precipitate emotional problems.

This theme is further discussed in chapter 11 of this volume by Jean E.

Denious and her colleagues, who explore the relationship between an individual's sex and health problems that develop throughout the life span. For example, men's being more apt to experience health problems holds true from birth to old age. The death rate for American men is higher than that for women in every decade of life. Women have an overall life expectancy that surpasses that of men at every age, regardless of race (Klonoff, Landrine, & Scott, 1995). On average, women visit physicians more often than men and are more likely to be admitted to hospitals and spend more days in a hospital than men.

Lung cancer now surpasses breast cancer as the leading cause of death for women. In adulthood, the mortality rates for men exceed those of women for most disorders, especially heart disease, cancer, accidents, and chronic pulmonary disease (Travis, 1993). The highest male-to-female death ratios occur for AIDS (approximately eight times more men than women), suicide (approximately four times more men), homicide (three times more men), accidents (twice as many men), and chronic liver disease (twice as many men).

Negative effects of socialization practices of boys and men have been linked to males' increased vulnerability to health problems (Klonoff et al., 1995). Anxiety associated with conforming to the masculine gender role, including the emphasis on competitiveness and achievement, may lead to development of compensatory behaviors that are hazardous to men's health, such as violence, smoking, excessive consumption of alcohol, drug abuse, and risk-taking behavior. Thus physical health is a social as well as a biomedical issue.

Susan Basow, in chapter 6 of this volume, on gender in the classroom, discusses another social institution that helps shape our views of what girls, boys, women, and men "should be like": education. Basow reviews the "hidden curriculum" in classrooms (i.e., what is being conveyed to girls and boys that reflects the culture's expectations about gender roles). Her review echoes the work by Myra Sadker and David Sadker (1994), who offered the following "snapshots" of an elementary school classroom:

Snapshot #1   Tim answers a question.
Snapshot #2   The teacher reprimands Alex.
Snapshot #3   Judy and Alice sit with hands raised while Brad answers a question.
Snapshot #4   Sally answers a question.
Snapshot #5   The teacher praises Marcus for skill in spelling.
Snapshot #6   The teacher helps Sam with a spelling mistake.
Snapshot #7   The teacher compliments Alice on her neat paper.
Snapshot #8   Students are in lines for a spelling bee. Boys are on one side of the room and girls are on the other. (p. 42)

Basow, as well as Sadker and Sadker, notes that such snapshots suggest a gender message and that the classroom is actually two: one of boys in action and one of girls not in action. She notes that boys are more involved in all aspects of an elementary school classroom, from answering questions to being reprimanded, while girls are relatively invisible. Basow concludes by noting:

> Without deliberate gender equity programs and teacher intervention, these messages will continue to be sent, often via the hidden curriculum. Such programs since the 1970s have affected the academic achievement and self-concept of girls, especially white girls, although more are needed. We also need to find ways to engage boys of all races and ethnicities in the educational enterprise, but on equal terms with girls. This task surely involves changing the cultural definition of masculinity to include equality with and respect for females. Educational achievement is not a zero-sum game, and we need both boys and girls to "win."

Deborah Tannen once quipped:

> If women speak and hear a language of connection and intimacy, while men speak and hear a language of status and independence, then communication between men and women can be like cross-cultural communication, prey to a clash of conversational styles. Instead of different dialects, it has been said they speak different genderlects.

In chapter 7 of this volume, on gender and verbal and nonverbal communication, Marianne LaFrance and Jennifer L. Harris discuss ways in which human communication has helped create a division between men and women. They focus their review on the ways in which gender stereotypes about women's and men's communication styles endure despite empirical research that reveals that actual differences in communication are more variable than stereotypes suggest. According to LaFrance and Harris:

> It appears that social contextual factors lead men and women to communicate differently in some situations and similarly in others. Men and women adopt similar communicative strategies when they are in the same role, engaged in the same task, and occupy the same status. They are more likely to demonstrate differences in line with stereotypes when gender is salient, when gender-stereotypic behavior is expected, and when men and women have different power.

LaFrance and Harris alert us to the fact that while women are often told to "communicate like a man," such behavior does not guarantee success in business, for this advice does not "provide women with the means to overcome descriptive stereotypical beliefs about gender and competency. Nor does it override prescriptive stereotypes that produce a negative response when women communicate in direct or assertive ways."

LaFrance and Harris's chapter suggests implications for interpersonal relationships discussed by DeSouza et al. and Castañeda and Burns-Glover, especially the ways in which adolescent boys and girls communicate about sexuality and sexual responsibility with their partners. Girls and boys do not share information about past or current sexual partners or practices. This is especially true with regard to the use of birth control and the prevention of sexually transmitted diseases (Amaro & Gornemann, 1992).

For many adolescents and adults, sexuality is a socially scripted activity. The expression of their sexuality is governed less by biological drives per se than by the expectations and social significance associated with certain patterns of sexual activity. This scripting is further governed by individuals' religious beliefs and ethnicity. For example, discussing sex is not typically appropriate behavior, especially for women, in many Latin American communities (Amaro & Gornemann, 1992).

Women may feel unable to assert themselves by suggesting that their partners wear a condom. As a result, they and their partners are at risk for sexually transmitted diseases as well as for pregnancy. Furthermore, if men suggest they use a condom, women may perceive them as wanting sex for pleasure—not for love or with the intention of marriage. Condoms may be seen only as a form of birth control and not as protection against sexually transmitted diseases. Use of birth control indicates deliberate sexual activity—something that many cultures disapprove of in adolescent girls but encourage and praise in adolescent boys. Individuals who feel comfortable discussing contraception are more likely to use it than those adolescents who are uncomfortable with such self-disclosure (Cunningham & Boult, 1996).

Hickman and Muehlenhard (1999) examined the ways in which women and men communicate sexual content. They reported that women and men attach different meanings to the same signal. Men reported signaling consent by using indirect nonverbal signals, statements about intoxication, and no response more frequently than women did. On the other hand, women reported using indirect verbal signals more frequently than men. Unfortunately, both women and men reported most often showing their consent to sex by making *no* response.

Placing Value on Women and Men

All of the contributors have addressed a common theme in the psychology of gender: more similarities between men and women than differences. This theme is further developed by Maureen McHugh and Lisa Cosgrove, in chapter 8 of this volume, on research methods in studying the psychology of gender. They call for a feminist orientation to conducting research that would eliminate the androcentric and antifemale biases from the study of the psychology of gender. First and foremost in this orientation is that research is viewed as taking place within a well-defined cultural and social context, never free from the concerns and values of the larger society. As Rhoda Unger (1995) noted:

> We need to begin to develop a "moral" basis for feminist psychology and its concern with diversity. To do so, we will need to move beyond our laboratory context, where issues of poverty and power are irrelevant. We will also need to leave our comfortable surroundings for much less pleasant realities so that we can better understand health coping in dire circumstances. (pp. 427–428)

In chapter 9 of this volume, on social role theory, Alice Eagly and Abigail Mitchell further discuss this perspective to help us understand gender comparisons. The main focus of this theory is its emphasis on "causes and consequences of the differential distribution of men and women into social roles within societies." Eagly and Mitchell discuss the psychology of gender as an interaction between biological differences between women and men and the cultural, ecological, and socioeconomic environment in which they were raised and now live. Eagly has applied this theory to several aspects of behavior, including leadership and partner selection preferences. In their chapter, Eagly and Mitchell apply social role theory to men's and women's sociopolitical attitudes and voting behavior, to explain why women typically vote Democratic and hold political attitudes that are more socially compassionate than men's.

"Plus ça change, plus c'est la même chose" (The more things change, the more they stay the same)

More work is needed on the individual, institutional, and societal levels to place value on both women and men. Contributors to this volume recognize that individuals don't change in a vacuum; rather, the social forces that surround them either prompt change or restrain it. Social institutions such as education, workplaces, politics, and physical health and health play a decisive role in creating the situations wherein individuals may choose to act. As Kahn and Gaeddert (1985) pointed out:

> In our society, men and women do have different status, and it is the status of women that must be improved if sex differences are to disappear and this will not be accomplished by changing perceptions or making women act more like men. (p. 141)

One way to accomplish the goals Kahn and Gaeddert recommend is to redefine the constructs typically used in studies of gender, an issue also addressed in this volume by all of the contributors. Thus, *work* needs to be redefined to include volunteer services, homemaking, and child rearing; *power* needs to be considered as a "capacity" rather than as a "thing" (Hartsock, 1983); and individuals who experience sexual violence need to be seen as "active help seekers," not as passive, helpless victims (Bowker, 1984).

This theme is echoed in chapter 10 in this volume, by William Gaeddert. Gaeddert focuses his discussion on the expression of gender in the workplace; specifically, the gender wage gap and discrimination in hiring and wage determination. He focuses on ways women and men strive to seek fairness and justice at work in terms of, among other things, salary and performance appraisals. Gaeddert concludes, "Although continued research on gender, racial, and ethnic biases is warranted, meaningful solutions are most likely to be based on political action."

Joan Chrisler and Christine Smith, in chapter 13 of this volume, note that political action is one form of feminist response to further change the psychology of gender. All of the contributors to this volume have taken a feminist perspective on their work. What is a feminist perspective? Sue Rosenberg Zalk (described in Paludi, 1992) developed the following exercise to inquire about individuals' attitudes toward feminism:

> You are at a social gathering talking to a small group of people you have just met. They all appear fairly educated, informed, and articulate. After some small talk about New York City's urban plight, the conversation turns to the accusations about gang rapes at St. Johns College and the growing realization that such incidents may be more common than previously thought. Everyone in the group agreed that it was scandalous although different motivations and explanations were attributed to the men's behavior. Finally, one of the men in the group laughed softly and stated, "I know feminists will have a field day with this, but

we can hardly generalize from the misdirected behavior of some boys trying to prove they are men, to the entire society." The nods to his comment were interrupted by the voice of one of the women. In a slightly raised voice, she announced "I am a feminist, and you are greatly underestimating the social meaning and impact of their behavior." She proceeded to explain her position. A few other women added comments, but you were most impressed with how articulate she was and the thoughtfulness of her argument.

Here are some questions to answer about this scenario:

How closely do you think the men listened to her argument?

How seriously was she taken by the men?

How closely do you think the women listened to her argument?

How seriously do you think she was taken by the women?

How assertive did the men think she was?

How assertive did the women think she was?

Do you think her behavior made her less attractive or interesting to the men?

Do you think the men found her threatening?

Do you think it mattered that she began with the words "I am a feminist"?

Why do you think she began this way?

Consider the substitution of the following sentence in the scenario. "I am not a feminist, but you are greatly underestimating the social meaning and impact of their behavior." Do you believe your answers to the questions would be different or the same? Further consider that instead of a woman making this statement, it was a man—who stated he was a feminist. Would your responses be different now?

Many individuals view the feminist woman as not being taken seriously by the men or the women. They also see her as not being listened to, as being perceived as very assertive by women and men, as not attractive, as threatening, and as not closely listened to. The woman who introduces herself as not being a feminist is viewed as being taken more seriously, as not assertive, as not threatening, as listened to, and as perceived as attractive.

Individuals, when asked to respond to the alternative in which a man identifies himself as a feminist, report that he was not listened to closely, was not taken seriously, was unassertive, was not threatening, and was unattractive. Responses from individuals who were provided the version with the man introducing his response with the words "I am not a feminist," however, were more positive; he was perceived as being listened to more closely, as taken more seriously, and as more attractive. Many individuals do not attach positive connotations to the word "feminist." Instead they list "man-hater," "angry," "militant," "lesbian," "unattractive." Feminism derivatively means *womanism*, valuing women in and of themselves. This valuing is unconditional. Women are valued for their caring, autonomy, relationships, commitment to children, nurturing of friends, education, love of family, and sexuality. Feminists believe that men and women should be economically, socially, politically, and legally equal. They also favor the social and legal changes that are necessary to achieve equality. Men as well as women may be feminists (McQuillan & Ferree, 1997).

Furthermore—a matter that Chrisler and Smith address—there are several types of feminism (Lorber, 1998). Lorber categorized feminism into three major areas: *gender-reform* feminism, *gender-resistance* feminism, and *gender-rebellion* feminism. Gender-reform feminism emphasizes similarities between women and men rather than focusing on differences between the sexes. Gender-resistance feminism holds that formal legal rights alone will not end gender inequality; male dominance is too ingrained into social relations. Gender-resistance feminists focus on how women and men are different—cognitively, socially, emotionally—and urge women to form women-centered organizations and communities. Gender-rebellion feminism looks at the interrelationships among inequalities of sex, race, ethnicity, social class, and sexual orientation.

Most individuals reject the term "feminist" when describing themselves, even though they support feminist principles. Why? Goldner's (1994) research provides some answers to this question. Her research noted that when women who hold feminist beliefs anticipate a negative reaction from their peers to the label "feminist," they will avoid using the term as a self-label. Goldner (1994) identifies the media as a primary source of negative images of feminists. It is common for newscasters, while discussing feminists, to accompany the text with photos of women only, and of women who have clenched fists and are yelling. These women are also shown as alone—without men. These images of feminists are rejected by many individuals, especially adolescent and young adult women, who are in the throes of identity development, in which the peer group and peer approval are important to their sense of self-esteem and self-concept.

Another answer to the "why" question we posed is that many younger women wish to view themselves as in control, as powerful, not as victims of injustice. They believe the term "feminist" implies a powerless position, something they reject (Rhode, 1997). In addition, many women of color continue to perceive feminism as a white women's movement that does not adequately address their concerns. Feminism is seen as a movement that does not deal with the experience of living with simultaneous multiple oppressions.

Chrisler and Smith note that taking courses on gender and reading books about the psychology of gender certainly have had an impact on the number of women and men who work toward feminist causes. Taking these courses and reading such texts are positively correlated with more positive gender role attitudes and behavior, including treating both sexes with respect and dignity. To answer the question posed at the beginning of this introduction, this is why another book on gender is needed.

We invite you to read the *Praeger Guide to the Psychology of Gender* in which each of the contributors encourages all of us to think critically about the psychology of gender, to value cultural experiences, and to integrate our knowledge of research and theories about the psychology of gender with our own life experiences. As Ethel Tobach reminds us:

> If the societal motivation for the research questions is designed to relate to policies and practices so that equity is possible for women and men, the relative valence of all process is important. To begin to understand the development of gender, questions asked about biochemical/physiological processes need to be answered as well as those about psychosocial/societal processes: education, training, family, and peer activities. Such research is demanding and challenging; but the demands and the challenges need to be met if the societal goal is to be achieved.

References

Amaro, H., & Gornemann, I. (1992). HIV/AIDS. Reported in Amarao, H. (1995). Love, sex and power: Considering women's realities in HIV prevention. *American Psychologist, 50,* 437–447.

Ashmore, R. (1998). Taking and developing pictures: Assessing the physical stereotypes of eight gender types. *Journal of Applied Social Psychology, 28,* 1611–1638.

Bowker, L. (1984). Coping with wife abuse: Personal and social networks. In A. R. Roberts (Ed.), *Battered women and their families* (pp. 168–191). New York: Springer.

Brannon, R. (1976). The male sex-role: Our culture's blueprint of manhood, and what it's done for us lately. In D. David & R. Brannon (Eds.), *The forty-nine percent majority: The male sex role.* Reading, MA: Addison-Wesley.

Campenni, C. (1999). Gender stereotyping of children's toys: A comparison of parents and nonparents. *Sex Roles, 40,* 121–138.

Cunningham, P., & Boult, B. (1996). Black teenage pregnancy in South Africa: Some considerations. *Adolescence, 31,* 691–700.

Deaux, K., & Kite, M. (1993). Gender stereotypes. In F. L. Denmark & M. Paludi (Eds.), *Psychology of women: Handbook of issues and theories.* Westport, CT: Greenwood Press.

Doyle, J. (1995). *The male experience* (3rd ed.). Madison, WI: Brown & Benchmark.

Doyle, J., & Paludi, M. (1998). *Sex & gender: The human experience* (4th ed.). Boston: McGraw-Hill.

Eccles, J. S., Wigfield, A., & Schiefele, U. (1999). Motivation to succeed. In N. Eisenberg (Ed.), *Handbook of child psychology,* Vol. 3, *Social, emotional and personality development* (pp. 1017–1095). New York: Wiley.

Fiske, S. (1993). Controlling other people: The impact of power on stereotyping. *American Psychologist, 48,* 621–628.

Fiske, S., & Stevens, L. (1993). What's so special about sex? Gender stereotyping and discrimination. In S. Oskamp & M. Costanzo (Eds.), *Gender issues in contemporary society* (pp. 173–196). Newbury Park, CA: Sage.

Goldner, M. (1994). Accounting for race and class variation in the disjuncture between feminist identity and feminist beliefs: The place of negative labels and social movements. Paper presented at the Annual Meeting of the American Sociological Association, Los Angeles.

Golge, Z., Yavuz, M., Muderrisoglu, S., & Yavuz, M. (2003). Turkish university students' attitudes toward rape. *Sex Roles, 49,* 653–661.

Hartsock, N. (1983). *Money, sex, and power: Toward a feminist historical materialism.* New York: Longman.

Heyman, G., & Legare, C. (2004). Children's beliefs about gender differences in the academic and social domains. *Sex Roles, 50,* 227–239.

Hickman, S. E., & Muehlenhard, C. L. (1999). "By the semi-mystical appearance of a condom": How young women and men communicate sexual consent in heterosexual situations. *Journal of Sex Research, 36,* 258–272.

Hughes, F., & Seta, C. (2003). Gender stereotypes: Children's perceptions of future compensatory behavior following violations of gender roles. *Sex Roles, 49,* 685–691.

Kahn, A., & Gaeddert, W. (1985). From theories of equity to theories of justice: The liberating consequences of studying women. In V. E. O'Leary, R. K. Unger, & B. S. Wallston (Eds.), *Women, gender and social psychology* (pp. 129–148). Hillsdale, NJ: Erlbaum.

Klonoff, E., Landrine, H., & Scott, J. (1995). Double jeopardy: Ethnicity and gender in health research. In H. Landrine (Ed.), *Bringing cultural diversity to feminist psychology: Theory, research and practice* (pp. 335–360). Washington, DC: American Psychological Association.

Levy, G., Sadovsky, A., & Troseth, G. (2000). Aspects of young children's perceptions of gender-typed occupations. *Sex Roles, 42,* 993–1006.

McQuillan, J., & Marx Ferree, M. (1997). The importance of variation among husbands and the benefits of feminism for families. In A. Booth (Ed.), *Men in families* (pp. 213–225). Mahwah, NJ: Erlbaum.

Murnen, S., Smolak, L., Mills, J., & Good, L. (2003). Thin, sexy women and strong, muscular men: Grade-school children's responses to objectified images of women and men. *Sex Roles, 49,* 427–437.

Nayak, M., Byrne, C., Martin, M., & Abraham, A. (2003). Attitudes toward violence against women: A cross-nation study. *Sex Roles, 49,* 333–342.

Niemann, Y. F., Jennings, I., Rozelle, R., Baxter, J., & Sullivan, E. (1994). Use of free response and cluster analysis to determine stereotypes of eight groups. *Personality and Social Psychology Bulletin, 20,* 379–390.

Paludi, M., & Paludi, C. A. (Eds.). (2003). *Academic and workplace sexual harassment: A handbook of cultural, social science, management and legal perspectives.* Westport, CT: Praeger.

Reid, P., & Paludi, M. (1993). Psychology of women: Conception of adolescence. In F. L. Denmark & M. A. Paludi (Eds.), *Psychology of women: A handbook of issues and theories* (pp. 191–212). Westport, CT: Greenwood Press.

Renk, K., Roberts, R., Roddenberry, A., Luick, M., Hillhouse, S., Meehan, C., Oliveros, A., & Phares, V. (2003). Mothers, fathers, gender role, and time parents spend with their children. *Sex Roles, 48,* 305–315.

Rhode, D. (1997). *Speaking of sex.* Cambridge, MA: Harvard University Press.

Rubin, J. Z., Provenzano, R., & Luria, Z. (1974). The eye of the beholder: Parents' views on sex of newborns. *American Journal of Orthopsychiatry, 44,* 512–519.

Russo, N. F. (1976). The motherhood mandate. *Journal of Social Issues, 32,* 143–153.

Sadker, M., & Sadker, D. (1994). *Failing at fairness: How America's schools cheat girls.* New York: Scribner's.

Sczesny, S. (2003). A closer look beneath the surface: Various facets of the think-manager-think-male stereotype. *Sex Roles, 49,* 353–363.

Travis, C. (1993). Women and health. In F. L. Denmark & M. A. Paludi (Eds.), *Psychology of women: A handbook of issues and theories* (pp. 284–323). Westport, CT: Greenwood Press.

Unger, R. K. (1979). Toward a redefinition of sex and gender. *American Psychologist, 34,* 1085–1094.

Unger, R. K. (1995). Cultural diversity and the future of feminist psychology. In H. Landrine (Ed.), *Bringing cultural diversity to feminist psychology: Theory, research, practice* (pp. 413–431). Washington, DC: American Psychological Association.

Walker, L. (1999). Psychology and domestic violence around the world. *American Psychologist, 54,* 21–29.

Wood, E., Desmarais, S., & Gugula, S. (2002). The importance of parenting experience on gender stereotyped toy play of children. *Sex Roles, 47,* 39–49.

Zalk, S. R. Feminism. Reported in Paludi, M. (2002). *The psychology of women.* Upper Saddle River, NJ: Prentice Hall.

Chapter 1

Learning Masculinity and Femininity: Gender Socialization from Parents and Peers across the Life Span

Shelly Marmion and Paula Lundberg-Love

The Effects of Parents on Gender Socialization

The earliest information available to children regarding what it means to be female or male comes from their parents. Parents influence their children's gender socialization both directly and indirectly via their interactions with their children, their gender attitudes, and the manner in which they model gendered behavior. This section of the chapter will describe how parents impact the development of their children's gender socialization from pregnancy through puberty. Specifically, we will address parental gender role reinforcement on the play behavior of children; the assignment of their chores; the development of independence, assertiveness, and compliance; their academic achievement levels; and the exhibition of aggression. Also we will describe the effects of paternal role modeling and maternal role modeling by identifying how maternal employment, father or mother absence, and having gay or lesbian parents affect gendered behavior.

Parental Gender Preferences and Stereotypes

While early studies indicated that in nearly all cultures the parental sex preference for their first child is a boy (Basow, 1992; Hoffman, 1977; Pooler, 1991; Williamson, 1976), more recent studies suggest that in the United States and Canada such a clear-cut pattern of sex preference no longer exists (Hamilton, 1991; Marleau & Saucier, 2002; McDougall, Dewit, & Ebanks, 1999). However, in studies where a sex preference was detected, it was mediated by the sex of previous children and the gender of the parent. In families where all prior children were girls, parents were more likely to continue having children, in contrast to families with boys only (Hoffman, 1977; Pooler, 1991). Pooler (1991) also reported that in a sample of college students, 83 percent of the males and only 41 percent of the females preferred a boy, and for males that preference was a strong one.

Parents have been shown to exhibit gender stereotyping behavior as early as twenty-four hours after a child's birth. They described their boys as strong, big, active, and alert, while they described their girls as small, soft, fine-featured, and inattentive even though the baby girls were matched to the boys on size, weight, and activity level (Rubin, Provenzano, & Luria, 1974). A more recent study (Karraker, Vogel, & Lake, 1995) also found that even though newborns were objectively similar in terms of size and health, parents of girls rated them as relatively weak, fine-featured, delicate, and feminine, while parents of boys rated them as relatively strong, large-featured, hardy, and masculine. In another study parents were shown a video of a nine-month-old apparently gender-neutral child playing with a card. Then an off-screen adult took the card away and the baby cried throughout the remainder of the video. Parents who had been told that they were watching a boy, as compared to those who were told they were watching a girl, rated the baby's behavior as quite angry (Condry & Condry, 1976). Subsequently, Plant and colleagues (2000) utilized this paradigm with men and women enrolled in a childbirth education class, and found that male participants who had strong gender stereotypes about emotions provided higher anger ratings for the "boy" condition. The remaining participants provided similar ratings in both gender conditions.

Parents attend to, stimulate, and interact with infants of the same sex more than they do with infants of the opposite sex (Parke, 1979). Fathers make more trips to the hospital to visit their newborn sons, engage in more play, and display more physical affection with them (Belsky, 1979; Field, 1978; Lamb, 1979; Weinraub & Frankel, 1977). Mothers tend to imitate, talk to, and play with their infant daughters more than with their sons. Such special interest of parents for the same-sex child may enhance the attractiveness of that parent for that child, making it more likely that the child will seek out that parent as a role model and companion.

Even the bedrooms of boys and girls are stereotypically decorated differently. Researchers surveyed the bedrooms of 120 girls and boys under the age of two (Pomerleau et al., 1990). They found that girls' rooms contained dolls, children's furniture, and toys for imitative manipulation. The color pink was prominent, although the bedding in the girls' rooms was more likely to be yellow. The boys' rooms had more sports equipment, tools, and vehicles, and the colors tended to be blue, red, and white.

Parental Impact on Children's Play Behavior

Jacklin and colleagues (Jacklin, Maccoby, & Dick, 1973) suggested that by the age of one year, girls often choose a doll or a stuffed animal, while boys prefer blocks or trucks. Bussey and Bandura (1992) found that children choose to play with same-sex toys from as young as thirty months. Boys are more strongly opposed to cross-sex toys than are girls. Sometimes boys even attempt to have the "feminine" toys removed rather than ignoring them. Frey and Ruble (1992) found that boys are more likely to restrict themselves to sex-typed toys even when the cross-sex toy is more attractive. Toy preferences appear to be shaped by parents' reactions to children's play with different types of toys.

Parents interact with boys and girls differently. For the first six months, infant boys rather than girls have more physical contact with their mothers, but by the time boys are six months old, this pattern reverses and girls receive more physical and nontactile contact (Lewis, 1972). Fathers spend less time with infants, but father–infant interaction is more playful and vigorous than mother–infant interaction (Clarke-Stewart, 1978; Parke, 1979). Mothers' play with infants is more intellectually oriented, involving verbalization and games like peek-a-boo. Mothers also are more likely than fathers to use toys to stimulate infants (Clarke-Stewart, 1978; Lamb, 1979; Parke, 1979).

Fagot, Leinbach, and O'Boyle (1992) found that toddlers and preschoolers who demonstrate a more pronounced tendency to discriminate nonhuman toys in gender-stereotyped ways have mothers who initiate more gender-type play and less "other-gender"-type play with them. Research also has shown that many parents actively discourage their children's interest in toys associated with the other sex (Antill, 1987; Fagot, 1978; Lytton & Romney, 1991). Boys may be persuaded not to play house or to cook, and girls may be dissuaded from engaging in vigorous, competitive play. Some parents even have trouble following researchers' instructions to utilize toys for the opposite gender when playing with their children, and when parents engage in atypical toy play, they play less enthusiastically (Caldera, Huston, & O'Brien, 1989).

Moreover, parental tolerance for other-sex play decreases during the second year of life at a faster rate for boys than for girls (Eisenberg et al., 1985; Fagot, 1978; Fagot & Hagan, 1991; Fagot & Leinbach, 1987). Thus children learn that if they want to play with an "engaged" adult, they should select a stereotyped toy. Boys, in particular, may decide that adult approval is contingent upon "appropriate" play. Both boys and girls (three to eight years of age) tend to avoid gender-inconsistent toys, and this behavior increases with age. Boys' avoidance is greater than girls', and boys show more avoidance behavior when an adult is present than when alone (Hartup, Moore, & Sager, 1963).

But different types of play can promote different types of thinking and interaction. Playing with different types of toys encourages boys and girls to develop different skills and competencies. Playing with dolls encourages quiet, nurturant interaction with another, physical closeness, and verbal communication. Playing with sports equipment, vehicles, and building equipment promotes independent activity and/or competitive play that requires less verbal interaction. Thus researchers caution parents not to limit their children's experiences to gender-stereotyped forms of play (Basow, 1992; Fagot, 1985).

Parental Impact on Children's Work Behavior

Even when both parents work outside the home, the division of household tasks remains gender-stereotyped. Women perform a larger number of household chores than do men (Bird, 1999; Gunter & Gunter, 1990). Early research found that women employed outside the home spent about thirty-three hours on household tasks, compared with thirteen hours for employed men with children (Scarr, 1984). A more recent study (Bird, 1999) reported that this household labor gender difference still exists, while other research suggests that the magnitude of the difference is smaller, with women spending about sixteen hours per week engaged in household work, compared with ten hours for men (Perkins & DeMeis, 1996). Nevertheless, as Rider (2000) cogently points out, such a difference in the division of household labor translates to women spending 832 hours per year on these tasks, which is 312 hours more than men. Over the course of a ten-year marriage, a woman will typically have performed 3,000 more hours of household work than her husband. It has been estimated (Blair & Lichter, 1991) that men would have to shift 60 percent of their family work time to achieve gender balance in the division of household labor.

Parents also assign chores to their children in a gender-biased manner. As early as age six many children are given responsibilities that reflect their parents' gender expectations (Antill et al., 1996; Huston, 1983; Huston & Alvarez, 1990; Lytton & Romney, 1991). Girls help with dinner preparations, laundry, making beds, cleaning, and sweeping, while boys are asked to mow the lawn, wash the car, take out the trash, shovel snow, or perform simple repairs (Burns & Homel, 1989; Goodnow, 1988; McHale et al., 1990; Rider, 2000). Similar to the difference in parental labor division, girls tend to have approximately fifty minutes less leisure time on a weekday than boys do. These findings regarding the differential assignment of responsibilities for girls and boys have important implications. Various tasks encourage particular types of activity and thinking. Domestic chores foster taking care of others and taking responsibility for them, and occur in small, interior spaces. Maintenance tasks, however, emphasize taking care of things instead of people, and tend to be performed in open spaces.

Children also learn about mothers' and fathers' responsibilities for child care. Research consistently indicates that mothers invest more time and constancy in child rearing than do fathers (Hochschild, 1989; Okin, 1989; Riessman, 1990). Even when both parents have full-time employment outside the home, only 20 percent of husbands do half of the child care and homemaking tasks (Hochschild, 1989), and mothers tend to do the daily activities of feeding, bathing, dressing, and supervising children, while fathers engage in occasional activities that tend to be more enjoyable (Burns & Homel, 1989; Hochschild, 1989). Hence it is not surprising that fathers tend to be the preferred playmates and mothers are the ones sought when help or comfort is needed (Thompson & Walker, 1989).

Parental Impact on the Development of Independence and Assertiveness

When a child begins to toddle and falls down, mothers tend to react differently according to the sex of the child. Brooks-Gunn and Matthews (1979) reported that when a son falls, the mother is likely to give him a hug, toss a toy across the room, and encourage him to fetch it, while the mother of a daughter hugs the girl, hands her a toy, and continues to cuddle her. By the age of two, girls are more likely to gather toys and bring them back to sit near a parent's chair. Boys are more likely to wander around the room and play, attempt to investigate electric outlets, and open forbidden cupboards (Brooks & Lewis, 1974). Parents are more likely to respond positively when their two-year-old daughters follow them around than when their sons do the same thing. Sons are left to play alone more than daughters are (Fagot, 1974, 1978).

Fathers tend to reinforce gender differences in the physical activity of their sons and daughters. Fathers involve boys in more active, physical play than girls (Rosen & Peterson, 1990). Fathers also are more likely to reward boys for assertiveness and girls for positive, compliant behavior (Kerig, Cowan, & Cowan, 1993). A strong relationship exists between boys' masculinity and their fathers' personalities. Boys who are "masculine" tend to have fathers who are more affectionate and powerful (Hetherington, 1967; Mussen & Rutherford, 1963; Payne & Mussen, 1956). However, the converse holds true for the mother–daughter relationship. Both mothers and fathers tend to view girls as more truthful and relate to them with more physical closeness and warmth. Boys are disciplined more harshly. Girls' requests for help are attended to by parents, whereas boys' attempts at assertiveness are reinforced by parents (Fagot et al., 1985; MacDonald & Parke, 1986; Ross & Taylor, 1989). The consequences of this parental assertiveness training are that boys may be more likely than girls to get into trouble and test their parents' limits (Bellinger & Berko-Gleason, 1982), and sons may be less likely than daughters to obey a request to stop engaging in certain behaviors (Minton, Kagan, & Levine, 1971; Snow, Jacklin, & Maccoby, 1983).

By the time children attend school, the behavior of girls becomes even more restricted than that of boys. Boys are given more independence. Girls tend to be picked up directly at school, required to play at home rather than in the neighborhood, forbidden to go to parks, libraries, and such on their own, and "grounded" as punishment. Parents of sons are more likely to report that they do not know where their child is (Newsom & Newsom, 1986). Parents judge that boys are able to accomplish tasks at an earlier age in spite of the fact that girls are actually more mature and less impulsive than their male peers (Callard, 1968; Hoffman, 1977). Parents think that girls are more fragile and more easily frightened, and need more protection even though girls are more physically resilient throughout childhood (Hoffman, 1977; Kuebli & Krieger, 1991). They also believe that girls are more vulnerable to assault (Newsom & Newsom, 1986), even though as many as one in six boys are at risk for sexual abuse (Hunter, 1990). One of the problems with these beliefs is that with greater independence, boys may have a greater opportunity than girls to develop self-confidence and a sense that they can cope with unexpected problems (Block, 1973, 1983).

The Impact of Maternal Employment

Since 1980 the results of research have indicated that children (age three years through adolescence) of employed mothers generally exhibit less stereotyped attitudes than do children of nonemployed mothers (Hoffman, 1979, 1989; Huston, 1983; Huston & Alvarez, 1990). Moreover, daughters of employed mothers have higher self-esteem, higher educational aspirations, greater expectancy of a career, and greater interest in more prestigious occupations than those of nonemployed mothers. That finding is consistent across ethnic groups (Donelson, 1999). Maternal employment appears to influence the attitudes, personalities, and behaviors of mothers and fathers in a manner different from those of parents where mothers are not employed (Wiesner, Garnier, & Loucky, 1994; Willetts-Bloom & Nock, 1994). Maternal employment is more likely to encourage independence, particularly in daughters, and the greater demands of running the household may change child-rearing practices.

The impact of maternal employment on the behavior of sons is less, which may reflect the greater influence of the salience of the father as role model for the sons (Beal, 1994). It has been speculated that perhaps in working-class families, maternal employment may signal to the son that mother has to work because father is not a "good enough" provider, and that may underlie the finding that these sons show more traditional gender attitudes (Flanagan, 1990; Katz, 1987). In middle-class and wealthy families the sons are less gender-stereotyped than the sons of women who are primarily home-makers. This may occur because these sons perceive that mothers work out of desire rather than necessity (Donelson, 1999).

The Impact of Single Parenting

Both parents in intact families are important for gender-typed development, but neither is irreplaceable (Huston, 1983; Jackson, Ialongo, & Stollak, 1986). As a result of death, divorce, or other circumstances many children are raised in a single-parent household. Although children of divorced and intact families differ, the magnitude of those differences is small, and the gender differences are more likely due to parenting styles than to any inherent determinant (Amato & Keith, 1991; Grych & Fincham, 1992).

Often the absent parent is the father. As we have seen, fathers tend to encourage gender-appropriate behavior more strongly than mothers, so we might expect that children reared in households headed by mothers would exhibit less gender-stereotyped behavior. Indeed, preschool boys in female-headed households are less aggressive and less likely to engage in stereotypical masculine rough-and-tumble play. Such a finding may be related to a mother's protective behavior or the absence of a father as a male role model who is more likely to encourage independence and risk-taking behavior (Leaper et al., 1991).

However, the male gender role encompasses a blending of assertiveness and restraint, so often a father provides a model of male self-control. Some studies have suggested that boys with an absent father exhibit increased hostility and aggression, classroom acting-out behavior, and difficulty delaying gratification as compared with boys who have a father in the home (Biller, 1981; Santrock, 1977). They also tend to have difficulty establishing close relationships, depend excessively on the male peer group, rebel against the authority of adult males, and avoid anything perceived to be feminine (Biller, 1981). A meta-analytic review found that older boys in homes where a male caretaker is absent tend to demonstrate more aggressive and other stereotypically masculine behavior (Stevenson & Black, 1988).

Perhaps because a father is not as salient a role model for female children, girls seem to be less directly influenced by father absence. However, during adolescence girls from female-headed households tend to have difficulty interacting with males. Girls from homes where the mother is widowed are more inept and anxious around males, and girls whose mothers are divorced behave in a more sexually assertive manner. Perhaps girls with divorced mothers have been more exposed to men because their mothers date. They may have observed their mothers behaving in a flirtatious manner and generalized this behavior as the way in which to socialize with males (Denmark, Rabinowitz, & Sechzer, 2000). Boys in the custody of their fathers are relatively high in maturity, independence, and self-esteem, but they are less communicative and less overtly affectionate, perhaps due to less exposure to the expressiveness modeled and taught by mothers (Hetherington, Stanley-Hagan, & Anderson, 1989).

While it might be expected that mother absence would be associated with a reversal of the traditional gender roles, such is not the case. Having a father as a primary caregiver has less impact on gender-role behavior, perhaps because the children come into contact with a female "parent figure." Children living with their fathers tend to have a more balanced experience in terms of male and female role models (Denmark et al., 2000). Also, a study of adolescents raised primarily by fathers indicated that father participation in child rearing contributes to more nontraditional gender views of parenting, although sons and daughters are differentially affected (Williams, Radin, & Allegro, 1992). Sons think their relationship with their fathers is enhanced, while daughters miss the contact with their mothers that they think they need.

Mothers and fathers may encourage different types of behaviors. However, either parent is capable of stepping in and filling a parental gap so that a daughter develops femininity or a son develops masculinity or both sexes develop both femininity and masculinity. What parents teach children in their custody is more likely due to social limitations than to biological differences (Jackson et al., 1986).

The Impact of Gay and Lesbian Parenting

Research indicates that the developmental outcomes of children reared in families with heterosexual parents as compared with those reared in families with one or both lesbian parents progress similarly (Patterson, 1992, 1994; Steckel, 1987). Children of gay and lesbian parents usually adopt the behaviors typical for their sex, are not confused about their sex, and have no interest in being of the opposite sex (Flaks et al., 1995; Golombok & Tasker, 1996; Patterson, 1992, 1994, 1995). Moreover, interviewers could not discern between children of lesbian mothers and children of single heterosexual mothers (Kirkpatrick, Smith, & Roy, 1981). If their childhood family was open and accepting of same-sex relationships, some children from lesbian families were more likely to explore same-sex relationships. However, the majority of children from lesbian families identified as heterosexual (Golombok & Tasker, 1996).

Children in homes with one or both lesbian mothers appeared to be less aggressive and more positive than children reared in homes with a heterosexual mother (Steckel, 1987). Patterson (1994), who has compared grade school children living with heterosexual mothers and those living with lesbian mothers, reported that children living with lesbian mothers expressed both their positive and their negative emotions more often than children in homes with heterosexual mothers. She suggested that children who are in homes with lesbian primary caregivers may be encouraged to recognize their affective states and verbalize their feelings and experiences (Patterson, 1994).

Learning from Siblings and Peers

The role of siblings in gender role socialization has received less attention than that of parents or peers, although siblings are the most frequent out-of-school companions for children and young adolescents (Updegraff, McHale, & Crouter, 2000). Older siblings appear to play a significant role in the gender development of their younger siblings (McHale et al., 2001). A longitudinal study in England found that both girls with older sisters and boys with older brothers displayed more gender-typed behaviors than only children of the same sex. The only children, in turn, were more gender-typed than children with other-sex older siblings (Rust, 2000). However, research on college students suggests that the effect may be somewhat different for boys and girls. A girl with an older brother is more likely to exhibit tomboy behaviors, but a boy with an older sister does not necessarily become more feminine, although he may display greater flexibility in his behavior (Graham-Bermann & Gest, 1991; Stoneman, Brody, & MacKinnon, 1986). If there are several children in the family, the picture becomes considerably more complex, since sibling influence is moderated by birth order and the child's need to differentiate himself or herself from siblings. Thus, a child with several older siblings of the same gender may "go in the other direction" in terms of gender role behaviors in order to establish a distinct identity within the family (Hoffman, 1991; Huston, 1983; Katz, 1987).

A major source of information about gender is the child's peer group, that is, other children of approximately the same age. As children interact in the larger environment of neighborhood and school, friends become increasingly important as tools by which to measure oneself. Behaviors are "tried out" on friends, and if they are rewarded, they will continue; if not, they will cease. Thus the little boy who enjoys having tea parties with his teddy bears and is jeered at by friends who call it "sissy" will probably stop engaging is this type of play (Witt, 2000). Encouragement from peers to enact traditional gender role behaviors has been found to be even stronger than adult reinforcement for young children (Katz & Walsh, 1991).

Matlin (2004) postulates that peers encourage gender typing in four major ways: (1) they reject children who act in a nonstereotypical fashion; (2) they encourage gender segregation; (3) they are prejudiced against children of the other sex; and (4) they treat boys and girls differently.

Rejection of Nontraditional Behavior

In general, children tend to reject peers who act in a fashion that is more characteristic of the other sex (Edwards, Knoche, & Kimuru, 2001). Within their respective play groups, girls and boys socialize each other into traditional gender role behavior by punishing deviations through critical remarks, abandoning play with the friend who persists in doing something that appears gender-inappropriate, or trying to get their friend to do something else. Children are more careful to play with gender-appropriate toys when another child is present than when they are alone, even if the peer is not actually interacting with them (Serbin et al., 1979). Those who adhere to gender boundaries are rated by their peers as more socially competent and have higher scores on a measure of friendship than children who violate gender boundaries (Sroufe et al., 1993).

Boys prefer boys with exclusively masculine behaviors, and their friendship ratings become increasingly negative with each addition of a feminine behavior to a boy's actions (Fagot, Rodgers, & Leinbach, 2000; Zucker et al., 1995). Peers make it quite clear that boys are supposed to act like boys, which means, above all, they must not show any signs of femininity, a rule that reinforces the cultural message that masculine is more valuable than feminine (Wood, 1994). Because academic success and/or studiousness may be associated with femininity, some boys may avoid, or attempt to disguise, high scholastic achievement (Renold, 2001). Pollack (1998) suggested that peers contribute to an unwritten boys' code, a set of rigid rules about how boys should speak and behave. He proposed that the code explicitly forbids boys to talk about anxieties, fear, and other "sensitive" emotions.

It is widely believed that the gender norm violations of boys are evaluated more negatively by their peers than those of girls (Levy, Taylor, & Gelman, 1995; Smetana, 1986; Zucker et al., 1995), though exceptions have been found (Carter & Patterson, 1982). Blakemore (2003) suggests that the pattern depends on what norms are violated and the acceptableness of the behavior in general, but that boys are much more negatively evaluated when appearance-related norms (dress and hairstyle) are violated.

Although peers are important to both sexes, they seem to play a larger role in boys' development of gender identity (Fagot & Leinbach, 1983; Maccoby & Jacklin, 1987), which may reflect the difference in parental same-sex models available to boys and girls. Male bonding tends to occur in adolescence and is extremely important in reinforcing and refining masculine identity (Gaylin, 1992; Raphael, 1988; Rubin, 1985; Wood & Inman, 1993).

Gender Segregation

The tendency to associate with other children of the same sex is seen for girls as early as age two years, and for boys by about age three years, and becomes stronger with age until early adolescence (Edwards et al., 2001; Gardiner, Mutter, & Kosmitzki, 1998; Maccoby, 1998; Martin & Fabes, 2001; Vaughn et al., 2001). In one such study, nursery school children spent three times more time with same-sex peers than with other-sex peers; in children two years older, the differential was more than ten. Even those children who are less strongly gender-typed are as likely to prefer same-sex playmates as are others, and gender segregation is greatest in situations that have *not* been structured by adults (Maccoby, 1990).

Boys and girls in mixed-sex friendships have to go underground to avoid teasing by their peers (Gottman, 1986), or they may enact the friendship in a neighborhood setting, but not at school (Thorne, 1993). Children who cross the "gender boundary" are unpopular with their peers, although there are certain conditions under which contact with the other gender is permissible. Often these involve playful teasing, pushing, and grabbing (Pellegrini, 2001). Segregation by sex seems to be cross-cultural but is minimized when there are few children of the same age available (Whiting & Edwards, 1988).

One problem with gender segregation is that these single-gender groups encourage children to learn gender-stereotyped behavior (Maccoby, 1998). Boys learn that they are supposed to be physically aggressive and not admit that they are sometimes afraid. Girls learn to focus their attention on clothing and glamour rather than on competence. Both groups learn that the boys' group has greater power and gives boys a sense of entitlement (Golden, 1998). Another major problem with gender segregation is that children who grow up playing only with same-sex peers will not learn the broad range of skills they need to work well with both females and males (Fagot et al., 2000).

One reason children prefer their own sex as playmates is that they simply get along better with others who possess similar styles of interaction and similar interests. For example, boys appear to enjoy rough-and-tumble play more than girls do, and are more likely to initiate it with each other. A key factor seems to be the partner's social responsiveness, with girls being more responsive and cooperative, whereas boys are more often assertive and domineering (Rosen & Peterson, 1990). Another reason for seeking out members of their own sex as playmates is the need to establish a gender identity. Shared gender membership is even more important to children than mutual interests, and most children are anxious for their peers to view them engaged in only gender-appropriate behavior (Denmark et al., 2000).

Gender Prejudice

A third way that peers encourage gender typing is with prejudice against members of the other sex (Boyatzis, Malis, & Leon, 1999). Thus, children's attitudes about peers are not based solely on the peers' actual behavior; they seem to think that peers of their own sex are good simply because of their sex, regardless of activity (Etaugh, Levine, & Mennella, 1984; Martin, Wood, & Little, 1990; Powlishta, 1995; Serbin, Powlishta, & Gulko, 1993). Such a same-sex bias appears to be stronger for girls than for boys and to increase during childhood (Powlishta et al., 1994; Serbin et al., 1993). For example, Hayden-Thompson and colleagues found that when elementary school students are asked to rate how much they like each of their classmates, girls like other girls more than boys like other boys, and overall, girls are liked more than boys are liked (Hayden-Thompson, Rubin, & Hymel, 1987).

Explanations for this pattern have included the lower status of girls and a resulting in-group favoritism (Van Knippenberg, 1984) and/or the fact that boys tend to dominate mixed-sex interactions and resist girls' attempts to influence them (Charlesworth & Dzur, 1987; Charlesworth & LaFreniere, 1983; Cramer & Skidd, 1992; Maccoby, 1988; Powlishta & Maccoby, 1990). Also, boys tend to try to get their way through physical means and direct commands, while girls use verbal persuasion and generally try to ease conflict in order to maintain harmony (Cramer & Skidd, 1992; Leaper, 1991; Maccoby, 1988; McCloskey & Coleman, 1992; Thorne & Luria, 1986). Both boys and girls are more fearful of boys than of girls (Brody, Hay, & Vandewater, 1990). Whatever the reasons for it, this sort of same-sex bias reinforces children's beliefs that females and males are very different kinds of people.

Differential Treatment

A fourth way in which peers promote gender typing is that they use different standards in their interactions with boys than with girls. One of the most interesting examples of differential treatment is that children respond to girls on the basis of their physical attractiveness, but attractiveness is largely irrelevant for boys. Gregory Smith (1985) observed middle-class European American preschoolers for five-minute sessions in a classroom setting on five separate days. He recorded the number of prosocial and physically aggressive behaviors directed at each child, and the relationship of these to the child's attractiveness. The results showed that attractiveness (as previously rated by college students) was correlated with the way the girls were treated. Specifically, attractive girls were much more likely to be helped, patted, and praised. In contrast, the less attractive girls received few of these positive responses. However, Smith found no correlation between attractiveness and prosocial treatment of boys; attractive and less attractive boys received a similar number of prosocial actions.

Smith (1985) also found a comparable pattern for physical aggression scores. That is, the less attractive girls were more likely to be hit, pushed, and kicked, whereas the cutest girls rarely received this treatment. However, attractiveness was not related to the aggression directed toward boys. Young girls learn a lesson from their peers that will be repeated throughout their lives: Physical attractiveness is important for females, and pretty girls and women will receive better treatment. Boys learn that physical attractiveness is not really relevant to their lives.

The influence of peers on gender typing has not been examined as thoroughly as the influence of parents. However, we have seen that, in several ways, children can influence others who are their own age. Specifically, they can reject nontraditional behavior in their peers. They can encourage gender segregation, so that boys and girls have minimal contact with one another. They can also express prejudice against children of the other sex. Finally, they can respond differently to girls and boys—for example, by emphasizing attractiveness for girls but not for boys.

The Development of Gender Knowledge and Behavior

Throughout childhood, children learn how to distinguish between the sexes, correctly label each, learn about and adopt gender roles, recognize gender constancy, and eventually become more flexible in applying gender rules to self and others. Research indicates that these elements are separable and that they develop at different times. Infants less than a year old are able to distinguish between men and women, apparently using hair length as a signal of sex (Fagot & Leinbach, 1994). However, toddlers younger than eighteen months are rarely consistent in gender labeling or in showing gender-typed behaviors. By twenty-seven months, about half can apply the labels correctly (Fagot & Leinbach, 1989). Those who succeed are more likely to have more gender-typed parents (Fagot, Leinbach, & O'Boyle, 1992).

Other aspects of gender knowledge, such as gender preferences, gender stability, gender consistency, and knowledge of gender stereotypes, are developed between the ages of three and six, usually in that order (Brannon, 2002). Gender stability is the knowledge that gender is a stable personal characteristic (i.e., girls grow into women and boys grow into men), and gender consistency is the knowledge that people retain their gender even when they adopt behaviors or superficial physical features or dress associated with the other gender. Some children show gender stability without gender consistency, but never the other way around (Martin & Little, 1990). In fact, it may be several years before a child's understanding of gender constancy becomes solid enough to avoid confusion when names, pronouns, or appearances of characters in stories are suddenly modified (Beal & Lockhart, 1989).

Children who have developed either component of gender constancy (stability or consistency) are generally very motivated to adopt gender-role behaviors, avoiding those associated with the other gender (Newman, Cooper, & Ruble, 1995). At an early age, children have clear ideas about the activities that are gender-consistent. For instance, when four and five year olds are given a choice of a picture to color, 75 percent of boys select a picture of a car, a baseball player, or some other masculine scene, whereas 67 percent of girls select a picture of a cat, a ballet dancer, or some other feminine scene (Boyatzis & Eades, 1999). Also, four year olds know that boys are "supposed to" like toy tools, whereas girls are "supposed to" like toy dishes (Raag, 1999). Many boys also report that their fathers would think it was wrong if they played with toy dishes (Raag & Rackliff, 1998), and adults have difficulty persuading children to play with toys considered appropriate for the other sex (Fisher-Thompson & Burke, 1998).

Children's images of sex play an important role in such areas as popularity in elementary school (Adler, Kless, & Adler, 1992; Powlishta et al., 1994), conceptions of personal power (Dyson, 1994), self-esteem (Orr & Ben-Eliahu, 1993), and motivation and personal goals for adolescents (Gibbons et al., 1993). All of these are salient in terms of personality formation and healthy adjustment (Denmark et al., 2000).

Gender role learning appears to be more punctuated than continuous, meaning that at transitional points in development, children appear to be particularly sensitive to gender lessons—for example, during the toddler stage and early adolescence (Beal, 1994). There is evidence that gender role development continues into adolescence and adulthood, but that gender-stereotyped behaviors and attitudes do not increase with gender knowledge in a linear fashion.

Gender role orientation may increase or decrease in flexibility in middle childhood and adolescence, depending on several factors. For example, Levy (1989) found that children who interact more with their parents show less gender role flexibility than children who spend less time with their parents, and children with fewer siblings show more gender role flexibility than those with more brothers and sisters. Some studies have found an increase in rigidity of gender role stereotypes in early adolescence (Basow & Rubin, 1999; Galambos, Almeida, & Peterson, 1990), sometimes referred to as *gender intensification.* Contributing to this intensification are the physical changes of puberty and resulting increased pressures from parents, peers, and other adults to display traditional gendered behaviors (Crouter, Manke, & McHale, 1995).

As gender intensification increases and adult standards become more salient, young women may internalize cultural devaluation of what they are supposed to become (Huston & Alvarez, 1990). It is during adolescence that eating disorders are likely to start among young women, and a gender gap emerges, with young women showing more depression and anxiety than young men (Nolen-Hoeksema & Girgus, 1994).

Cognitive changes make adolescents more aware of gender expectations and more concerned about what others think of them (Crockett, 1991), and when adolescents begin to date and enter romantic relationships, they may increase their gender-stereotypical behavior in order to enhance their appeal to the other sex. Jackson and Tein (1998) found that inflexibility increases as traditional young men approach high school graduation and begin to contemplate marriage and careers.

Other research, on the other hand, indicates that gender role flexibility may increase or decrease during adolescence, depending on several factors, including gender and social environments (Katz & Ksansnak, 1994). Girls tend to be more flexible than boys in their preferences for engaging in gender-typical or gender-atypical behavior, as well as in their standards for the behavior of others, as are adolescents who perceive their social environment to be flexible rather than gender-traditional. Alfieri, Ruble, and Higgins (1996) found that gender role flexibility may depend on whether social environments change or remain stable, with a change in environment (e.g., from elementary to middle school or junior high) creating, at least temporarily, increased gender-role flexibility.

It may not be until adulthood, when peer pressure decreases, that people, especially men, become comfortable with exhibiting behaviors associated with the other sex (Block, 1973; Werrback, Grotevant, & Cooper, 1990). Some research has investigated the correlates of gender flexibility in adults. Men who reject stereotypically masculine and feminine roles are more likely to have had nurturing fathers and mothers in the workforce, and to have had at least one adult relationship with a feminist woman (Christian, 1994). Adherence to gender roles may increase after the arrival of children. Married or cohabiting couples with children tend to follow fairly traditional gender role norms of the female nurturer and the male provider, a phenomenon Gutmann (1987) calls the *parental imperative,* although there is no evidence that successful child rearing is related to men and women adopting stereotypical gender roles. Once children are grown, the imperative lessens, allowing both men and women to adopt more traits associated with the other gender. Likewise, considerable research suggests that in adulthood, the traits displayed by a person have less to do with sex and more to do with role characteristics—for example, whether it is a position of dominance or submissiveness (Epstein, 1988).

Thus, gender role development appears to be a lifelong process. Early childhood sees a sharp increase in gender knowledge and the fairly rigid application of gender-related rules. With continuing maturity, the relationship between age and gender role flexibility is toward greater flexibility over the life span, although social environment, roles, and life circumstances may produce periods of gender intensification or increased rigidity, resulting in a relationship that is complex and nonlinear.

Conclusions

In this chapter we have considered the many ways in which parental behaviors affect the gendering of children. These included adults' gender preferences and the differential treatment of newborns, gendered interactions and the impact on children's play, the modeling of gendered divisions of labor and the assignment of children's chores, and parental behaviors that produce gender differences in such traits as independence and assertiveness. We also considered the impact of maternal employment, single-parent households, and gay/lesbian parenting on the development of sex-role behaviors in children.

We next considered the role that peers, including siblings, play in gender-role development. A child's peers affect gender-role development by rejecting nontraditional behaviors and the children who continue to exhibit them, through play that is usually segregated along gender lines, by displaying a preference for their own sex over the other, and in reinforcing the differential treatment of boys and girls.

The learning of gender knowledge and the production of gendered behavior follow differing patterns over the life span. In the last section of this chapter we traced the typical stages of gender knowledge development during childhood and beyond. While knowledge about gender roles is gained early in life, the display of gendered behaviors will reflect considerable individual difference, as well as varying degrees of flexibility, during different life stages and circumstances. No matter the individual choices made, no one escapes the constant cultural messages regarding gender. In addition to influences considered in this chapter, many others have impact, including gendered institutions such as schools, workplaces, and sports; various forms of media, such as television, books, and magazines; and one's constant exposure to gendered linguistic forms and conventions. Expectations of gendered behavior and related cultural messages are the sea that we swim in. Whether one adopts behaviors consistent with these messages, or struggles against them, they impact our lives in countless and long-lasting ways.

References

Adler, P. A., Kless, S. J., & Adler, P. (1992). Socialization to gender roles: Popularity among elementary school boys and girls. *Sociology of Education, 65,* 169–187.

Alfieri, T., Ruble, D., & Higgins, E. T. (1996). Gender stereotypes during adolescence: Developmental changes and the transition to junior high school. *Developmental Psychology, 32,* 1129–1137.

Amato, P. R., & Keith, B. (1991). Consequences of parental divorce for the well-being of children: A meta-analysis. *Psychological Bulletin, 110,* 26–46.

Antill, J. K. (1987). Parents' beliefs and values about sex roles, sex differences, and sexuality: Their sources and implications. In P. Shaver & C. Hendrick (Eds.), *Sex and gender* (pp. 294–328). Newbury Park, CA: Sage.

Antill, J. K., Goodnow, J. J., Russell, G., & Cotton, S. (1996). The influence of parents and family context on children's involvement in household tasks. *Sex Roles, 34,* 215–236.

Basow, S. A. (1992). *Gender stereotypes and roles* (3rd ed.). Pacific Grove, CA: Brooks/ Cole.

Basow, S. A., & Rubin, L. R. (1999). Gender influences on adolescent development. In N. G. Johnson, M. C. Roberts, & J. Worell (Eds.), *Beyond appearance: A new look at adolescent girls* (pp. 25–52). Washington, DC: American Psychological Association.

Beal, C. (1994). *Boys and girls: The development of gender roles.* New York: McGraw-Hill.

Beal, C. R., & Lockhart, M. E. (1989). The effect of proper name and appearance changes on children's reasoning about gender constancy. *International Journal of Behavioral Development, 12,* 195–205.

Bellinger, D. C., & Berko-Gleason, J. (1982). Sex differences in parental directives to young children. *Sex Roles, 8,* 1123–1139.

Belsky, J. (1979). Mother–father–infant interaction: A naturalistic observation study. *Developmental Psychology, 15,* 601–607.

Biller, H. B. (1981). Father absence, divorce, and personality development. In M. E. Lamb (Ed.), *The role of the father in child development* (2nd ed.) (pp. 489–552). New York: Wiley.

Bird, C. E. (1999). Gender, household labor, and psychological distress: The impact of the amount and division of housework. *Journal of Health and Social Behavior, 40,* 32–45.

Blair, S. E., & Lichter, D. T. (1991). Measuring the division of household labor: Gender segregation of housework among American couples. *Journal of Family Issues, 12,* 91–113.

Block, J. H. (1973). Conceptions of sex role: Some cross-cultural and longitudinal perspectives. *American Psychologist, 28,* 512–526.

Block, J. H. (1983). Differential premises arising from differential socialization of the sexes: Some conjectures. *Child Development, 54,* 1335–1354.

Boyatzis, C. J., & Eades, J. (1999). Gender differences in preschoolers' and kindergartners' artistic production and preference. *Sex Roles, 41,* 627–638.

Boyatzis, C. J., Mallis, M., & Leon, I. (1999). Effects of game type on children's gender-based peer preferences: A naturalistic observational study. *Sex Roles, 40,* 93–105.

Brannon, L. (2002). *Gender: Psychological perspectives* (3rd ed.). Boston: Allyn & Bacon.

Brody, L. R., Hay, D. H., & Vandewater, E. (1990). Gender, gender role identity, and children's reported feelings toward the same and opposite sex. *Sex Roles, 23,* 363–387.

Brooks, J., & Lewis, M. (1974). Attachment behavior in thirteen-month-old opposite-sex twins. *Child Development, 45,* 243–247.

Brooks-Gunn, J., & Matthews, W. S. (1979). *He & she: How children develop their sex-role identity.* Englewood Cliffs, NJ: Prentice Hall.

Burns, A., & Homel, R. (1989). Gender division of tasks by parents and their children. *Psychology of Women Quarterly, 13,* 113–125.

Bussey, K., & Bandura, A. (1992). Self-regulatory mechanisms governing gender development. *Child Development, 63,* 1236–1250.

Caldera, Y. M., Huston, A. C., & O'Brien, M. (1989). Social interactions and play patterns of parents and toddlers with feminine, masculine, and neutral toys. *Child Development, 60,* 70–76.

Callard, E. D. (1968). Achievement motive of four-year-olds and maternal achievement expectancies. *Journal of Experimental Education, 36,* 14–23.

Carter, D. B., & Patterson, C. J. (1982). Sex roles as social conventions: The development of children's conceptions of sex role stereotypes. *Developmental Psychology, 18,* 812–824.

Charlesworth, W. R., & Dzur, C. (1987). Gender comparisons of preschoolers' behavior and resource utilization in group problem solving. *Child Development, 58,* 191–200.

Charlesworth, W. R., & LaFreniere, P. (1983). Dominance, friendship utilization and resource utilization in preschool children's groups. *Ethology and Sociobiology, 4,* 5–18.

Christian, H. (1994). *The making of anti-sexist men.* London: Routledge.

Clarke-Stewart, K. A. (1978). And Daddy makes three: The father's impact on mother and young child. *Child Development, 49,* 466–478.

Condry, J. C., & Condry, S. (1976). Sex differences: A study of the eye of the beholder. *Child Development, 47,* 812–819.

Cramer, P., & Skidd, J. E. (1992). Correlates of self-worth in pre-schoolers: The role of gender stereotyped styles of behavior. *Sex Roles, 26,* 369–390.

Crockett, L. J. (1991). Sex roles and sex-typing in adolescence. In R. M. Lerner, A. C. Petersen, & J. Brooks-Gunn (Eds.), *Encyclopedia of adolescence,* vol. 2 (pp. 1007–1017). New York: Garland.

Denmark, F., Rabinowitz, V., & Sechzer, J. (2000). *Engendering psychology* (pp. 145–168). Boston: Allyn & Bacon.

Donelson, F. E. (1999). *Women's experiences: A psychological perspective.* Mountain View, CA: Mayfield.

Dyson, A. H. (1994). The Ninjas, the X-men, and the ladies: Playing with power and identity in an urban primary school. *Teachers College Record, 96* (2), 219–239.

Edwards, C. P., Knoche, L., & Kimuru, A. (2001). Play patterns and gender. In J. Worrell (Ed.), *Encyclopedia of women and gender* (pp. 807–815). San Diego, Academic Press.

Eisenberg, N., Wolchick, S. A., Hernandez, R., & Pasternak, J. F. (1985). Parental socialization of young children's play: A short-term longitudinal study. *Child Development, 56,* 1506–1513.

Epstein, C. F. (1988). *Deceptive distinctions: Sex, gender, and the social order.* New Haven, CT: Yale University Press.

Etaugh, C., Levine, D., & Mennella, A. (1984). Development of sex biases in children: 40 years later. *Sex Roles, 10,* 911–922.

Fagot, B. I. (1974). Sex differences in toddlers' behavior and parental reaction. *Developmental Psychology, 10,* 554–558.

Fagot, B. I. (1978). The influence of sex of child on parental reactions to toddler children. *Child Development, 49,* 459–465.

Fagot, B. I. (1985). Beyond the reinforcement principle: Another step toward understanding sex role development. *Developmental Psychology, 21,* 1092–1104.

Fagot, B. I., & Hagan, R. (1991). Observations of parent reactions to sex-stereotyped behaviors: Age and sex effects. *Child Development, 62,* 617–628.

Fagot, B. I., & Leinbach, M. D. (1983). Play styles in early childhood: Consequences for boys and girls. In M. B. Liss (Ed.), *Social and Cognitive skills: Sex roles and children's play* (pp. 93–116). New York: Academic Press.

Fagot, B. I., & Leinbach, M. D. (1987). Socialization of sex roles within the family. In B. Carter (Ed.), *Current conceptions of sex roles and sex typing: Theory and research* (pp. 89–100). New York: Praeger.

Fagot, B. I., & Leinbach, M. D. (1989). The young child's gender schema: Environmental input, internal organization. *Child Development, 60,* 663–672.

Fagot, B. I., & Leinbach, M. D. (1994). Gender role development in young children. In M. R. Stevenson (Ed.), *Gender roles through the life span: A multidisciplinary perspective* (pp. 3–24). Muncie, IN: Ball State University Press.

Fagot, B. I., Leinbach, M. D., & O'Boyle, C. (1992). Gender labeling, gender stereotyping, and parenting behaviors. *Developmental Psychology, 28*(2), 225–230.

Fagot, B. I., Rodgers, C. S., & Leinbach, M. (2000). Theories of gender socialization. In T. Eckes & H. M. Trautner (Eds.), *The developmental social psychology of gender* (pp. 65–89). Mahwah, NJ: Erlbaum.

Field, T. (1978). Interaction behaviors of primary versus secondary caretaker fathers. *Developmental Psychology, 14,* 183–184.

Fisher-Thompson, D., & Burke, T. A. (1998). Experimenter influences and children's cross-gender behavior. *Sex Roles, 39,* 669–684.

Flaks, D. K., Ficher, I., Masterpasqua, F., & Joseph, G. (1995). Lesbians choosing motherhood: A comparative study of lesbian and heterosexual parents and their children. *Developmental Psychology, 31,* 105–114.

Flanagan, C. A. (1990). Change in family work status: Effects on parent–adolescent decision-making. *Child Development, 61,* 163–177.

Frey, K. S., and Ruble, D. N. (1992). Gender constancy and the "cost" of sex-typed behavior: A test of the conflict hypothesis. *Developmental Psychology, 28*(4), 714–721.

Galambos, N. L., Almeida, D. M., & Peterson, A. C. (1990). Masculinity, femininity, and sex role attitudes in early adolescence: Exploring gender intensification. *Child Development, 61,* 1905–1914.

Gardiner, H. W., Mutter, J. D., & Kosmitzki, C. (1998). *Lives across cultures: Cross-cultural human development.* Boston: Allyn & Bacon.

Gaylin, W. (1992). *The male ego.* New York: Viking.

Gibbons, J. L., Lynn, M., Stiles, D. A., De Berducido, E. J., Richter, R., Walker, K., & Wiley, D. (1993). Guatemalan, Filipino, and U.S. adolescents' imges of women as office workers and homemakers. *Psychology of Women Quarterly, 17*(4), 373–388.

Golden, C. (1998, December). Separate and unequal [review of the book *The two sexes: Growing up apart, coming together*]. *Women's Review of Books, 16,* 24–25.

Golombok, S., & Tasker, F. (1996). Do parents influence the sexual orientation of their children? Findings from a longitudinal study of lesbian families. *Developmental Psychology, 32,* 3–11.

Goodnow, J. J. (1988). Children's household work: Its nature and functions. *Psychological Bulletin, 103,* 5–26.

Gottman, J. M. (1986). The world of coordinated play: Same- and cross-sex friendship in children. In J. M. Gottman & J. G. Parker (Eds.), *Conversations of friends: Speculations on affective development*. Cambridge: Cambridge University Press.

Graham-Bermann, S., & Gest, S. (1991). *Sibling and peer relations in socially rejected, average, and popular children*. Paper presented at the biennial meeting of the Society for Research in Child Development, Seattle, WA.

Grych, J. H., & Fincham, F. D. (1992). Interventions for children of divorce: Toward greater integration of research and action. *Psychological Bulletin, 111*, 434–454.

Gunter, N. C., & Gunter, B. G. (1990). Domestic division of labor among working couples: Does androgyny make a difference? *Psychology of Women Quarterly, 14*, 355–370.

Gutmann, D. (1987). *Reclaimed powers: Toward a new psychology of men and women in later life*. New York: Basic Books.

Hamilton, M. C. (1991). *Preference for sons or daughters and the sex role characteristics of the potential parents*. Paper presented to the annual meeting of the Association for Women in Psychology, Hartford, CT.

Hartup, W. W., Moore, S. G., & Sager, G. (1963). Avoidance in appropriate sex-typing by young children. *Journal of Consulting Psychology, 27*, 467–473.

Hayden-Thompson, L., Rubin, K. H., & Hymel, S. (1987). Sex preferences in sociometric choices. *Developmental Psychology, 23*, 558–562.

Hetherington, E. M. (1967). The effects of familial variables on sex-typing, on parent–child similarity, and on imitation in children. In J. P. Hill (Ed.), *Minnesota symposia on child psychology*, vol. 1 (pp. 82–107). Minneapolis: University of Minnesota Press.

Hetherington, E. M., Stanley-Hagan, M., & Anderson, E. R. (1989). Marital transitions: A child's perspective. *American Psychologist, 44*, 303–312.

Hochschild, A. (1989). *The second shift: Working parents and the revolution at home*. New York: Viking.

Hoffman, L. W. (1977). Changes in family roles, socialization, and sex differences. *American Psychologist, 32*, 644–657.

Hoffman, L. W. (1979). Maternal employment. *American Psychologist, 34*, 859–865.

Hoffman, L. W. (1989). Effects of maternal employment in the two-person family. *Employee Responsibilities and Rights Journal, 10*, 263–275.

Hoffman, L. W. (1991). The influence of the family environment on personality: Accounting for sibling differences. *Psychological Bulletin, 110*, 187–203.

Hunter, M. (1990). *The sexually abused male: Prevalence, impact, and treatment*, vol. 1. Lexington, MA: Lexington Books.

Huston, A. C. (1983). Sex-typing. In E. M. Hetherington (Ed.), *Handbook of Child Psychology*. Vol. 4, *Socialization, personality, and social development* (4th ed., pp. 387–467). New York: Wiley.

Huston, A. C., & Alvarez, M. (1990). The socialization context of gender development in early development. In R. Montemayor, G. R. Adams, & T. P. Gullota (Eds.), *From childhood to adolescence: A transitional period?* (pp. 156–179). Newbury Park, CA: Sage.

Jacklin, C. N., Maccoby, E. E., & Dick, A. E. (1973). Barrier behavior and toy preference: Sex differences (and their absence) in the year-old child. *Child Development, 44,* 196–200.

Jackson, D. W., and Tein, J. (1998). Adolescents' conceptualization of adult roles: Relationships with age, gender, work goal, and maternal employment. *Sex Roles, 38,* 987–1008.

Jackson, L. A., Ialongo, N., & Stollak, G. (1986). Parental correlates of gender role: The relations between parents' masculinity, femininity, and child-rearing behaviors and their children's gender roles. *Journal of Social and Clinical Psychology, 4,* 202–224.

Katz, P. A. (1987). Variations in family constellation: Effects on gender schemata. In L. S. Liben & M. L. Signorella (Eds.), *Children's gender schemata* (pp. 39–56). San Francisco: Jossey-Bass.

Katz, P. A., & Ksansnak, K. R. (1994). Developmental aspects of gender role flexibility and traditionality in middle childhood and adolescence. *Developmental Psychology, 30*(2), 272–282.

Katz, P. A., & Walsh, V. (1991). Modification of children's gender-stereotyped behavior. *Child Development, 62,* 338–351.

Kerig, P. K., Cowan, P. A., & Cowan, C. P. (1993). Marital quality and gender differences in parent–child interaction. *Developmental Psychology, 29*(6), 931–939.

Kirkpatrick, M., Smith, C., & Roy, R. (1981). Lesbian mothers and their children: A comparative survey. *American Journal of Orthopsychiatry, 51,* 545–551.

Kuebli, J., & Krieger, E. (1991, April). *Emotion and gender in parent–child conversations about the past.* Paper presented at the biennial meeting of the Society for Research in Child Development, Seattle, WA.

Lamb, M. E. (1979). Parental influences and the father's role. *American Psychologist, 34,* 938–943.

Leaper, C. (1991). Influence and involvement in children's discourse: Age, gender, and partner effects. *Child Development, 62,* 797–811.

Leaper, C., Smith, L., Sprague, R., & Schwartz, R. (1991). *Single parent mothers, married mothers, married fathers, and the socialization of gender in preschool children.* Paper presented at the biennial meeting of the Society for Research in Child Development, Seattle, WA.

Levy, G. D. (1989). Relations among aspects of children's social environments, gender schematization, gender role knowledge, and flexibility. *Sex Roles, 21,* 803–823.

Levy, G. D., Taylor, M. G., & Gelman, S. A. (1995). Traditional and evaluative aspects of flexibility in gender roles, social convention, moral rules, and physical laws. *Child Development, 66,* 515–531.

Lewis, M. (1972). Parents and children: Sex-role development. *School Review, 80,* 229–240.

Lytton, H., & Romney, D. M. (1991). Parents' differential socialization of boys and girls: A meta-analysis. *Psychological Bulletin, 109,* 267–296.

Maccoby, E. E. (1988). Gender as a social category. *Developmental Psychology, 26*, 755–765.

Maccoby, E. E. (1990). Gender and relationships: A developmental account. *American Psychologist, 45*, 513–520.

Maccoby, E. E. (1998). *The two sexes: Growing up apart, coming together.* Cambridge MA: Belknap Press of Harvard University Press.

Maccoby, E. E., & Jacklin, C. N. (1987). Gender segregation in childhood. In H. W. Reese (Ed.), *Advances in child development and behavior* (pp. 239–287). New York: Academic Press.

MacDonald, K., & Parke, R. D. (1986). Parent-child physical play: The effects of sex and age of children and parents. *Sex Roles, 15*, 367–378.

Marleau, J. D., & Saucier, J. F. (2002). Preference for a first-born boy in Western societies. *Journal of Biosocial Science, 34*, 13–27.

Martin, C. L., & Fabes, R. A. (2001). The stability and consequences of young children's same-sex peer interactions. *Developmental Psychology, 37*, 431–446.

Martin, C. L., & Little, J. K. (1990). The relation of gender understanding to children's sex-typed preferences and gender stereotypes. *Child Development, 61*, 1427–1439.

Martin, C. L., Wood, C. H., & Little, J. K. (1990). The development of gender stereotype components. *Child Development, 61*, 1891–1904.

Matlin, M. W. (2004). *The psychology of women* (5th ed.) (pp. 72–106). Belmont, CA: Wadsworth.

McCloskey, L. A., & Coleman, L. M. (1992). Difference without dominance: Children's talk in mixed- and same-sex dyads. *Sex Roles, 27*, 241–257.

McDougall, J., DeWit, D. J., & Ebanks, C. E. (1999). Parental preferences for sex of children in Canada. *Sex Roles, 41*, 615–626.

McHale, S. M., Bartko, W. T., Crouter, A. C., & Perry-Jenkins, M. (1990). Children's housework and psychosocial functioning: The mediating effects of parents' sex-role behaviors and attitudes. *Child Development, 61*, 1413–1426.

McHale, S. M., Updegraff, K. A., Helms-Erikson, H., & Crouter, A. C. (2001). Sibling influences on gender development in middle childhood and early adolescence: A longitudinal study. *Developmental Psychology, 37*, 115–125.

Minton, C., Kagan, J., & Levine, J. A. (1971). Maternal control and obedience in the two-year-old child. *Child Development, 42*, 1873–1894.

Mussen, P. H., & Rutherford, E. (1963). Parent–child relations and parental personality in relation to young children's sex-role preferences. *Child Development, 34*, 489–507.

Newman, L. S., Cooper, J. N., & Ruble, D. N. (1995). Gender and computers II. The interactive effects of knowledge and constancy on gender-stereotyped attitudes. *Sex Roles, 33*, 325–351.

Newsom, J., & Newsom, W. (1986). Family and sex roles in middle childhood. In D. J. Hargreaves & A. M. Colley (Eds.), *The psychology of sex roles* (pp. 142–158). New York: Harper & Row.

Nolen-Hoeksema, S., & Girgus, J. S. (1994). The emergence of gender difference in depression during adolescence. *Psychological Bulletin, 115,* 424–443.

Okin, S. M. (1989). *Justice, gender, and the family.* New York: Basic Books.

Orr, E., & Ben-Eliahu, E. (1993). Gender differences in idiosyncratic sex-typed self-images and self-esteem. *Sex Roles, 29*(3/4), 271–296.

Parke, R. D. (1979). Perspectives on father–child interaction. In J. D. Osofsky (Ed.), *Handbook of infant development* (pp. 549–590). New York: Wiley.

Patterson, C. (1992). Children of lesbian and gay parents. *Child Development, 63,* 1025–1042.

Patterson, C. (1994). Children of the lesbian baby-boom: Behavioral adjustment, self-concepts, and sex-role identity. In B. Greene & G. M. Herek (Eds.), *Lesbian and gay psychology: Theory, research, and clinical applications* (pp. 157–175). Thousand Oaks, CA: Sage.

Patterson, C. J. (1995). Sexual orientation and human development: An overview. *Developmental Psychology, 31,* 3–11.

Payne, D. E., & Mussen, P. H. (1956). Parent–child relations and father identification among adolescent boys. *Journal of Abnormal & Social Psychology, 52,* 358–362.

Pellegrini, A. D. (2001). A longitudinal study of heterosexual relationships, aggression, and sexual harassment during the transition from primary school through middle school. *Applied Developmental Psychology, 22,* 119–133.

Perkins, H. W., & DeMeis, D. K. (1996). Gender and family effects on the "second shift" domestic activity of college educated young adults. *Gender and Society, 10,* 78–93.

Plant, E. A., Hyde, J. S., Keltner, D., & Devine, P. G. (2000). The gender stereotyping of emotions. *Psychology of Women Quarterly, 24,* 81–92.

Pollack, W. (1998). *Real boys: Rescuing our sons from the myths of boyhood.* New York: Random House.

Pomerleau, A., Bolduc, D., Malcuit, G., & Cossette, L. (1990). Pink or blue: Environmental stereotypes in the first two years of life. *Sex Roles, 22,* 259–267.

Pooler, W. S. (1991). Sex of a child preference among college students. *Sex Roles, 25,* 569–576.

Powlishta, K. K. (1995). Intergroup processes in childhood: Social categorization and sex role development. *Developmental Psychology, 31,* 781–788.

Powlishta, K. K., & Maccoby, E. E. (1990). Resource utilization in mixed-sex dyads: The influence of adult preference and task type. *Sex Roles, 23,* 223–240.

Powlishta, K. K., Serbin, L. A., Doyle, A. B., & White, D. R. (1994). Gender, ethnic, and body type biases: The generality of prejudice in childhood. *Developmental Psychology 30*(4), 526–536.

Raag, T. (1999). Influences of social expectations of gender, gender stereotypes, and situational constraints on children's toy choices. *Sex Roles, 41,* 809–831.

Raag, T., & Rackliff, C. L. (1998). Preschoolers' awareness of social expectations of gender: Relationships to toy preferences. *Sex Roles, 38,* 685–700.

Raphael, R. (1988). *The men from the boys: Rites of passage in male America.* Lincoln: University of Nebraska Press.

Renold, E. (2001). Learning the "hard" way: Boys, hegemonic masculinity and the negotiation of learning identities in primary school. *British Journal of Sociology of Education, 22,* 369–385.

Rider, E. A. (2000). *Our voices: Psychology of women.* Belmont, CA: Wadsworth.

Riessman, C. K. (1990). *Divorce talk: Women and men make sense of personal relationships.* New Brunswick, NJ: Rutgers University Press.

Rosen, B. N., & Peterson, L. (1990). Gender differences in children's outdoor play injuries: A review and an integration. *Clinical Psychology Review, 10,* 187–205.

Ross, H., & Taylor, H. (1989). Do boys prefer Daddy or his physical style of play? *Sex Roles 20*(1/2), 23–31.

Rubin, J. Z., Provenzano, F., & Luria, Z. (1974). The eye of the beholder: Parents' views on sex of newborns. *American Journal of Orthopsychiatry, 44,* 512–519.

Rubin, L. (1985). *Just friends: The role of friendship in our lives.* New York: Harper & Row.

Rust, P. C. (2000). Bisexuality: A contemporary paradox for women. *Journal of Social Issues, 56,* 205–221.

Santrock, J. W. (1977). Effects of father absence on sex typed behaviors in male children: Reason for absence and age of onset of the absence. *Journal of Genetic Psychology, 130,* 3–10.

Scarr, S. (1984). *Mother care, other care.* New York: Basic Books.

Serbin, L. A., Connor, J. M., Buchardt, C. J., & Citron, C. C. (1979). Effects of peer presence on sex-typing of children's play behavior. *Journal of Experimental Child Psychology, 27,* 303–309.

Serbin, L. A., Powlishta, K. K., & Gulko, J. (1993). The development of sex-typing in middle childhood. Chicago, IL: Society for Research in Child Development.

Smetana, J. G. (1986). Preschool children's conceptions of sex-role transgressions. *Child Development, 57,* 862–871.

Smith, G. J. (1985). Facial and full-length ratings of attractiveness related to the social interactions of young children. *Sex Roles, 12,* 287–293.

Snow, M. E., Jacklin, C. N., & Maccoby, E. E. (1983). Sex-of-child differences in father-child interaction at one year of age. *Child Development 54* (1), 227–232.

Sroufe, L. A., Bennett, C., Englund, M., Urban, J., & Shulman, S. (1993). The significance of gender boundaries in preadolescence: Contemporary correlates and antecedents of boundary violation and maintenance. *Child Development, 64,* 455–466.

Steckel, A. (1987). Psychosocial development of children of lesbian mothers. In F. N. Bozett (Ed.), *Gay and lesbian parents* (pp. 75–85). New York: Praeger.

Stevenson, M. R., & Black, K. N. (1988). Paternal absence and sex-role development: A meta-analysis. *Child Development, 59*(3), 793–814.

Stoneman, Z., Brody, G. H., & Mackinnon, C. E. (1986). Same-sex and Cross-sex siblings: Activity choices, roles, behavior, and gender stereotypes. *Sex Roles, 15,* 495–511.

Thompson, L., & Walker, A. J. (1989). Gender in families: Women and men in marriage, work, and parenthood. *Journal of Marriage and the Family, 51,* 845–871.

Thorne, B. (1993). *Gender play: Girls and boys in school.* New Brunswick, NJ: Rutgers University Press.

Thorne, B., & Luria, Z. (1986). Sexuality and gender in children's daily worlds. *Social Problems, 33,* 176–190.

Updegraff, K. A., McHale, S. M., & Crouter, A. C. (2000). Adolescents' sex-typed friendships: Does having a sister versus a brother matter? *Child Development, 21,* 1597–1610.

Vaughn, B. E., Colvin, T. N., Azria, M. R., Caya, L., & Krzysik, L. (2001). Dyadic analyses of friendships in a sample of preschool-age children attending Head Start: Correspondence between measures and implications for social competence. *Child Development, 72,* 862–878.

Weinraub, M., & Frankel, J. (1977). Sex differences in parent–infant interaction during free play, departure, and separation. *Child Development, 48,* 1240–1249.

Werrback, G. B., Grotevant, H. D., & Cooper, C. R. (1990). Gender differences in adolescents' identity development in the domain of sex role concepts. *Sex Roles, 23,* 349–362.

Whiting, B. B., & Edwards, C. P. (1988). *Children of different worlds: The formation of social behavior.* Cambridge, MA: Harvard University Press.

Wiesner, T. S., Garnier, H., & Loucky, J. (1994). Domestic tasks, gender equalitarian values and children's gender typing in conventional and nonconventional families. *Sex Roles, 30,* 23–54.

Willetts-Bloom, M. C., & Nock, S. L. (1994). The influence of maternal employment on gender role attitudes of men and women. *Sex Roles, 30,* 371–389.

Williams, E., Radin, N., & Allegro, T. (1992). Sex-role attitudes of adolescents raised primarily by their fathers: An 11-year follow-up. *Merrill-Palmer Quarterly, 38*(4), 457–476.

Williamson, N. E. (1976). *Sons or daughters: A cross-cultural survey of parental preferences.* Beverly Hills, CA: Sage.

Witt, S. D. (2000). The influence of peers on children's socialization to gender roles. *Early Child Development and Care, 162,* 1–7.

Wood, J. T. (1994). *Gendered lives: Communication, gender, and culture.* Belmont, CA: Wadsworth.

Wood, J. T., & Inman, C. (1993). In a different mode: Recognizing male modes of closeness. *Journal of Applied Communication Research, 21*(August), 279–295.

Zucker, K. J., Wilson-Smith, D. N., Kurita, J. A., & Stern, A. (1995). Children's appraisals of sex-typed behavior in their peers. *Sex Roles, 33,* 703–725.

Chapter 2

Cultural Perspectives on Gender

Janet Sigal and Maureen Nally

Although there is considerable research related to gender differences, gender roles may have a greater impact in the United States and cross-culturally than gender does. In this chapter we will contrast traditional gender roles with more egalitarian roles and examine possible conceptual frameworks for understanding the development and maintenance of gender roles throughout the world. Factors affecting the development of gender roles will be discussed along with examples from the United States and other countries.

Culture influences perceived appropriate gender roles for women and the status of women in different societies. In the second part of this chapter, we will examine the effects of gender roles, patriarchal cultures, and related concepts on the incidence of domestic violence or spousal abuse worldwide.

Gender roles can be defined as "people's beliefs about the appropriate roles and obligations of women and men" (Frieze et al., 2003, p. 256). The traditional gender role scenario states that men basically are responsible for the economic security of the family; that is, men are seen as the breadwinners, and women are pictured as being dependent on men. Women primarily have responsibilities within the home, including raising the children, whereas men's responsibilities are outside the home, in the workplace. Stemming from this traditional approach, men are perceived as possessing greater status and power, and control over women. The nontraditional gender role framework pictures a more egalitarian sharing of responsibilities and power between men and women.

Whether a culture reinforces a traditional or a nontraditional gender role orientation varies among different countries. Each culture incorporates aspects of gender roles specific to that culture ("emic") and universal characteristics of gender roles ("etic"). Even the dichotomous traditional versus nontraditional culture distinction is too simplistic. Cultures vary in terms of how traditional or nontraditional gender roles are. However, cultures that generally incorporate a more traditional gender role structure often are supportive of attitudes that reinforce men's domination over women. In particular, patriarchal cultures that legitimize and legislate men's superior status and power can be characterized by attitudes implying that women are inferior, sex discrimination against women in the workplace, and extensive controls over women in society. In countries with more egalitarian gender role norms, women are able to achieve greater career success and increased control over their lives.

Gender stereotypes, or characteristics expected of men and women, often are associated with gender role conceptualizations. In traditional cultures, men are seen as strong, virile, dominant, and agentic, whereas women are characterized as weak, submissive, passive, and dependent. More positively, women are seen as caring and compassionate, and men are expected to be strong (the "sturdy oak"), successful ("big man"), and dependable. These stereotypes are prescriptive; in other words, when men or women fail to fulfill these expected norms, they generally are punished by being devalued or by attempts to change their behavior so it becomes "appropriate." In more egalitarian cultures, men and women can adopt whatever characteristics suit their situation or their personality without fearing repercussions for violating these stereotypes.

Conceptual Frameworks

Cross-culturally, one of the most important and relevant conceptual approaches to explaining gender roles is the identification of cultures that are patriarchal. As indicated above, patriarchal cultures tend to reinforce more traditional gender roles than do nonpatriarchal cultures. According to Haj-Yahia (2002), there are two aspects to patriarchal societies: (1) Patriarchal structure of the society—the "hierarchical organization" (p. 283) reflects the patriarchal nature of entire nations. In other words, all workplaces, governments, organizations, and interpersonal relations are structured in a top-down pattern. This pattern is reinforced through financial, social, and legal statutes in patriarchal countries. Generally, patriarchal societies foster domination by men in power positions both within and outside the home. The term "patriarch of the family" implies that the male head of the family rules the family, and his word is law. Along with these concepts are the sometimes implicit, but at times explicitly stated, rules that women will be restricted to the traditional domestic role and will have low status in society. (2) Ideology—Haj-

Yahia suggests that in patriarchal societies, norms, attitudes, and accepted cultural mores reinforce men's dominant status and women's inferior status.

A second, related concept is the "culture of honor." Although all cultures incorporate some idea of honor, according to Vandello and Cohen (2003), in some cultures, honor becomes the ideal around which the entire society is organized. It is a relative distinction, in that cultures are seen as forming a continuum of honor (i.e., honor is a more central or less of a core value in the society) rather than as valuing or not valuing this concept. Many Asian cultures, for example, emphasize the honor of a family, community, workplace, and nation, and the culture is organized around the importance of avoiding shame or slurs on the honor of the individual or collective. However, in some cultures, honor has another association that is directly connected to gender roles. Honor is related to the reputation of individuals, particularly males in a patriarchal society. A man's honor is based on his ability to protect his "own"; that is, a man must be capable of protecting his family and his possessions, especially the honor of his family. In some societies, the honor of the family is directly connected to controlling the chastity of the women in a man's family (Wasti et al., 2000). If a male head of the family permits a woman (e.g., wife or daughter) to damage the honor of the family by adultery or by being raped, this action brings dishonor to the entire family, but particularly to the patriarch. Therefore, the role of the male head of the family goes beyond simply exercising his ability to make decisions and run the family. It becomes the male head's responsibility to curtail the activities of the women in the family in order to avoid any "straying" from appropriate chaste behavior and to maintain the honor of the family. Thus, "cultures of honor" in a sense go beyond traditional gender role orientations supported in patriarchal societies to enforce the subordinate status of women and strictly confine them to the domestic realm. Vandello and Cohen (2003) identify Middle Eastern and Latin American countries as examples of "cultures of honor."

Factors Affecting Development and Maintenance of Traditional Gender Roles

Socialization

Socialization is a major factor contributing to the development and maintenance of gender roles, and plays a very important part in countries characterized by traditional gender roles and patriarchal structures. In patriarchal societies, children are taught to adhere to traditional cultural norms, including respect for authority figures and "appropriate behavior" for men and women (i.e., traditional gender roles). For example, Talbani and Hasanali (2000) suggest that socialization focuses on differentiating between boys and girls in terms of the general preferential treatment and extensive freedom given to boys by their parents, and the increased control over the lives of girls in families. The authors hypothesize that arranged marriages may contribute to perpetuation of the traditional differentiation of male and female behaviors. According to the researchers, in some South Asian nations, women's basic role is to enter into early arranged marriages, and women's educational and career goals are seen as important only because that status will enhance their value as a marriage partner or contribute to the financial stability of their family. Talbani and Hasanali indicate that these traditions often are carried through to other countries when South Asian nationals migrate. Again, socialization is facilitated by limiting female children's range of social contacts to those within the culture of the country of origin.

Modernization

Another factor related to the type of gender role development concerns the degree of modernization and the type of government characterizing a culture. Chia, Allred, and Jerzak (1997) suggest that when a country emerges from rural isolationism and enters a more modern phase, particularly a country with a democratic government, nontraditional gender roles may become more accepted. To some extent, their research comparing participants from Taiwan with those from mainland China, a less modern society, endorses this assumption, in that women in China support more traditional gender roles than women in Taiwan. However, the study reveals some contradictory indications that ancient Chinese traditions may still influence modern Chinese attitudes toward gender roles, creating conflict for individuals in Taiwan.

Similar findings are reported by Tang and Tang (2001), who examined attitudes of Chinese residents in Hong Kong. For example, successful women in Hong Kong are supposed to be assertive and competent while still exhibiting traditional female characteristics of submissiveness and dependency. Tang and Tang indicate that women in positions of power continually have to prove that they have earned the authority associated with these positions, but still will "act like a woman." Such dual demands can cause stress for career women in Hong Kong and other modernized Chinese societies. Tang and Tang suggest that this type of stress may contribute to the development of psychological problems, including depression and eating disorders. In addition, according to the authors, in these cultures the most acceptable model of the family still is portrayed as the man as breadwinner and the woman as restricted to domestic activities at home.

Another interesting example of conflicting tendencies in a country characterized by a democratic government, but influenced by traditional as well as nontraditional factors, is described by Wasti et al. (2000) in their analysis of Turkey. The authors suggest that although Turkey is a collectivist culture (i.e., one in which the good of the whole is more important and valued than the rights of the individual) and can be classified as a "culture of honor," there are women in prestige professions in percentages comparable with those of Western countries. However, the researchers also point out that there is a "bipolar pattern" of employment of women in Turkey: There are women at the top of the employment status hierarchy in some professions, and many women at the bottom of the hierarchy in unskilled jobs, but very few women in the middle of the continuum. Wasti et al. conclude that women still are viewed as lower in status than men; in fact, women are not seen as a major part of the workforce, and traditional gender roles continue to be the ideal in Turkish society.

Gender Differences

One significant factor that appears to be consistent across cultures relates to gender differences in attitudes toward appropriate roles for men and women. Throughout the world, women apparently endorse more liberal and nontraditional gender role conceptualizations than men do. For example, Chia et al. (1997) found that women in the United States and in Taiwan have more liberal attitudes toward gender roles than men. Even in very traditional and restrictive societies, women have begun movements to gain more power and control over their lives. For example, in Afghanistan, while the Taliban was in power, some women opened schools for girls even though the penalties for this opposition to Taliban law were extreme. It seems reasonable to assume that women would be more egalitarian in their gender role attitudes, since men may be motivated to maintain the status quo (i.e., dominance of men in the workplace and the political arena).

Religion

Finally, a few studies indicate that religion also may be a factor in determining which types of gender roles are preferred in a society. Frieze et al. (2003), for example, found that religious observance is somewhat related to traditional gender role preference, and that men from Croatia, which is a very religious Catholic country, reflect less egalitarian gender role attitudes, as do men from Slovenia, when compared with American men. Frieze et al. found it interesting that although Slovenia was part of the original Soviet Union, a system that ostensibly fostered gender equality, in actuality women there hold low-status jobs and perform all domestic duties, regardless of work demands.

Immigrants and Cross-Cultural Examples

Immigrants to the United States and other countries represent a special case that is relevant to the discussion of gender roles. Talbani and Hasanli (2000) suggest that immigrants often maintain the culture from their country of origin when they settle in another country. Dasgupta (1998) describes Sue and Sue's (1971) analysis of the immigrant experience thus: (1) "Traditionalists" are immigrants who continue to espouse the culture of their original country and do not incorporate any aspects of the new culture; (2) "assimilationists" internalize the aspects of the new culture and reject the characteristics of the original culture; (3) "biculturalists" attempt to integrate characteristics of both cultures; (4) "marginalists" reject both cultures. According to Okazaki (1998), for Asian Americans, biculturalism presents special problems because the traditional gender role conceptualizations are so prominent in Asian countries. Many of these cultures are strongly patriarchal and are organized around central concepts of respect for authority, the honor of the family, the need to "save face" or preserve that honor at any cost, and the idea that members of the family are very committed to and "obligated" to each other. For example, in one family, conflicts between an immigrant wife and her husband's family were resolved by the intervention of a "neutral" male relative. According to both Okazaki and Dasgupta, daughters of immigrant parents are most at risk of experiencing stress and conflict between the traditional gender role norms of their original culture and the less traditional norms of the American culture. Okazaki suggests that the ideal situation would be to identify ways to enable Asian American women to achieve more equality with men, at least in terms of attaining certain rights and privileges similar to those attained by American women, while still adhering somewhat to the gender role characterizations of their country of origin.

Even in countries that appear to have a rigid traditional gender role society, the picture may be rather complex. In a study analyzing cultural patterns in Nigeria, Onyeizugbo (2003) reports that the apparent traditional society image is somewhat misleading when different generations are compared. She indicates that young married women are expected to adhere to the stereotypical female role of dependence and submissiveness. However, over the years married women, as a result of their dominance in domestic issues in the home, acquire much greater power and often are able to enter professions and start businesses when they are older. In fact, in her study, when she questioned 214 married women who were working, the author found that older women were higher in assertiveness than younger women or older men. Onyeizugbo also suggests that the situation for women may be changing slowly in Africa.

Gender Roles, Culture, and Spousal Abuse

Wallace (1999) defines spousal abuse as "any intentional act or series of acts that cause injury to a spouse" (p. 178). The definition includes both physical and emotional abuse. Araji and Carlson (2001) expand Wallace's definition to a more inclusive term of family violence: "any physical or mental acts that can result in short- and/or long-term injury or death to a family member" (p. 588). We will limit our consideration to spousal abuse, because most of the research deals with this behavior.

It is impossible to compare spousal abuse incidence rates cross-culturally because figures are difficult to obtain, particularly in countries that do not compile official statistics. Even in the United States, statistics may be misleading because many victims do not report abuse. For example, Gelles (1997) reports that almost 30 percent of all marriages involve at least one instance of spousal abuse during the course of the marriage. Oliver (2000) suggests that as many as 2 million females experience domestic abuse or violence every year. As a result of the impossibility of verifying existing statistics of abuse and the lack of data in some countries, we will consider attitudes toward spousal abuse and possible origins of these attitudes. Even in countries where domestic violence rates may be comparable, considerable variation exists in terms of attitudes toward the abuse as well as in perceptions of the responsibility of a society to deal with the abuse and to help the victims.

Conceptual Approaches Related to Attitudes Toward Spousal Abuse

Wallace (1999) suggests that three factors are related to the incidence of spousal abuse: (1) most important is the concept of power of the abuser over the abused spouse; (2) the dependency of the victim on the abuser; (3) if there is stress within or outside the marriage, spousal abuse is more likely to occur.

We will examine these three determinants of spousal abuse within the conceptual framework of the culture of honor, through studies of immigrant populations and the cross-cultural research.

Culture of Honor

Although the patriarchal culture was conceptualized as contributing significantly to the development of traditional gender roles, the culture of honor that characterizes some patriarchal cultures is more closely associated with tolerance for spouse abuse. As described earlier, Vandello and Cohen (2003) indicate that in societies that promulgate the "culture of honor," a man's reputation can be harmed if his "woman" (e.g., wife, daughter, mother) is not faithful. He may be seen as "less of a man." Even if his wife is raped, this act will bring "dishonor" on the head of the family. There are honor cultures in which there is no legislation outlawing spousal abuse. In fact, some societies have laws that support a man's right to punish his spouse if she has "strayed" or has been sexually attacked. In this manner, a man's honor may be upheld through violence against his spouse when he "washes the honor with the blood" (Vandello & Cohen, 2003, p. 999). Since the traditional female role is to be passive and submissive, the wife is supposed to remain with the husband regardless of the severity of the abuse.

The most extreme example of this "honor code" is the "honor killing." A recent newspaper article (Winik, 2003) reported that approximately 5,000 murders of women a year have been identified as "honor killings." For example, Araji and Carlson (2001) describe a case in Jordan in which a young girl was raped by her brother. When she revealed this incident to another brother, the eldest in the family, this brother killed her as his relatives watched and applauded his "cleansing the family's honor" (p. 591). Cultural support for this type of killing also is illustrated by a case in which a father killed his daughter for having an affair. His sentence was extremely lenient (he was jailed for six days). In general, sentences for "honor killings" tend to be very light. Similar cases have been observed in Nigeria, where women have been stoned to death for committing adultery.

Both dependency of the female spouse and power of the husband over his spouse, two conditions specified by Wallace, clearly contribute to "honor killings." Haj-Yahia (2002) also suggests that cultural norms affect attitudes toward spousal abuse. For example, in his study conducted with 356 married women in Jordan, a culture of honor, participants perceived wife abuse as justified, in that women deserved the beating because they did not obey or respect their husbands. Subjects also felt that the women who were abused would become "better wives" as a result of the beatings. Spouse batterers were not seen as responsible for the abuse, or at least were not expected to be punished for the abuse (e.g., "men will be men; it is their nature"). In addition, these participants in the study indicated that the abuse is a family problem and should not be handled by any type of social or government agency outside the family.

One controversial aspect of any discussion of "honor cultures" and domestic abuse is the contribution of religion to these cultural attitudes or norms. In the Haj-Yahia (2002) study, Jordan is identified as a predominantly Islamic culture in which religion plays a significant part. Kikoski (2000) analyzes the complex nature of the Islamic culture by postulating a somewhat dichotomous classification: (1) traditionalists and fundamentalists interpret Islamic religious teachings as reinforcing the patriarchal structure of society and legitimizing the power of men over women; (2) modernists and feminists in Islamic societies emphasize that the Prophet Muhammad was a supporter of equal rights for men and women. According to Kikoski, at present the fundamentalist view dominates, particularly in Arab societies with strong patriarchal hierarchical structures. However, Kikoski suggests that some of these cultures are slowly changing. For example, in Egypt divorce laws are evolving so that the law that in the past permitted Egyptian men to obtain a divorce by saying "I divorce you" three times in public, now requires the husband to go to court, and also allows women to obtain divorces. And in Jordan, there is royal support for abolishing "honor killings." Although honor killings have been examined primarily within the context of the Islamic communities, a newspaper article (Winik, 2003) revealed that individuals of other religions, including Christians and Sikhs, have committed these types of murders.

Vandello and Cohen (2003) describe cultures in areas besides the Middle East where religion is an important part of the society and honor plays a major role. In Latin America, for example, a man's honor also is connected to the fidelity of his wife. According to Nazzari (1998), women should remain "virgins until they married, wives should be faithful, and widows chaste" (p. 104). "Marianismo" describes the expected behavior of Hispanic women as submissive and loyal. Machismo, which is a core concept in these cultures, is tied directly to a man's honor. Since men are permitted extensive sexual freedom (also part of the machismo culture), a man must protect his women from male "sexual predators."

Vandello and Cohen also identify the importance of the "honor culture" within subcultures of the United States. They indicate that men living in the southern part of the United States tend to believe in a "culture of honor" more than residents of the northern part. Consistent with this assumption, Cohen et al. (1996) found that white males in the South responded more aggressively to provocation than did white males in the North, because their honor was attacked. One such tragic incident occurred in Texas several years ago. A Japanese couple rang the wrong doorbell while attempting to find a party. When the homeowner opened the door and ordered the couple to "freeze," they didn't comprehend these instructions, and he shot them. He was acquitted of murder because he was defending his "honor."

Immigrants

Dasgupta (1998b) suggests that for many immigrants from patriarchal cultures and cultures of honor, values of the dominant American culture conflict with the values from the country of origin in complex ways. In particular, helping professionals, the police, and the legal system may perceive women from these types of cultures as contributing to their victimization by accepting and internalizing the traditional submissive gender role. Dasgupta relates two examples that illustrate the additional stresses experienced by immigrant women from patriarchal cultures when the American legal system is involved. In the first case, a woman from Pakistan asked for a restraining order to prevent her husband from abusing her, despite the intense pressures from her family and the community to remain quiet about the abuse. In return, her husband asked for a restraining order that was in fact totally unjustified. The family court judge voided both restraining orders, although he acknowledged that the wife definitely was abused and that the husband's order was absurd. He justified his legal stand by stating that norms in the Pakistani culture supported the husband's right to treat his wife in that manner. The second example was the case of a Chinese immigrant male who killed his wife when she committed adultery. The judge administered a lenient penalty of five years' probation, stating that the individual was "driven to the murder" because, according to Chinese culture, he had "lost his manhood" as a result of his wife's behavior. These examples suggest that spousal abuse in immigrant communities may be responded to differently by the legal process than that in the dominant American culture.

Dasgupta also indicates that immigrant women from patriarchal societies are particularly reluctant to seek help when abused. These women have been socialized to accept the traditional values of submission and loyalty to their husbands, and fear ostracism and lack of support from their families and their communities if they go outside the culture to seek refuge from their abusive relationship. Many of these cultures disapprove of divorce, and women who attempt to break the cycle of abuse are subjected to family pressures to remain within the abusive relationship. In Asian cultures, for example, a woman who leaves her abusive husband is guilty of "bringing shame and dishonor" to the family. Families may urge the victim to "give him another chance" and suggest that a "good woman" (one who is loyal and submissive) may change a man's behavior. In addition to these pressures to remain loyal to the abuser, the victim is deprived of family support that in the country of origin may help constrain the abuser's behavior.

Another factor that contributes to the immigrant female's dependence on her husband, and that may prevent her from seeking help when she is abused, is related to the legal status of the wife. In American immigration law, the Marriage Fraud Act specifies that the only way a wife of a legal immigrant resident, or of an American citizen, may be offered temporary residency is if the husband begins the process by supporting or initiating her case. In this way, the abuser gains extreme power over the wife because he can use the threat of deportation to convince her to remain silent about the abuse. There is a clause exempting battered women from this act, but many immigrant women are unfamiliar with the laws, may not speak English, and may be too economically dependent on the husband even to consider using this option.

Asian Immigrant Communities

Many Asian countries are characterized by a patriarchal structured society that does not denounce men's violence against their spouses. Rhee (1997) identifies Korean women as representing the highest percentage of domestic abuse victims among Asian immigrants in Los Angeles. Rhee attributed this high rate to three possible factors:

1. A strong patriarchal dominance of men over women in the Korean culture.

2. Extensive stress of the immigration experience; Korean men generally lose occupational status in America as compared with their jobs in Korea. In addition, women are forced to work for economic reasons, but this behavior conflicts with the strong patriarchal expectation that women will remain in the home. Apparently, Korean men continue to emphasize male dominance despite the fact that the wives are working and performing domestic duties.

3. Social acceptance of the use of alcohol by men in the Korean culture. Drinking has been associated with increased probability of spousal abuse, although in a complex manner (Wallace, 1999).

Rhee suggests that all of the above factors provide a situation that has a high potential for abuse. In addition, when the women go to work, they come into contact with American views that favor equality over patriarchy in gender roles. As a result, the two cultures clash, producing a volatile family situation.

Yoshihama (2002) raises an issue related to treatment of abused spouses. The researcher suggests that professionals often advocate that only direct coping responses to abuse, such as involving the police and/or leaving the abuser, are effective. However, this advice conflicts with Japanese immigrant women's convictions that adopting these behaviors will produce a loss of support from their community. Once again, it is recommended that the helping professional attempt to develop strategies that will be acceptable to Asian women and will prevent future abuse.

Latina Immigrant Women

Perilla, Bakeman, and Norris (1994) examined abuse in a sample of Latina women who had contacted social services for assistance in dealing with the problem. As discussed earlier, the Hispanic culture is characterized by a patriarchal structure, although Perillo et al. indicate that this traditional gender role approach may be changing in immigrant populations. As in the Korean sample described above, the husband's drinking is associated with increased risk for abuse. However, an interesting pattern emerges with respect to the wife's dependence on the husband. When the wife works, she contributes to the economic well-being of the family. In this situation, it might be assumed that this economic contribution would create a more equal partnership between the husband and wife (i.e., a less patriarchal structure), which in turn might be associated with a decreased risk of abuse. However, Perilla et al. found, at least in the family's current situation, that her economic contribution actually increased the risk that the wife would be abused by the husband. In the short term, this economic independence conflicted with the important machismo value of the man being the sole provider for the family. Perilla et al. suggested that once the situation stabilized, the wife's economic contributions might translate into a gradual change in the unequal gender power-sharing traditionally associated with the Hispanic culture.

Cross-Cultural Findings

Yoshihama (2002) analyzes the issue of domestic abuse and attitudes toward wife battering in Japan. The author indicates that although domestic violence is a serious problem in Japan, there were no laws related to prevention of spouse battering until 2001. A "web of silence and abuse" is described in which the battered spouse is blamed for her victimization by the abuser, her family, and society, and there are few services available to help the battered spouse. In addition to the lack of support from the community, there is a tradition of requiring "conciliation" if one spouse refuses to grant a divorce. Therefore, abused spouses are unlikely to successfully sue for divorce without going through the conciliation process. According to Yoshihama, this mandated conciliation process may imply that divorce is unacceptable, and thus many abused spouses may see little chance of escaping from the abuse.

Conclusions

In this chapter we have examined the importance of culture in the development and maintenance of gender role attitudes and behaviors in America and cross-culturally. In particular, patriarchal and honor cultures are reinforced throughout socialization and continue to characterize cultures of immigrants from these types of societies. In the latter part of the chapter, we analyzed the role of patriarchal and honor cultures, as well as environmental stress, in spousal abuse, in addition to attitudes toward the abuse. These factors and others were discussed within the American culture, within immigrant cultures, and cross-culturally.

In conclusion, it is very important to consider culture when looking at gender roles and the part they play in spousal abuse. In addition, when designing interventions for abused spouses, it becomes very difficult to determine how to implement positive interventions that will not circumvent or conflict with cultural values of different communities. In the cases where it is impossible to integrate these proactive programs with cultural considerations, it may be necessary to rely on the illegality of spousal abuse in America to change norms supportive of abuse. Before that approach is implemented, however, considerable research must be conducted to clarify the complex impact of cultural gender role attitudes on domestic abuse and other destructive behaviors.

References

Araji, S. K., & Carlson, J. (2001). Family violence including crimes of honor in Jordan: Correlates and perceptions of seriousness. *Violence against Women, 7,* 586–621.

Chia, R. C., Allred, L. J., & Jerzak, P. A. (1997). Attitudes toward women in Taiwan and China. *Psychology of Women Quarterly, 21,* 137–150.

Cohen, D., Nisbett, R. E., Bowdle, B. F., & Schwarz, N. (1996). Insult, aggression, and the Southern culture of honor: An "experimental ethnography." *Journal of Personality and Social Psychology, 70,* 945–960.

Dasgupta, S. D. (1998). Women's realities: Defining violence against women by immigration, race and class. In R. K. Bergen (Ed.), *Issues in intimate violence* (pp. 209–219). Thousand Oaks, CA: Sage.

Frieze, I. H., Ferligoj, A., Kogousek, T., Rener, T., Horvat, J., & Sarlija, N. (2003). Gender-role attitudes in university students in the United States, Slovenia, and Croatia. *Psychology of Women Quarterly, 27,* 256–261.

Gelles, R. J. (1997). *Intimate violence in families* (3rd ed.). Thousand Oaks, CA: Sage.

Haj-Yahia, M. M. (2002). Beliefs of Jordanian women about wife-beating. *Psychology of Women Quarterly, 26,* 282–291.

Kikoski, C. K. (2000). Feminism in the Middle East: Reflections on ethnographic research in Lebanon. *Journal of Feminist Family Therapy, 11,* 131–146.

Nazzari, M. (1998). An urgent need to conceal. In L. L. Johnson & S. Lipsett-Rivera (Eds.), *The faces of honor: Sex, shame, and violence in colonial Latin America* (pp. 103–126). Albuquerque: University of New Mexico Press.

Okazaki, S. (1998). Teaching gender issues in Asian American psychology: A pedagogical framework. *Psychology of Women Quarterly, 22,* 33–52.

Oliver, W. (2000). Preventing domestic violence in the African-American community: The rationale for popular culture interventions. *Violence against Women, 6,* 533–549.

Onyeizugbo, E. U. (2003). Effects of gender, age, and education on assertiveness in a Nigerian sample. *Psychology of Women Quarterly, 27,* 12–16.

Perilla, J. A., Bakeman, R., & Norris, F. H. (1994). Culture and domestic violence: The ecology of abused Latinas. *Violence and Victims, 9,* 325–339.

Rhee, S. (1997). Domestic violence in the Korean immigrant family. *Journal of Sociology and Social Welfare, 24,* 63–77.

Sue, S., & Sue, D. (1971). Chinese American personality and mental health. *Amerasia Journal, 1,* 36–49.

Talbani, A., & Hasanali, P. (2000). Adolescent females between tradition and modernity: Gender role socialization in South Asian immigrant culture. *Journal of Adolescence, 23,* 615–627.

Tang, T. N., & Tang, C. S. (2001). Gender role internalization, multiple roles, and Chinese women's mental health. *Psychology of Women Quarterly, 25,* 181–196.

Vandello, J. A., & Cohen, D. (2003). Male honor and female fidelity: Implicit cultural scripts that perpetuate domestic violence. *Journal of Personality and Social Psychology, 84,* 997–1010.

Wallace, H. (1999). Spousal abuse. In H. Wallace (Ed.), *Family violence: Legal, medical, and social perspectives* (2nd ed.) (pp. 175–208). Boston: Allyn & Bacon.

Wasti, S. A., Bergman, M. E., Glomb, T. M., & Drasgow, F. (2000). Test of the cross-cultural generalizability of a model of sexual harassment. *Journal of Applied Psychology, 85,* 766–778.

Winik, L. W. (2003, November 9). Honor killings reach England. "The Record," *Parade,* p. 14.

Yoshihama, M. (2002). Breaking the web of abuse and silence: Voices of battered women in Japan. *Social Work, 47,* 389–400.

Chapter 3

A Latin American Perspective on the Study of Gender

Eros R. DeSouza, John Baldwin,
Sílvia H. Koller, and Martha Narvaz

A tradition of research is growing in the area of gender roles (Thompson, Pleck, & Ferrera, 1992), with long-standing interest in masculinity/femininity of minority groups (Baca Zinn, 1982). In this chapter, the term *Latinos* refers to men, and Latinas to women, from Latin American countries. The dominant U.S. culture (white Anglos) often characterizes Latinos as hypermasculine or macho (Marín & Marín, 1991). Yep (1995) defines machismo as "the assumed cultural expectation for men to be dominant in social relationships" (p. 202). Some Latinas are guided by *marianismo* (known as *modelo de Maria* in Brazil), which is the counterpart of machismo. *Marianismo* refers to the woman being framed as self-sacrificing, submissive to her man, and a "good" mother and wife (Baldwin & DeSouza, 2001); she is the *mujer sufrida* (suffering wife/woman) of Latin cultures. Thus, Latinas are dichotomized as "saints" (virtuous, pure, and asexual) or as "fallen creatures" to be pursued for pleasure only (Arcaya, 1999). This dichotomy reflects a sexual double standard. Men are expected to seek sex and pleasure, but women are not. For example, in a 1992 study by Marín and Gómez (as cited in VanOss-Marín et al., 1997) utilizing focus groups, Latinos/as stated that it would be dangerous for a woman to know as much about sex as a man and that a man would be disrespectful if he talked about sex to a woman. In fact, Latinos have been reported to maintain the negotiating power within heterosexual relationships, giving women little opportunity to discuss sex-related topics (DeSouza & Hutz, 1995; Maldonado, 1991).

Balls-Organista and Organista (1998) suggest that traditional psychological research on Latinos/as, and other ethnic groups, is often sexist and racist. For example, some Latin American cultural values (e.g., machismo and *marianismo*) are misunderstood and are framed as problematic, as issues to be "dealt with" by researchers and clinicians. In addition, researchers often assume that Latin American constructions of gender roles are static characteristics, failing to recognize regional and class subtleties of masculinities and femininities or universal similarities in the same constructions (Casas et al., 1995). Thus, the purpose of this chapter is to discuss gender roles and family violence in Latin America, particularly Brazil, which is the largest and most populous Latin American country.

Machismo

The literature on gender roles and identity in Latin America suggests that these countries are *machista* cultures. González (1982) contends that "the essence of machismo" is constituted by "a system of behavioral traits characterized by exaggerated manliness that eschews any type of female role or feminine activity" (p. 331). Some argue that what differentiates Latinos from mainstream U.S. culture is the higher degree of these stereotyped or male-dominated gender roles (Baird, 1993; Casas et al., 1995; DeSouza & Hutz, 1995; Marín & Gómez, 1995; Marín, Gómez & Hearst, 1993; Padilla, 1987).

Traditionally, machismo has included the notion (erroneous or not) that Latinos have greater sexual prowess and dominance over women; this has been framed as a key aspect of the machismo construct (Bernal & Alvarez, 1983; Parillo, 1980). Machismo also has referred to such things as a man's ability to control his alcohol consumption, to physical aggressiveness, and to verbal aloofness. The Mexican essayist Octavio Paz (1959) describes this verbal aloofness as the mask of invulnerability of Mexican men. He explains:

> Ideal "manhood" consists in never "giving in" (*rajarse*). Those who "open up" (*abren*) are cowards. The Mexican [male] can bend, humble himself, "stoop" (*agacharse*), but never "*rajarse*," that is, permit the outside world to penetrate his private life (*intimidad*). (p. 26, internal quotes in original)[1]

As expected, in addition to being a key aspect of Latino identity, notions of machismo impact gendered relationships. Generally, the attribute most Latinos choose to describe their ethnicity is "to maintain control and authority over their wives," while Latinas express submission, such as showing "public affection and respect towards their husbands" (Salgado de Snyder & Padilla, 1982, p. 360). Triandis et al. (1984) summarize Latinos' domination in intimate relationships thus:

Husband–wife relations among Hispanics are frequently described in terms of the husband's patriarchal dominance and the wife's submissive obedience. Men are idealized as masters, as stronger, more intelligent, more reliable, less emotional, and so forth. Women are presented as chaste, subdued, self-sacrificing, respectful, nurturant, and needing to be sheltered. (pp. 299–300)

Some research corroborates the above construction of machismo (González, 1982; Lara-Cantú, 1989; Sorenson & Siegel, 1992): Mexican American men with hypermasculinity have been reported to engage in unsafe sexual practices, even if such behaviors harm themselves or their families (Casas et al., 1995), such as having several sexual partners, infrequent condom use, and control over condom use (Maldonado, 1991; Mikawa et al., 1992). Moreover, we also see the influence of machismo in same-sex sexual relationships: In Latin America, men who are passive and penetrable are perceived, like women, to be feminine, while men who are active and impenetrable are perceived to be masculine (Magaña & Carrier, 1991; Parker, 1993). Thus, passive men who assume the receptive role in anal intercourse are stigmatized and labeled as homosexuals, while active men who play the insertive role are not perceived as homosexual.

Since machismo is defined in terms of that which is not feminine, it seems apparent that it reflects, as a mirror, the social construction of women in Latin America. *Marianismo* or, in Brazil, *modelo de Maria* (DeSouza, Baldwin, & da Rosa, 2000), reinforces women's views that they should tolerate the infidelities of their husbands/boyfriends. Based upon the chaste and maternal image of the Virgin Mary (Stevens, 1973), the ideal woman should be passive, pure, forgiving, and patient (Pescatello, 1973). These female characteristics constitute what Lara-Cantú and Navarro-Arias (1987) call the "syndrome of the self-sacrificing [Latin] woman" (pp. 332–333).

Defining machismo and *marianismo* creates twin difficulties. First, since machismo refers to traits associated with "manhood," especially as defined in Latin America, and *marianismo*, to traits associated with womanhood, both terms entail a wide array of beliefs and behaviors, as noted above. Second, while certain behaviors are associated with machismo and *marianismo*, none in and of itself defines manhood or womanhood. Thus, a man can be verbally nonexpressive or drink heavily and still not be seen as macho. A woman might be passive but not self-denying (indeed, in most cultures, there are different ideological archetypes of womanhood, including the contrasting images of saint and seductress). However, critiques of the traditional treatment of machismo and *marianismo* in academic literature run even deeper than this.

Some recent scholarship, for example, has challenged the above view of machismo as too simple and based, possibly, on white North American stereotypes of Latinos as womanizers, domineering, and sexually callous. Stephenson (2003) contends that the traditional concept of machismo "has a decidedly racist origin" and "first arose partly as prejudice directed against Mexican immigrants in the United States" (pp. 84–85). Baca Zinn (1982) also has argued that the traditional notion of machismo in Latin American cultures is a stereotypic myth, citing, for example, research that shows that decision-making in Latin American homes is likely to be more egalitarian than male-dominated.

Mirandé (1985) screened out the more negative aspects of machismo (e.g., cowardice, abusiveness, shamelessness, and drunkenness) and, instead, defined machismo as encompassing "the pride, dignity, and tenacity of the Chicano people as they have resisted the onslaught of economic, political, and cultural control" (p. 179). Several authors have pointed out positive aspects of machismo, such as its emphasis on a noble education, self-confidence, nurturance, and dedication to the protection of the family (Bernal & Alvarez, 1983; González, 1982; Lara-Cantú, 1989; Mirandé, 1985; Ruiz, 1981; Sorenson & Siegel, 1992; Valdes, Baron, & Ponce, 1987). While the ideology of machismo implies that to be a "true man," one should not cry in public or appear weak, it also invokes notions of honor, responsibility, and protection of individuals weaker than oneself (Stephenson, 2003). In sum, like most cultural values, machismo has both positive and negative elements, and both should be considered in research, as well as in clinical and preventive work.

Similarly, women's behavioral roles are very complex in Latin America; they are not formed simply as a reaction to machismo or male dominance (Chaney, 1979). Chaney says that the dependent, subordinate, and sacrificial mother has an alter ego. Latinas "sometimes wield formidable power within certain restricted spheres, principally behind the high walls and closed doors that guard the sacred and private family circle" (pp. 47–48). In sum, a view that describes Latin American gender roles primarily or only in terms of machismo or *marianismo* is limiting, because it frames social reality using male hegemony. Moreover, we cannot state that machismo is strictly negative, or that Latin American sexual identity is uniform or uncomplicated.

A second challenge to the traditional notion of Latin American machismo is that the same traits that have been called "machismo" in the literature on Latinos seem to be alive and well in other cultures. Researchers have called this set of attitudes and behaviors "traditional masculinity" (Bunting & Reeves, 1983), hypermasculinity, or "masculinity ideology" (Pleck, Sonenstein, & Ku, 1993a, 1993b). Research on the "universal" aspects of machismo has associated extreme masculinity or hypermasculinity with lack of emotion and aloofness from family (Pasick, Gordon, & Meth, 1990), alcohol and drug abuse (Burda & Vaux, 1987; Pasick et al. 1990), unsafe sexual practices (Bunting & Reeves, 1983; Eisler & Skidmore, 1987), aggression or violence toward self and others (Eisler & Skidmore, 1987), reluctance to seek help from others (Metz & Seifert, 1990), and the likelihood to use power and control to validate one's masculinity (O'Neil, 1982). Men scoring high on scales of machismo are more likely to use physical force in intimate relationships and to feel more isolated because of a decreased ability to hold close personal relationships (Koval, Ponzetti, & Cate, 1982; Neuhouser, 1989). Further, Pleck et al. (1993a) found that, after controlling for socioeconomic status (SES) and ethnicity, *machista* men (in all groups studied) reported more sexual partners during a year, used condoms less consistently, viewed condoms more negatively (e.g., as reducing sexual pleasure), were less concerned with whether a partner wanted him to use a condom, believed less in male responsibility for contraception, and believed more strongly that impregnating a woman would validate a man's masculinity compared with non-*machista* men.

Indeed, some research is challenging our traditional notions of comparative machismos in the Americas: Acuña and Bruner (2001) compared men and women in Mexico and the United States on the Bem Sex Role Inventory, with some contradictory results: U.S. men rated more highly "masculine" than Mexican men, and U.S. women more highly "feminine" than Mexican women. DeSouza and Hutz (1996) compared U.S. and Brazilian college students' perception of a fictitious female's sexual intent when she consistently or inconsistently said no to a man's sexual advances. When participants continued the story in their own words, content analyses of their written responses indicated that Brazilian students had a stronger consensual sexual-intercourse scenario (45.2 percent) compared with U.S. students (28.2 percent), whereas U.S. students had a stronger date rape scenario (27.1 percent) compared with Brazilian students (3.4 percent), regardless of the scenario received. DeSouza and Hutz (1996) suggest that "in a rapidly changing society [like Brazil], token resistance to sex might simply be an acceptable avenue for Brazilian women to initiate and/or negotiate sexual contact with men, without being labeled 'loose'" (p. 561).

Overall, Burda and Vaux (1987) suggest that men in the U.S. culture (without reference to ethnicity):

can be characterized by restricted emotional expression, a drive to utilize control, and engage in competition in order to gain power and status, an irrational fear of femininity and homosexuality, a need to maintain an invulnerable and independent image, a fear of genuine intimacy, and poor health care maintenance. (p. 32)

As stated earlier, many researchers contend that Latinos, in general, hold more male-dominated and stereotypical gender beliefs than white North Americans (Baird, 1993; Casas et al., 1995; Marín & Gómez, 1995; Marín et al., 1993). Yet, in Brazil, Barker and Loewenstein (1997) studied many young men of low SES in the city of Rio de Janeiro who did not accept the traditional gender roles. Cultures differ regarding the acceptable deviation from social roles (Gudykunst & Kim, 2003). This deviation seems, in part, to be due to the salience of competing discourses regarding these roles. The exponential increase of books on the social construction of masculinity (e.g., Brod, 1987; Connell, 1995; Craig, 1992; Horrocks, 1994), and their availability in academia, suggest that competing discourses (and, thus, heterogeneity of social roles) are present across cultures.

Gender Schema Theory and a Layered Perspective of Gendered Identities

Critiquing laundry-list approaches that merely enumerate the aspects of machismo, Casas et al. (1995) argue for theory-driven empirical research to better understand machismo among Latinos. They propose Bem's (1981, 1985) gender schema theory as a valuable lens through which to view machismo. This approach admits the influence of culture on *machista* values, as well as individuals' ability to cognitively process gender schemata. Children learn to evaluate themselves in terms of gender schemata and match their behaviors, attitudes, and personal characteristics to prototypes of the gender models they have seen. But they may also refuse those gender schemata. Thus, women and men may differ in the degree to which they subscribe to cultural notions of femininity and masculinity, actually exhibit those traits (Thompson et al., 1992), base their self-concepts on gender-based dimensions (Bem, 1985), or match their ideology to their behavior (Weisbuch, Beal, & O'Neal, 1999).

By incorporating explanatory factors from both psychology and sociology, the model proposed by Casas et al. (1995) addresses a growing call to consider the intersections between traditional disciplines as they address complex social issues (Baldwin & Hecht, 1995). The holographic layered approach (HLA), while not an axiomatic theory with specific predictions (Hecht & Baldwin, 1998), suggests the need to look for complex aspects of social phenomena at the individual, social, and discursive (rhetorical) levels. Thus, HLA may help researchers crystallize some of the aspects of machismo suggested by Casas et al. (1995).

The HLA encourages using the views of multiple disciplines to examine a particular social reality (Baldwin, 1998), such as machismo or *marianismo*. The HLA derives from Talbot's (1991) discussion of holographic film. When the film is cut into tiny pieces, each piece contains the image of the whole. The more the film is cut, however, the more distorted the image. This suggests that one might look at one piece of the "film" of machismo/*marianismo*—either at one culture or through one disciplinary window—and see an image, a microcosm, of extreme masculinity or femininity throughout a society or throughout the world. However, the multiplication of cultural, methodological, and disciplinary views provides a much clearer view of the phenomenon. The complexity of machismo/*marianismo* requires collaboration among researchers because gender identity exists intrapsychically, is constructed in dyadic and relational communication, and is reproduced in communal memory through media, law, and ritual (Collier & Thomas, 1988; Gilmore, 1990; Hecht, 1993; Hecht, Jackson, & Ribeau, 2003). Thus, machismo/*marianismo* is likely to be influenced not just by psychodynamics and cognitive processes, but also by social (economic structure, ethnicity, immigration patterns), political (power distribution, legal sanction), rhetorical (media and interpersonal constructions, popular culture), and biological factors.

The HLA also accounts for the cross-cultural similarities in masculinities and femininities by proposing that some social phenomena have a shared reality, a similarity in theme, across cultures and time. The underlying theme of machismo/*marianismo* might derive from the common history of societies as agricultural or gathering communities that relied on men's physical labor (leading both to men's control of resources and competition between men). Evolutionary descriptions of gender roles (e.g., Buss, 1998) suggest that men's physical strength and lack of expressiveness have helped them compete in the public sphere against other men and have been maintained as functional, or that men's desire for multiple sex partners is related to the propagation of the gene pool. It may simply be that men's larger size and greater physical force have enabled them to get away with controlling sexual activity or decision-making in the home.

Another possible explanation for universal similarities in machismo derives from sociological theory. Baca Zinn (1982) proposed that Mexican machismo is an attempt to reclaim power for a disempowered group. Mexican American men in the United States, she contends, express machismo because of disempowerment before the dominant white Anglo culture. Other researchers support the possibility of machismo being related to disempowerment. For example, working-class white men in one Chicago suburb ("Teamsterville") embraced "masculine" values of aggression toward women, children, and cultural "others"—to do otherwise would not be "speaking like a man" (Philipsen, 1975). Men in other lower SES contexts, such as pool halls, motorcycle clubs, and shop floors, attempted to embody "true masculinity," perhaps as a result of a "subordinate order-taking position in relation to higher status males" (Pyke, 1996, p. 531). For Pyke, notably, there are different masculinities. Lower-status masculinity, she urged, is compensatory, relying on "physical endurance and tolerance of discomfort, . . . pervasive talk of their sexual prowess and a ritualistic put-down of women" (pp. 531–532). She contrasted this with different masculinities held by men in more privileged positions.

At the same time, the HLA considers the discursive influences that construct gender roles differently in each culture and change them across time. Many researchers across disciplines hold that "machismo is a socially constructed, learned, and reinforced set of behaviors comprising the content of male gender roles in Latino society" (De la Cancela, 1986, p. 291). Even some evolutionary theorists admit that complex social phenomena, such as racism and gender oppression, must be understood in terms of competing visions of reality and ideologies (Van der Dennen, 1987). While there may be social, cognitive, and even biological roots to male gender schemata among Latinos and in other cultures, these schemata are also ideological, in that they are situated within the socially constructed mental frameworks, which consist of thought images, concepts, assumptions, and systems of representation shared by specific groups of individuals (Hall, 1996; Van Dijk, 1998). Ideologies of "masculinity" and "femininity" are socially constructed through culturally specific discourses (Foucault, 1978; Hollway, 1984; Tiefer, 1995) that are passed on through family and friends (social learning, everyday communication), popular culture (media images, popular music, novels, etc.), textbooks, and regulations (laws, organizational policies).

Several current gender theories view the masculine gender as an active discourse process, produced and reproduced daily in a culture (Hare-Mustin & Marecek, 1990; Unger, 1990; West & Zimmerman, 1987). One aspect of this discourse is the "male sexual drive" discourse (Hollway, 1984). Zilbergeld (1978) identified several themes of this particular discourse: Sex is a male performance; the man is responsible for initiating sex; a man always wants and is always ready to have sex; for a man, all physical contact must lead to sex; and birth control is the woman's responsibility.

Discourse also constructs women's gender. We can see this, for example, through the lens of the sexual double standard. This standard exists in many cultures. For example, at many U.S. universities, if the man walks home from the women's residential hall in the morning, he walks the "walk of fame," but if the woman returns from the men's hall, she walks the "walk of shame." The man with multiple (female) sexual partners is a "stud," but the woman with multiple male partners is a "slut." A Brazilian family law expert (Lopes de Oliveria) summarizes how such a double standard plays out in Brazilian society:

> When a man violates the conjugal loyalty he does that by futile desire. That doesn't destroy the love of the woman, or the fundament of conjugal society. The woman's adultery, on the contrary, affects the family's internal order, compromising the stability of the conjugal life. The woman's adultery is more serious, not only for the scandal it causes, but also because it hurts many values and the law more deeply. There is danger of her introducing strange children into her home. (Americas Watch, 1991, p. 22)

The above quote illustrates that at least in social custom, if not before the law, female adultery is socially unacceptable, because it goes against the socially constructed "natural" role of women as mothers and, through their service to the family, as progenitors of the nation; on the other hand, men are free to fulfill their personal desires almost with social impunity (Neuhouser, 1989). The "honesty" (understood as chastity) of women is still frequently a major issue in rape cases in Brazil (Thomas & Beasley, 1993). In regard to the family, the man is seen typically as the provider, the supporter, and the legal representative (Americas Watch, 1991). To put it simply, social institutions have historically acted to deny women the right to exercise their power publicly. Men conquer the workplace and dominate in the legal sphere, while women are framed as mothers and valued if they are "honest" (chaste).

Combined, the discourses of masculine and feminine identity lead to a set of common themes about sexuality in Latin America: Male sexuality is uncontrollable; women are responsible for male sexuality; sex is a force of nature; and men are dominant and women are submissive. These themes limit women's sexuality and give men sexual freedom (e.g., more types and frequency of sexual partners, greater frequency of intercourse, and less responsibility for birth control); however, the same language of "natural uncontrollability" in male sexuality also imprisons men by not allowing them to refuse sex, lest they be accused of being sexually inadequate, impotent, or homosexual (Reinholtz et al., 1995).

Future research should investigate the relationship between machismo and other cultural norms, such as sexual conservatism (Baca Zinn, 1982), views on gay sex (Balls-Organista & Organista, 1998; DeSouza, Madrigal, & Millan, 1999), and notions of male virility (González, 1982; Lara-Cantú, 1989; Sorenson & Siegel, 1992), which may lead Latin men to have unsafe sex with prostitutes, intimate partners, and other men.

The Cycle of Violence in the Family:
The Example of Brazil

Machismo and *marianismo*, however they are constructed, can be applied to all Latin American countries (Portuguese- and Spanish-speaking), though we expect nuances of differences between countries (as well as between racial, ethnic, and regional cultures). If we look more closely at individual countries or cultures, we can better see the convergence of social and historical factors that helped to shape gender roles. Further, we will see gender violence situated within the gender roles and the social contexts in which it occurs. In this section, then, we will look specifically at the Brazilian social construction of gender in the family and the relationship of that construction to violence.

The Historical Context of the Family in Brazil

The configuration of women's roles has been changing in Brazilian society. However, the path to change is very slow and hard, since the patriarchal family was the economic base of colonial Brazil. Wealthy white men owned vast tracts of land and many slaves. The family of the white man was organized around him and had the purpose of satisfying his needs and desires, in face of the power that he had. On the other hand, even white women were property of the patriarch, and they played limited roles in society. Marriages were arranged. Married women were supposed to take care of the house and to serve their husbands as good childbearers, thus supporting the patriarch's role in society (Corrêa, 1994).

During the colonial period in Brazil, the supposition that women were "biologically inferior" became a settled and accepted ideology. Besides being fragile, women were seen as men's property (Corrêa, 1994). Arranged marriages treated women as merchandise, without their own will and subject to patriarchal fathers and to future husbands (new patriarchs in the woman's new family). Not only women's will, but also their bodies, were subordinated, for they did not have sexual choice, and their sexual life was an expression of subservience to men.

In the nineteenth century, the maintenance of the patriarchal family did not serve the dominant interests in Brazil. Capitalism needed consolidation, and for such consolidation of capital to take place, a necessary change in the family was imposed. Urban life intensified and forced adjustments in family structure and functioning. One of the first changes was a move from arranged marriages to romantic love. The man stopped being seen as the owner of his family and became instead the material provider (breadwinner) for the wife and their offspring. The woman stopped being seen as property and became instead the children's mother and educator, as well as the nurturer of the husband and of the home (D'Incao, 2001). However, women were still viewed as submissive and passive, adopting a caretaker (maternal) role, whereas men remained dominant, active, and enterprising. Intimacy and matrimonial partnership, both in the relationship between the spouses and in the care and raising of children, led to an affectionate estrangement between man and woman.

The twentieth century witnessed more dramatic changes in women's social and family history. At the beginning of the twentieth century, the Brazilian Civil Code still guaranteed men's power over women and restricted women's entrance into the workplace. However, women (especially white women) have systematically enlarged their areas of influence. White women began to enter the job market and to have access to formal education. The birth-control pill appeared, giving women more control over their body and reproduction. The feminist movements in the United States and in Europe began to produce effects in Brazil, as well as other Latin American countries, in the 1950s; Brazilian women struggled for new laws and for the modification of the Brazilian Civil Code, so that they could achieve the right to enter the workplace (Alvarez, 1990).

The World Conference of the United Nations designated 1975 as Women's International Year. In the same year, March 8 was established as Woman's International Day in Latin America. In Brazil, despite a struggle against the military dictatorship, the feminist movement progressed, and women started to participate actively in politics, collaborating with women of the whole world in the fight for visibility and against exclusion. The family concept also changed, especially after the year 2002, when the Brazilian Civil Code was revised. The power in the family that was exercised by the man is now shared between woman and man. A new world is open for human rights—not only for women's rights—since men as well as women will have to find their new roles and positions in this society. One of the key issues that men and women will have to face in Brazil is the raising of children under new, more egalitarian structures, as Brazilians produce a new picture of family and gender issues in the future. Thus, we now turn to violence in the Brazilian family.

Violence in the Brazilian Family

Gender violence involves "unified actions or circumstances that submit individuals, physically and/or emotionally, consciously and/or unconsciously as a function of their sex" (Werba & Strey, 2001, p. 72). However, some recent feminist work places traditional ideologies of what it is to be men (e.g., control of sexuality, reticence to communicate regarding relationships, view of women as sex objects) on a continuum that links such ideologies to violence against women (DeFrancisco, 1997). That is, as gender roles play out in society and in the family, they may be linked to violence against women in several ways. It is important to note that while physical and sexual abuse constitute the most overt forms of violence, DeFrancisco sees all oppression of women as violence. Thus, we could extend her view of violence to the silencing of women's voices through ridicule of their speaking styles, to unequal wages, to sexual harassment, or to barriers in the workplace.

Through the HLA (Hecht & Baldwin, 1998; Talbot, 1991) we can also examine family interactions in terms of gender issues in everyday life. That is, we can examine one small piece (e.g., turn-taking patterns in family communication, women's poetry about suppression or oppression in their relationships) to figure out the full picture of how violence plays out in the home. Because the HLA indicates multiple fronts (individual/psychological, communicative, relational, communal, legal, and structural) for addressing intolerance, it has great potential for transformation that a family can go through as a remedy for violence against women.

The family, according to Narvaz and Koller (in press), is our primary social group (see also Camilo Osório, 1997). There we learn our social and gender roles. It should be a place where we learn in safety and security—a place of protection and intimacy. Yet women have been victims of gender violence in their own families through generations. This transgenerationality of violence implies that women experience violence collectively (Narvaz & Koller, in press). Such violence is often institutionalized. For example, in Brazil the sexual double standard described above has changed little since colonial times. In those days, female adulterers were punished by death, while men received little punishment for relations with single women, prostitutes, or slaves (Araújo, 1993). Men who commit adultery are only expressing their "natural" maleness. Some reports suggest that, though illegal, the "honor defense" (in which a man kills a woman or her lover for adultery), is still accepted on 80 percent of the occasions on which it is used in Brazil (Americas Watch, 1991; Thomas & Beasley, 1993).

A completely new world is open to "denaturalize" gender violence and establish equivalent relationships between human beings. Those violent events have been histories of encounters and misunderstandings, crowded by secrets and traditional practices, "naturally" installed in the education of girls and women. Gender-abusive families rewrite histories of complicities and connivances, marked with domination and submission.

The victimization of women negates their rights. As women seek to re-dress gender violence, they also uncover the hidden and petrified areas of vi-olence in their own families of origin and cultures (Andolfi & Angelo, 1989). Thus, the cycle of violence begins to break down when women seek em-powerment (Koller, 1999). Macho men are often present in the typical fam-ily environment of abusive systems to the extent that these systems reflect more rigid gender roles that correspond to patriarchal systems in Latin Amer-ica. The fact that violence toward women is so often supported, at least im-plicitly, by the larger social structure suggests that violence in the home is not the father's domain, but the domain of men in general, commonly con-doned by Western culture (Jones, 1994).

Feminist family theory (Jones, 1994) foreshadows a possible overlap with the ecological approach to human development (Bronfenbrenner, 1979) and the HLA (Hecht & Baldwin, 1998; Talbot, 1991). The common base of fem-inist theory and the ecological approach of human development is centered in the understanding that the personal problems of a family depend on the context. This context exists at the interface of national, cultural, ethnic, and class factors, for some research suggests that egalitarianism among men may vary depending on class and the region of a country (Muraro, 1983). But the family itself may be a relevant context, for while it is influenced by its sur-rounding culture, the family can also develop its own culture (Dodd & Bald-win, 2002). The family is a privileged context of ideological reproduction, in which we learn social roles and gender roles (Reis, 1985; Schützenberger, 1997). The family has to be contextualized, and observed through the lens of gender issues, so that one can capture the full picture of beliefs and myths and, from this picture, develop strategies for change.

Since its origin, the term "family" has demarcated an association with tra-ditional forms of family organization. The Latin word *famulus* designates the "things and belongings of someone," mostly related to a man's belongings, which include his wife and children (Camilo Osório, 1997). Such a defini-tion ignores the balance in the gender relationships and guarantees the man's sense of ownership toward the family (Koller, 1999). Until recently, all fam-ily members used the man's family name, and he was legally considered the family provider and the guardian of all. This picture of male hegemony has prevailed since the days of the patriarchal structures in Latin America. Such configuration reproduced the norms of masculine power and ownership, which were dictated by the masculine, and allowed by the feminine, through generations. Most Latin American countries, as well as other cultures, re-produce this picture (Goodrich et al., 1988).

However, this situation is changing, as experts in women's rights are framing violence against women as human rights for fair conditions to protect women. Jones (1994) claims that different people should not be treated as equal, but as equivalent. Oppression based on gender, and based on ethnicity and social class as well, permeates diverse societies. The use of some tactics to deal with gender issues is similar to other forms of oppression that sustain discriminatory practices, such as racism, homophobia, and all other kinds of exclusion. In every way, such oppression can happen as relationships of power reproduce themselves through the family, which socializes its members according to the dictates of the mainstream culture. Thus, the family internalizes, reproduces, and hides the actual oppression (Grossi, 2001).

Family Ideologies and Structures of Power

Ideally, in the traditional family, the submission processes and acceptance of the parents' control are presented as natural and necessary. The submission that women learn from their early life evidences a pattern of relationship (one can read "dominance") that is transferred to other spheres of their lives. It produces obedient girls—future citizens without voice, submissive to all and without authority. Symbolic and ideological forms produce and reproduce these mechanisms of dominance (Reis, 1985). The family is but one locus of the (re)production of gender ideology, as parents treat boys and girls in ways that assume a hierarchy in which men are above women. Such ideological mechanisms of reproduction of the asymmetrical relationships of power in the family, especially relative to gender issues, have been discussed thoroughly by feminists and academicians in some Latin American cultures, who have tried to redress them (Narvaz & Koller, in press).

The supremacy of masculinity has favored unequal, unjust, and asymmetrical power relationships, in which it has been hard for men and women to share spaces for interplay of care and reciprocal responsibilities. If dominance can be understood as relationship, it is only a relationship of expropriation of power in which one removes, in an asymmetrical or unjust way, the power and the rights of others (Grossi, 2001). The historical primacy of the masculine over the feminine engenders some of the explanations of masculine dominance, the passive feminine role, and women's victimization in gender relationships through time. Gender ideology legitimates a form of power that justifies heterosexual masculine ascendancy, naturalizing differences that actually are built by society through discourse (talk, media, law, etc.). Moreover, it converts differences into inequalities and oppressions (Werba & Strey, 2001).

Defining women as wives and mothers stimulates feminine dependence as it does the compulsory nature of permanent care for others. The basic requirements of these roles compel women to submit to and to take care of others. Dependence appears as the operative methodology of patriarchal dominance (Gilligan, 1979, 1982). Women, from an early age, are socialized to respond to the needs of men (parents and siblings) and not to their own or to those of their daughters. The role that is transmitted to them guarantees a supposedly ideal family and engenders a mythic view of women (*marianismo*) as caretakers and self-denying, altruistic, and dedicated. Men and children, especially sons, are the main recipients of their care.

Another culturally transmitted ideal is based on a belief that men are sexual beings who cannot be controlled. Even if it is not explicit, the formulation of this ideology seems to be that "men should be served," and never contradicted; men should be assisted in all their needs, even (or especially) the sexual ones. These social laws, framed as natural, are deemed to be the ones to which women and daughters ought to submit. They will supposedly guarantee that the family survives intact (Narvaz & Koller, in press).

Gender issues are central to the maintenance of women and men as social subjects; furthermore, they are implicated in the perpetuation of gender violence. Thus, they become an important topic for analysis and for our understanding of the organization of interpersonal relationships, especially within Latin American families (De Antoni & Koller, 2000; Koller, 1999; Narvaz, 2001, 2002a, 2002b; Narvaz, Berwanger, Moraes, & Rose, 2000). Here we see the important juncture of power and domination, which are not synonymous. Rather, power can be good, useful, and enjoyable; it involves choice, and is much more fluid than domination (Narvaz & Koller, in press). Perhaps it is for this reason that Chaney (1979), as noted above, argues that women in Latin America do have power, but of a different kind than men do. There is power in everyday life, in folkloric culture (Adorno, 1991), in journals and networking and feminine communication (Kramarae, 1981). It is the power that women have—relational power, collective power, and, with increasing frequency, power in the political, literary, workplace, and academic domains—that allows the possibility of resistance and provides a bulwark against all forms of violence and oppression (Narvaz & Koller, in press).

Resisting Dominance and Violence

Such resistance must be multifaceted, since oppression has many dimensions (Hecht & Baldwin, 1998). As with other forms of cultural intolerance, any solution aimed only at information and education assumes that the problem is based solely on ignorance. Rather, relational and sexual violence are about power; further, that power not only exists at the dyadic level of the relationship, but also is reinforced and inscribed by societal power structures (division of labor, laws, material relations, cultural ideologies). Solutions to dominance must be multifaceted and integrated. Thus, for each of several areas of violence, we offer suggestions for women and for their male allies.

In the Family

Women are redrafting the transgenerationality of being abused because of their gender. That is, they are transforming the patterns of socialization to generate relationships of equality and cooperation, instead of contexts that legitimate the feminine dominance, in their dyadic communication and social relationships. So, too, education should emphasize the *equivalence* of men and women as human beings; that is, men and women are not equal, but they are equivalent. They each have idiosyncrasies and similarities, but a man or a woman is always at some point an icon of his or her gender. The new configuration of families would show new pictures of organization and values that may lessen the odds of gender violence and empower family members to reorganize their relationship on the basis of other issues.

Social Violence

Women and girls, according to several studies, are more frequently victims of social violence (Narvaz, 2003; Werba & Strey, 2001); girls and women are abused at home, and societies often condone such abuse through silence. A million children in the world have been victims of domestic violence and of sexual exploitation, with poverty being seen as the primary cause; in Brazil alone, 100,000 children and women are sexually exploited every year (Nunes, 2003). Child abuse and violence against women have been hidden through socially established pacts (such as family secrets) that mask the reality of abuse. Family secrets need to stop, and women (as well as male allies) need to start fighting against gender violence.

A wider approach—one that involves variables such as economic, political, or social contexts as provided by the HLA—allows us to better understand women's behavioral response to violence (Dutton, 1997). The proclivity of societies and cultures to sexual violence engenders scarcity of resources, ineffectiveness of policies, and one-sidedness of information concerning women's human rights (Strey, 2001). This proclivity disguises a prejudicial society that believes it is acceptable for men to provoke and harass women, and that the guilt for this harassment should be attributed to women (Vigarello, 1998). Changing society's focus to the aggressor's responsibility would demonstrate how we have implicitly blamed the victims in such cases.

Communication Expectations

Women are also submitted to the masculine pattern in their personal relations. If women act resigned and passive, this may be interpreted as indulgence and complicity. Yet if they adopt men's communicative styles, they are often seen as "bitches." Thus, society uses forms such as criticizing women's speech patterns to silence them (Kramarae, 1981).[2] It is necessary to evaluate the communicative resources that woman have in order to rupture the silence, which is intertwined with sexual violence.[3] Zuwick (2001) emphasizes the unbearable shame of a victimized woman, who feels that any resistance to domination may eventually work against her. She believes she will be silenced once again for not holding to the rules of her domination, and thus turns down networking support. Even if she belongs to a supportive society, sometimes an attacked woman does not fight for her own needs: "To understand the woman's reason to stay with the one who attacks her, it becomes necessary to reveal that hidden reality that oppresses the woman daily and maintains her in the extreme point of subordination" (Cardoso, 1997, p. 136). In some cases, ignorance and anomie lead a woman even to contemplate her partner raping their own daughter without reacting and without denouncing the act (Corsi, 1997). Researchers and activists should also consider how Latin American cultures are complicit with violent practices against women and minorities. Society becomes an accomplice because it does not give visibility to the problem (Koller, 1999). In response, efforts against violence should be aimed not only at the individual family but also at laws, educational systems, and other social structures.

Men are often socialized in families in which women are seen as male property, that is, as sex objects. Sexual aggression is defined more as an exercise of power than of gender differences (Madanes, 1991). Male sexual aggressors assume characteristics and attitudes considered traditionally masculine, tending to have difficulty expressing feelings or having empathic attitudes. These men tend to justify their beliefs and myths concerning sexual violence and to believe in violence in general as a means of conflict resolution (Martín, 2000). It is necessary that we make this communication of problematic beliefs visible. Women and men should be called by their names and not by their roles, an issue that becomes especially apparent when women are reduced to the maternal or conjugal role. Women stop being merely "mothers" or "wives" to guarantee their personal singularity. Women should not be made responsible only for the structure and function of the family, nor should they be relegated to the cultural position of being responsible for the construction of family patterns (Ravazzola, 1999). Rather, in our media, in our homes, in our national constitutions, in the terms we use for women, we should construct them as individuals with choice and freedom—be that the freedom to work primarily within the home or the freedom to seek more expansive social roles.

Conclusions

As we have seen in this chapter, many writers on Latin American gender roles speak of traditionally accepted gender archetypes, such as machismo (an exaggerated masculinity for men) and *marianismo* (a passive, nurturing role for women). Each of these constructs includes an array of meanings and behavioral characteristics. However, we also note that these constructs are problematic in some regards, since women or men may possess only some of the traits assigned to the archetype, and because power and sexual identities are more complex in Latin America than these roles often describe. Certainly, one of the difficulties in defining gender roles is that Latin American countries underwent rapid changes in gender roles during the latter part of the twentieth century. However, there is still a wide disparity between the rich and the poor.

We have also seen that violence against women can be understood broadly to include any form of exclusion, harassment, or abuse. Further, we note that this violence is multifaceted. Certainly, to borrow from the HLA (Hecht & Baldwin, 1998), it exists in both physical and verbal treatment and in the media. While both men and women are victims of relational violence, violence against women is supported by the social structure (laws, policies, social practices). Prejudice against women is still blatant in work settings in Latin America (DeSouza & Solberg, 2003). According to the Caipora Women's Group (1993), until recently the women's movement in Brazil ignored black women, the majority of whom live in poverty. Criticisms from the left charge that middle-class feminism diverts attention from the real issue of class conflict (Hahner, 1990).

These criticisms have also been voiced in the United States regarding middle-class bias in women's studies and male bias in racial/ethnic studies (Weber, 1998). Weber states that race, class, gender, and sexuality are contextually entrenched in history and geography. Thus, they are socially constructed, not biologically determined. They also should be examined ecologically, from macrostructural systems of oppression (e.g., racism, class inequalities, homophobia) to the micro social-psychological levels (e.g., domestic violence). Weber adds that race, class, gender, and sexuality hierarchies exist within power relationships, as we described above. Since gender violence exists within these hierarchies, any solution to that violence must address the problem at psychological, communicative, and social structural levels.

In sum, if we are to have a world that values every individual as a human being, we need to develop an interdisciplinary and cross-cultural perspective to address all social inequalities. We need a psychology with practical significance that does not limit itself solely to individual thought and behavior, but that considers how these are informed by—and themselves inform—a more holistic view of social reality. Thus, the progress of women (and men) in Brazil is also tied to the progress of women (and men) in other Latin American countries as well as in North America, because we are part of a global village linked together by interdependent economies, technologies, and societies (DeSouza, Baldwin, & da Rosa, 2000).

Notes

1. Translation from Spanish is our own. *Rajarse* is especially problematic to translate, since it is a slang word that changes meaning from place to place, meaning such things as "flee" (Argentina), "spend a lot" (United States), "be wrong" (Colombia), "not keep one's word," "brag," or "speak badly or lie about others." The meanings that seem most appropriate here would be to "give in" or to "be a coward," though the rest of the quotation suggests a figurative reading of "to split oneself open" (*Pequeño Larousse*, 1982, p. 867).

2. The current status of communication between men and women in the United States is controversial; for example, Weatherall (1996) concludes from her study that women are not silenced in public discourse.

3. The level of power that women have to combat or resist power structures is a topic of debate. Some feel that women, by enacting the cultural patterns or ideologies of *marianismo*, participate in their own subjugation. Others feel that women have learned these patterns—often as their only option—and thus have no alternative to the patterns of subjugation and violence.

References

Acuña, L., & Bruner, C. A. (2001). Estereotipos de masculinidad y femineidad en México y en Estados Unidos [Stereotypes of masculinity and femininity in Mexico and in the United States]. *Interamerican Journal of Psychology, 35,* 31–51.

Adorno, T. W. (1991). *The culture industry*, (Ed. J. M. Bernstein). London: Routledge.
Alvarez, S. E. (1990). *Engendering democracy in Brazil: Women's movements in transition politics*. Princeton, NJ: Princeton University Press.
Americas Watch (1991). *Criminal injustice: Violence against women in Brazil*. New York: Human Rights Watch.
Andolfi, M., & Angelo, C. (1989). *Tempo e mito em terapia familiar* [Time and myth in family therapy]. Pôrto Alegre, Brazil: Artes Médicas.
Araújo, E. (1993). *O teatro dos vícios: Transgressão e transigência na sociedade urbana colonial* [The theater of vices: Transgression and endurance in colonial urban society]. Rio de Janeiro: José Olympio.
Arcaya, J. (1999). Hispanic American boys and adolescent males. In A. M. Horne & M. S. Kiselica (Eds.), *Handbook of counseling boys and adolescent males: A practitioner's guide* (pp. 101–116). Thousand Oaks, CA: Sage.
Baca Zinn, M. (1982). Chicano men and masculinity. *Journal of Ethnic Studies, 10,* 20–44.
Baird, T. L. (1993). Mexican adolescent sexuality: Attitudes, knowledge, and sources of information. *Hispanic Journal of Behavioral Sciences, 15,* 402–417.
Baldwin, J. R. (1998). Tolerance/intolerance: A multidisciplinary view of prejudice. In M. L. Hecht (Ed.), *Communicating prejudice* (pp. 24–56). Thousand Oaks, CA: Sage.
Baldwin, J. R., & DeSouza, E. (2001). Modelo de Maria and machismo: The social construction of gender in Brazil. *Interamerican Journal of Psychology, 35,* 9–29.
Baldwin, J. R., & Hecht, M. L. (1995). The layered perspective of cultural (in)tolerance(s): The roots of a multidisciplinary approach. In R. L. Wiseman (Ed.), *Intercultural communication theory* (pp. 59–91). Thousand Oaks, CA: Sage.
Balls-Organista, P., & Organista, K. C. (1998). Culture and gender sensitive AIDS prevention with Mexican migrant workers: A primer for counselors. In P. Balls-Organista, K. M. Chun, & G. Marín (Eds.), *Readings in ethnic psychology* (pp. 240–248). New York: Routledge.
Barker, G., & Loewenstein, I. (1997). Where the boys are: Attitudes related to masculinity, fatherhood, and violence toward women among low-income adolescents and young adult males in Rio de Janeiro, Brazil. *Youth & Society, 29,* 166–196.
Bem, S. L. (1981). *Bem Sex-Role Inventory: Professional Model*. Palo Alto, CA: Consulting Psychologists Press.
Bem, S. L. (1985). Androgyny and gender schema theory: A conceptual model and empirical integration. In T. B. Sonderegger (Ed.), *Psychology and gender* (pp. 179–226). Lincoln: University of Nebraska Press.
Bernal, G., & Alvarez, A. I. (1983). Culture and class in the study of families. In C. J. Falicov (Ed.), *Cultural perspectives in family therapy* (pp. 33–50). Rockville, MD: Aspen Systems.
Brod, H. (Ed.). (1987). *The making of masculinities: The new men's studies*. Boston: Allen and Unwin.

Bronfenbrenner, U. (1979). *The ecology of human development: Experiments by nature and design*. Cambridge, MA: Harvard University Press.

Bunting, A. B., & Reeves, J. B. (1983). Perceived male sex orientation and beliefs about rape. *Deviant Behavior, 4*, 281–295.

Burda, P. C., & Vaux, A. C. (1987). The social support process in men: Overcoming sex-role obstacles. *Human Relations, 40*, 31–44.

Buss, D. M. (1998). Sexual strategies theory: Historical origins and current status. *Journal of Sex Research, 35*, 19–31.

Caipora Women's Group. (1993). *Women in Brazil*. London: Latin American Bureau.

Camilo Osório, L. (1997). A família como grupo primordial [The family as the primordial group]. In D. E. Zimerman & L. Camilo Osório (Eds.), *Como trabalhamos com grupos* [How we work as groups] (pp. 49–59). Pôrto Alegre, Brazil: Artes Médicas.

Cardoso, N. M. (1997). Mulher e maus-tratos [Women and mistreatment]. In M. N. Strey (Ed.), *Mulher: Estudos de gênero* [Women: Gender studies] (pp. 127–138). São Leopoldo, Brazil: Unisinos.

Casas, J. M., Wagenheim, B. R., Banchero, R., & Mendoza-Romero, J. (1995). Hispanic masculinity: Myth or psychological schema meriting clinical consideration. In A. M. Padilla (Ed.), *Hispanic psychology: Critical issues in theory and research* (pp. 231–244). Thousand Oaks, CA: Sage.

Chaney, E. M. (1979). *Supermadre: Women in politics in Latin America*. Austin: University of Texas Press.

Collier, M. J., & Thomas, M. (1988). Cultural identity in inter-cultural communication: An interpretive perspective. In Y. Y. Kim & W. B. Gudykunst (Eds.), *Theories in intercultural communication* (pp. 94–120). Newbury Park, CA: Sage.

Connell, R. W. (1995). *Masculinities*. Berkeley: University of California Press.

Corrêa, M. (1994). Repensando a família patriarcal brasileira [Rethinking the Brazilian patriarchal family]. In A. Arantes (Ed.), *Colcha de retalhos: Estudos sobre a família no Brasil* [A patchwork quilt: Studies on the family in Brazil] (pp. 51–68). Campinas, Brazil: Unicamp.

Corsi, J. (1997). *Violência familiar: Una mirada interdisciplinaria sobre un grave problema social* [Family violence: An interdisciplinary look at a serious social problem]. Buenos Aires: Paidós.

Craig, S. (Ed.). (1992). *Men, masculinity, and the media*. Newbury Park, CA: Sage.

De Antoni, C., & Koller, S. H. (2000). A visão de família entre as adolescentes que sofreram violência intrafamiliar [The vision of family among adolescents who suffer intrafamily violence]. *Estudos de Psicologia (Natal)* [Psychological studies (Natal)], *5*, 347–382.

DeFrancisco, V. (1997). Gender, power and practice: Or, putting your money (and your research) where your mouth is. In R. Wodak (Ed.), *Gender and discourse* (pp. 37–56). London: Sage.

De la Cancela, V. (1986). A critical analysis of Puerto Rican machismo: Implications for clinical practice. *Psychotherapy, 23*, 291–296.

DeSouza, E., Baldwin, J. R., & da Rosa, F. H. (2000). A construção social dos papéis sexuais femininos [The social construction of feminine sexual roles]. *Psicologia: Reflexão e Crítica, 13,* 485–496.

DeSouza, E., & Solberg, J. (2003). Incidence and dimensions of sexual harassment across cultures. In M. Paludi & C. A. Paludi, Jr. (Eds.), *Academic and workplace sexual harassment: A handbook of cultural, social science, management, and legal perspectives* (pp. 3–30). Westport, CT: Praeger.

DeSouza, E. R., & Hutz, C. S. (1995). Responses towards sexual stimuli in Brazil as a function of one's gender role identity and sex. *Interamerican Journal of Psychology, 29,* 13–21.

DeSouza, E. R., & Hutz, C. S. (1996). Reactions to refusals of sexual advances among U.S. and Brazilian men and women. *Sex Roles, 34,* 549–565.

DeSouza, E. R., Madrigal, C., & Millan, A. (1999). A cross-cultural validation of the multidimensional condom attitudes scale. *Interamerican Journal of Psychology, 33,* 191–204.

D'Incao, M. A. (2001). Mulher e família burguesa [Woman and the bourgeois family]. In M. Del Priore (Ed.), *História das mulheres no Brasil* [History of women in Brazil] (pp. 78–90). São Paulo: Contexto.

Dodd, C. H., & Baldwin, J. R. (2002). Family culture and relationship differences as a source of intercultural communication. In J. Martin, T. Nakayama, & L. Flores (Eds.), *Readings in cultural contexts* (2nd ed.) (pp. 279–288). Boston: McGraw-Hill.

Dutton, M. A. (1997). La mujer maltratada y sus estrategias de respuesta a la violencia [The mistreated woman and her response strategies to violence]. In J. L. Edleson & Z. C. Eisikovits (Eds.), *Violencia doméstica: La mujer golpeada y la familia* [Domestic violence: The battered woman and her family] (pp. 153–178). Buenos Aires: Granica.

Eisler, R. M., & Skidmore, J. R. (1987). Masculine gender role stress: Scale development and component factors in the appraisal of stressful situations. *Behavior Modification, 11,* 123–136.

Foucault, M. (1978). *The history of sexuality.* New York: Pantheon.

Gilligan, C. (1979). Woman's place in man's life cycle. *Harvard Educational Review, 49,* 431–446.

Gilligan, C. (1982). *In a different voice: Psychological theory and women's development.* Cambridge, MA: Harvard University Press.

Gilmore, D. (1990). *Manhood in the making: Cultural concepts of masculinity.* New Haven, CT: Yale University Press.

González, A. (1982). Sex-roles of the traditional family: A comparison of Chicano and Anglo students' attitudes. *Journal of Cross-Cultural Psychology, 13,* 330–339.

Goodrich, T., Rampage, C., Ellman, B., & Halstead, C. (1988). *Terapia feminista da família* [Feminist family therapy]. Pôrto Alegre, Brazil: Artes Médicas.

Grossi, P. K. (2001). Por uma nova ótica e uma nova ética na abordagem da violência contra mulheres nas relações conjugais [Toward a new view and a new ethics in the treatment of violence against women in conjugal relations]. In P. K. Grossi & G. C. Werba (Eds.), *Violências e gênero: Coisas que a gente não gostaria de saber* [Violence and gender: Things we didn't want to know] (pp. 19–45). Pôrto Alegre, Brazil: EDIPUCRS.

Gudykunst, W. B., & Kim, Y. Y. (2003). *Communicating with strangers: An approach to intercultural communication* (4th ed.). Boston: McGraw-Hill.

Hahner, J. E. (1990). *Emancipating the female sex: The struggle for women's rights in Brazil, 1850–1940.* Durham, NC: Duke University Press.

Hall, S. (1996). The problem of ideology: Marxism without guarantees. In D. Morley & K. H. Chen (eds.), *Stuart Hall: Critical dialogues in cultural studies* (pp. 25–46). London: Routledge. Earlier published in B. Matthews (Ed.). (1983). *Marx: 100 years on* (pp. 57–84). London: Lawrence and Wishart.

Hare-Mustin, R. T., & Marecek, J. (Eds.). (1990). *Making a difference: Psychology and the construction of gender.* New Haven, CT: Yale University Press.

Hecht, M. L. (1993). 2002: A research odyssey—Toward the development of a communication theory of identity. *Communication Monographs, 60,* 76–82.

Hecht, M. L., & Baldwin, J. R. (1998). Layers and holograms: A new look at prejudice. In M. L. Hecht (Ed.), *Communicating prejudice* (pp. 57–84). Thousand Oaks, CA: Sage.

Hecht, M. L., Jackson, R. L., II., & Ribeau, S. A. (2003). *African American communication: Exploring identity and culture* (2nd ed.). Mahwah, NJ: Erlbaum.

Hollway, W. (1984). Gender differences and the production of subjectivity. In J. Henriques, W. Hollway, C. Urwin, C. Venn, & V. Walkerdine, (Eds.), *Changing the subject* (pp. 227–263). London: Methuen.

Horrocks, R. (1994). *Masculinity in crisis: Myths, fantasies, and realities.* New York: St. Martin's.

Jones, E. (1994). Feminismo e terapia de família: Os casamentos complicados podem dar certo? [Feminism and family therapy: Can troubled marriages work out?] In R. J. Perelberg & A. C. Miller (Eds.), *Os sexos e o poder nas famílias* [Gender and power in families] (pp. 75–93). Rio de Janeiro: Imago.

Koller, S. H. (1999). Violência doméstica: Uma visão ecológica [Domestic violence: An ecological view]. In Amencar (Ed.), *Violência doméstica* [Domestic violence] (pp. 32–42). Brasília: UNICEF.

Koval, J. E., Ponzetti, J. J., & Cate, R. M. (1982). Programmatic interventions for men involved with conjugal violence. *Family Therapy, 9,* 147–154.

Kramarae, C. (1981). *Women and men speaking: Frameworks for analysis.* Rowley, MA: Newbury House.

Lara-Cantú, M. A. (1989). A sex-role inventory with scales for "machismo" and "self-sacrificing woman." *Journal of Cross-Cultural Psychology, 20,* 386–398.

Lara-Cantú, M. A., & Navarro-Arias, R. (1987). Self-descriptions of Mexican college students in response to the Bem Sex Role Inventory and other sex role items. *Journal of Cross-Cultural Psychology, 18,* 331–344.

Madanes, C. (1991). *Sex, love and violence.* New York: Norton.

Magaña, J. R., & Carrier, J. M. (1991). Mexican and Mexican American male sexual behavior and spread of AIDS in California. *Journal of Sex Research, 28,* 425–441.

Maldonado, M. (1991). Latinas and HIV/AIDS: Implications for the 90s. *SIECUS Report, 19,* 11–15.

Marín, B. V., & Gómez, C. A. (1995). Latino culture and sex: Implications for HIV prevention. In J. Garcia & M. Zea (Eds.), *Psychological interventions and research with Latino populations* (pp. 73–93). Needham Heights, MA: Allyn & Bacon.

Marín, B. V., Gómez, C. A., & Hearst, N. (1993). Multiple heterosexual partners and condom use among Hispanics and non-Hispanic Whites. *Family Planning Perspectives, 25,* 170–174.

Marín, G., & Marín, B. (1991). *Research with Hispanic populations.* Newbury Park, CA: Sage.

Martín, A. F. (2000). La coerción y la violencia sexual en la pareja [Coercion and sexual violence among couples]. In J. N. Góngora & J. P. Miragaia (Eds.), *Parejas en situaciones especiales* [Couples in special situations] (pp. 87–120). Buenos Aires: Paidós.

Metz, M. E., & Seifert, M. H., Jr. (1990). Men's expectations of physicians in sexual health concerns. *Journal of Sex and Marital Therapy, 16,* 79–88.

Mikawa, J. K., Morones, P. A., Gómez, A., Case, H. L., Olsen, D., & González-Huss, M. J. (1992). Cultural practices of Hispanics: Implications for the prevention of AIDS. *Hispanic Journal of Behavioral Sciences, 14,* 421–433.

Mirandé, A. (1985). *The Chicano experience: An alternative perspective.* Notre Dame, IN: University of Notre Dame Press.

Muraro, R. M. (1983). *Sexualidade da mulher brasileira: Corpo e classe social no Brasil* [Sexuality of Brazilian women: Body and social class in Brazil] (2nd ed.). Petrópolis, Brazil: Vozes.

Narvaz, M. (2001). Violência familiar [Family violence]. In M. R. Nunes (Ed.), *Sobre as crianças e os adolescentes—nosso olhar, nosso compromisso* [About children and adolescents: Our view, our commitment] (pp. 18–22). Pôrto Alegre, Brazil: Assembléia Legislativa do Rio Grande do Sul.

Narvaz, M. (2002a). Abusos sexuais e violências de gênero [Sexual abuse and gender violence]. In M. R. Nunes (Ed.), *Os direitos humanos das meninas e das mulheres: Enfoques feministas* [Human rights of girls and women: Feminist perspectives] (pp. 29–33). Pôrto Alegre, Brazil: Assembléia Legislativa do Rio Grande do Sul.

Narvaz, M. (2002b). A transmissão transgeracional da violência [The transgenerational transmission of violence]. *Insight, 11*(18), 17–22.

Narvaz, M. (2003). Quem são as mães das vítimas de incesto? [Who are the mothers of incest victims?] *Nova Perspectiva Sistêmica, 12*(21), 2003.

Narvaz, M., Berwanger, C., Moraes, R., & Rosa, M. I. (2000). Abuso sexual infantil: Compartilhando dores na esperança de reescrever uma nova história. Uma experiência com grupos multifamiliares [Child sexual abuse: Sharing the pain in hopes of rewriting a new history. An experience with multifamily groups]. *Nova Perspectiva Sistêmica, 18*(9), 31–38.

Narvaz, M. & Koller, S. H. (in press). Famílias, gêneros e violências: Desvelando as tramas da transmissão transgeracional da violência de gênero [Family, gender, and violence: Uncovering the trauma of transgenerational transmission of gender violence]. In M. Strey (Ed.), *Gênero e violência* [Gender and violence]. Pôrto Alegre, Brazil: EDIPUCRS.

Neuhouser, K. (1989). Sources of women's power and status among the urban poor in contemporary Brazil. *Signs, 14,* 685–702.

Nunes, M. R. (2003). *Violência sexual contra meninos e meninas: Abuso sexual intrafamiliar e a exploração sexual commercial* [Sexual abuse of boys and girls: Intrafamily sexual abuse and commercial sexual exploitation]. Pôrto Alegre, Brazil: Boletim do Gabinete da Deputada Federal Maria do Rosário do PT/RS.

O'Neil, J. M. (1982). Gender-role conflict and strain in men's lives: Implications for psychiatrists, psychologists, and other human-service providers. In K. Solomon & N. B. Levy (Eds.), *Men in transition: Theory and therapy* (pp. 5–44). New York: Plenum.

Padilla, E. (1987). Sexuality among Mexican Americans: A case of sexual stereotyping. *Journal of Personality and Social Psychology, 52,* 5–10.

Parillo, V. N. (1980). *Strangers to these shores: Race and ethnic relations in the United States.* Boston: Houghton Mifflin.

Parker, R. G. (1993). "Within four walls": Brazilian sexual culture and HIV/AIDS. In H. Daniel & R. Parker (Eds.), *Sexuality, politics and AIDS in Brazil: In another world?* (pp. 65–84). London: Falmer.

Pasick, R. S., Gordon, S., & Meth, R. L. (1990). Helping men understand themselves. In R. L. Meth & R. S. Pasick (Eds.), *Men in therapy: The challenge of change* (pp. 152–180). New York: Guilford.

Paz, O. (1959). *El labirinto de la soledad* [The labyrinth of solitude]. Mexico City: Fondo de Cultura Económica.

Pequeño Larousse ilustrado. (1982). Mexico City: Ediciones Larousse.

Pescatello, A. (1973). The *brasileira*: Images and realities in writings of Machado de Assis and Jorge Amado. In A. Pescatello (Ed.), *Female and male in Latin America: Essays* (pp. 29–58). Pittsburgh, PA: University of Pittsburgh Press.

Philipsen, G. (1975). Speaking "like a man" in Teamsterville. *Quarterly Journal of Speech, 61,* 14–22.

Pleck, J. H., Sonenstein, F. L., & Ku, L. C. (1993a). Masculinity ideology: Its impact on adolescent males' heterosexual relationships. *Journal of Social Issues, 49,* 11–29.

Pleck, J. H., Sonenstein, F. L., & Ku, L. C. (1993b). Problem behavior and masculinity ideology in adolescent males. In R. D. Ketterlinus & M. E. Lamb (Eds.), *Adolescent problem behaviors: Issues and Research* (pp. 165–186). Hillsdale, NJ: Erlbaum.

Pyke, K. D. (1996). Class-based masculinities: The interdependence of gender, class, and interpersonal power. *Gender & Society, 10,* 527–549.

Ravazzola, M. C. (1999). *Historias infames: Los maltratos en las relaciones* [Infamous histories: Mistreatment in relationships]. Buenos Aires: Paidós.

Reinholtz, R. K., Muehlenhard, C. L., Phelps, J. L., & Satterfield, A. T. (1995). Sexual discourse and sexual intercourse: How the way we communicate affects the way we think about sexual coercion. In P. J. Kalbfleisch & M. J. Cody (Eds.), *Gender, power, and communication in human relationships* (pp. 141–162). Hillsdale, NJ: Erlbaum.

Reis, J. R. T. (1985). Família, emoção e ideologia [Family, emotion, and ideology]. In S. T. M. Lane & W. Codo (Eds.), *Psicologia social: O homem em movimento* [Social psychology: Man (People) in motion] (pp. 99–124). São Paulo: Brasiliense.

Ruiz, R. (1981). Cultural and historical perspectives in counseling Hispanics. In D. W. Sue (Ed.), *Counseling the culturally different: Theory and practice* (pp. 186–214). New York: Wiley.

Salgado de Snyder, N., & Padilla, A. M. (1982). Cultural and ethnic maintenance of interethnically married Mexican Americans. *Human Organization, 41,* 359–362.

Schützenberger, A. A. (1997). *Meus antepassados: Vínculos transgeracionais, segredos de família, síndrome de aniversário e prática do genossociograma* [My ancestors: Transgenerational bonds, family secrets, birthday syndrome, and the practice of genograms]. São Paulo: Paulus.

Sorenson, S. B., & Siegel, J. M. (1992). Gender, ethnicity, and sexual assault: Findings from a Los Angeles study. *Journal of Social Issues, 48,* 93–104.

Stephenson, S. (2003). *Understanding Spanish-speaking South Americans: Bridging hemispheres.* Yarmouth, ME: Intercultural Press.

Stevens, E. (1973). Machismo and marianismo. *Society, 10,* 57–63.

Strey, M. N. (2001). Violência e gênero: Um casamento que tem tudo para dar certo [Violence and gender: A marriage that has everything it needs to work out]. In P. K. Grossi & G. C. Werba (Eds.), *Violências e gênero: Coisas que a gente não gostaria de saber* [Violence and gender: Things that we didn't want to know] (pp. 47–70). Pôrto Alegre, Brazil: EDIPUCRS.

Talbot, M. (1991). *The holographic universe.* New York: HarperCollins.

Thomas, D. Q., & Beasley, M. E. (1993). Domestic violence as a human rights issue. *Human Rights Quarterly, 15,* 36–62.

Thompson, E. H., Pleck, J. H., & Ferrera, D. L. (1992). Men and masculinities: Scales for masculinity ideology and masculinity-related constructs. *Sex Roles, 27,* 573–607.

Tiefer, L. (1995). *Sex is not a natural act and other essays.* Boulder, CO: Westview Press.

Triandis, H. C., Marín, G., Hui, C. H., Lisansky, J., & Ottati, V. (1984). Role perceptions of Hispanic young adults. *Journal of Cross-Cultural Psychology, 15,* 297–320.

Unger, R. K. (1990). Imperfect reflections of reality. In R. T. Hare-Mustin & J. Marecek (Eds.), *Making a difference: Psychology and the construction of gender* (pp. 102–149). New Haven, CT: Yale University Press.

Valdes, L., Baron, A., & Ponce, F. (1987). Counseling Hispanic men. In M. Scher, M. Stevens, G. Good, & G. Eichenfield (Eds.), *Handbook of counseling & psychotherapy with men* (pp. 203–217). Newbury Park, CA: Sage.

Van der Dennen, J.M.G. (1987). Ethnocentrism and in-group/out-group differentiation: A review and interpretation of the literature. In V. Reynolds, V. Falger, & I. Vine (Eds.), *The sociobiology of ethnocentrism: Evolutionary dimensions of xenophobia, discrimination, racism and nationalism* (pp. 1–47). London: Croom Helm.

Van Dijk, T. A. (1998). *Ideology: A multidisciplinary approach*. London: Sage.

VanOss-Marín, B., Gómez, C. A., Tschann, J. M., & Gregorich, S. E. (1997). Condom use in unmarried Latino men: A test of cultural constructs. *Health Psychology, 16,* 458–467.

Vigarello, G. (2001). *The history of rape: Sexual violence in France from the 16th to the 20th centuries*. Malden, MA: Polity Press.

Weber, L. (1998). A conceptual framework for understanding race, class, gender, and sexuality. *Psychology of Women Quarterly, 22,* 13–32.

Weisbuch, M., Beal, D., & O'Neal, E. C. (1999). How masculine ought I to be? Men's masculinity and aggression. *Sex Roles, 40,* 583–592.

Werba, G. C., & Strey, M. N. (2001). Longe dos olhos, longe do coração: Ainda a invisibilidade da violência contra a mulher [Out of sight, out of mind [lit. heart]: The continued invisibility of violence against women]. In P. K. Grossi & G. C. Werba (Eds.), *Violências e gênero: Coisas que a gente não gostaria de saber* [Violence and gender: Things we didn't want to know] (pp. 71–82). Pôrto Alegre, Brazil: EDIPUCRS.

West, C., & Zimmerman, D. H. (1987). Doing gender. *Gender and Society, 1,* 125–151.

Wetherall, A. (1996). Language about women and men: An example from popular culture. *Journal of Language and Social Psychology, 15,* 59–75.

Yep, G. A. (1995). Communicating HIV/AIDS risk to Hispanic populations. In A. M. Padilla (Ed.), *Hispanic psychology: Critical issues in theory and research* (pp. 196–212). Thousand Oaks, CA: Sage.

Zilbergeld, B. (1978). *Male sexuality*. Boston: Little, Brown.

Zuwick, A. N. (2001). O corpo violado [The violated body]. In P. K. Grossi & G. C. Werba (Eds.), *Violências e gênero: Coisas que a gente não gostaria de saber* [Violence and gender: Things we didn't want to know] (pp. 83–94). Pôrto Alegre, Brazil: EDIPUCRS.

Chapter 4

Gender, Sexuality, and Intimate Relationships

Donna Castañeda and Alyson Burns-Glover

In Western societies, gender is a defining aspect of individual identity. It has a profound influence on our lives from the moment we are born, and we enact its social and cultural meanings at every level from the intrapsychic to the legal and political levels. One arena in which gender meanings may be particularly important is in the development and expression of sexuality within ongoing relationships. Gender effects may seem most obvious in heterosexual relationships, but because they have been subject to the same gender socialization as persons in heterosexual relationships, lesbians and gay men are not immune to the influence of traditional gender expectations in their sexuality and close relationships (Huston & Schwartz, 1996).

Here we define close relationships as partnered relationships between adults that include sexuality and in which the ongoing processes in the relationship are key (Duck, 1993; Scanzoni et al., 1989). These processes (e.g., intimacy, communication, conflict, sexuality) may then be enacted within the social structures that define and legitimate relationships such as marriages and civil unions—heterosexual, gay, or lesbian. Another assumption we maintain is that humans have a basic drive and survival need to seek out and maintain attachments with others (Baumeister & Leary, 1995; Harlow, 1958). Relationships play an important role in our lives, and although relationship quality and quantity can certainly vary across a given individual's life, this need to belong is a basic aspect of being human.

Below we discuss several areas of research that reliably demonstrate ways in which gender socialization, expectations, and ideologies may influence sexuality-related behavior in close relationships, including the sexual double standard, sexual desire, gender differences in sexual attitudes and behavior, sexual satisfaction and problems, sexual scripts, and sexual violence in relationships. We discuss how the individual-level experience of sexuality is linked to violence in relationships. We also discuss how the individual-level experience of sexuality is linked to gendered power differentials at the social and political levels, and to culturally based conceptions of gender and sexual orientation. But first, to frame our discussions of gender differences in sexuality within relationships, a brief overview of statistical trends in marriage, cohabitation, and divorce is provided

Trends in Marriage, Cohabitation, and Divorce

Since the mid-1970s dramatic changes have occurred in the structure of relationships in society. For example, heterosexual relationships are frequently institutionalized through marriage, but marriage rates in the United States are declining. According to the U.S. Census, married couples with or without children declined from 70.6 percent of the population in 1970 to 52.8 percent in 2000. In fact, the percentage of persons never married increased from 22 percent among women and 28 percent among men in 1970 to 25 percent and 31 percent, respectively, for women and men in 2000. Women and men are waiting longer before they marry: the median age at first marriage for women increased from 20.8 years in 1970 to 25.1 years in 2000; among men the median age at first marriage increased from 23.2 in 1970 to 26.8 in 2000. The age at first marriage is now the oldest since such data began to be reported in 1890 (Fields, 2001).

Another change in the structure of relationships has been an increase in the number of couples who cohabit, or live together as unmarried partners, and also have a close personal relationship. In 2000, 5.5 million couples, about 5 percent of all households, were living together but were not married, up from 3.2 million in 1990. The majority of these cohabiting couples, 89 percent, were made up of cross-sex partners, but about one in nine of these couples were of the same sex, 51 percent male couples and 49 percent female couples (Simmons & O'Connell, 2003).

The United States has one of the highest divorce rates in the world. Between 1960 and 1980, the rate of divorce doubled to one out of two marriages ending in divorce, although since 1980 the divorce rate has remained relatively stable. The remarriage rate, although initially high in response to the divorce rate, has declined in a manner similar to the decline in first marriages, but these couples still make up a significant proportion of the households in the United States. Currently, in about four out of ten marriages in the United States, at least one partner has been married previously (Norton & Miller, 1992).

These data indicate changes related to marriage, cohabitation, and divorce, but they should not be interpreted to mean that marriage is obsolete. The popularity of marriage remains strong: 74 percent of women and men have been married by age thirty-five, and 95 percent have been married by age sixty-five.

With legal rulings in Canada, the United States, and Europe that now allow same-gender couples to enter civil unions and to get married, the future will likely show changes in same-gender marriage, cohabitation, and divorce. Whether these changes will be similar to or different from those among cross-gender couples is yet to be seen.

Sexuality, the Individual, and Society

During our intimate sexual interactions within relationships we may feel most ourselves, most free from the influences of larger social and cultural prescriptions for behavior. However, even in these intensely personal interactions, gender meanings can affect behavior. Because psychology focuses on individual-level behavior and psychological experience, the fact that sexuality occurs within a broader social and political context, where efforts to contain, control, and limit women's sexuality (and, ultimately, their reproduction) are constantly under way, is easily overlooked (Forbes, 1996). Although women today appear to have greater freedom of sexual expression than in the past, their sexuality is still a contested topic intricately linked to systems of power. This is most apparent in political and legal debates surrounding issues such as abortion, the "morning-after pill," adolescents' access to condoms and safer sex information, prevention of teenage pregnancy, and access to overall reproductive health care. These debates reveal serious power struggles in society regarding women's sexual and reproductive self-determination that can have direct consequences upon their sexual and reproductive rights and freedoms.

Moreover, women's (and men's) sexuality continues to be defined and organized predominantly by institutionalized heterosexuality. This refers, first, to the myriad ways that sexuality is conceptualized in heterosexual terms (e.g., "sex" is defined as penetration, women should be sexually passive, and men's sexual pleasure is most important) and, second, to how traditional femininity and masculinity ideologies are socially constructed so that they maintain these heterosexual forms of sexuality (Espín, 1997; Rich, 1983; Tolman, Striepe, & Harmon, 2003). Institutionalized heterosexuality limits women's sexual options and closes off many avenues for sexual autonomy, knowledge, pleasure, and desire.

Cultural Diversity in Gender and Sexual Orientation

The majority of research on sexuality and relationships has been done with a limited segment of humanity: college-age, primarily middle-class, European American persons. Most researchers come from this background. Therefore, alternative conceptions of gender and sexuality have been much less present in this body of research. But when perspectives from other ethnic/racial, sexual identity, cultural, and social class groups are examined, the tidy assumptions of discrete categories of gender and sexual identity are brought into question. For instance, terms may not even be available, at least in English, to describe the differing categories, conceptions, or shifting identities of gender and sexual orientation in other cultural groups (Blackwood, 2000; Tafoya, 1997). Native Americans have historically viewed gender and sexual orientation as more fluid and context-bound, and less a static feature of the individual. Reflecting this, Tafoya (1997), in a study of interracial same-sex couples, found that Native Americans showed higher rates of bisexuality than other ethnic groups.

Yet another example comes from a review of women's same-sex sexuality across world cultures by Evelyn Blackwood (2000). She shows that the categories of homosexual, heterosexual, and bisexual, as they are understood in Europe or North America, have little cross-cultural reliability. For instance, among Creole women in Suriname, *mati* work, or erotic attachments among women, is common. But *mati* women do not identify themselves as lesbians, and they continue to have relationships with men through marriage, concubinage, or visiting relationships. In this case, sex with both women and men is part of their sexuality. *Mati* work reflects an ideology of sexuality for Surinamese women and men that is fluid and multiply defined, and this ideology serves to produce quite different sets of ideas about women's and men's sexual desire. Blackwood (2000) also shows that cultural arrangements and institutions such as religion, living arrangements, availability of paid work outside the home and economic self-sufficiency of women, kinship systems, and rules of inheritance not only create different possibilities for women's and men's sexual desire, but also affect their access to sexual partners.

The Sexual Double Standard

The double standard, in which the social rules and expectations surrounding sexual behavior are different for women and for men, is still alive and well in the early twenty-first century (Crawford & Popp, 2003; Muehlenhard et al., 2003). Attitudes about sexuality, at least in the United States and Western Europe, have become more egalitarian since the 1960s and 1970s (Crawford & Popp, 2003; DeLameter, 1987; Haavio-Mannila & Kontula, 2003; Oliver & Shibley Hyde, 1993), but the sexual double standard has not faded completely. Crawford and Popp (2003), in their review of studies since 1980 on the sexual double standard, concluded that overt expressions of an absolute double standard have declined, and the contemporary sexual double standard may be more subtle in its expression, although no less effective in influencing and controlling sexual behavior. Many times these sexual double standards are "local social constructions" (Crawford & Popp, 2003, p. 20) existing in specific situations, schools, communities, and social and cultural groups, and they intersect with aspects of the individual such as age, education, race/ethnicity, sexual orientation, social class, and education level.

Among Latinas/os and Asian Americans, adherence to the sexual double standard may be stronger because deviations from these sexual rules affect not only individual women but also their family's honor and social standing (Faulkner, 2003; Okazaki, 2002). Furthermore, differential attitudes about acceptable sexual behavior of women and men continue to be reflected in language use, which itself exerts a powerful influence on behavior. Sexual slang in English demeans women more often than men (Crawford & Popp, 2003; Richardson, 1997). One study, for example, found that the slang terms for women's genitals are less numerous than those for men, but the ones for women tend to be more derogatory. In addition, terms for female genitals that evoke disgust are more easily generated by men than by women (Braun & Kitzinger, 2001).

Inconsistent results regarding the presence of the double standard have to do with differences across studies in measurements, study design, and sample characteristics (Crawford & Popp, 2003; Milhausen & Herold, 1999). Experimental studies, which are more likely to utilize European–American, college-age samples, are less likely to show the presence of a sexual double standard, possibly because much of the meaningful social context is removed from the decision-making task in experimental designs (Gentry, 1998). These studies may not adequately simulate the day-to-day experience of many women and men, where negative evaluations of women who are perceived to be sexually experienced are not uncommon.

Qualitative studies (i.e., those utilizing interviews, focus groups, or ethnographies) are more likely to utilize samples diverse in age, race/ethnicity, and social class, and they are more likely to demonstrate the presence of a sexual double standard. Also, studies may not distinguish between people's own beliefs regarding the sexual double standard and their perception of how pervasive it is among others. This is important to do because at least one study found that college-age women perceived the sexual double standard as still existing at the societal level, but when questioned about their own beliefs and values, they showed they did not support it (Milhausen & Herold, 1999).

The sexual double standard is important to study, understand, and ultimately change because it has profound implications for sexual behavior, particularly that of women. In their efforts to remain socially desirable, women are influenced by the sexual double standard to suppress their own sexual needs and desires, and ultimately to be less connected to their own sexuality (Crawford & Popp, 2003; Katz & Farrow, 2000; Tolman, 2001; Tolman & Debold, 1994). Although condom use can prevent unwanted pregnancy, HIV, and sexually transmitted diseases, women may be more reluctant than men to produce a condom in sexual interactions because they know they may be perceived less positively. Some evidence supports this—for example, women, more than men, report that they would be embarrassed to purchase condoms (Helweg-Larsen & Collins, 1994) and believe they would be negatively evaluated if they produced a condom before a sexual interaction (Hynie & Lydon, 1995). Latina/o, compared with non-Latina/o, college students, both women and men, rate a female who introduces a condom into an ongoing sexual interaction as more promiscuous than a male who does the same (Castañeda & Collins, 1998); and Chinese Americans, compared with European Americans, react more negatively to a female who initiates condom use (Conley, Collins, & Garcia, 2000). Being prepared for sexual encounters by purchasing and introducing condoms makes sense, but for women these behaviors can send a message that they are, or have been in the past, willing to engage in casual sex.

Sexual Desire

A common perception is that men are more interested in sex than in relationships, while the reverse is true of women—they are more interested in relationships than in sex. This difference is thought to be related to women's and men's differing levels of sexual desire. In reality, the concept of sexual desire is still little understood, and many times it is confused with the need for intimacy or to be loved, or even with sexual arousal and overt sexual behavior (Regan & Berscheid, 1996). When heterosexual women and men are asked to define sexual desire, they tend to offer a similar definition—that it is primarily a psychological experience characterized by a sense of longing, urge, yearning, need, or want, but they differ in what they consider to be the goals and objects of sexual desire (Regan & Berscheid, 1996). Women emphasize love, emotional intimacy, and commitment as the goals of sexual desire more than men do, while men are more likely than women to specify a physically and/or sexually attractive other as the object of sexual desire.

But do women overall have less desire for sex than men do? One gauge of the potential difference between women and men in terms of sexual desire may be masturbation, because with masturbation one does not need a partner (Peplau, 2003). In a meta-analytic study of sexual behavior, Oliver and Shibley Hyde (1993) found that men were more likely than women to masturbate and they engaged in masturbation more frequently, an indication that men may have a greater desire for sex than women. Baumeister, Catanese, and Vohs (2001) attempted to answer this question by reviewing studies not only of masturbation but also of spontaneous thoughts about sex, frequency and variety of sexual fantasies, desired frequency of intercourse, desired number of partners, liking for various sexual practices, willingness to forgo sex, initiating versus refusing sex, making sacrifices for sex, and other measures. Across these studies, men showed more frequent and intense desire for sex than women did. Baumeister et al. concluded that men have a stronger sex drive than women, although they were careful to differentiate their conception of sex drive from other sexuality-related constructs, such as sexual or orgasmic capacity, enjoyment of sex, or extrinsically motivated sex.

On the other hand, large surveys of sexual behavior indicate that the difference between women's and men's desire for sexual intercourse has gotten smaller over time (e.g., Levin & Levin, 1975; Pesman, 1991). Furthermore, although Oliver and Shibley Hyde (1993) found a significant difference between women and men in masturbation, this was one of the few gender differences in sexual behavior across the large number of studies they included in their meta-analysis.

In a study that examined the role of close relationships in sexual desire, Hendrick and Hendrick (2002) found that love was considered primary over sex by both women and men. This is not to say that sexuality was unimportant to individuals in ongoing relationships, but that love was even more important; and it appeared to be the element that drove sexual desire and sexual satisfaction in relationships (Hendrick & Hendrick, 2002). This study points to the critical role of relationships in sexuality, and although one need not be in love to experience sexual desire and to have a satisfying sexual encounter, loving someone is linked to sexually desiring that person for both sexes (Hendrick & Hendrick, 2002; Regan & Berscheid, 1999).

Since they grow up in a society where an ideology of men's greater need and desire for sex is part of both women's and men's sexual socialization, whether women and men differ in their level of sexual desire is difficult to determine. As a group with less power than men, women are not as free to openly express sexual desire without the potential for negative physical, emotional, or social consequences. Desire and the search for sexual pleasure are certainly part of women's sexuality, but in contrast to men, women's sexuality has always contained elements of both pleasure and danger. As Carol S. Vance wrote in 1985, "Although the boundaries of the safe zone have somewhat been renegotiated since the nineteenth century to include relatively respectable forms of unmarried and non-procreative heterosexuality, gross and public departures from 'good' woman status such as lesbianism, promiscuity, or non-traditional heterosexuality still invite, and are thought to justify, violation" (pp. 3–4). This observation is as valid today as it was in 1985.

Sexual Scripts

In psychology, "scripts" refers to schemata, or cognitive representations, of organized knowledge of particular events (Schank & Abelson, 1977). Scripts include not only understandings of specific behavior associated with an event, but also information about props, roles, and the rules regarding the ordered sequence of behaviors. These scripts are then used as guides to behavior, especially in new or ambiguous situations. A *sexual* script refers to schemata about how sexual encounters are supposed to unfold, and knowledge of these scripts helps guide behavior in sexual encounters (Miller et al., 1993).

The traditional sexual script contains quite specific and gendered prescriptions for sexual behavior of women and men in heterosexual relationships. Part of women's and men's socialization surrounding sexuality includes messages that men are the initiators of sexual activity and women are in charge of determining how far a sexual encounter will proceed. Furthermore, in the traditional sexual script, women and men are seen as adversaries; men are supposed to utilize multiple strategies to overcome women's objections to sex, and women respond with multiple strategies to avoid having sex.

This adversarial approach to heterosexual sexual interactions can set the stage for forced sex. Men adhering to the traditional sexual script may be inclined to ignore women's protests or view them as token resistance. Women, on the other hand, may not define an experience of forced sex as rape because elements of the situation fit the traditional sexual script (Littleton & Axsom, 2003).

Traditional sexual scripts not only act to guide initiation of sexual encounters by men and the refusal/permission function assigned to women, but also encompass affective responses to specific sexual acts based on the congruence between an individual's sexual script and a particular behavior (Mosher & MacIan, 1994). For example, women's sexual script may be more likely to contain expressions of love, cuddling behavior, sensuality, and greater foreplay, whereas that of men may contain lesser amounts of these behaviors and a greater genital focus. A partner's behavior that is less congruent with one's sexual script can lead to less positive affect and less sexual arousal in a given sexual encounter (Mosher & MacIan, 1994).

Despite being a fairly entrenched aspect of the sexual socialization of women and men, aspects of the traditional sexual script can wane as a relationship progresses. As partners become more knowledgeable about and comfortable with one another, sexual behavior may become more flexible, and in established relationships, who actually initiates sex is sometimes difficult to determine. Furthermore, lesbians and gay men tend to be less constrained by the traditional sexual script even in sexual encounters with a new partner (Huston & Schwartz, 1996; Rose & Zand, 2002; Rose, Zand, & Cini, 1993), although the partners in some lesbian and gay male relationships may establish a pattern where one partner is more often the initiator than the other (Huston & Schwartz, 1996).

Gender, Sexual Attitudes, and Sexual Behaviors

With regard to a range of sexual behaviors and attitudes, research has demonstrated that although differences between women and men have lessened quite a bit since the mid-1960s, some differences still exist. Overall, men tend to have more permissive attitudes than women regarding casual premarital sexual behavior (Oliver & Shibley Hyde, 1993), are more likely to view having sex outside of a committed relationship as more acceptable (DeLamater, 1987), to be willing to engage in more unusual or experimental sexual behavior (Hatfield et al., 1988), and to engage in masturbation more frequently and at an earlier age than women (Oliver & Shibley Hyde, 1993). Men also report engaging in sexual fantasies more frequently than women (Leitenberg & Henning, 1995) and, for those currently in a heterosexual relationship, a greater proportion of men's fantasies involve someone other than their current partner (Hicks & Leitenberg, 2001).

In terms of the frequency of sexual activity in relationships, married persons in their twenties report that, on average, they engage in sexual intercourse two to three times per week, but with the passage of time this frequency declines (Blumstein & Schwartz, 1983; Call, Sprecher, & Schwartz, 1995; Michael et al., 1994). When comparing heterosexual, gay male, and lesbian couples in frequency of sexual interactions, gay male couples tend to report more sexual activity than heterosexual couples, and lesbian couples tend to report less sexual activity than gay male or heterosexual couples (Blumstein & Schwartz, 1983). This last finding regarding sexuality among lesbian couples has not been found in all, or even most, studies of lesbian sexuality (see Iasenza, 2002). Much of the research on frequency of sexual activity has focused on sexual interactions, primarily intercourse, leading to orgasm. This narrow conception of sexuality has obscured insight into sexual behavior within lesbian couples (Iasenza, 2002), particularly understanding of the phenomenon of "lesbian bed death," a term applied to the supposed sharp decline in sexual activity that occurs in lesbian relationships.

Despite a fair amount of empirical evidence to the contrary (see Iasenza, 2002), the notion that women are less interested in sex than men and that two women together would have difficulty maintaining a passionate sex life persists. However, studies of lesbian sexual behavior show that lesbian couples, compared with heterosexual couples, tend to have a greater whole body/whole person approach to sexual interactions, to have sexual interactions of much greater duration, to show greater concern for reciprocity of pleasure, and to use a wider variety of sensual techniques and behaviors (see Iasenza, 2002). The truth is that couples in general show a decline in sexual behavior over time, and the frequency of sexual activity is extremely variable across couples, regardless of whether they are in same- or cross-gender relationships.

Another gender difference that is consistently seen in the research literature is that men report a higher number of sexual partners than women (Brown & Sinclair, 1999; Oliver & Shibley Hyde, 1993; Smith, 1992). This difference between women and men is interesting because when considering heterosexual partners, theoretically the number of sexual partners of women and men should be the same. This paradox may be due to women and men answering differently when asked about how many sexual partners they have had, with men making general estimates and showing a preference for numbers that end in 0 or 5, and women actually counting partners (Brown & Sinclair, 1999; Weiderman, 1997). When the time frame for reporting numbers of partners is shortened to the last year, as opposed to lifetime number of partners, the number of sexual partners for women and men becomes much more similar, going from 5.36 and 17 sexual partners in a lifetime for women and men, respectively, to 0.89 and 1.25 sexual partners in the last year for women and men, respectively (as cited in Stombler & Baunach, 2004).

The difference in number of reported sexual partners may also reflect self-presentation strategies in response to the sexual double standard (Alexander & Fisher, 2003). One tenet of the sexual double standard is that men can and should have many sexual partners and women should have few sexual partners. Thus, women may be motivated to understate, and men to exaggerate, their number of sexual partners. Evidence that this occurs was found in a study that used the bogus pipeline methodology (Alexander & Fisher, 2003). In this methodology, participants are attached to a nonfunctioning polygraph device (they are unaware it is nonfunctioning) and are led to believe that the device can detect dishonest answers. In this study the direction of the difference in number of lifetime sexual partners actually reversed for women and men connected to the bogus pipeline, with men reporting fewer sexual partners than women.

Another important and consistent difference in sexuality between women and men is that women, more often than men, report a preference that sexuality occur within the context of a relationship (Peplau, 2003). This difference is also found between lesbians and gay men, where lesbians have less permissive attitudes toward casual sex and sex outside the relationship than gay men do. Gay men in committed relationships are also more likely than lesbians or heterosexuals to have sex with persons outside their primary relationship.

The greater preference by women, compared with men, for sexuality within the context of a relationship is a theme that runs throughout the research on gender and sexuality. This does not mean that men do not value sexuality within relationships or that women do not value sexual pleasure in and of itself, but may have to do with differing goals for sexual behavior. Men are more likely to view the goal of sex as sexual gratification, while women are more likely to view intimacy as the goal of sexual interaction (Peplau, 2003; Regan & Berscheid, 1996, 1999). Reasons for this difference are still to be uncovered, but they likely involve a combination of biological, cultural, and individual experiential factors (Peplau, 2003).

Women and men also differ in their sexual behavior in relationships in that women are more often the sexually compliant partner. Sexual compliance refers to consensual *unwanted* sex, where an individual who is less interested in sex agrees to engage in sex with the partner who is more interested in sex (Impett & Peplau, 2003). It does not refer to forced, coerced, or nonconsensual sex, although the line between what is consensual and nonconsensual sex may be very thin at times.

Impett and Peplau (2003) reviewed explanations for why women in heterosexual relationships are more often the compliant sexual partner that fell into three categories. The first category is explanations due to gender. Adherence to traditional sexual scripts, where men are always expected to initiate sexual interactions and women to wait until their male partner does so before engaging in sex, is an example of a gender-related reason for greater sexual compliance among women.

The second category of explanations is relationship-based. For example, the degree of commitment to a relationship can increase the potential for engaging in compliant sex, especially by the partner with higher commitment (Impett & Peplau, 2003). Why this should be the case is not clear, but may have to do with the belief that if one makes a sacrifice for a partner, and engaging in unwanted consensual sex can be thought of as a sacrifice, then the commitment level of the less committed partner, who understands a sacrifice has been made for her or him, will increase. Although commitment enhancement may be a reason behind some compliant sex situations, Impett & Peplau (2003) indicate that more research needs to be done to determine if this sexual sacrifice is actually successful in changing a partner's level of commitment.

A third category is motivationally based explanations for sexual compliance. These are based on approach or avoidance strategies—whether people are motivated to pursue positive or pleasurable experiences or to avoid negative or painful outcomes. For example, sexual compliance may occur to avoid rejection, separation, or angering a potentially violent partner; to rekindle passion in a relationship; or because a woman may be interested in becoming a parent, though the timing for conception may be on a day when she has little desire for sexual intercourse.

An important point to keep in mind about sexual compliance is that even though women appear to engage in compliant sex to a greater degree than men, a great deal of overlap between women and men exists in both rates of compliant sex and reasons each gender gives for this behavior. The concept of sexual compliance highlights the fact that both women and men engage in sex for many reasons other than sexual pleasure or desire, and that sexual behavior, even in couples with seemingly established sexual routines and patterns, is a complex process.

Sexual Satisfaction in Relationships

Women are sometimes believed to be less interested in sexual satisfaction than men. Research demonstrates, however, that sexual satisfaction is as important to women as it is to men, and in heterosexual relationships both women and men report they are satisfied with sexuality (Henderson-King & Veroff, 1994; Sprecher & Regan, 2000). Furthermore, persons in lesbian, gay, and heterosexual relationships show no difference in level of sexual satisfaction (Christopher & Sprecher, 2000).

Something that many couples already realize is that sexual satisfaction in a relationship does not occur in a vacuum—it is related to satisfaction with the overall relationship for both women and men; African Americans and European Americans; heterosexuals, gay men, and lesbians; and married and unmarried couples (Blumstein & Schwartz, 1983; Byers, Demmons, & Lawrence, 1998; Henderson-King & Veroff, 1994; Oggins, Leber, & Veroff, 1993; Peplau, Cochran, & Mays, 1997; Sprecher, 2002; Sprecher & Regan, 2000). In fact, changes in the quality of a relationship are associated with changes in sexual satisfaction (Edwards & Booth, 1994). One study of un-married heterosexual couples found that higher sexual satisfaction was linked to greater relationship stability, that is, less likelihood of breaking up (Sprecher, 2002). Because specific aspects of relationships, such as commit-ment and love (Sprecher, 2002), intimacy (Sprecher & Regan, 2000), and quality of both general and sexual communication within the couple (Cu-pach & Comstock, 1990; Sprecher & Regan, 2000), are associated with sex-ual satisfaction as well as relationship satisfaction, the direction of causality is not clear, but undoubtedly sexual and overall relationship satisfaction go hand-in-hand.

One situation in which men report greater sexual satisfaction than women is first sexual intercourse (Darling, Davidson, & Passarello, 1992; Thomp-son, 1984). Men also report greater emotional satisfaction with this experi-ence than women and less guilt, even though women most often experience first intercourse within the context of an ongoing relationship (Darling et al., 1992). Lesbians do not necessarily report that their first sexual encounters were less sexually satisfying (Thompson, 1984, 1990). First heterosexual in-tercourse may be less satisfying for girls because of physical discomfort and pain, but it may also be because of, as narratives of these encounters show, the absence of desire. In some instances this absence of desire may be de-velopmental (i.e., girls may have sex before they are sexually ready), because of coercion and lack of choice, or due to lack of adequate stimulation that would make the encounter more sexually pleasurable (Darling et al., 1992; Thompson, 1984, 1990). First heterosexual intercourse may also be less sat-isfying for girls because they do not feel a right to desire, to sexual pleasure (Thompson, 1984, 1990; Tolman, 2001). For girls the recognition of, and a sense of entitlement to, sexual desire may be difficult in a social and cultural context that, while it highly sexualizes and objectifies women's bodies, al-lows little room for them to fully articulate, seek, and experience sexual plea-sure. In many ways, as women grow and mature, they struggle to come to terms with this contradiction in their own sexual lives.

Sexual Problems

Just as satisfaction with sexuality is connected to the quality of the relation-ship, so sexual problems are often related to aspects of the relationship, par-ticularly feelings about the partner (Bancroft, Loftus, & Long, 2003; Henderson-King & Veroff, 1994; Laumann, Paik, & Rosen, 1999; Oggins et al., 1993). This view tends to be neglected in the prevailing medical model ap-proach to sexual problems reported by women and men (Tiefer, 1996, 2001).

The medical model stresses correct genital performance—which involves sexual desire, genital arousal, and orgasm, occurring in that sequence—and the ability to enjoy vaginal penetration (Tiefer, 2001). The response by researchers to sexual problems has been to expend great efforts to produce medical remedies, such as a pill, that will improve genital functioning, with little attention "devoted to assessment or education about sexual motives, scripts, pleasure, power, emotionality, sensuality, communication, or connectedness" and the effect they may have on sexuality (Tiefer, 2001, p. 90).

Particularly problematic for women is that their sexual problems have tended to be approached from the perspective that women and men experience, both physically and emotionally, the elements of sexual response, and thus sexual problems, in the same way. However, this approach may hinder rather than contribute to understanding of women's sexual distress. For example, a recent representative national survey of African American and European American women in heterosexual relationships found that negative emotional feelings during sexual interaction with the partner, as well as lack of emotional well-being (e.g., depression, tiredness, general unhappiness), were stronger predictors of sexual distress than physiological aspects of female sexual response, such as pain or lack of lubrication (Bancroft et al., 2003). This study did not include men, but, as the authors of this study note, men would likely be quite disturbed by impaired physiological response in sexual interactions. Despite such evidence, subjective emotional elements like the ones uncovered in the study of Bancroft et al. are not included in the *DSM-IV* categories of female sexual dysfunction (i.e., hypoactive sexual desire disorder, female sexual arousal disorder, female orgasmic disorder, dyspareunia, and vaginismus); rather, the emphasis is on impaired physiological functioning.

Violence in Close Relationships

Close relationships, whether with partners of the same or a different gender, are fraught with contradictions: emotional security versus vulnerability; passionate desire versus boredom; and limiting of the self versus expansion of the self, among others. Another contradiction within relationships is that while they can include intense caring and love, they can also include violence, fear, and coercion. This intimate partner violence can be physical (shoving, punching, kicking, etc.), emotional (threats, extreme controlling behavior, jealousy, social isolation, ridicule, etc.), financial (forcing economic dependence, damaging or stealing property, preventing partner from accessing financial resources, going to work, or school); or sexual (sexual coercion or forced sex); these different types of violence often occur together.

When looking specifically at the prevalence of sexual violence, or rape, of adult women, prevalence estimates range from 14 to 25 percent (Koss, 1993). These estimates are higher than police reports of rape, but rape is a crime that is highly underreported. Studies of rape by intimate male partners show prevalence rates that are startling and disturbing. For example, studies in Canada and the United States have found that, as a proportion of all rapes, prevalence rates for rape by intimate partners range from 19 to 30 percent (George, Winfield, & Blazer, 1992; Kilpatrick, Edmunds, & Seymour, 1993; Randall & Haskell, 1995; Ullman & Siegal, 1993). In fact, a woman is more at risk for rape by an intimate partner than by a stranger (for a review, see Mahoney & Williams, 1998), and a married woman is more likely to be raped by her husband than by a stranger (Russell, 1990).

A burgeoning body of research has documented that violence, including sexual abuse, also occurs in same-sex relationships. Although estimates are difficult to make when the true population of lesbians and gay men is unknown, a number of studies have found rates of intimate partner violence among same-sex couples that are high. One study found a 17 percent prevalence rate of abuse among lesbians (Loulan, 1987), but others have found rates of 52 percent (Lie & Gentlewarrier, 1991) and 73 percent (Lie et al., 1991). One of the few prevalence studies of intimate partner violence among gay men found that 26.1 percent of respondents reported they had used violence in their current or most recent male–male relationship, and 25.5 percent reported that their partner had (Harms, 1995, as cited in Merrill & Wolfe, 2000).

The patterns, forms, and frequencies of violence seen in same-sex relationships are similar to those seen in heterosexual relationships (Merrill & Wolfe, 2000). However, one study found that, unlike many heterosexual women in abusive relationships, gay and bisexual men were unlikely to report being financially trapped as a reason for staying in the relationship (Merrill & Wolfe, 2000). Another difference between same-sex and heterosexual relationships is that in same-sex relationships, a partner can threaten to or actually engage in "outing" a relationship partner's lesbian or gay identity to family, employer, or others in her or his social network as a form of emotional abuse (McLaughlin & Rozee, 2001; Poorman, 2001). Lesbian and gay men in relationships may also be much less informed about domestic violence than those in heterosexual relationships (Merrill & Wolfe, 2000; McLaughlin & Rozee, 2001; Poorman, 2001). The lack of awareness of the prevalence and seriousness of violence in lesbian and gay male couples—in contrast to heterosexual couples, among whom awareness of this problem is much greater—can prevent abused partners in same-sex couples from naming their experience as abuse and thereby taking the first step to seek help.

The experience of violence in relationships of lesbians and gay men is also different from that in heterosexual relationships in that lesbians and gay men may be much more reluctant to turn to the police or shelters for help due to extensive homophobia in the legal and social service delivery systems, feelings of shame or fear of retaliation from a partner, and concerns about revealing ones's sexual orientation (Poorman, 2001; West, 1998). Moreover, the belief that service providers would be unresponsive to victims of violence in lesbian and gay male relationships is grounded in reality; few agencies have programs or personnel trained to deal with violence in same-sex couples (Renzetti, 1996), and the experience of many lesbian and gay men victims of relationship violence who have turned to the legal and social service systems for help has been negative (see Poorman, 2001).

The causes of violence in intimate relationships are multiple and complex (for a review, see Kantor & Jasinski, 1998), but because women are the primary targets of this violence in heterosexual relationships, a feminist perspective has emphasized the role of gendered power differentials, patriarchy, and male privilege in society as causal elements (Kaschak, 2001). Thus, a key factor in the reduction of violence against women is reduction of male power and privilege, particularly through political action; if relationship violence is seen as legitimate at the highest levels of power in society, its eradication at the relationship level is difficult. When women and men are most equal in society, less gender-based violence is seen in relationships.

In relationships of same-sex couples, however, this perspective is less useful and may actually play a role in the invisibility and lack of adequate response by service providers to lesbian and gay men victims of partner violence (Ristock, 2001). The convenient fiction that women in relationships cannot really hurt or sexually assault each other, or that men in relationships can always defend themselves, has been difficult to dislodge from the minds of many. However, within same-sex couples, power can be based upon elements other than male power and privilege, such as ethnicity/race, social class, education, and other socially defined sources of hierarchy (Kaschak, 2001). Unfortunately, an alternative theory that can better explicate violence in same-sex couples is still lacking, and even feminist-identified therapists may rely upon norms surrounding heterosexual relationship dynamics in treatment of victims and perpetrators of abuse in same-sex couples (Ristock, 2001). As one researcher says, "We need more spaces and a language to talk about lesbian relationships and lesbian abuse that move us beyond European American, heteronormative frameworks if we are to develop truly inclusive services and appropriate therapeutic practice" (Ristock, 2001, pp. 69–70). Though this author is speaking specifically about lesbians, her statement can easily be applied to the relationships of gay men as well.

Conclusion

This chapter has attempted to offer a brief sketch of some of the ways in which gender socialization, expectations, and ideologies influence how sexuality is enacted, understood, and subjectively experienced by women and men, particularly those in intimate relationships. Of course, sexuality is affected by multiple individual and social factors, such as personal history and characteristics, morality, biological and health issues, values and beliefs concerning reproduction, and the facts that it is women, not men, who bear children, and that women are most often sexually objectified and exploited. Sexuality is also intricately involved in our economy and politics, and the debates surrounding it are in many ways contests over social control, power, and self-determination. This has been the case throughout history (D'Emilio & Freedman, 1988). Thus sexuality, such a personal and private experience, is never just a personal act; it is a reflection of many elements that come together to influence behavior. This does not mean, however, that persons are trapped in fixed sexual lives that may be unfulfilling, abusive, or without meaning. Rather, greater insight into the many factors influencing sexuality strengthens us to be better able to transform our sexual lives and relationships, thereby creating sexuality that sustains mutuality and equality, rather than traditional gender prescriptions (Levitt, Gerrish, & Hiestand, 2003; Ramazanoglu, 1992; Rose & Zand, 2002; Segal, 1994).

References

Alexander, M. G., & Fisher, T. D. (2003). Truth or consequences: Using the bogus pipeline to examine differences in self-reported sexuality. *Journal of Sex Research, 40,* 27–35.

Bancroft, J., Loftus, J., & Long, J. S. (2003). Distress about sex: A national survey of women in heterosexual relationships. *Archives of Sexual Behavior, 32,* 193–208.

Baumeister, R. F., Catanese, K. R., & Vohs, K. D. (2001). Is there a gender difference in strength of sex drive? Theoretical views, conceptual distinctions, a review of relevant evidence. *Personality and Social Psychology Review, 5,* 242–273.

Baumeister, R. F., & Leary, M. P. (1995). The need to belong: Desire for interpersonal attachments as a fundamental human motivation. *Psychological Bulletin, 117,* 497–529.

Blackwood, E. (2000). Culture and women's sexualities. *Journal of Social Issues, 56,* 223–238.

Blumstein, P., & Schwartz, P. (1983). *American couples: Money, work, sex.* New York: William Morrow.

Braun, V., & Kitzinger, C. (2001). "Snatch," "hole," or "honey-pot?" Semantic categories and the problem of nonspecificity in female genital slang. *Journal of Sex Research, 38,* 146–158.

Brown, N. R., & Sinclair, R. C. (1999). Estimating number of lifetime sexual partners: Men and women do it differently. *Journal of Sex Research, 36,* 292–297.

Byers, E. S., Demmons, S., & Lawrence, K. (1998). Sexual satisfaction within dating relationships: A test of the interpersonal exchange model of sexual satisfaction. *Journal of Social and Personal Relationships, 15,* 257–267.

Call, V., Sprecher, S., & Schwartz, P. (1995). The incidence and frequency of marital sex in a national sample. *Journal of Marriage and the Family, 57,* 639–652.

Castañeda, D., & Collins, B. (1998). Effects of gender, ethnicity, and a close relationship theme on perceptions of condom introducers. *Sex Roles, 39,* 369–390.

Christopher, E. S., & Sprecher, S. (2000). Sexuality in marriage, dating, and other relationships: A decade review. *Journal of Marriage and the Family, 62,* 999–1017.

Conley, T. D., Collins, B. E., & Garcia, D. (2000). Perceptions of women condom proposers among Chinese Americans, Japanese Americans, and European Americans. *Journal of Applied Psychology, 30,* 389–406.

Crawford, M., & Popp, D. (2003). Sexual double standards: A review and methodological critique of two decades of research. *Journal of Sex Research, 40,* 13–26.

Cupach, W. R., & Comstock, J. (1990). Satisfaction with sexual communication in marriage: Links to sexual satisfaction and dyadic adjustment. *Journal of Social and Personal Relationships, 7,* 179–186.

Darling, C. A., Davidson, J. K., & Passarello, L. C. (1992). The mystique of first intercourse among college youth: The role of partner, contraceptive practices, and psychological reactions. *Journal of Youth and Adolescence, 21,* 97–117.

DeLamater, J. (1987). Gender differences in sexual scenarios. In K. Kelley (Ed.), *Females, males, and sexuality: Theories and research* (pp. 127–139). Albany: State University of New York Press.

D'Emilio, J., & Freedman, E. B. (1988). *Intimate matters: A history of sexuality in America.* New York: Harper & Row.

Duck, S. (Ed.). (1993). *Social context and relationships.* Newbury Park, CA: Sage.

Edwards, J. N., & Booth, A. (1994). Sexuality, marriage, and well-being: The middle years. In A. S. Rossi (Ed.), *Sexuality across the life course* (pp. 233–259). Chicago: University of Chicago Press.

Espín, O. M. (1997). *Latin realities: Essays on healing, migration, and sexuality.* Boulder, CO: Westview Press.

Faulkner, S. L. (2003). Good girl or flirt girl: Latinas' definitions of sex and sexual relationships. *Hispanic Journal of Behavioral Sciences, 25,* 174–200.

Fields, J. (2001). *America's families and living arrangements: March 2000.* Current Population Reports, ser. P-20, no. 537. Washington, DC: U.S. Census Bureau.

Forbes, J. S. (1996). Disciplining women in contemporary discourses of sexuality. *Journal of Gender Studies, 5,* 117–129.

Gentry, M. (1998). The sexual double standard: The influence of number of relationships and level of sexual activity on judgements of women and men. *Psychology of Women Quarterly, 22,* 505–511.

George, L. K., Winfield, I., & Blazer, D. G. (1992). Sociocultural factors in sexual assault: Comparison of two representative samples of women. *Journal of Social Issues, 48,* 105–125.

Haavio-Mannila, E., & Kontula, O. (2003). Single and double standards in Finland, Estonia, and St. Petersburg. *Journal of Sex Research, 40,* 36–49.

Harlow, H. F. (1958). The nature of love. *American Psychologist, 13,* 673–685.

Harms, B. (1995). *Domestic violence in the gay male community.* Unpublished master's thesis, San Francisco State University, Department of Psychology.

Hatfield, E., Sprecher, S., Pillemer, J. T., Greenberger, D., & Wexler, P. (1988). Gender differences in what is desired in the sexual relationship. *Journal of Psychology and Human Sexuality, 1,* 39–52.

Helweg-Larsen, M., & Collins, B. E. (1994). The UCLA Multidimensional Condom Attitudes Scale: Documenting the complex determinants of condom use in college students. *Health Psychology, 13,* 224–237.

Henderson-King, D. H., & Veroff, J. (1994). Sexual satisfaction and marital well-being in the first years of marriages. *Journal of Social and Personal Relationships, 11,* 509–534.

Hendrick, S. S., & Hendrick, C. (2002). Linking romantic love with sex: Development of the perceptions of love and sex scale. *Journal of Social and Personal Relationships, 19,* 361–378.

Huston, M., & Schwartz, P. (1996). Gendered dynamics in the romantic relationships of lesbians and gay men. In J. T. Wood (Ed.), *Gendered relationships* (pp. 163–176). Mountain View, CA: Mayfield.

Hynie, M., & Lydon, J. E. (1995). Women's perception of female contraceptive behavior: Experimental evidence of the sexual double standard. *Psychology of Women Quarterly, 19,* 563–581.

Iasenza, S. (2002). Beyond "lesbian bed death": The passion and play in lesbian relationships. In S. M. Rose (Ed.), *Lesbian love and relationships* (pp. 111–120). New York: Harrington Park.

Impett, E. A., & Peplau, L. A. (2003). Sexual compliance: Gender, motivational, and relationship perspectives. *Journal of Sex Research, 40,* 87–100.

Kantor, G. K., & Jasinski, J. L. (1998). Dynamics and risk factors in partner violence. In J. L. Jasinski & L. M. Williams (Eds.), *Partner violence: A comprehensive review of 20 years of research* (pp. 1–43). Thousand Oaks, CA: Sage.

Kaschak, E. (Ed.). (2001). *Intimate betrayal: Domestic violence in lesbian relationships* (pp. 1–5). Binghamton, NY: Haworth.

Katz, J., & Farrow, S. (2000). Discrepant self views and young women's social and emotional adjustment. *Sex Roles, 42,* 781–796.

Kilpatrick, D. G., Edmunds, C. N., & Seymour, A. K. (1993). *Rape in America: A report to the nation.* Charleston: Crime Victims Research and Treatment Center, Medical University of South Carolina.

Koss, M. P. (1993). Detecting the scope of rape: A review of prevalence research methods. *Journal of Interpersonal Violence, 8,* 98–122.

Laumann, E. O., Paik, A., & Rosen, R. C. (1999). Sexual dysfunction in the United

88 Praeger Guide to the Psychology of Gender

States: Prevalence and predictors. *Journal of the American Medical Association, 281,* 537–544.

Leitenberg, H., & Henning, K. (1995). Sexual fantasies. *Psychological Bulletin, 117,* 469–496.

Levin, R. J., & Levin, A. (1975, October). The Redbook report on premarital and extramarital sex. *Redbook, 45,* 38–40, 190–192.

Levitt, H. M., Gerrish, E. A., & Hiestand, K. R. (2003). The misunderstood gender: A model of modern femme identity. *Sex Roles, 48,* 99–113.

Lie, G. Y., & Gentlewarrior, S. (1991). Intimate violence in lesbian relationships: Discussion of survey finding and practice implications. *Journal of Social Service Research, 15,* 41–59.

Lie, G. Y., Schilit, R., Bush, J., Montagne, M., & Reyes, L. (1991). Lesbians in currently aggressive relationships: How frequently do they report aggressive past relationships. *Violence and Victims, 6,* 121–135.

Littleton, H. L., & Axsom, D. (2003). Rape and seduction scripts of university students: Implications for rape attributions and unacknowledged rape. *Sex Roles, 49,* 465–475.

Loulan, J. (1987). *Lesbian passion: Loving ourselves and each other.* San Francisco: Spinsters/Aunt Lute.

Mahoney, P., & Williams, L. M. (1998). Sexual assault in marriage: Prevalence, consequences, and treatment of wife rape. In J. L. Jasinski & L. M. Williams (Eds.), *Partner violence: A comprehensive review of 20 years of research* (pp. 113–162). Thousand Oaks, CA: Sage.

McLaughlin, E. M., & Rozee, P. D. (2001). Knowledge about heterosexual versus lesbian battering. In E. Kaschak (Ed.), *Intimate betrayal: Domestic violence in lesbian relationships* (pp. 39–58). Binghamton, NY: Haworth.

Merrill, G. S., & Wolfe, V. A. (2000). Battered gay men: An exploration of abuse, help-seeking, and why they stay. *Journal of Homosexuality, 39,* 1–30.

Michael, R. T., Gagnon, J. H., Laumann, E. O., & Kolata, G. (1994). *Sex in America.* Boston: Little, Brown.

Milhausen, R. R., & Herold, E. S. (1999). Does the sexual double standard still exist? Perceptions of university women. *Journal of Sex Research, 99,* 361–368.

Miller, L. C., Betancourt, B. A., DeBro, S. C., & Hoffman, V. (1993). Negotiating safer sex: Interpersonal dynamics. In J. B. Pryor & G. D. Reeder (Eds.), *The social psychology of HIV infection* (pp. 85–123). Hillsdale, NJ: Erlbaum.

Mosher, D. L., & MacIan, P. (1994). College men and women respond to X-rated videos intended for male or female audiences: Gender and sexual scripts. *Journal of Sex Research, 31,* 99–113.

Muehlenhard, C. L., Peterson, Z. D., Karwoski, L., Bryan, T. S., & Lee, R. S. (2003). Sexuality and gender: The importance of context. *Journal of Sex Research, 40,* 1–3.

Norton, A. J., & Miller, L. F. (1992). *Marriage, divorce, and remarriage in the 1990s.* Current Population Reports, ser. P-23, no. 180. Washington, DC: U.S. Census Bureau.

Oggins, J., Leber, D., & Veroff, J. (1993). Race and gender differences in black and white newlyweds' perceptions of sexual and marital relations. *Journal of Sex Research, 30,* 152–162.

Okazaki, S. (2002). Influences of culture on Asian Americans' sexuality. *Journal of Sex Research, 39,* 34–41.

Oliver, M.B., & Shibley Hyde, J. (1993). Gender differences in sexuality: A meta-analysis. *Psychological Bulletin, 114,* 29–51.

Peplau, L.A. (2003). Human sexuality: How do women and men differ? *Current Directions in Psychological Science, 12,* 37–40.

Peplau, L.A., Cochran, S.D., & Mays, V.M. (1997). A national survey of the intimate relationships of African American lesbians and gay men: A look at commitment, satisfaction, sexual behavior, and HIV disease. In B. Greene (Ed.), *Psychological perspectives on lesbian and gay issues.* Vol. 3, *Ethnic and cultural diversity among lesbians and gay men* (pp. 11–38). Thousand Oaks, CA: Sage.

Pesman, C. (1991, November). Love and sex in the '90s: Our national survey. *Seventeen,* 63–68.

Poorman, P.B. (2001). Forging community links to address abuse in lesbian relationships. In E. Kaschak (Ed.), *Intimate betrayal: Domestic violence in lesbian relationships* (pp. 7–24). Binghamton, NY: Haworth.

Ramazanoglu, C. (1992). Love and the politics of heterosexuality. *Feminism and Psychology, 2,* 444–447.

Randall, M., & Haskell, L. (1995). Sexual violence in women's lives. *Violence against Women, 1,* 6–31.

Regan, P.C., & Berscheid, E. (1996). Beliefs about the state, goals, and objects of sexual desire. *Journal of Marital and Sexual Therapy, 22,* 110–120.

Regan, P.C., & Berscheid, E. (1999). *Lust: What we know about human sexual desire.* Thousand Oaks, CA: Sage.

Renzetti, C.M. (1996). The poverty of services for battered lesbians. In C.M. Renzetti & C.H. Miley (Eds.), *Violence in gay and lesbian domestic partnerships* (pp. 61–68). New York: Harrington Park.

Rich, A. (1983). Compulsory heterosexuality and lesbian experience. In A. Snitow, C. Stansell, & S. Thompson (Eds.), *Powers of desire: The politics of sexuality* (p. 177–205). New York: Monthly Review Press.

Richardson, L. (1997). Gender stereotyping in the English language. In L. Richardson, V. Taylor, & N. Whittier (Eds.), *Feminist frontiers IV* (pp. 115–122). New York: McGraw-Hill.

Ristock, J.L. (2001). Decentering heterosexuality: Responses of feminist counselors to abuse in lesbian relationships. In E. Kaschak (Ed.), *Intimate betrayal: Domestic violence in lesbian relationships* (pp. 59–72). Binghamton, NY: Haworth.

Rose, S., & Zand, D. (2002). Lesbian dating and courtship from young adulthood to midlife. In S.M. Rose (Ed.), *Lesbian love and relationships* (pp. 85–109). New York: Harrington Park.

Rose, S., Zand, D., & Cini, M. (1993). Lesbian courtship scripts. In E. D. Rothblum
    & K. A. Brehony (Eds.), *Boston marriages: Romantic but asexual relation-
    ships among contemporary lesbians* (pp. 70–85). Amherst: University of Mas-
    sachusetts Press.
Scanzoni, J., Polonko, K., Teachman, J., & Thompson, L. (1989). *The sexual bond:
    Rethinking families and close relationships.* Newbury Park, CA: Sage.
Schank, R. C., & Abelson, R. P. (1977). *Scripts, plans, goals, and understanding: An
    inquiry into human knowledge structures.* Hillsdale, NJ: Erlbaum.
Segal, L. (1994). *Straight sex: Rethinking the politics of pleasure.* Berkeley: Univer-
    sity of California Press.
Simmons, T., & O'Connell, M.. (2003). *Married-couple and un-married partner
    households, 2000.* Census 2000 Special Reports. Washington, DC: U.S. Cen-
    sus Bureau.
Smith, T. (1992). Discrepancies between men and women in reporting number of sex-
    ual partners: A summary from four countries. *Social Biology, 39,* 203–211.
Sprecher, S. (2002). Sexual satisfaction in premarital relationships: Association with sat-
    isfaction, love, commitment, and stability. *Journal of Sex Research, 39,* 190–196.
Sprecher, S., & Regan, P. C. (2000). Sexuality in a relational context. In C. Hendrick
    & S. S. Hendrick (Eds.), *Close relationships: A sourcebook* (pp. 217–227).
    Thousand Oaks, CA: Sage.
Stombler, M., & Baunach, D. M. (2004). Doing it differently: Women and men's es-
    timates of their number of lifetime sexual partners. In M. Stombler, D. M.
    Baunach, E. O. Burgess, D. Donnelly, & W. Simonds (Eds.), *Sex matters: The
    sexuality and society reader* (pp. 48–49). Boston: Pearson A and B.
Tafoya, T. (1997). Native gay and lesbian issues. In B. Greene (Ed.), *Psychological
    perspectives on lesbian and gay issues.* Vol. 3, *Ethnic and cultural diversity
    among lesbians and gay men* (pp. 1–8). Thousand Oaks, CA: Sage.
Thompson, S. (1984). Search for tomorrow: On feminism and the reconstruction of
    teen romance. In C. S. Vance (Ed.), *Pleasure and danger: Exploring female
    sexuality* (pp. 350–384). Boston: Routledge & Kegan Paul.
Thompson, S. (1990). Putting a big thing into a little hole: Teenage girls' accounts
    of sexual initiation. *Journal of Sex Research, 27,* 341–361.
Tiefer, L. (1996). The medicalization of sexuality: Conceptual, normative, and pro-
    fessional issues. *Annual Review of Sex Research, 7,* 252–282.
Tiefer, L. (2001). A new view of women's sexual problems: Why new? Why now?
    Journal of Sex Research, 38, 89–96.
Tolman, D. L. (2001). Echoes of sexual ojectification: Listening for one girl's erotic
    voice. In D. L. Tolman & M. Brydon-Miller (Eds.), *From subjects to subjec-
    tivities: A handbook of interpretive and participatory methods* (pp. 130–144).
    New York: New York University Press.
Tolman, D. L., & Debold, E. (1994). Conflicts of body and image: Female adoles-
    cents, desire, and the no-body body. In P. Fallon, M. Katzman, & S. Wooley
    (Eds.), *Feminist perspectives on eating disorders* (pp. 301–317). New York:
    Guilford.

Tolman, D. L., Striepe, M. I., & Harmon, T. (2003). Gender matters: Constructing a model of adolescent health. *Journal of Sex Research, 40,* 4–12.

Ullman, S. E., & Siegel, J. M. (1993). Victim–offender relationship and sexual assault. *Violence and Victims, 8,* 121–134.

Vance, C. S. (1985). Pleasure and danger: Toward a politics of sexuality. In C. S. Vance (Ed.), *Pleasure and danger: Exploring female sexuality* (pp. 1–27). Boston: Routledge and Kegan Paul.

Weiderman, M. (1997). The truth must be in here somewhere: Examining the gender discrepancy in self-reported lifetime sexual partners. *Journal of Sex Research, 34,* 375–386.

West, C. M. (1998). Leaving a second closet: Outing partner violence in same-sex couples. In J. L. Jasinski & L. M. Williams (Eds.), *Partner violence: A comprehensive review of 20 years of research* (pp. 163–183). Thousand Oaks, CA: Sage.

Chapter 5

Gender and Mental Health: Incidence and Treatment Issues

Rudy Nydegger

Introduction

Certainly, most people would believe and agree that there are relationships between mental health and gender. However, when one begins to look at some of the reasons, complicating factors, and implications of this assumption, it becomes much more complex. The simple fact that there may be differences in mental health issues does not address the important factors that are essential in the understanding of this major health care concern.

To examine this vital area, it is important to evaluate a number of considerations and a broad range of literature. Some of the questions that need to be asked and answered include the following:

1. Are there differences in the rates of psychological and emotional conditions between men and women? If so (or not), why is this so?

2. Are there differences in the types of psychological and emotional problems that men and women suffer, and if so (or not), why is this so?

3. Are there differences between men and women in their access to and/or utilization of mental health services, and if so (or not), why is this so?

4. Are there differences in responses to mental health treatment between men and women, and if so (or not), why is this so?

5. Are there differences in mental health policy, reimbursement issues, and social factors that may affect women and men differently?

6. Are there differences in gender distribution in the various mental health professions, and how might this affect the care and treatment of patients with mental health problems?

Clearly, these are complex issues that deserve serious treatment, and either to dismiss them as irrelevant or to imply that these considerations do not warrant attention, is to miss an opportunity to improve our understanding of mental health issues. We hope that improved understanding will lead to better diagnosis and treatment, and improved care for those in need of mental health services. Even more important, better understanding of these issues may lead us to better methods of preventing or minimizing the terrible effects of mental health problems in society. This is not an issue only in the United States; it is increasingly being recognized as a major problem in the rest of the world, including the developing nations.

As we begin the examination of gender and mental health issues, it immediately becomes clear that there are differences in how we think about mental health relative to gender differences, and that this varies from culture to culture and from subculture to subculture. Clearly, the perception of mental health or illness depends on the prevailing culture, and since sex roles and other gender issues are based, at least in part, on culture, then clearly culture has something to do with how we think about mental health and gender.

Before we begin discussing the gender differences in prevalence of mental health problems, it might be interesting to look at some of the factors that the World Health Organization (WHO) (2000) feels are important in protecting people against mental health problems, especially depression: (1) having some degree of autonomy and some control when responding to severe events in one's life; (2) having access to resources that give a person the opportunity to have choices when confronting severe life events; and (3) having support from family and friends as well as health providers when confronting difficult life situations is "powerfully protective." The extent to which these protective factors may be differentially relevant to men and women will also impact the rates and types of problems that various people experience.

To examine the relationship between gender and mental health, we will start by reviewing relevant literature related to the prevalence of psychological and emotional problems. That is, do women and men differ in the rates at which they experience mental health problems, and if so, what differences exist, and why?

Gender and the Prevalence of Mental Health Problems

In looking at the various studies that have been done, it is very clear that psychological and emotional problems are some of the most significant and costly health problems in the world today. According to Robins and Regier

(1991), there is a 32 percent lifetime incidence of mental illness around the world, and a 20 percent annual incidence. This means that at any given time, about one person in five has a diagnosable mental condition, and that over a person's lifetime there is about a one-in-three chance of suffering from such a condition. Robins and Regier also point out that earlier studies demonstrating that women have a higher rate of mental illness represent what they refer to as "institutionalized sexism in the social definition of mental disorders." They make this assertion because while women tend to have higher rates of mental illness in general, this holds only if substance use disorders and personality disorders are not included in the statistics. When these two types of disorders are added, the rates for men and women are about equal, with men predominating in some conditions and women in others (Robins & Regier, 1991). Stereotypically, women are expected to have more mental disorders than men, and this tendency is assumed to increase with age. Thus, the stereotypic psychiatric patient should be a middle-aged woman with anxiety or depression. However, across many different studies done in a variety of cultures, it was found is that there is little gender difference in overall rate of mental illness, with men having a slightly higher lifetime rate. In any given year about 20 percent of men and 20 percent of women will have a psychiatric disorder. However, over their lifetimes about 36 percent of men and 30 percent of women will suffer from such a disorder. These statistics include both substance use disorders and personality disorders (Robins & Regier, 1991).

It is also true that females report many more medical complaints than men, and symptoms judged to be of a somatoform nature are twice as common in women as in men. Further, women are more likely to be diagnosed with hypochondriasis, and to have higher rates of disorders with somewhat vague symptoms and unknown causes, such as irritable bowel syndrome, chronic fatigue syndrome, and fibromyalgia. It is suggested that a history of physical and or sexual abuse may play a role in this, and also that the cultural pattern typified by male stoicism and resistance to asking for help may contribute to these patterns (Kroenke & Spitzer, 1998).

In general, women tend to predominate in anxiety and depressive disorders, somatoform disorders, and co-morbidity with other medical and psychological problems (WHO, 2003). With respect to anxiety disorders, including panic disorder, obsessive-compulsive disorder, post-traumatic stress disorder, phobias, and generalized anxiety disorder, women outnumber men in everything but social phobia and obsessive-compulsive disorder (Robins & Regier, 1991; Bourdon et al., 1988).

With regard to depressive disorders, unipolar depression is twice as common in women as in men (WHO, 2003). It is found in about 12 percent of women and 6.6 percent of men (Regier et al., 1993), and is the leading cause of disease burden in females age five and older worldwide (Murray & Lopez, 1996). It is estimated by the WHO (2003) that unipolar depression will be the second leading cause of disability worldwide by 2020. Currently, the WHO (2003) estimates that depressive disorders account for 41.9 percent of the disability from neuropsychiatric disorders in women, compared with 29.3 percent in men. It should also be pointed out, however, that doctors are more likely to diagnose a woman with depression, even when they score the same on tests for depression and present with the same symptoms as men (WHO, 2003).

A problem sometimes related to depression is suicide, and we find differential rates based on sex in this as well. In studies conducted across nine different countries, women reported attempting suicide about two to three times as often as men. The WHO (2003) reports that at sites all over the world, women attempt suicide more frequently than men, and the world rate is 3.5 to 1. However, it is also reported that except in China and parts of India, men commit suicide more frequently than women do. The world rate for suicide completion is 3.5 men to each woman. In the United States men are four times more likely to commit suicide than women (Hoyert, Kochanek, & Murphy, 1999). Finally, Murray and Lopez (1996) report that self-inflicted injury, including suicide, is the ninth leading cause of disease burden for females age five and older worldwide.

Although most of the studies on prevalence of mental health conditions have been done in industrialized countries, it is estimated that up to 20 percent of those accessing primary health care in developing countries suffer from anxiety and depressive disorders, and that most of these patients are female (WHO, 2000). This type of finding also crosses age groups. According to the WHO (2000), the leading mental health problems of the elderly are depression, organic brain syndromes, and dementia. In all of these disorders, women outnumber men. Another article, however, discussed the fact that since men in many cultures do not express their feelings as easily as women, they tend to have greater problems during bereavement (WHO, 2003).

Also, we find gender differences in children. The WHO (2003) reports that in general, girls' psychological symptoms tend to be inner-directed, and boys tend more to acting out. Specifically, girls show more depression, more suicidal ideation, and more suicide attempts than boys (WHO, 2000), and a higher incidence rate of eating disorders in most cultures (American Psychiatric Association 2000; WHO, 2003). The WHO (2003) also reports that lower self-esteem and more concern for body image among girls lead to pressures that result in higher depression rates and higher rates of eating disorders.

Boys, on the other hand, are likely to have problems with anger, high-risk behaviors, conduct disorders, and antisocial behaviors, and to commit suicide more often than girls (WHO, 2003). One interesting study found that as adults, women are diagnosed with psychological problems at as least as high a rate as men and are more frequently given psychotropic medications; however, Gardner et al. (2002) found that compared with girls, boys are more likely to be labeled by a primary care physician as suffering from a mental health condition. While this may be due in part to the way that the boy's behaviors are described by their parents, it is also true that boys are diagnosed with ADHD and conduct disorders more frequently than girls, and are given psychotropic medications more often. Boys show a lower rate of internalizing types of disorders, but have much higher rates of behavioral and acting-out types of problems. It was also reported that in most cases, children receive care for mental health problems in the primary care setting (Gardner et al., 2002).

Prior (1999) has an interesting observation on these findings. She suggests that deviant behaviors in females are more often labeled as "mad," whereas deviant behaviors in males tend to be labeled as "bad." Thus, in most cases, females (and especially adult women) tend to be labeled with mental health explanations for their problems, and are treated accordingly. Males are more likely (especially as adults) to be labeled as "bad," and thus are treated in the legal system more frequently than in the mental health system. Of course, as pointed out above, in the primary care setting, boys may be labeled as having mental health problems more frequently, but even then, the problems that get them labeled are usually the ones that result from acting out and externalizing types of difficulties.

In most literature, men have higher rates of certain personality disorders and of substance use disorders. It is also true that men tend to use alcohol to manage stress more frequently than women, and that they are far more likely to develop alcohol dependence. This is also true in emergent nations. Over the lifetimes of patients, about one-fifth of men and one-twelfth of women in developing countries will develop a diagnosable problem with alcohol. Also, that men are more likely to disclose alcohol problems to health care providers than women are (WHO, 2003).

In terms of personality disorders, one diagnostic category that definitely shows a preponderance in males is antisocial personality disorder. Men have a rate that is three times greater than that of women (WHO, 2003). Women will show higher rates of personality disorders such as hysterical personality disorder and borderline personality disorder because the symptoms are more consistent with the stereotypical female role in many societies. Paris (1993) found that three-quarters of patients diagnosed with borderline personality disorder were female—and this study had tried to eliminate some of the complicating effects of gender bias. It must be pointed out, however, that many of the diagnoses of personality disorders are colored by bias or expectations of the diagnosing professionals. The diagnostic categories for personality disorders allow for considerable individual differences between patients; they are very complex; they often coexist with Axis I disorders; they rarely exist in pure form; and the categories tend to be unreliable. Clearly, many personality disorders depend upon sex-linked traits; the diagnoses are often made by men using clinical judgment; and even if there is not bias in the definitions of the disorders, there may well be bias in the ways they are applied. In fact, many of the diagnostic tests and procedures that are used may complicate this problem further (Widger, 2000).

Regarding more serious mental illnesses, some interesting patterns have emerged as well. For example, we know that men and women suffer from schizophrenia at about the same rate (less than 2 percent of the population for both). However, men tend to show an earlier onset of the disorder (WHO, 2003). It has also been found that schizophrenia tends to be more disabling in men than in women, and that men are more susceptible to serious developmental disorders like retardation and autism. Schizophrenic men not only seem to have more disabling symptoms, but their symptoms tend to be more difficult to treat (Waddington et al., 1998). This may be due in part to the fact that since men tend to develop schizophrenia at an earlier age, they may not have as long a period of time of learn appropriate social behavior, and may not be as psychologically resilient because they had a shorter premorbid history, thus giving them fewer resources with which to deal with such a disabling condition. Waddington et al. (1998) also suggest that these gender differences may be due in part to the role of female hormones (especially estrogen), which may act as neurotransmitters in parts of the brain. While schizophrenia is usually thought of as a disease of young adults, it often emerges in women in their forties, as their estrogen levels begin to decrease. Some have even suggested that in female schizophrenic patients, their symptoms tend to fluctuate with their menstrual cycles, which also suggests the possibility of a protective role of female hormones in the development of schizophrenic symptoms.

Since the rates for men and women are about the same overall, it is not likely that schizophrenia is a sex-linked disorder, but the different ways in which the disease is manifested in men and women may be due in part to cultural factors such as gender role differences and socialization patterns. These differences may also have something to do with sex-specific factors like hormones. Another interesting conclusion, drawn by Goldstein et al. (1998), was based on studies that showed that schizophrenic men do worse on tests of attention, language, verbal memory, and executive functions. Men are equal with women in nonverbal memory, visual–spatial ability, and motor speed. Schizophrenic men perform worse than their controls on all measures. Women schizophrenics are worse than their controls in all but language, verbal memory, and visual–spatial ability. The authors suggest that these differences may be due to brain function, and that women may not be damaged as much by schizophrenia as men are.

Another serious mental illness is bipolar disorder, and men and women have approximately similar rates of this disorder. However, in contrast to schizophrenia, women may have a higher rate of the more serious forms of bipolar disorder (WHO, 2003).

With respect to other serious mental disorders, various forms of dementia also have some gender-related issues. It appears to be true that the rates of dementia are about the same for men and women, and that the frequencies are fairly evenly split among the mild, moderate, and severe forms (Skoog et al., 1993). However, the main risk factor in the dementias is age, and while the rates are about the same for men and women, since women tend to live longer than men, there will always be more female dementia patients at any given time than male patients (National Institute on Aging, 1999; WHO, 2003).

A related and important factor when looking at chronic and disabling conditions such as schizophrenia and dementia is the impact that these disorders have on families and caregivers. Schulz et al. (1995) found that caregivers are more likely to suffer from depression than the average person; and, as McCann et al. (1997) point out, in most cultures, caregivers are usually family members, frequently wives or daughters. Since women seem to be more susceptible to depression in general, if they also have to fulfill the role of caregiver, then this significantly affects their risk of becoming depressed (Schulz et al., 1995). Patel (2002) further notes that in caring for others with terminal conditions such as HIV/AIDS, there is a significant burden on the caregivers, which leads to an increased risk for depression. Women, who are frequently the caregivers for people with these conditions, suffer considerable mental and physical health problems as a result of caregiving, and depression is the most common problem.

In summary, it is quite apparent that mental and emotional problems affect men and women worldwide, and that these problems are a significant health problem. It is also quite clear that men and women may experience these types of problems at about the same general rate, but there are definite differences between men and women with respect to how they experience these problems, and the nature of the problems from which they suffer. Women tend to suffer from anxiety, depressive, and somatoform disorders more frequently, and men tend to suffer from substance-related problems and some personality disorders more frequently. Although men and women may suffer from schizophrenia at about the same rates, men tend to have an earlier onset of the disorder, and typically are more negatively impacted than are women. Similarly, both men and women suffer from bipolar disorder at about the same rate, but women may be prone to the more serious variants of this disorder at a higher rate. Also, while men and women are diagnosed with dementia at about the same rates, since women tend to live longer, there are more women with these types of disorders at any given time. Women also tend to attempt suicide and self-destructive behaviors more often than men, but men tend to succeed in committing suicide at a higher rate.

While it is clear that there may be differential rates in the diagnosis and distribution of various psychiatric disorders between men and women, the reasons for these differences are not so clear. In the next section we will examine some of the apparent reasons why men and women may experience psychological and emotional difficulties differently.

Some Factors Related to Gender Differences in Mental Illness

Research has convincingly demonstrated that there are different rates of various forms of psychopathology between men and women, and it is essential to try to understand some of the reasons for these differences. One area of inquiry that has been explored is the evaluation of the role of hormonal factors and reproductive health on mental health and illness. Interestingly, there appears to be a gender issue in this area. Specifically, we can find substantial amounts of research from around the world that examines reproductive health and its relationship to mental health in women, but there are very few studies examining the role of reproductive health in the mental health of men (WHO, 2003). That being said, however, there are some interesting studies regarding the role of these factors on the mental health of women.

Several studies have found that before adolescence and late in life, males and females experience depression at about the same rate (Bebbington et al., 1998; Birmaher et al., 1996). Since it appears, then, that gender differences in depression in women are not seen until after puberty and before menopause, it is hypothesized that hormonal factors may be involved in women's greater vulnerability to this disorder. However, as tempting as this hypothesis may be, there are other factors that operate here as well. Such things as stress caused by multiple roles in the home and at work, the increased probability of women's being poor, the risk of women's being victims of violence and abuse, and the fact that women frequently raise children alone also clearly play a role (Sherrill et al., 1997).

Postpartum depression, or postnatal depression, has been studied primarily in industrialized countries, and is found in about 10 to 20 percent of mothers (Patel, 2002). However, it has also been discovered that postnatal depression is found, frequently at higher rates than expected, in developing nations as well. This has a severe impact on the health of both mothers and their babies (Patel et al., 2000). However, it must be noted that in both developing and industrial countries, other gender-related factors, such as marital disharmony and violence, have been reported as risk factors for postnatal depression (Patel, 2002).

Another "female" problem that is related to psychological and emotional functioning is premenstrual syndrome (PMS), which is sometimes referred to as premenstrual dysphoric disorder (PMDD). It is estimated that 3 to 4 percent of women suffer PMS symptoms that significantly interfere with work and social functioning (Johnson, McChesney, & Beanu, 1988; Rivera-Tovar & Frank, 1990). It would appear that PMS is an abnormal response to hormone changes, and that women predisposed to depression are more vulnerable to the mood-shifting effect of hormones (Schmidt et al., 1998). It must be pointed out, however, that even if hormones are a factor in PMS, social, cultural, family, relationship, and other health factors play a role in this disorder as well.

Finally, research has demonstrated some relationship between other genitourinary factors and mental health issues. For example, infertility and hysterectomy have been found by some to increase a woman's risk for depressive and anxiety disorders. Even bladder control problems have been found to lead to higher rates of emotional distress, and these, too, are more common in women (WHO, 2003). Reproductive tract surgery may lead to emotional problems because of the identification of the reproductive organs with sexuality and with a woman's identity. It is suggested that inadequate concern for women's identities may be a key factor in adverse mental health consequences that are related to reproductive tract surgeries (Patel, 2002).

Of course, it is apparent that there are many other factors that contribute to differential rates of psychopathology in men and women, and many of them are social and/or cultural. According to the WHO (2003), gender-specific risk factors for common psychological disorders that affect women more than men include violence against women, socioeconomic disadvantage, income inequality and lower income levels, lower social status, and continuous and unrelenting care of others. Patel et al. (2000) also found that certain disorders, including anxiety and depressive problems, are associated with economic deprivation resulting from unemployment, being in debt, or belonging to a low-income group of society. Patel et al. (2000) further suggested that those who are already vulnerable are at high risk for suffering from conditions that will disable them even further, and it is likely that women will suffer these problems at a greater rate than men.

Gender inequality in mental health and illness goes far beyond the statistics that we have cited. In literature and art, over time and in many different cultures, women are often portrayed as irrational and emotional, and men as rational and in control. Thus, "madness" is often seen as a female problem (Showalter, 1987). It is also clear that in many cultures the normal healthy adult is judged by male norms. A woman who either rejects or adheres too closely to the prevailing cultural norms is often judged as "mentally ill" (Ussher, 1992).

One fact that is becoming increasingly obvious is that psychological and emotional problems are not simply associated with the high-stress life of industrialized countries; in fact, many of the problems that we are discussing are found at even higher rates in areas where reasonable and accessible care is almost nonexistent. It is true that gender is a crucial element in physical health inequities in emerging nations, and this is true of mental health as well. In most cultures, gender influences the amount of control men and women have over the determinants of their health. For example, such things as economic position and socioeconomic status, as well as access to resources and treatment opportunities in society, are factors that can create problems in the access and use of mental health treatments (WHO, 2000). One very important set of studies, conducted by Broadhead and Abas (1998), looked at some of the social factors related to mental health and illness. Their comparisons involved studies conducted on women in Harare, Zimbabwe, and in Camberwell, England (a deprived district in inner London thought to have a high rate of depression). Some very compelling findings came out of these studies. For example, in Harare, 31 percent of the women had depressive or anxiety disorders, as opposed to 9 percent of the women in Camberwell, and more women in Harare had experienced severe life events (54 percent), compared with the women in Camberwell (31 percent). Notable in these findings was that in Harare there was a much higher proportion of events involving humiliation and entrapment.

There are apparently other factors that may predispose women to have some differences in the rate and type of psychological difficulties that they experience. Some writers have suggested that gender-specific roles may well contribute to the manifestation of psychological problems. For example, most forms of somatization are more common in women, and some argue that this comes from training for the female role that makes women more willing to express feelings and symptoms, and to seek help for them. Others would say that this is a kind of "inarticulate protest" against the lack of power many women feel, and the sense of oppression that characterizes many women. Statistically, in developing countries men have poorer health than women, and also have a higher death rate at every age. However, women are more likely to feel ill and to report being ill. Also, while women have a higher rate of depression (as noted above), this is particularly true when the physical symptoms of depression are included. Similarly, women tend to react more physically to the effects of trauma than do men (Illness without disease, 1999).

There do appear to be consistent relationships in most cultures between family, personal, and social stresses and psychopathology. It has been found in China that personal distress from things like arranged marriages, unwanted abortions, and an enforced nurturing role often leads to higher rates of psychological problems (WHO, 2003). This, of course, suggests that powerlessness and oppression are clearly factors that may lead to emotional problems, and when these are more related to female roles, one would expect higher rates of psychological disorders (at least of certain types) in women. Cooper et al. (1999) state that because of the varying expectations and evaluations of the roles of men and women, mental illness in women may attract more shame and dishonor than in men. It would also be expected that psychological problems in women would have a greater impact on family life, given that in most cultures the woman tends to have most of the responsibility for household and family functioning.

The WHO (2003) reports that in most cultures the communication between female patients and health care workers tends to be very authoritarian, making a woman's disclosure of emotional distress difficult and often stigmatized. It is suggested that in many cultures, when women disclose their mental health problems to health care workers, these workers may have gender biases that lead them either to overtreat or to undertreat women. In looking at the effect of gender roles on psychopathology, one study found some interesting results. An article from the Press Association (2003) reported that women who stay single have better mental health than those who are married or divorced. The opposite is true for men—married men have fewer mental health problems than either divorced or single men.

As discussed above, many studies have demonstrated that men tend to have higher rates of substance use problems, and also of some types of personality disorders, such as antisocial personality disorder. Prior (1999) suggests that the reason for these higher rates may be due, at least in part, to masculine roles. Pleck (1981) claims that while the male role may be oppressive to women, it is also oppressive to men. This makes sense when one looks at the differential rates of certain conditions from which men suffer and at the relationship between these types of problems and the prevailing masculine roles in the societies in question. Other writers (Connell, 1995; Edley & Wetherall, 1995) have pointed out that the current psychiatric system is not "man friendly," and is not flexible enough to be helpful to men who are having problems related to the male role or identity. Also, men are often reluctant to seek help for fear of appearing weak. Thus, it seems clear that while there are characteristics of traditional female roles in many cultures that predispose women to certain types of psychological problems, there are also aspects of traditional male roles that predispose men to psychological difficulties—but problems different from those women may suffer.

As one might expect, there appears to be substantial evidence that other environmental and cultural factors may be related to psychopathology. While it was pointed out that certain biological factors, such as hormonal fluctuations, may have some impact on rates of psychological problems, it is obvious that other factors must be at work as well. Patel (2002) reported variations in the rates of depression in men and women between different cultures. The highest difference was found in Santiago, Chile: a rate of depression of 4.7 women to one man. In Ibadan, Nigeria, this rate was 3.8 women to 5.3 men, which is unusual but clearly important. This range clearly suggests that biological factors alone cannot explain the different rates of depression—or any other psychopathology, for that matter. Social and cultural factors obviously are also important to the understanding of these problems.

According to the WHO (2003), women's exposure to social problems such as low income lead to depression, while in men, they tend to lead to alcohol and drug abuse and violence. However, it has been pointed out that about 80 percent of the approximately 50 million people affected by violent crime, civil war, disasters, and displacement are women and children (WHO, 2003). Further, there is a lifetime prevalence rate of violence against women ranging from 16 to 50 percent, depending upon the culture and the study, and it is estimated that about one-fifth of women experience rape or attempted rape over their lifetime (WHO, 2003).

The WHO (2003) also suggests that the high prevalence of sexual violence toward women and the resulting higher rate of post-traumatic stress disorder (PTSD) make women the largest group affected by this disorder. In fact, Breslau et al. (1991) report that women are twice as likely to develop PTSD as men following trauma. It is also true that the harmful effects of sexual violence and abuse in children have been shown to lead to higher rates of psychopathology in adulthood (Patel, 2002). Finally, it is also true that women are more likely to develop long-term PTSD and to have higher rates of co-morbidity for both medical and psychiatric problems as well (Breslau et al., 1992).

There are many studies documenting the negative impact that trauma, abuse, deprivation and hardship, social ills, and other social factors have on the mental health of any individual. Fischback and Herbert (1997) found that among the most disabling and long-lasting health effects of violence are the mental health effects, such as PTSD and depression. However, they also found higher rates of other problems—eating disorders, sexual dysfunction, and suicidal behavior—as the result of violence.

Even such things as social policies have an impact on the mental health of a population. According to the WHO (2000), economic and social policies that cause sudden, disruptive, and severe changes in income and employment, and that cannot be controlled or avoided significantly, increase gender in-equality and the rates of psychological problems in society. That is, when so-cial and economic policies create social and financial problems, this will lead to higher rates of psychological and emotional problems, and these problems will affect women more than they will men. We also know that stressful life events, such as domestic violence and being denied educational and occupa-tional opportunities, also increase the type of stress that will cause more men-tal health problems, and that more women will be affected by these factors than men. In fact, it may not be surprising that more women suffer the men-tal health effects of this type of discrimination than men; rather, it may be more surprising that even more women are not affected. In writing about women in India, Davar (1999) states that oppressive relationships, in a cul-ture of discrimination against women, are significant risk factors for depres-sion in women. Women also bear the brunt of economic disadvantage in this culture, which increases their vulnerability to depression (Davar, 1999). In the Indian culture women also suffer more rejection for mental illness than do men. Mentally ill men are usually cared for in their homes by their wives. Mentally ill wives, however, are typically returned to their parents, deserted, or divorced (Davar, 1999).

It seems clear that in addition to the differential rates of psychopathology for men and women, there are also different reasons for these rates. While there is some evidence that biological factors such as hormones may play a role in some types of psychopathology, there are many other factors at work as well. Traditional male and female roles may lead to differential rates of certain types of disorders. Family stress, violence, and abuse lead to psy-chological problems, as do cultural factors such as violence, deprivation, and discrimination. While it does seem to be true that family, social, and cultural factors may impact women more negatively than men, it is also true that men are impacted by these factors as well. Thus, all of these factors can affect anyone in one way or another, but it does seem that many of these apparent causal factors disproportionately affect women. This would also imply that the solution to some of these difficulties may be more social than individual. That is, removing the differential effects of these types of problems in the long term probably requires improved social conditions, decreased discrimination, better prevention and control of conditions that spawn violence, and more educational and preventive programs—rather than simply more available treatment after the problems have occurred. Certainly better treatments, and better access to these treatments, are vital, but in some respects the psychological problems that result from social ills and crises are merely symptoms of the deeper societal problems that produce them.

Gender Differences in the Treatment of Psychopathology

In recent years there has been an increase in the number of psychiatric beds in both public and private acute care hospitals. This is due in large part to the decrease in the number of beds in specifically psychiatric facilities. The trend toward deinstitutionalization that began in the 1960s has resulted in a dramatic decrease in beds in psychiatric hospitals. In fact, today there are fewer than half the number of beds in psychiatric facilities than there were in the 1950s (Prior, 1999). This trend is likely due to several factors. First, there are better treatments available today, and people are kept out of hospitals because of better care. Also, medications that provide some symptom relief are prescribed very commonly, and even though these medications rarely "cure" psychological problems, they often control symptoms well enough to keep people out of psychiatric hospitals even if they are not fully relieved of their problems. Finally, changes in the reimbursement systems for mental health services have resulted in decreased hospital care for psychiatric patients. Managed care specifically tends to force patients out of hospitals and into outpatient care even when they might benefit from longer inpatient care. Clearly, there is need for and use of mental health treatment in general, but are there differences between men and women in the use of psychological and psychiatric treatments?

In general, it seems clear in most reporting cultures, women predominate in the use of all mental health services (Prior, 1999). One interesting finding is that women tend to use mental health services more frequently, whereas men tend to seek treatment later in the course of their psychological problems, and thus their symptoms tend to be more severe and difficult to treat (WHO,

2003). Further, men are more likely to be involuntarily committed to psychiatric facilities (Prior, 1999). The WHO (2003) suggests that at least in industrialized countries, women tend to have an advantage in terms of residential independence in psychiatric treatment. Since women tend to have later onset of serious mental illness such as schizophrenia, they have more time to learn social skills and coping mechanisms, as well as to develop better support systems, than their male counterparts. Further, since men tend to wait longer to get treatment, it may be that by waiting until symptoms are more severe, they are likely to require more intensive (inpatient) treatment. The WHO further reports that women are more likely to report psychological distress, and are also more likely to be diagnosed with a mental health condition than are men with the same symptoms. However, after men admit that they have a problem, they are as likely as women to get help. The problems seem to be in men admitting that they have a problem, and that health professionals are less likely to perceive men's problems as psychological. When these difficulties are accounted for, men are as likely as women to get help (WHO, 2003).

The WHO (2003) reports other gender differences in the seeking of mental health care. Women are far more likely to report mental health problems to their primary care physicians, and to seek treatment for these problems. Men, on the other hand, seek care later, are more likely to seek specialist care, and are the principal users of inpatient care. In the United States and many other cultures, men tend to be noncommunicative, competitive, and nongiving. Their success is measured by achievement and acquisitions, and appearing "weak" and seeking help are neither typically expected nor supported. Thus, it is not surprising that men more frequently turn to street drugs and alcohol to self-medicate their psychological problems.

In treatment settings there appear to be some gender differences as well. Doctors are more likely to perceive physical illness as psychological if the patient is female. Also, in ads for psychotropic medications, the patients are usually female, while in the ads for nonpsychotropic medications, the patients are more frequently male (Ashton, 1991). It also appears that in planning treatment and in the provision of mental health services, there is a gender bias so that women are overrepresented in treatment statistics (Prior, 1999). It should be pointed out, however, that even with the apparent gender differences in treatment, which are found in all parts of the world, for both women and men, most mental health problems are neither detected nor treated (WHO, 2003).

Some other findings relative to the treatment of mental disorders also have points to add to our understanding. First, and most generally, Sartoris, Nielson, and Stomgren (1989) found that women tend to respond more positively to mental health care and treatment programs. Thus, not only are women more likely to seek treatment, but they also are more likely to benefit from it. This could be due to several factors. For example, men tend to ask for help much later in the course of their problems, and this complicates treatment. Further, because of the traditional male role, which makes asking for help somewhat of a problem, they may not be as comfortable with the care that they receive, and may tend to leave treatment prematurely. Finally, methods of treatment often involve taking medications and talking about problems. It may well be that many men in many cultures simply find psychological and/or psychiatric treatment too uncomfortable to tolerate.

Another interesting finding emerged from the work of Schmidt et al. (2000). As mentioned above, there are some researchers and clinicians who suggest that female hormones may play a role in depression, postpartum depression, and PMDD. Schmidt et al. suggest that in the early stages of menopause, estrogen may be an alternative to antidepressant medications for some women. While the use of hormones has risks and concerns, the use of antidepressant medications does as well. There are many who feel that psychotropic medications are inappropriately and excessively used, and this, too, may disproportionately affect women.

According to the WHO (2003), gender is a significant predictor in the prescribing of psychotropic medications, and this trend is also appearing in the developing nations (Astbury, 2001). A study done in Finland showed that women are more likely to use psychotropic medications to help them function normally, and that men are more likely to use alcohol to manage stress. Thus, while medications certainly have a role in the treatment of psychological problems, there are concerns that they may be overused and/or misused on occasion, and that this problem may well affect women more than men, although men may seek nonmedical but chemical relief from their problems.

Along this line, Prior (1999) argues that there has been a "medicalization" of women's problems, and that this has led to more treatment and a higher use of drugs for women than for men. The problem with this is that we have evolved a treatment system that tends to treat women symptomatically rather than dealing with issues that will restore them to health (Prior, 1999). As far back as 1961, Thomas Szasz, a psychiatrist, felt that we were developing a system of care that was using medical treatments for "problems in living," thus clouding the issues that have created circumstances that produce an unhappy life for many women. As demonstrated earlier, there is no question that a wide variety of social, family, and relationship factors put women at higher risk for mental health problems. Clearly, the real "cure" for many of these issues is social, not medical or psychological. However, "medicalizing" women's problems diverts attention from the difficulties that may actually be more responsible for creating the problems.

Gender and the Providers of Mental Health Care

Although there are clear indications that some of the approaches and biases that have led to differential diagnosis and treatment of mental health conditions were dominated by male perspectives and values, some interesting trends regarding the people who are providing mental health services are evolving.

Traditionally, social work has been considered a "female profession." Even in 1961, 68 percent of social workers were women, and the figure had increased to 77 percent in 1977 (Gibelman & Schervish, 1993). In 1994 more than 77 percent of the National Association of Social Workers were female, and this was expected to increase. In 1992–1993, 86 percent of B.S.W. and 82 percent of M.S.W. graduates were female.

Psychology is a very diverse field, so we will focus only on the areas that are most involved with mental health treatment—clinical and counseling psychology. In 1976, 31.1 percent of clinical psychology graduates were women and 34.1 percent of counseling graduates were female. However, in 1997, 71.1 percent of the clinical graduates and 64.7 percent of the counseling graduates were women. Clearly there is a continuing and increasing trend for women to enter the field of psychology—at least in the areas that are typically involved with the treatment of psychological conditions and emotional difficulties.

Psychiatry continues to be more male in its composition, but even this difference is changing. In 1977–1978, 32 percent of the psychiatry residents were women; this increased to 41 percent in 1988, and the trend has continued. Interestingly, in 1988, when these numbers were compiled, most of the female residents were under the age of thirty-five.

What are the implications of these findings? First, by getting more women in these fields, it could be hoped that less gender bias and insensitivity might occur in the provision of mental health services. For this to occur, however, it is not just a selection issue, but a training issue as well. Simply training anyone, male or female, in the traditional methods and models will only serve to perpetuate the problems that we have discovered. Not only do we need to foster diversity in the selection of people to provide mental health services— and I mean diversity in the broadest sense—but we also need to train these people to be aware of the issues and difficulties in the provision of mental health care to both men and women *by* both men and women. A more unfortunate implication of the changing demographics of mental health providers is the relative decrease in the salaries paid to mental health service providers. Although psychiatrists seem to hold their own relative to their physician colleagues, psychologists and social workers are finding their earnings decreasing relative to the market forces. Obviously managed care is responsible for most of this, but it also reflects the values of a society where mental health issues are not seen as being as important as other medical issues. At this juncture we need to be mindful of the importance of having appropriately selected and trained men and women who reflect the composition of the society in which they practice. This also suggests that other issues of diversity (e.g., age, race, ethnicity, and subculture) are equally important in the selection and training of mental health professionals. However, regardless of the intentions and the success of the training institutions in attracting and graduating well-trained and diverse groups of mental health professionals, if we do not provide services in a reasonable manner to all of the segments of society that need the care, we are still falling far short of what we need to be doing.

Summary

To recap what we have found, let us return to the questions that were asked at the beginning of this chapter. First, are there differences in the rates of psychological and emotional conditions between men and women, and why is this so? Clearly, this is a complex issue, but in the past the tendency was to find women more frequently diagnosed with psychological disorders. However, this was due in part to the ways in which society viewed gender-specific behavior. Traditionally, according to Prior (1999), women who were deviant from society's norms were seen as "mad," and men who deviated from these norms were seen as "bad." However, if we include substance abuse and personality disorders as valid categories of psychological disturbance, the differences in the rates between men and women vanish. Thus, it would appear that in general it is cultural values and perceptions that have resulted in the apparent (but not real) differences between men and women in the frequency of psychological problems. Further, this has been perpetuated in medical practice, where women's problems tend to be attributed to psychological factors more frequently than the same problems when the presenting patient is male.

We also asked if there were differences in the types of psychological problems suffered by men and women, and if so, why that might be. Once again it is clear that there are in fact differences in the types of problems that are experienced. Women tend to be diagnosed with anxiety and depressive disorders, as well as various types of somatoform disorders, at a greater rate than men, and men tend to be diagnosed more frequently with substance abuse problems and with certain types of personality disorders (e.g., antisocial personality disorder). Some other personality disorders (e.g., histrionic personality disorder and borderline personality disorder) are more common in women. In the serious mental illnesses such as schizophrenia and bipolar disorder, there are no differences between men and women in the morbidity rates, although some interesting trends have been found. For example, men tend to develop schizophrenia earlier and are more difficult to treat. In bipolar disorder, the rates are about the same, but women seem more prone to the more serious variants of this disorder.

These types of differences are likely due to factors ranging from biological to social/cultural. With respect to the personality disorders, there may be some biological factors involved with some of them, but more likely it is the cultural factors related to male and female roles that are largely responsible for these differences. If one looks at some of the personality disorders as exaggerations of stereotypic male and female roles in society, then it helps to make some sense of why these differences would exist. Other factors, such as poverty, social roles and conditions, being victims of abuse and violence, and being caretakers, also seem to affect women more than men; and these factors, too, impact both the rates of morbidity and the types of problems that are suffered by men and women.

Finally, there is some evidence that biological factors such as hormones may impact men and women in such a way as to result in different rates of certain types of disorders. For example, it is assumed that female hormones, and specifically estrogen, may be a contributing factor in the different rates of depression for men and women. As mentioned above, women have higher rates of depression than men except before puberty and after menopause. Also, postpartum depression and PMS are conditions for which hormonal influences are felt to be contributing, if not simply causal, factors.

In terms of treatment, it seems clear that in most cultures, women are more likely to be diagnosed with psychological problems, and to be referred for treatment of these conditions, than are men. This is both a good and a bad thing. First, it reflects some bias in the ways in which women's behavior is evaluated by medical and mental health professionals. However, it also means that more women than men are receiving treatment. Further, men tend to be more reluctant to seek help for these types of conditions, and they tend to be diagnosed and referred less often. This may also mean that men are *undertreated* for mental health problems, and that may be one reason why men tend to be disabled by their psychological problems more frequently than are women. It has also been found that women tend to respond more positively to treatment than do men, regardless of the type of treatment. One final note regarding treatment is that women tend to be prescribed psychotropic medications far more frequently than men, and this, too, has positive and negative aspects. Although it does mean that they may be receiving treatment more frequently than men, it also suggests perceptual differences that result in the "pathologizing" and "medicalization" of women's problems. As Szasz (1961) pointed out, by treating "problems in living" as illness, we may be missing what the real problems are.

In examining the social factors that contribute to gender issues in mental health, researchers have found numerous social and cultural factors that relate to gender differences in mental health and illness, and typically these factors affect women more than men. Thus, poverty, nutritional difficulties, violence and abuse, gender-specific roles, and other factors mentioned above are obviously related to the incidence and distribution of psychological and emotional conditions. Therefore, it is clear that to deal with the mental health problems resulting from these social conditions, we must start to focus our attention on these types of factors and try to ameliorate the conditions that lead to the exacerbation of the emotional conditions from which people suffer. However, as Prior (1999) points out, the situation involving gender, race, and social factors is so complex that it is difficult to develop good social policy. She goes on to suggest that effective and helpful social policy must address the needs of all segments of society, and it must take into account all socioeconomic factors that create mental anguish and impede the recovery from psychological conditions.

The final question that we asked involved the gender distribution of mental health care providers. While social work has traditionally been a "female profession," it has become even more so in recent years, with more than three-quarters of people receiving degrees in social work being female. Psychology was traditionally male in the past, but today in clinical and counseling psychology far more than half of the providers are female. Only psychiatry remains primarily male, but even this is changing, with more women opting into this medical specialty as well. As pointed out above, having a greater representation of women in the mental health professions may result in increased sensitivity to gender issues in the diagnosis and treatment of psychological problems. This, however, is not enough. We also need to ensure that mental health professionals are trained in such a way that they are aware of gender and other diversity issues as legitimate concerns in mental health care.

Regardless of patient or provider sex, there are some real concerns about mental health treatment that cut across all treatment groups. One very frightening scenario that is emerging today is largely the result of the failure of the "for-profit" experiment in health care that has been a part of the American scene since the 1980s. Managed care as a new approach to health care has been, by almost all accounts, an abysmal failure, particularly in the area of mental health. The care (or lack of care, actually) is making things worse than they have ever been. Prior (1999) suggests that managed care in the

United States is evolving into a system where the rich will be the only ones who can afford private care, and the poor will have to use public care and facilities. While a two-or-more-tiered health care system may not bother some people, this type of system will end up costing society dearly in the long run. Given the fact that there are more women and children in poverty in this country than there are men, this implies that women and children will differentially be relegated to public forms of treatment that may not be as comprehensive or of as high a quality as they might need. This is not an indictment of either public health or publicly funded types of treatment or facilities. However, it is morally and ethically wrong, in my judgment, to have the provision of care be dictated entirely by ability to pay; and if this is something that discriminates on the basis of gender, age, race, or similar criteria, then it is simply wrong. To make quality health care, and more specifically mental health care, a privilege is a step in the direction of social change that seems counter to the values that have traditionally typified the United States. Of course, it may have always been the case that people with money could afford more and better care, but to institutionalize this and concretize it in such a way as to make it policy strikes me as being morally bankrupt, and we as a society must acknowledge and deal with this fact if it is not to become a larger problem than it already is.

Finally, it is clear that the relationship between gender and mental health is a complex medical, psychological, and social problem. Understanding these issues is the first step toward dealing with them. From my standpoint, a responsible and reasonable society will look at health care as a right of all citizens. The cost to society in lost talent, higher medical and mental health costs, and supporting people on disability and social services who might be able to contribute to society, and the cost of living in a society that devalues some of its members because of their gender, age, race, country of origin, religion, lifestyle, socioeconomic status, or mental/emotional condition are issues that must be confronted and addressed. To neglect these things further will create problems and costs that we have not yet begun to appreciate.

References

American Psychiatric Association. (2000). Work group on eating disorders: Practice guidelines for the treatment of patients with eating disorders (revision). *American Journal of Psychiatry, 157*(1, supp.), 671–675.

American Psychological Association. (2003). Ph.D. recipients in psychology from U.S. universities by gender and subfield: 1920–1997. [On-line]. Retrieved February 24, 2001. Available: http://www.apa.org/pi/wpo/wapa/table1.pdf

Ashton, H. (1991). Psychotropic drug prescribing to women. *British Journal of Psychiatry, 158*(supp. 10), 30–35.

Astbury, J. (2001). Gender disparities in mental health. In *Mental health: A call for action by world health ministers* (pp. 73–92). Geneva: World Health Organization.

Bebbington, P. E., Dunn, G., Jenkins, R., et al. (1998). The influence of age and sex on the prevalence of depressive conditions: Report from the National Survey of Psychiatric Morbidity. *Psychological Medicine, 28*(1), 9–19.

Birmaher, B., Ryan, N. D., Williamson, D. E., et al. (1996). Childhood and adolescent depression: A review of the past 10 years. Part I. *Journal of the American Academy of Child and Adolescent Psychiatry, 35*(11), 1427–1439.

Bourdon, K. H., Boyd, J. H., Rae, D. S., et al. (1988). Gender differences in phobias: Results of the ECA Community Survey. *Journal of Anxiety Disorders, 2,* 227–241.

Breslau, N., Davis, G. C., Andreski, P., et al. (1991). Traumatic events and post-traumatic stress disorder in an urban population of young adults. *Archives of General Psychiatry, 48*(3), 216–222.

Broadhead, J., & Abas, M. (1998). Life events and difficulties and the onset of depression among women in low-income urban settings in Zimbabwe. *Psychological Medicine, 28,* 29–38.

Connell, R. W. (1995). *Masculinities.* Berkeley: University of California Press.

Cooper, P., Tomlinson, M., Swartz, L., Woolgar, M., Murray, L., & Molteno, C. (1999). Post-partum depression and the mother–infant relationship in South African peri-urban settlement. *British Journal of Psychiatry, 175,* 554–558.

Davar, B. (1999). *The mental health of Indian women: A feminist agenda.* New Delhi and Thousand Oaks, CA: Sage.

Edley, N., & Wetherell, M. (1995). *Men in perspective: Practice, power and identity.* London: Prentice Hall, Harvester Wheatsheaf.

Fischback, R. L., & Herbert, B. (1997). Domestic violence and mental health: Correlates and conundrums with and across cultures. *Social Science and Medicine, 45,* 1161–1170.

Gardner, W., Pajer, K. A., Kelleher, K. J., Scholle, S. H., & Wasserman, R. C. (2002). Child sex differences in primary care clinician's mental health care of children and adolescents. *Archives of Pediatric and Adolescent Medicine, 156,* 454–459.

Gibelman, M., & Schervish, P. H. (1993). *What we earn: 1993 NASW salary survey.* Washington, DC: NASW Press.

Goldstein, J. M., Seidman, L. J., Goodman, J. M., Koren, D., Lee, H., Weintraub, S., & Tsuang, M. T. (1998). Are there sex differences in neuropsychological functions among patients with schizophrenia? *American Journal of Psychiatry, 155,* 1358–1364.

Hoyert, D. L., Kochanek, K. D., & Murphy, S. L. (1999). *Deaths: Final data for 1997.* National Vital Statistics Reports, 47(9). DHHS Publication no. 99–1120. Hyattsville, MD: Nation Center for Health Statistics.

Illness without disease—Part II. (1999). *Harvard Mental Health Letter, 16*(4), 2–3.

Kroenke, K., & Spitzer, R. (1998). Gender differences in the reporting of physical and somatoform symptoms. *Psychosomatic Medicine, 60,* 150–155.

McCann, J. J., Gebert, L. E., Bennett, D. A., Skull, V., & Evans, D. A. (1997). Why Alzheimer's disease is a women's health issue. *Journal of the American Medical Women's Association, 52*(3), 132–137.

Murray, C.J.L., & Lopez, A. D. (Eds.). (1996). *The global burden of disease: A comprehensive assessment of mortality and disability from disease, injuries, and risk factors in 1990 and projected to 2020.* Cambridge, MA: Harvard School of Public Health.

National Association of Social Workers. (2003). Women in the social work profession. [On-line]. Retrieved January 31, 2003. Available: http://www.social-workers.org/da/da2005/documents/womsocworkprof.pdf

National Institute on Aging. (1999). *Progress report on Alzheimer's disease 1999.* NIH Publication no. 99-4664. Bethesda, MD: National Institute on Aging.

Paris, J. (Ed.). (1993). *Borderline personality disorder: Etiology and treatment.* Washington, DC: American Psychiatric Press.

Patel, V. (2002). Gender and mental health research in developing countries. *Global Forum for Health Research,* Arush: 1–10.

Patel, V., Araya, R., Luvio, G., & Swartz, L. (2000). Socio-economic factors and mental health. In *Mental health: A call for action by world health ministers.* Geneva: World Health Organization.

Pleck, J. (1981). *The myth of masculinity.* Cambridge, MA: MIT Press.

Press Association. (2003). Women stay single to stay sane. Press Association Ltd.

Prior, P. M. (1999). *Gender and mental health.* New York: New York University Press.

Robins, L., & Regier, D. (Eds.). (1991). *Psychiatric disorders in America: The Epidemiologic Catchment Area study.* New York: Maxwell Macmillan International.

Sartoris, N., Nielson, J., & Stomgren, E. (1989). Changes in frequency of mental disorders over time: Results of repeated surveys of mental disorder in the general population, *Acta Psychiatrica Scandinavica, 79*(supp. 348), 1–87.

Schmidt, P. J., Nieman, L. K., Danaceau, M. A., et al. (1998). Differential effects of gonadal steroids in women with and those without pre-menstrual syndrome. *New England Journal of Medicine, 338*(4), 209–216.

Schmidt, P. J., Nieman, L., Danaceau, M. A., Tobin, M., Rocca, C., Murphy, J., & Rubinow, D. R. (2000). Estrogen replacement in perimenopause-related depression: A preliminary report. *American Journal of Obstetrics and Gynecology, 183*(2), 414–420.

Schulz, R., O'Brien, A. T., Bookwala, J., & Fleissner, K. (1995). Psychiatric and physical morbidity effects of dementia caregiving: Prevalence, correlates, and causes. *Gerontologist, 35*(6), 771–791.

Sherrill, J. T., Anderson, B., Frank, E., Reynolds, C. F., Tu, X. M., Patterson, D., Ritnour, A., & Kupfer, D. (1997). Is life stress more likely to provoke depressive episodes in women than in men? *Depression and Anxiety, 6*(3), 95–105.

Showalter, E. (1987). *The female malady: Women, madness, and English culture 1830–1980*. New York: Penguin.

Skoog, I., Nilsson, L., Palmertz, B., et al. (1993). A population-based study of dementia in 85-year-olds. *New England Journal of Medicine, 328,* 153–158.

Szasz, T. (1961). *The myth of mental illness: Foundations of a theory of personal conduct*. New York: Hoeber-Harper.

Ussher, J. (1992). *Women's madness: Mysogyny or mental illness?* Amherst: University of Massachusetts Press.

Waddington, J. L., Lane, A., Scully, P. J., et al. (1998). Neurodevelopmental and neuroprogressive processes in schizophrenia. *Psychiatric Clinics of North America, 2*(1), 123–149.

Widger, T. A. (2000). Personality disorders—Part II. *Harvard Mental Health Letter, 16*(10), 5–7.

World Health Organization. (2000). *Women's mental health: An evidence based review*. WHO/MSD/MHP/00.1. Geneva: World Health Organization.

World Health Organization. (2003). Gender and women's mental health. [On-line]. Retrieved December, 14, 2003. Available: http://www.who.int/mental_health/prevention/genderwomen/en/

Chapter 6

The Hidden Curriculum: Gender in the Classroom

Susan Basow

A great deal of concern has been expressed recently about boys' education. Titles such as The New Gender Gap (Conlin, 2003), *The War against Boys: How Misguided Feminism Is Harming Our Young Men* (Sommers, 2000), and *What about the Boys? Issues of Masculinity in Schools* (Martino & Meyenn, 2001) suggest that boys are being neglected, mistreated, or even punished by an education system geared to support girls at the expense of boys. In this chapter, we will examine such claims by first examining what the education system in the United States teaches boys and girls about gender. Then we will look at how boys and girls fare in the education system in the United States. Overall, we will see that although there has been a shift in some aspects of education toward more gender equity (e.g., graduation rates), boys and girls in general still learn, and are reinforced for, traditional gendered behaviors. In other words, along with the three R's there is a hidden curriculum of gender.

The Gender Curriculum

Students learn about gender both directly, through instructional material, and indirectly, through observation and differential treatment. In her book *We've All Got Scars*, Raphaela Best (1983) described the results of her four years of observation in an elementary school. She noted three areas that taught students about gender: the actual academic curriculum, with its sexist materials and gender typing of academic skills; the behavioral curriculum, wherein boys and girls played different roles and engaged in different activities; and the sexual curriculum, which emphasized different roles for males and females (for example, "getting it" for boys, "being careful" for girls). We will examine the first two areas in more detail. Underlying all gender instruction is the belief in differential gender roles.

Traditional Gender Roles

Traditionally, the male gender role is one of dominance, while the female gender role is one of subordination. Males are the actors, the doers, the leaders, the authority; females are the audience, the watchers, the followers, the subordinates. These gender roles are endemic to patriarchies, the gender system existing in nearly all cultures of the world today. What does vary is the degree of male dominance.

Until the second wave of the women's movement in the early 1970s, the education system was a strong socializing agent furthering male dominance and female subordination. Boys were the stars of the education system, the winners of academic and athletic awards, and they were encouraged to prepare for their role as family breadwinner. This meant that they were encouraged to pursue those jobs earning the most money, whether through advanced education or technical training. Boys were required to take shop classes and learn useful manual skills, and they were assumed to be the more capable sex in math and science. They were called on more in class, encouraged to speak up, chosen as class leaders and class presidents. Their lives were reflected in the literature and history they studied, and in the "generic" male language itself.

Girls, in contrast, were trained in submission. They were assumed to be more compliant, and often ran errands for teachers. All girls were expected to take home economics, and learn at least rudimentary cooking and sewing skills for their future primary role as housewife. If they were career-oriented at all, they were encouraged to pursue careers in education, nursing, or secretarial work, jobs that would be compatible with their assumed caretaking tendencies and eventual maternal roles. These were relatively low-paying jobs with no career track or room for advancement. Girls were cheerleaders and onlookers for boys' teams, and played the same role in most storybooks and textbooks.

The second wave of the women's movement challenged this gender curriculum. Starting in the 1970s, laws were passed banning unequal educational opportunities for boys and girls (Title IX of the Education Amendments of 1972, the Women's Educational Equity Act of 1974, the Vocational Educational Act of 1976, and the Career Incentive Act of 1977). Discrimination on the basis of sex in education programs receiving federal financial assistance was outlawed. In addition, educational institutions were required to initiate programs to overcome sex discrimination and sex stereotyping in education programs. Tracking students by gender was expressly prohibited: Girls now could take shop, and boys could take home economics. Biased teaching practices, generally privileging boys, also were challenged, as was biased career counseling. The content of the curriculum was challenged as well. New nonsexist materials were developed that promoted gender equity; Women's History Month and women's studies became established. These acts and activities eliminated some of the grossest inequities that had existed, but many would argue that the academic curriculum is still biased toward males.

Academic Curriculum

Even with the availability of newer nonsexist materials, many schools still use materials in which males play the dominant role. For example, in a 1989 study of 1,883 stories used in schools, Purcell and Stewart (1990) found that although the ratio of male to female human characters was relatively equal, animal characters were 75 percent male and story illustrations were 66 percent male. Furthermore, females were depicted as less adventurous than males, in fewer occupations, and more in need of being rescued. These differences continue in more recent books (Gooden & Gooden, 2001). In general, males in children's books are more likely than females to be active agents, while girls more often play the role of observer or cheerleader or the one who needs help.

In upper grades, history books still primarily chronicle the activities of men in terms of lines of succession, wars, conquests, politics, and so on. There may be sections or chapters or a whole month devoted to women's history, but women are still treated as outsiders in "regular" history or in terms of exceptions to the rule. For example, extraordinary women like Queen Elizabeth or Marie Curie may be mentioned, but their exceptional status is highlighted. True integration of women into the curriculum has yet to be accomplished, and this is true on the college level as well (Koch, 2003; McIntosh, 1983).

Academic areas still are gender-typed, with math, science, and computers being viewed as more appropriate for males than for females, and English, foreign languages, and the arts being viewed as more appropriate for females than for males. In high school, more boys than girls take computer design and advanced placement (AP) science courses, and more girls than boys take AP courses in English, biology, and foreign languages (Koch, 2003). College majors reflect this gendering of academic interests, with females being overrepresented in the humanities, social sciences, and biology. In contrast, males are overrepresented in the physical and computer sciences and engineering.

Gender Segregation

Children enter the education system with years of gender socialization, mainly from family members, peers, toys, and the media. One major message that children learn early is that boys and girls are different. Because of previous differential experience with toys and activities (such as playing with dolls or blocks), boys and girls often gravitate to different play areas during preschool and recess. Thus, children start segregating themselves into same-sex groups, which reinforce gendered behaviors (Maccoby, 1998; Thorne, 1993). The activities girls engage in, such as playing house or hopscotch, tend to be cooperative and verbal; boys' activities and games tend to be more competitive and physical. Teachers, who tend to believe such differences are natural, typically support such gender segregation. They may even encourage such segregation by organizing activities based on sex ("the girls against the boys").

Children themselves tend to reinforce such segregation as well, often ignoring or discouraging play by an other-sex child. Unless this tendency is explicitly and repeatedly counteracted by committed teachers, children become increasingly limited, in terms of the range of their behaviors, skills, communication styles, and friendships, to same-gender patterns (Koch, 2003). This means that both boys and girls are disadvantaged in developing their full capacities as humans: Girls often fail to learn the gross motor and assertiveness skills utilized in male groups; boys often fail to learn the fine motor and empathy skills utilized in female groups.

Sexual Harassment

Sexual harassment is "unwanted and unwelcome sexual behavior that interferes with your life" (AAUW, 2001b, p. 2). In a 2001 survey conducted by the Harris Poll for the AAUW, 83 percent of girls and 79 percent of boys reported having experienced such behaviors during their school years, usually from male peers. Boys receive a great deal of taunting and accusations of "being gay," the most negative thing a boy can be called. Such blatant homophobia serves as a social control mechanism to keep boys conforming to a restricted and extreme definition of masculinity, one in which they must be tough, unemotional, aggressive, and heterosexually focused (Kehily, 2001; Pharr, 1988). Girls, too, may be accused of being "queer" or a "dyke" if they express disinterest in or disapproval of male behavior, but such intended slurs tend to occur later for girls (high school and college) than for boys.

Unwanted and unwelcome sexual behaviors, such as being "felt up," or taunted, can begin in elementary school and often occur in the presence of teachers, who may view such actions as "boys being boys." Yet such behaviors can have serious negative consequences, especially for girls, who are more likely than boys to change emotionally and behaviorally as a result (AAUW, 2001b). For example, compared with boys, girls report feeling more embarrassed and self-conscious, as well as less confident, because of an incident of harassment. Girls also are more likely to avoid the person who harassed them and to keep silent in classes.

Sexual harassment contributes to a pattern of dominant boys and silent girls that is evident in many classrooms and on playgrounds across the country (Koch, 2003). It also contributes to girls' negative feelings about their bodies, especially as puberty hits. Girls, especially white girls, tend to develop an objectified body consciousness; that is, they view their body as if it were an object (Fredrickson & Roberts, 1997). This objectification is an internalization of the larger culture's portrayal of female bodies and is associated with greater body dissatisfaction. Teachers, too, tend to pay more attention to girls' appearance than to boys' (Koch, 2003). Body dissatisfaction can lead to eating disorders, which occur nine times more often in girls than in boys. Depression, which is correlated with both body dissatisfaction and sexual harassment, affects females three times more often than males, beginning at puberty. Thus, in school, girls and boys are having very different experiences as well as different reactions to similar experiences.

Education Structure

The structure of the education system reflects traditional gender roles. As status increases, so does the percentage of males in higher positions. Female teachers are most represented in the lower grades, while male teachers appear most often in the upper grades, especially teaching math, science, and shop classes. Men also dominate the faculties of colleges and universities, being most represented at research universities and less represented at two-year colleges. Furthermore, at every level the highest-status positions—principal, superintendent, college president—are most likely filled by males.

There has been gradual improvement in gender representation since the mid-1970s. For example, women now are 40 percent of college faculty, compared with 22 percent in 1974 (National Center for Education Statistics, 1983, 2002). Still, as rank and status increase, the percentage of women decreases.

Students are aware of which positions are the most respected and powerful, and thus their direct instruction regarding the gender hierarchy is augmented by their observational learning of this hierarchy in the education system, as well as in other institutions of the culture (for example, business and politics).

Gender Dynamics in the Classroom

Perhaps the most profound lessons students receive about gender take place indirectly, through classroom dynamics. There have been many observational studies from elementary school to college that indicate that male students get more teacher attention and talk more in class than do female students (Harris, 1997; Sadker & Sadker, 1994). Most of this research is from the 1980s and 1990s, and more recent research does suggest some change in this area (e.g., Kleinfeld, 1998). Nonetheless, the general pattern remains. Boys tend to receive both more praise and more reprimands than do girls, and girls tend to receive teacher approval mainly for being quiet and compliant.

In a three-year study of more than 100 fourth-, sixth-, and eighth-grade classrooms in several communities, Myra and David Sadker (1994) found that boys clearly and consistently dominated classroom interactions. Teachers called on and encouraged girls less often than they did boys. For example, if a student gave an incorrect answer, the teacher was more likely to help the child discover the correct answer if the child was a boy. If the child was a girl, the teacher was more likely to move on to another student. For a correct answer, boys tended to receive praise ("excellent!"), while girls tended to get a simple acknowledgment ("ok"). Girls often were reprimanded for calling out in class, whereas boys who did the same thing often were attended to. The general message sent by these teacher behaviors was that boys are more capable academically and their voices should be heard, whereas girls should be more passive learners.

This general classroom dynamic appears to be invisible to students, who typically report that teachers pay more attention to girls (Kleinfeld, 1998). Teachers, too, sometimes report that girls participate more than boys in their classrooms (Sadker & Sadker, 1994). Yet when objective observers examine actual classroom behaviors, the male-dominant pattern appears (Duffy, Warren, & Walsh, 2001; Harris, 1997; Sadker & Sadker, 1994). This is particularly true in math and science classrooms, subject areas gender-typed as male (Altermatt, Jovanovic, & Perry, 1998; Jovanovic & King, 1998). Perhaps this lower involvement of girls contributes to women's consistent underrepresentation in science- and math-related careers.

This pattern of teachers paying more attention and giving more encouragement to their male students than their female students occurs primarily for white students. African American males fare particularly poorly in the classroom, which may account for their withdrawal from academic involvement. For example, African American males are viewed as having the lowest academic potential and receive the fewest opportunities to respond, compared with females of both races and with white males (Grant, 1985;

Ross & Jackson, 1991). African American females enter school with more active behaviors than their white counterparts, but the lack of academic feedback from their teachers often causes them to withdraw as well (Wilkinson & Marrett, 1985). Either they silence themselves to fit in with the academic environment, or they reject academic achievement in order to maintain strong self-esteem (Fordham, 1996). The latter choice would contribute to the decline in academic self-esteem over the adolescent years for African American girls as well as to their high school dropout rate (AAUW, 1992).

Gender and race stereotypes become internalized and can negatively affect achievement, especially when a stigmatized identity is made salient. For example, in groups where an individual's race or gender is salient because of small numbers, or where boys are pitted against girls, or even when race or gender information is asked before a test, the stigmatized group may experience *stereotype threat* that impairs performance (Inzlicht & Ben-Zeev, 2000; Steele & Aronson, 2000). For example, for girls or for African Americans, taking a math test when such a group is a minority in the room may lead to poorer performance than when the same test is taken in a group consisting of similar peers.

Colleges and Universities

Gendered classroom dynamics occur at all grade levels through college. In general, compared with their male peers, female college students receive less encouragement for speaking, are called on less frequently, and often have their ideas credited to others (Sadker & Sadker, 1994). In addition, they are interrupted, ignored, and devalued more often. The Association of American Colleges' Project on the Status and Education of Women (Hall & Sandler, 1982; see also Whitt et al., 1999) concluded that the classroom climate is a "chilly" one for many female students. This "chill" may make some female college students feel like imposters, contribute to the drop in self-esteem that women in coed colleges seem to experience, and affect their choice of classes, majors, and professors. This, in turn, will affect their future career opportunities.

The classrooms in which female college students are most likely to receive less teacher encouragement tend to be large (as opposed to small or medium-sized), more masculine-relevant (e.g., physical sciences), and more male-dominated in terms of student gender ratio (Brady & Eisler, 1999). The most gender equity is found in classes that are smaller, more interactive, and in more feminine-relevant or androgynous subjects, and have a more balanced or female-dominant student gender ratio. Other factors that facilitate more equal female and male participation are a more cooperative rather than more competitive classroom environment, being allowed to take one's time to respond, and receiving respect and recognition when one does so.

The qualities that seem to facilitate more gender equity in the classroom
are more likely to be found in classes of female rather than male instructors
(Brady & Eisler, 1999; Canada & Pringle, 1995). And, indeed, female college students participate more and report feeling more comfortable in classes
taught by women than by men (Crawford & McLeod, 1990). Although subject matter differences may account for some of these findings (women faculty are more likely to be teaching in the humanities; men faculty, in the
physical sciences), there also is evidence that male and female faculty may
bring different teaching styles to the same subject matter. For example,
Statham, Richardson, and Cook (1991) interviewed fifteen women and fifteen men who were matched for rank, discipline, and gender ratio of their
departments at a large state university. The researchers found that compared
with their male counterparts, female faculty tended to be more student-
oriented and to engage students more in discussions, regardless of discipline.
In contrast, male faculty were more likely than female faculty to assert their
authority in the classroom through public reprimands and corrections.

Different teaching styles may appeal to different students. There is some
evidence that female students may particularly appreciate female professors,
being more likely than male students to nominate a female instructor as
"best" (Basow, 2000) and frequently rating female professors higher than
male students do on evaluation forms (Basow, 1998). Traditional pedagogical styles appear to benefit male students more than female students (Gabriel
& Smithson, 1990), whereas "female-friendly" styles (such as those involving more cooperation than competition) benefit both sexes (e.g., Rosser,
1997). Thus, the increasing number of women on college faculties may be
helping to increase gender equity in the classrooms, and may partially account for the increased retention of female students in higher education.

On the other hand, although female faculty seem to be particularly appreciated by female students, such is not the case with male students. Male students are less likely to cite a female faculty member as their best instructor
than would be expected on the basis of the number of female professors they
had, and they frequently rate female faculty lower than female students do
and lower than they rate male faculty (Basow, 1998, 2000). Given the nature
of gender roles, with males having more status than females and masculinity being defined as "not-feminine" (Basow, 1992), it perhaps is not surprising that male college students value male faculty more than female faculty.
A similar process is at work with respect to other cultural figures: Boys are
less likely than girls to read books or watch television shows or movies with

predominantly female main characters, and are less likely to cite a female role model as influential. Girls, in contrast, watch, read about, and choose role models of both sexes.

This antipathy that many boys have toward girls and women may partially explain the greater difficulty boys have adjusting to school. If boys learn to avoid anything feminine in order to become men, and if schooling is associated with females (because of the greater number of female teachers in the lower grades and the emphasis on being compliant to adults), then boys may consider school and school achievement as antithetical to being "real boys" and "real men." Certainly, something is going on that has led to a backlash against gender equity programs and goals.

Gendered Educational Outcomes: Endangered Boys?

After thirty years of gender equity laws and programs, is the educational system finally gender-neutral, or is it, as some writers currently argue, privileging girls at the expense of boys (Evelyn, 2002; Martino & Meyenn, 2001; Sommers, 2000)?

As reported in *Business Week* (Conlin, 2003), girls outnumber boys in high school extracurricular activities such as student government, music/performing arts, yearbook/newspaper, and academic clubs, while males still outnumber females in athletics. In terms of academics, girls get higher grades, do better on reading tests, and are less likely to be special education students than are boys. Males, however, still score higher than girls on both the verbal and math sections of the SAT. Women of every ethnicity are more likely than their male counterparts to get bachelor's degrees and master's degrees, and these differences are expected to increase over the next ten years. In 2002, women earned half of all doctoral degrees for the first time (Smallwood, 2003). Women also make up half of medical and law school classes. It is understandable, given the changing demographics of higher education over the last thirty years, to wonder what is happening to males.

Several things are important to keep in mind. Until the 1980s, fewer females than males went to college despite the fact that girls had higher high school grades than did boys. The situation then might suggest that girls were being discouraged, or at least not actively encouraged, to pursue higher education to develop their minds as well as expand their job opportunities. The current statistics, which appear to reflect women's potential more accurately than the statistics of the 1970s and earlier, are exactly the same statistics used as evidence that there is a "war against boys." Certainly we should be concerned about students of whatever sex or race or ethnicity or class being limited in their opportunities to develop to their full potential. But to transform this worthy goal into a zero-sum game where only one group can "win" is both inaccurate and misleading.

Something else to keep in mind is that the changing sex demographics hide a changing racial/ethnic demographic. White Americans are becoming an increasingly smaller percentage of the population. And the biggest gender gaps in terms of educational achievement are for African Americans and Hispanics. Thus, although women now earn 57 percent of all bachelor's degrees, the rate is only 55 percent for white students, while it is 58 percent for Hispanic students and 85 percent of African American students (Conlin, 2003). Thus some of the decline in "male" academic achievement is due to the decreasing percentage of white males in the statistics. This group, the dominant one in the culture and the one still given the most attention in the classroom, appears to be achieving at rates relatively similar to those in the past. What has changed, and what is affecting the overall gender demographic, is the increased participation of females of all races in bachelor's and master's programs.

In terms of doctoral degrees, however, the actual number awarded to women has not changed since the turn of the twenty-first century. Fewer men are earning this degree; the result is that the actual number of earned doctorates is at its lowest point since the mid-1990s (Smallwood, 2003). The decrease has been most pronounced in the physical sciences and engineering, and part of the reason for the drop in male enrollment may be due to the potential for men to earn high salaries in technological fields without a doctoral degree.

Why have boys in general fallen behind academically in all areas except physical science and computing? Why are girls more likely to be school leaders except in athletics? As we've seen, it is not the case that teachers are ignoring boys, at least white boys, in favor of girls. Nor is it the case that educational practices that benefit girls somehow hurt boys. Gender equity programs and materials can benefit both sexes, although their effects are complex (Koch, 2003). The real issues involve factors that interact with educational practices, such as cultural messages about masculinity and race and ethnicity.

As traditional female gender roles have been challenged and programs have been developed to empower girls and women, the traditional cultural construction of masculinity has become less attainable. No longer automatically assumed to be superior, boys are struggling to define themselves as males. Many are focusing on sports and physical aggressiveness as ways to achieve dominance, encouraged by the media ("gangsta rap," extreme sports, superheroes) and the toy industry (extreme G.I. Joe, etc.). Boys enter school with fewer school-related skills than do girls: the ability to listen, sit still, pay attention, utilize fine motor skills, cooperate with peers (Childs & McKay, 2001; Koch, 2003). Yet their culturally constructed need to be dominant means they often are both highly verbal and aggressive in the classroom, behaviors that may interfere with the educational curriculum and cause teachers to focus on them, as we have seen. In other words, rather than schools privileging girls to the detriment of boys, it is actually gender socialization that is alienating boys from school culture (AAUW, 2001a). Even among college students, women are more engaged in learning than are men, as reported in a survey conducted at over 400 four-year colleges (Young, 2003).

African American and Hispanic boys in particular may be viewed as not academically inclined, especially by their communities and by their primarily white teachers (AAUW, 2001a). Although girls from these minority groups also may suffer from racial and ethnic stereotypes, they tend to be viewed with less hostility and suspicion than their brothers. Academic achievement may be viewed as a "white thing," as well as a "female thing" (Fordham, 1996). No wonder men from these minority groups feel alienated from school.

We need to move "beyond the 'gender wars'" (AAUW, 2001a) and find ways to reach all children (boy/girl, majority/minority, urban/suburban) in the school system. Boys' achievements should not come at the expense of girls', and girls' achievements should not be viewed as incompatible with boys'.

Summary

School is both a reflection and a shaper of our culture. As a reflection, it incorporates cultural messages regarding the nature of boys and girls, masculinity and femininity. This can be seen in the gendered structure of the educational system; the academic curriculum itself; children's own gendered beliefs, experiences, and behaviors; and teachers' expectations of and behavior toward each gender in the classroom. All of these aspects of the education system also reinforce traditional cultural messages regarding gender: that boys and girls are different, with different interests, abilities, and potential; that boys and men are more aggressive and dominant, and have higher status; that girls and women are more silent and compliant, and have lower status.

Without deliberate gender equity programs and teacher intervention, these messages will continue to be sent, often via the hidden curriculum. Such programs since the 1970s have positively affected the academic achievement and self-concept of girls, especially white girls, but more is needed. We also need to find ways to engage boys of all races and ethnicities in the educational enterprise, on equal terms with girls. This task surely involves changing the cultural definition of masculinity to include equality with and respect for females. Educational achievement is not a zero-sum game, and we need both boys and girls to "win."

The current situation, with more women than men receiving bachelor's and master's degrees and equal numbers of women and men receiving doctoral and professional degrees, signals a cultural shift. Rather than decry these changes as signaling the downfall of civilization because there won't be enough men to be leaders of business and other cultural institutions (Fletcher, 2002), we might celebrate these changes as potentially leading to a diminution, if not the end, of male dominance. Although this would be a major cultural shift, only those most wedded to patriarchy would view it as disastrous.

References

Altermatt, E. R., Jovanovic, J., & Perry, M. (1998). Bias or responsivity? Sex and achievement-level effects on teachers' classroom questioning practices. *Journal of Educational Psychology, 90,* 516–527.

American Association of University Women. (1992). *How schools shortchange girls: The AAUW report.* Washington, DC: AAUW Education Foundation/National Education Association.

American Association of University Women. (2001a). *Beyond the "gender wars:" A conversation about girls, boys, and education.* Washington, DC: AAUW Education Foundation.

American Association of University Women. (2001b). *Hostile hallways: Bullying, teasing, and sexual harassment in schools.* Washington, DC: AAUW Education Foundation.

Basow, S. (1998). Student evaluations: The role of gender bias and teaching styles. In L. H. Collins, J. C. Chrisler, & K. Quina (Eds.), *Career strategies for women in academe: Arming Athena* (pp. 135–156). Thousand Oaks, CA: Sage.

Basow, S. A. (1992). *Gender stereotypes and roles* (3rd ed.). Pacific Grove, CA: Brooks/Cole.

Basow, S. A. (2000). Best and worst professors: Gender patterns in students' choices. *Sex Roles, 43,* 407–417.

Best, R. (1983). *We've all got scars: What boys and girls learn in elementary school.* Bloomington: Indiana University Press.

Brady, K. L., & Eisler, R. M. (1999). Sex and gender in the college classroom: A quantitative analysis of faculty–student interactions and perceptions. *Journal of Educational Psychology, 91,* 127–145.

Canada, K., & Pringle, R. (1995). The role of gender in college classroom interactions: A social context approach. *Sociology of Education, 68,* 161–186.

Childs, G., & McKay, M. (2001). Boys starting school disadvantaged: Implications from teachers' rating of behaviour and achievement in the first two years. *British Journal of Educational Psychology, 71,* 303–314.

Conlin, M. (2003, May 26). The new gender gap. *Business Week online.* [On-line]. Retrieved May 26, 2003. Available: http://www.businessweek.com/print/magazine/content/03_21/b3834001_mz001.html

Crawford, M., & McLeod, M. (1990). Gender in the college classroom: An assessment of the chilly climate for women. *Sex Roles, 23,* 101–122.

Duffy, J., Warren, K., & Walsh, M. (2001). Classroom interactions: Gender of teacher, gender of student, and classroom subject. *Sex Roles, 45,* 579–593.

Evelyn, J. (2002, June 28). Community colleges start to ask, where are the men? *Chronicle of Higher Education,* A32.

Fletcher, M. A. (2002, June 25). Degrees of separation: Gender gap among college graduates has educators wondering where the men are. *Washington Post,* A01.

Fordham, S. (1996). *Blacked out: Dilemmas of race, identity, and success at Capital High.* Chicago: University of Chicago Press.

Fredrickson, B. L., & Roberts. T. A. (1997). Objectification theory: Towards understanding women's lived experience and mental health risks. *Psychology of Women Quarterly, 21,* 173–206.

Gabriel, S. L., & Smithson, I. (Eds.). (1990*). Gender in the classroom: Power and pedagogy.* Urbana: University of Illinois Press.

Gooden, A. M., & Gooden, M. A. (2001). Gender representation in notable children's picture books: 1995–1999. *Sex Roles, 45,* 89–101.

Grant, L. (1985). Race–gender status, classroom interaction, and children's socialization in elementary school. In L. C. Wilkinson & C. B. Marrett (Eds.), *Gender influences in classroom interaction* (pp. 57–77). Orlando, FL: Academic Press.

Hall, R. M., & Sandler, B. R. (1982). *The classroom climate: A chilly one for women?* Washington, DC: Project on the Status and Education of Women, Association of American Colleges.

Harris, L., and Associates. (1997). *The Metropolitan Life survey of the American teacher 1997: Examining gender issues in public schools.* New York: Louis Harris and Associates.

Inzlicht, M., & Ben-Zeev, T. A. (2000). A threatening intellectual environment: Why females are susceptible to experiencing problem-solving deficits in the presence of males. *Psychological Science, 11,* 365–371.

Jovanovic, J., & King, S. S. (1998). Boys and girls in the performance-based science classroom: Who's doing the performing? *American Educational Research Journal, 35,* 477–496.

Kehily, M. (2001). Bodies in school: Young men, embodiment, and heterosexual masculinities. *Men & Masculinities, 4,* 173–185.

Kleinfeld, J. S. (1998). *The myth that schools shortchange girls: Social science in the service of deception.* Prepared for the Women's Freedom Network. (Available from Susan Basow, College of Liberal Arts, University of Alaska Fairbanks, Fairbanks, AK 99775).

Koch, J. (2003). Gender issues in the classroom. In W.M. Reynolds & G.E. Miller (Eds.), *Handbook of psychology.* Vol. 7, *Educational psychology* (pp. 259–281). Hoboken, NJ: Wiley.

Maccoby, E. E. (1998). *The two sexes: Growing up apart, coming together.* Cambridge, MA: Belknap Press of Harvard University Press.

Martino, W., & Meyenn, B. (Eds.). (2001). *What about the boys?: Issues of masculinity in schools.* Buckingham, UK, and Philadelphia: Open University Press.

McIntosh, P. (1983). *Interactive phases of curricular re-vision: A feminist perspective.* Working Paper no. 124. Wellesley, MA: Wellesley College Center for Research on Women.

National Center for Education Statistics. (1983). *Faculty salaries, tenure, and benefits survey.* Washington, DC: National Center for Education Statistics.

National Center for Educational Statistics. (2002). *Gender and racial/ethnic differences in salary and other characteristics of postsecondary faculty: Fall 1998.* Washington, DC: National Center for Education Statistics.

Pharr, S. (1988). *Homophobia: A weapon of sexism.* Inverness, CA: Chardon.

Purcell, P., & Stewart, L. (1990). Dick and Jane in 1989. *Sex Roles, 22,* 177–185.

Ross, S. I., & Jackson, J. M. (1991). Teachers' expectations for Black males' and Black females' academic achievement. *Personality and Social Psychology Bulletin, 17,* 78–82.

Rosser, S. V. (1997). *Re-engineering female friendly science.* New York: Teachers College Press.

Sadker, M., & Sadker, D. (1994). *Failing at fairness: How our schools cheat girls.* New York: Scribner's.

Smallwood, S. (2003, December 5). Women take lead in number of U.S. doctorates awarded, as total falls again. *Chronicle of Higher Education,*

Sommers, C. H. (2000). *The war against boys: How misguided feminism is harming our young men.* New York: Simon & Schuster.

Statham, A., Richardson, L., & Cook, J. (1991). *Gender and university teaching: A negotiated difference.* Albany: State University of New York Press.

Steele, C. M., & Aronson, J. (2000). Stereotype threat and the intellectual test performance of African Americans. In C. Stangor (Ed.)., *Stereotypes and prejudice: Essential readings* (pp. 369–389). Philadelphia: Psychology Press.

Thorne, B. (1993). *Gender play: Girls and boys in school.* New Brunswick, NJ: Rutgers University Press.

Whitt, E. J., Edison, M. I., Pascarella, E. T, Nora, A., & Terenzini, P. T. (1999). Women's perceptions of a "chilly climate" and cognitive outcomes in college: Additional evidence. *Journal of College Student Development, 40,* 163–177.

Wilkinson, L.C., & Marrett, C.B. (Eds.). (1985). *Gender influences in classroom interaction.* Orlando, FL: Academic Press.

Young, J.R. (2003, November 14). Student "engagement" in learning varies significantly by major, survey finds. *Chronicle of Higher Education.* [On-line]. Retrieved November 10, 2003. Available: http://chronicle.com/weekly/v50/i12/12a03701.htm

Chapter 7

Gender and Verbal and Nonverbal Communication

Marianne LaFrance and Jennifer L. Harris

A common belief about men and women is that they communicate differently. Indeed, this perception is widely promulgated in best-selling books such as *You Just Don't Understand* (Tannen, 1990) and *Men Are from Mars, Women Are from Venus* (Gray, 1992). But among researchers, the issue is considerably more complex than popular views would have it. These two facts—persistence of stereotypic beliefs about gender differences in communication and mixed empirical findings—present some challenges in the attempt to convey how gender intersects with verbal and nonverbal communication.

Consider, for example, the assertiveness training movement that emerged to great fanfare in the 1980s. Assertiveness training proponents argued that effective and influential communication requires one to communicate in a straightforward manner (Crawford, 1995). Women especially were counseled to stop speaking in equivocal "feminine" ways that limited their effectiveness and curbed their leadership potential in the professional world. Apparently, women rely on linguistic devices such as hedges, disclaimers, tag questions, imperatives phrased as questions, and rising intonation at the end of declarative sentences. The effect seemingly is to make women appear hesitant and uncertain (Gervasio & Crawford, 1989; McMillan et al., 1977). Women were also chastised for overuse of linguistic intensifiers like the adverb "so" and surplus expressive nonverbal communication, both of which were seen to detract from communicational clarity (Henley, 1977; McMillan et al., 1977). Assertiveness training advocates advised women to imitate the communication style commonly attributed to men. Instead of indirect statements or hints, women were advised to use declarative statements and straightforward requests. Instead of coupling refusals with excuses and requests with apologies, women were instructed to be plain and unadorned when they spoke (Gervasio, 1987; Gervasio & Crawford, 1989; Wilson & Gallois, 1993).

Assertiveness training is no longer in ascendance, in part because its assertions were overly simplified in some places and just plain wrong in others. Nevertheless, its endorsement over a considerable period of time illustrates some important and ongoing issues in the domain of gender and communication. For example, what accounts for the persistent belief that sex differences are large and pervasive? Why are some modes of communication believed to be more effective than others? Does one sex substantially and reliably employ these modes more than the other? When and where are gender differences observed? How are we to explain them when they do occur? What are we to make of situations when they do not occur?

The study of gender and communication encompasses a wide variety of behaviors besides *what* people talk about. Specifically, psychologists and other social scientists have been concerned with studying the *how* of communication. They have studied speech attributes such as interruptions, intonation, tempo, verbal fillers, talk time, and pauses. They have also examined nonverbal communicational attributes such as facial expressions, paralanguage, gesture, posture, eye contact, and touch. The size of the resulting literature is such that it cannot be summarized in a single chapter. However, several recurring concepts, issues, and explanations can be described. So instead of attempting a comprehensive review, we focus on one area of gender and communication—the use of direct and indirect communication styles—to illustrate the theoretical and methodological issues that characterize the field as a whole.

Direct and Indirect Communication

Direct communication can be differentiated from indirect communication by the degree to which the speaker uses an assertive or declarative mode versus a more mitigated or qualified one. In a direct communication style, the speaker uses straightforward and uncomplicated commands, statements, and queries. In contrast, an indirect style draws on suggestions and hints or qualifies statements of fact with a questioning intonation. Indirect forms include hedges, such as "perhaps," "you know," or "I guess"; tag questions, or questions eliciting agreement at the end of a statement; and compound requests, such as sentences beginning with "Won't you . . . ?" or "Would you mind . . . ?" Indirect communication can also be reflected in nonverbal channels and take the form of facial expressions such as smiling, rising intonation at the end of a sentence, and gestural accompaniments, all of which can serve to soften the effect of communication content.

Beliefs about Gender and Communication

The most common belief about sex differences in communication is that men are more direct in how they communicate. For example, Kramer (1977) found that both sexes believe men are more demanding, loud, authoritarian, forceful, and blunt, while women are more polite, gentle, and emotional, and smile a lot when talking. As noted previously, the direct and assertive mode has tended to be evaluated more positively than the more indirect (and presumably feminine) mode.

In the 1920s Jesperson (1922) pointed to problems associated with women's mode of communication and proposed that men's more direct style made them more effective communicators. Fifty years later, Lakoff (1975) again called attention to the problems of "woman's language." In her influential book *Language and Woman's Place,* Lakoff argued that indirect forms of communication give the impression of a speaker "not being really sure of himself, of looking to the addressee for confirmation, even of having no views of his own" (p. 17). According to Henley (1977), several modes of nonverbal communication, such as greater smiling and constrained posture and gesture, also communicate powerlessness.

Communication Style and Attributions of Competence

One consequence of the presumed link between sex and communication style is that certain sets of personality traits are attributed to people who communicate in a particular way (Broverman et al., 1972; Erickson et al., 1978; Kramer, 1977; Mulac, Lundell, & Bradac, 1986). For example, direct forms of speech lead observers to attribute agentic traits such as aggressiveness, dominance, decision-making ability, leadership, and self-confidence to the speaker (Broverman et al., 1972). In contrast, indirect forms lead perceivers to attribute more communal traits, such as tactfulness, gentleness, awareness of others' feelings, and lack of decision-making ability.

Consider the study done by Mulac et al. (1986). Participants read transcripts of speeches made by students whose sex was not known, and were asked to rate the speakers on a number of trait dimensions. The speeches by females tended to use more fillers, oppositions, and negations. Observers rated these transcripts high on "socio-intellectual status" and "aesthetic quality." Speeches made by males, on the other hand, contained more present-tense verbs and judgmental adjectives. These speakers were judged to possess more "dynamic" traits, including strength, activity, and aggressiveness. Bradley (1981) demonstrated that women who argued their position on an issue using qualifying phrases, such as tag questions and disclaimers, were rated as less dynamic, knowledgeable, and intelligent than women who did not use such qualifiers.

Other data indicate that it is the style per se that is associated with particular attributes. One study showed that both sexes are judged to be less confident, powerful, competent, intelligent, and knowledgeable when they adopt qualifying communicational features (Carli, 1990). In a study of courtroom communication, frequent use of hedges, hesitations, polite language, and questioning intonation by both male and female witnesses led to their being seen to have lower credibility than witnesses who used these forms less often (Erickson et al., 1978).

In sum, findings indicate that a direct style of communication is associated with attributions of agency and ability. Thus it makes sense that some would advocate that women should learn to "talk like a man." We shall see, however, that such suggestions are not so easily carried out; nor are they inevitably more positively evaluated.

Effectiveness of Direct and Indirect Communication Styles

Despite the apparent benefits of direct communication, there are indications that it is not always constructive. Findings from several studies show that there are many circumstances where direct speech acts violate politeness norms and where indirect linguistic forms are more appropriate and effective (Crawford, 1995; Fishman, 1980; Gervasio, 1987; Gervasio & Crawford, 1989; Holmes, 1995; McMillan et al., 1977; Mulac et al., 1986; Tannen, 1994; Wilson & Gallois, 1993). Indirect forms are often more effective when speakers need to express beliefs and make requests without appearing aggressive. Indirect forms also acknowledge that listeners may have different perspectives. And indirect forms solicit, rather than prescribe, input from others, and thus promote interaction and conversation flow. Nonverbal expressiveness also can promote conversational engagement, which in turn can contribute to communicational accuracy (Hall, 1978, 1984; LaFrance, Hecht, & Paluck, 2003). In sum, indirect modes of communication are also effective.

Research also suggests that a direct style may not always increase women's effectiveness, even in professional situations. A meta-analysis of research on gender and leadership style showed that women managers are more likely to adopt a democratic, participatory style than an autocratic, directive style, presumably because they have found it to be more effective (Eagly & Johnson, 1990). Carli (1990) found that while an assertive message presented by a woman speaker was indeed more influential for female listeners, tentative messages were more influential for male listeners. In fact, Wilson and Gallois (1993) argued that women are more likely to achieve their goals by communicating in a less direct and more polite manner.

Finally, some research suggests that variations in communication matter more for women than for men. Contrary to the results for women speakers, Bradley (1981) showed that men who used qualifiers were rated virtually the same on knowledge and intelligence as men who did not use qualifiers. Carli (1990), too, found that tentative language use by men had no effect on their ability to influence either men or women. Hence, while it is commonly believed that men are more direct than women in how they talk, and that directness is more effective than indirectness, it is not necessarily the case that women can achieve greater communicational efficacy simply by becoming more direct.

Gender Differences in Direct/Indirect Behaviors

What other evidence is there that men and women communicate differently? Researchers have found, for example, that women use more tag questions (e.g., Crosby & Nyquist, 1977; Fishman, 1980; Holmes, 1995; McMillan et al., 1977; Mulac et al., 1986); hedges and disclaimers (e.g., Crosby & Nyquist, 1977; Hirschman, 1973; Holmes, 1995; McMillan et al., 1977; Mulac et al., 1986); mitigated directives, such as imperatives in question form (e.g., Fishman, 1980; Holmes, 1995; McMillan et al., 1977; Mulac et al., 1986), and high, rising intonation than do men (Holmes, 1995). In the nonverbal communication literature, studies indicate that females are more facially expressive (Hall, 1978, 1984), evidence greater amounts of smiling (LaFrance et al., 2003), are better at decoding nonverbal cues in others, and show facial expressions that can be more easily read by others (Hall, 1978, 1984).

Several studies have shown that communication composites are gender-linked. For example, Mulac et al. (1986) demonstrated that a weighted combination of twenty gender-linked linguistic features shows sex-linked patterns. E-mail messages can also be correctly linked to a sender's sex through a constellation of linguistic features (Thomson & Murachver, 2001). Women were found to use more questions, modals, and subordinating conjunctions, while males were found to use more opinions, adjectives, and insults. Although the researchers found only small differences in any single individual feature, a combination of features led to higher accuracy in ascertaining a sender's sex.

Gender differences in communication style have been documented in preadolescents. Goodwin (1980) compared the speech of boys and girls in same-sex groups during task activities and found that boys tend to use more commands and express more personal desires, while girls' directives involve more suggestions for future action and reasons why an action should be undertaken. Goodwin found that girls often used indirect linguistic forms such as "let's" do something and modal verbs such as "can" or "could," sometimes preceded by the even more tentative "maybe." Gender differences in some linguistic features have been found in even younger groups. In a study of the language of five year olds during play situations with a same-sex partner, Sachs (1987) found that the majority of obliges by girls (i.e., phrases designed to elicit a response from the other child) were in mitigated forms, such as tag questions, joint utterances such as the use of "let's," and pretend directives (i.e., "Pretend he's sick"), compared with 34 percent of the obliges of boys. Conversely, 42 percent of boys' obliges were in unmitigated forms, such as simple imperatives (e.g., "Lie down" or "Gimme your arm") and prohibitions (e.g., "Don't take my things"), compared with 17 percent of those by girls. Another study of problem-solving communication by preschool children found that preschool girls tended to use mitigation tactics much more than boys, including giving suggestions and offering a joint plan or a reason for a course of action (Holmes-Lonergan, 2003). Indeed, differences in communication style have been found in girls and boys as young as three years old. During joint play situations, three-to-five-year-old girls used questions to elicit agreement for their course of action, while boys made statements without expecting a response (Sheldon, 1993).

Evidence therefore supports the general conclusion that males and females use several different linguistic forms. Nonetheless, a more precise rendering of the data is that such differences do not occur in all situations. In the next section, we discuss the situational nature of gender differences in communication style.

Gender Differences across Situations

Given the volume of research on sex differences in communication style and the number of explanations that have been offered for what is found, the most surprising finding is the extent of *similarity* between men and women. For example, a meta-analysis of 162 research reports on gender differences in smiling found a moderate effect size (d = 0.41), with females tending to smile more than males (LaFrance et al., 2003). But an effect size of 0.41 indicates a 60 percent overlap between the sexes. In other words, although there is a modest difference in how much women and men smile, the overlap between the sexes is greater than the difference.

The amount of smiling during conversation, as for many other direct and indirect forms of communication, depends in good measure on the whole interaction context rather than merely on the sexes of the communicators. For example, situational dimensions such as sex composition, type of task, group members' status and popularity, experimental setting, and awareness of being observed have all been shown to affect the likelihood that gender differences in communicational style will be observed. Moreover, a person's sex is only one of a number of individual characteristics that can influence how much he or she smiles, or uses other direct or indirect communication features, in a given situation. A person's culture, ethnicity, and age can also significantly influence communication style. In the following sections, we show how several contextual factors affect the degree to which gender differences are found.

Sex Composition

Research provides broad evidence of the power of context in moderating gender differences in direct and indirect forms of communication, with the sex composition of the dyad or group appearing to be especially powerful. Findings indicate that the sex of the recipient may be as important as the sex of the sender, with speakers adjusting their communication style according to the sex of the person they are communicating with. Several studies have demonstrated that females tend to use significantly more direct syntactical forms in mixed-sex settings and more indirect forms in same-sex settings. Women in same-sex groups tend to use more intensifiers, modal and imperative constructions, and tag questions than women in mixed-sex groups, while men use slightly more intensifiers and tag questions in mixed-sex than in same-sex groups (McMillan et al., 1977). Mulac et al. (1988) found that women and men use more gender-stereotypical language in same-sex than in mixed-sex dyads, and females actually speak more assertively than males in mixed-sex discussions. Gender differences in the amount of smiling are also significantly higher in same-sex pairs (LaFrance et al., 2003). In addition, Carli (1989) found that the sex of the partner affected conversational style, with both men and women exhibiting more disagreements when trying to influence a man than a woman.

Studies of children have also shown significant effects of sex composition on language use. Among preschool children engaged in a problem-solving task, both girls and boys in mixed-sex dyads engaged in more controlling verbal and nonverbal interactions than children in same-sex dyads (Holmes-Lonergan, 2003). In addition, both boys and girls were more likely to agree with a female partner than with a male partner. Leaper (1991) found that girls in middle childhood (ages six to nine) used more controlling speech acts with a male partner and more cooperative and collaborative speech acts in female dyads. Boys, however, used more cooperative and controlling types of speech acts with a female partner and more domineering acts with a male partner. In conflict situations, girls used direct commands and heavy-handed persuasion more often when arguing with boys than with girls (Goodwin, 1980; Miller, Danaher, & Forbes, 1986). Boys' behavior, however, did not change much when dealing with boys or girls (Miller et al., 1986). Maccoby (1990) concluded that all types of sex differences in children vary according to the sex composition of the interacting group. With children, as well as adults, the sex of the person on the receiving end often accounts more for what style is used than does the sex of the sender.

Social Role

An individual's social role plays an important part in determining the amount of gender-stereotypical communication behavior that will be displayed. For example, Brown (1993) observed Tenejapa, a peasant Mayan community in southern Mexico, and found that women are expected to be extremely polite, to suppress signs of conflict, and to avoid eye contact in public. In contrast, men are permitted to be direct and straightforward, and are allowed to express conflict. However, in a courtroom setting, these expectations disappear; both sexes exhibit direct eye contact, use aggressive gestures, and openly challenge opponents.

In the United States, both male and female clients were found to use tag questions and hedges with police (Crosby & Nyquist, 1977). Another study showed similar behavior by both sexes when they were in the same role. In powerful roles, both sexes used tag questions to encourage others to talk; in "powerless" roles, both sexes used them to ascertain agreement (Cameron, McAlindon, & O'Leary, 1988). Among children, girls used direct commands more often when playing teacher or mother and when telling younger siblings what to do (Goodwin, 1980), as well as when instructing boys in a task (e.g., jumping rope) in which they were viewed as holding more expertise (Goodwin, 2001). Both sexes were found to show comparable amounts of smiling when assigned to different social roles (LaFrance et al., 2003).

Task

The task to be done also appears to affect whether the sexes will differ in how they communicate. For example, both male and female speakers use tag questions when their task is to facilitate interaction (Hochschild, 1983), but both become more direct when they are in competitive or achievement situations (Goodwin, 1980).

Tasks also influence parents' use of language with their sons and daughters. Both mothers and fathers use more assertive speech acts during a goal-directed play activity (e.g., constructing a toy car) than during an affiliative play activity (e.g., playing store) (Leaper & Gleason, 1996). Meta-analyses of parent–child interactions have shown that unstructured activities are more likely to produce significant gender differences than structured tasks (Anderson, & Leaper, 1998; Leaper, Anderson, & Sanders, 1998).

One interpersonal task is, however, associated with larger gender differences in communicational directness. Women use indirect forms of communication more than men when attempting to influence or persuade others. When instructed to influence men, women tend to use significantly more tentative language (disclaimers, tag questions, and hedges) than men do (Carli, 1990). Females also smile more, and men smile less, in the attempt to be persuasive (LaFrance et al., 2003).

Experimental Condition

Meta-analyses of gender differences demonstrate the importance of the experimental condition in affecting the magnitude of gender differences that are found. In studies of conversational interruptions and parent–child interactions, naturalistic conditions produce larger sex differences than laboratory settings (Anderson & Leaper, 1998; Gleason, 1987; Leaper et al., 1998). Additionally, the belief that one is being observed increases the likelihood that females will show more smiling than males (LaFrance et al., 2003). In studies of leadership, however, laboratory situations tend to produce stronger gender differences than naturalistic settings (Eagly & Johnson, 1990; Eagly & Karau, 1991).

Cultural Differences

Many Asian and Arabic cultures are believed to value indirectness in both men and women compared with Western cultures (Holmes, 1995; Ma, 1992; Nelson, Batal, & Bakary, 2002). In a literature review of the indirect communication style common to East Asian cultures, Ma (1992) concluded that an indirect mode of communication is valued especially during negotiations. Speakers are expected to be nonassertive and nonargumentative, to communicate very little explicit information, and to avoid confrontation. According to Holmes (1995), in many Pacific cultures both men and women use a more cooperative style of conversation. She describes the high, rising intonation and interactive politeness devices used by both male and female members of the Maori culture in New Zealand. The Maori conversational style is more similar to that attributed to women rather than to men in the Anglo New Zealand culture. Gender differences in smiling are found in every country in which research was conducted, but the differences are the largest for Canadian and U.S. samples and smallest for British samples (LaFrance et al., 2003).

But some other cultures and nonwhite ethnicities may place greater value on direct styles of communication by both men and women. Tannen (1994) suggests that Americans of Eastern European Jewish and Greek descent view arguing between women and men as a sign of intimacy. Researchers also have suggested that directness is more valued among African–American women than among white women in the United States. The gender differences in smiling are largest for Caucasians and smaller for African–American samples (LaFrance et al., 2003). A study comparing all-black with all-white task-oriented, mixed-sex groups of eighth graders demonstrated that white females tend to use more tentative and polite language than either white males or black males and females (Filardo, 1996). In this study, sample sizes were small (N = 10) and many of the differences were not statistically significant. Nonetheless, white females used the highest percentage of mitigated speech (i.e., language that softened the force of their statements and/or considered the listener's point of view), and the lowest percentage of aggravated speech (i.e., language that demonstrated a lack of consideration of the other's point of view, asymmetrical rights, and/or assumed compliance). Black females in these groups did demonstrate significantly more mitigated speech acts than black males, but the percentage of aggravated speech acts for black females was similar to that of both black and white males.

Age

Age is another individual factor that alters the likelihood of finding direct and indirect styles of communication. Leaper (1991) found few gender differences in controlling and collaborative speech acts in her study of children between the ages of four and six, but did find them in older children (ages six to nine). Gender differences in smiling appear to be strongest among teenagers and tend to decrease with age (LaFrance et al., 2003). The smallest gender differences were found in samples of adults over age sixty-five.

In sum, gender differences in particular linguistic features vary depending on the situation and other characteristics of the individual. In the next section, we discuss several theoretical explanations that have been offered for why the observed gender differences take the form that they do.

Theories of Gender and Communication

Perceived sex differences in communication styles have generated considerable debate about why men and women differ in how direct they are. One explanation, based on dominance and power, begins with the assumption of gender inequality. Indirectness characterizes women's communication style because indirection is the style of subordinates. Direct communication style characterizes men's communication patterns because directness is the mode of the more powerful. In contrast, a cultural explanation posits that early socialization experiences cause men and women to have different communication goals. A third explanation focuses on current context factors. According to a social context explanation, the influence of socialization is not limited to early socialization experiences, but includes the impact of ongoing sex-role prescriptives for appropriate communicative behavior and concurrent participation in sex-segregated social and occupational roles.

Dominance and Power

Lakoff (1975) proposed dominance as an explanation for gender differences in communication. She contended that little girls are taught to be polite as a signal of deference to the addressee and as a sign of their own inferiority. Henley (1977) proposed that speech styles characteristic of women, including hesitancy and qualifying phrases, represent the speech styles of subordinated groups. In addition, nonverbal cues can convey dominance and submission. Direct nonverbal communication behaviors, such as staring, loud speech, interrupting, and not smiling mirror the behaviors exhibited by men toward women and by the powerful toward the powerless.

The dominance approach has relied on showing parallels between having power and being male and having little power and being female. In discussing why, in cross-sex conversations, male speakers are significantly more likely to interrupt, and females are more likely to remain silent following these interruptions, Zimmerman and West (1975) concluded that "men deny equal status to women as conversational partners" (p. 125). Fishman (1980) saw women's more common use of questions as deriving from their lack of power: "Women's conversational troubles reflect not their inferior social training but their inferior social status" (p. 258). Henley and LaFrance (1984) proposed that women's superior ability in interpreting nonverbal cues results from their need to win approval or meet the needs of those with higher status.

Social Cultural Approach

In contrast to an explanation based on power differences, Maltz and Borker (1982) proposed a "cultural approach to male–female miscommunication." Building on the work of the anthropologist Gumperz (Gumperz & Cook-Gumperz, 1982), Maltz and Borker borrowed the idea that speakers from different cultures follow different rules of conversation. They proposed that boys and girls, too, come from different cultures and learn how to conduct friendly conversations in gender-segregated groups at school. Girls' culture focuses on close friendships between equals and discourages criticism, competition, and conflict. Boys' culture, on the other hand, is based on a hierarchy in which boys learn to assert themselves and use speech to express dominance. As a result of early socialization experiences, Maltz and Borker argued, women use conversation to express affiliation and tend to view direct and unmitigated styles of communication as negative and disruptive. Men, on the other hand, view competitive forms of conversation, such as arguing and issuing commands, as a conventional way to hold a conversation.

Tannen articulated a variation of the cultural approach in her popular book *You Just Don't Understand: Women and Men in Conversation* (1990). She proposed that women use language to create rapport, while men use language to establish hierarchy and maintain their independence. Women tend to favor cooperative forms of communication, such as agreeing, supporting the listener, and making suggestions. Men are more likely to engage in direct conflict when they converse, and may even use verbal opposition to express solidarity (Tannen, 1990, 1994).

Critics responded that the cultural approach ignores the difference in power between men and women (Crawford, 1995). In response to her critics, Tannen (1994) argued that linguistic strategies are relative and ambiguous. For example, depending on one's point of view, direct linguistic forms can be interpreted as a sign of either power or solidarity. According to Tannen, one needs to know the intent of the speaker.

Dominance and Social Culture

More recent research emphasizes the validity of both the dominance and the cultural points of view. According to Holmes (1995), men are more competitive *and* use more direct and challenging language for the purpose of dominating others and asserting their status. Women, however, use language to make contact and strengthen relationships *and* convey deference. As a result, men tend to dominate women in conversation. In addition, "Women's subordinate societal status may account not so much for how women talk, as for the way their talk is interpreted and perceived" (Holmes, 1995, p. 111). For example, women tend to use tag questions more to facilitate conversation, while men use them more to express uncertainty. In addition, women use qualifiers, such as "you know," "I think," and "sort of," more often to express politeness and warmth toward the addressee, whereas men use them more often as a hedge. Men therefore assume that women's greater use of these linguistic forms is due to greater tentativeness and uncertainty. Romaine (1999) argued that women may hedge more due to both a greater sensitivity to personal relationships and the experience of being subordinate. The differences in communication styles of men and women reflect different concerns *and* unequal positions in society.

Socialization of Gender-Appropriate Behavior

Both dominance and social cultural theories of gender differences in communication acknowledge the importance of early socialization experiences that teach children how to communicate in ways that conform to society's expectations for males and females. In particular, social learning theory emphasizes the key role that parents and peers play in modeling gender-appropriate behavior for boys and girls (Bandura, 1977, 1986; Mischel, 1966).

Research shows that fathers and mothers model scripts specifying that males should communicate directly and females, indirectly. Fathers use nearly twice as many direct commands and threats than mothers do, and they use them more often with sons than with daughters (Gleason, 1987). Similarly, mothers use more question forms and polite imperatives. By the age of four, the children observed in this study used the same directives as their same-sex parent. In two meta-analyses of parents' language with their children, mothers used more statements of approval, agreement, acknowledgment, and collaboration, and fewer directives and informing speech forms than fathers (Anderson & Leaper, 1998; Leaper et al., 1998). Mothers also talked more and used more supportive speech with their daughters than with their sons. But parenting takes place in a context. One study found that daughters of employed mothers perceived significantly smaller differences between men and women on both competence and warmth-expressiveness measures than daughters of mothers who were not employed (Broverman et al., 1972).

Same-sex play groups, common among pre-adolescents, provide a powerful education for learning and practicing gender-stereotypical communication behaviors (Goodwin, 1980; Maccoby, 1990; Maltz & Borker, 1982). In these groups, boys and girls are viewed as opposites and gender differences are exaggerated (Thorne, 1993). Children who do not conform are teased, and nonconforming boys are assigned the humiliating label of "sissy."

Same-sex groups of boys and girls exhibit different social organizations, and these organizations dictate appropriate forms of communication (Goodwin, 1980). Boys' groups are more likely to be organized in hierarchies, and the accompanying talk reflects asymmetrical relationships with an emphasis on "you" or "me." In contrast, girls organize themselves in a more egalitarian manner, and their speech stresses symmetrical relationships with a focus on "we." Females in sex-segregated groups learn to avoid or limit direct forms of self-assertion, even in competitive or conflict situations. In fact, the gender-stereotypical communication patterns of children in same-sex peer groups mirror those found in all-male and all-female adult dyads and groups.

Moreover, when given the choice, both boys and girls as young as age three tend to prefer to play in same-sex groups, and same-sex play preferences peak in adolescence (Maccoby & Jacklin, 1987). There is some evidence that girls reject the competition and dominance common in boys' play groups (Maccoby, 1988). Girls find that their cooperative style of influence is effective with each other and with adults, but becomes increasingly ineffective with boys because they become less responsive to polite suggestion with age.

The rules for self-assertion taught in these play groups are strongly endorsed by adults. Wilson and Gallois (1993) found that men and women subscribe to different social rules about appropriate communicative behavior. Men are expected to "defend yourself against unfair criticism by telling others they're unfair" and "state problems directly when letting others know they cause you problems." Women, however, are expected to "defend yourself against unfair criticism by giving your explanation." Researchers noted no male-specific rules for avoiding conflict, but females had five specific rules, including "agree to reasonable requests," "accept some unfair criticism," "when criticized fairly, show you're willing to change behavior," and "be indirect and hint when letting others know they cause you problems." In relationship rules, women are expected to "be polite and tactful when letting others know they cause you problems." The authors suggest that women endorse these self-expression rules because they are more compatible with expected feminine gender roles, and thus more likely to be evaluated positively by both men and women.

Contextual Theories of Gender and Communication

In contrast to theories of gender differences based on power or social cultural factors, a third theoretical position holds that sex differences in communication style emerge as a function of contingencies in particular contexts. Contextual theories stress the combination of active expectations and situational characteristics in explaining why, in any particular context, gender differences are or are not expected.

Social Role Theory

Eagly (1987) proposed social role theory to explain many observed gender differences. According to Eagly, the typical distribution of men and women into different social roles is the underlying cause of gender differences and related gender stereotypes about male and female characteristics. Specifically, women tend to occupy domestic and lower-status roles in which a communal orientation is required, while men tend to occupy employee and higher-status roles that demand an agentic orientation. These social roles and gender stereotypes, in turn, lead to gender differences in social behaviors due to skills and beliefs learned during implementation of their different roles. In addition, men and women receive positive reinforcement from others when they behave according to gendered expectations. Reinforcement, in turn, affects people's self-concepts and individuals regulate their own behavior accordingly. Women become skilled at being communal and are rewarded for expressive, sensitive, and interpersonally oriented communication styles. Men learn to excel at styles that communicate leadership, self-confidence, and forcefulness. As support, Eagly and Steffen (1984) demonstrated the link between social roles and gender stereotypes. They found that subjects rated men and women who held domestic roles as possessing more communal traits, and those who were employed as possessing more agentic traits. In addition, higher-status individuals within an organization were viewed as more agentic than lower-status individuals.

Expectations States Theory

Like social role theory, expectations states theory (also known as status characteristics theory) proposes that gender stereotypes affect interpersonal behavior (Ridgeway & Smith-Lovin, 1996; Wagner & Berger, 1998). However, expectations states theory holds that gender is a diffuse status characteristic. In other words, sex, like other group characteristics, is stratified in terms of the status it is assumed to have and leads to expectations of people's capabilities. Some groups (e.g., males, whites, highly educated people) are afforded higher status. Higher-status individuals receive more opportunities from other group members to contribute to a given task and are more likely to receive positive evaluation for the contributions they make. As a result, they are more successful at influencing others and appear more competent. When sex becomes salient in a group (i.e., when it forms a basis for discrimination between group members, such as in a mixed-sex group) and when assumed gender characteristics are relevant to the group task, men and women tend to be rewarded for more gender-stereotypic behavior. As a result, in task groups women are expected to be less competent, so they are given fewer opportunities to participate and their contributions are valued less. These results, in turn, reinforce gender stereotypes.

Gender-in-Context and Doing Gender

According to gender-in-context theory, three factors predict gendered behavior in a given situation: expectations of others, especially if gender becomes salient; individual gender identity; and situational context (Deaux & Major, 1987). "Gender is not static but flexible, and its meaning becomes clear in the beliefs that people hold and in the context of social interaction, where those beliefs are manifested, rather than in any inherent qualities of the male or female" (Deaux & Kite, 1987, p. 111). Similarly, West and Zimmerman (1987) propose that gender is not a property of individuals, but a feature of social situations. The situation creates gender roles because we "do gender" to manage how others judge and respond to us. From early childhood, we learn to monitor our own conduct and that of others regarding appropriate gendered behavior in a variety of situations.

Contextual Explanations for Gender Differences in Communication

Social role theory, expectations states theory, and gender-in-context/ doing gender theories emphasize the importance of context and others' expectations in explaining many of the variable and seemingly contradictory results found in studies of sex differences. They help explain why sex differences are apparent in some contexts but not in others. For example, laboratory studies in which participants do not know each other tend to produce larger gender differences because, without any additional information about appropriate roles, gender will become salient and individuals will tend to behave according to gendered expectations. Similarly, situations in which individuals hold well-defined social roles or greater status may override gender expectations and lead to less gender-stereotypical behavior.

Contextual theories also help explain why assertiveness training did not help women to establish success in the professional world. Aries (1996) proposed that efforts to change individual communication style "failed to recognize the extent to which gender differences are produced and maintained by forces outside the individual, namely by contextual-situational variables. This conceptualization creates the illusion that individual change will be sufficient to achieve equality between men and women" (p. 20). As expectations states theorists would argue, women who exhibit directive or controlling behaviors, even if they possess legitimate status superiority, may encounter resistance and negative reactions because they are violating the expected gender hierarchy. Carli (1990) noted that an indirect communication style by women likely developed as a way to exert influence in situations of low status. In addition, women who conform to stereotypes and communicate using a more indirect style may find their behavior rewarded by others, and this approval, in turn, tends to reinforce a stereotypical communication style.

Conclusion

Stereotypes in Anglo-American culture hold rather simply that men are direct and women are indirect in how they communicate. Socialization surely accounts for some of why this might be the case, and even genetic factors may account for why extremes of directness or indirectness are more likely to be shown by men and women, respectively. For example, recent research indicates that certain hormones that produce a "tend-and-befriend" response to stress are found more in women than in men (Taylor et al., 2000). Thus women's communal behaviors and more indirect communication style may have a biological basis. Nonetheless, a biological explanation alone cannot explain situational differences in communication style or the extent of overlap between actual communication techniques of men and women.

Actual gender differences in communication style tend to be more variable than either stereotypes or a simple genetic basis would suggest. It appears that social contextual factors lead men and women to communicate differently in some situations and similarly in others. Men and women adopt similar communicative strategies when they are in the same role, engaged in the same task, and occupy the same status. They are more likely to demonstrate differences in line with stereotypes when gender is salient, when gender-stereotypic behavior is expected, and when men and women have different power.

The research on the links between sex and communicational directness also explains why assertiveness training did not lead to greater effectiveness or increases in perceived leadership abilities of women in the professional world. According to Heilman (2001), both descriptive and prescriptive stereotypes continue to reinforce a "glass ceiling" in the professional world. Simply "communicating like a man" does not provide women with the means to overcome descriptive stereotypical beliefs about gender and competence. Nor does it override prescriptive stereotypes that produce a negative response when women communicate in direct or assertive ways. Nor, in the final analysis, does it deal with findings that show that directness is not always the best communicative strategy. Effective interpersonal communication calls for directness on some occasions, and subtlety on others, by both women and men.

Research still needs to explore the question of why beliefs about gender differences in communication and the resulting attributions of competence persist, even though data clearly show the contextual and situational nature of gender-stereotypical communication styles. Research must also address requirements for changing these beliefs. A meta-analysis of females' ratings of their own assertiveness demonstrates that some change may have occurred, at least in the internalization of prescriptive stereotypes about assertive behavior (Twenge, 2001). From 1965 to 1993, women's assertiveness scores increased moderately, and the difference between scores for men and women decreased significantly. Twenge demonstrates that this increase in assertiveness followed an increase in women's educational attainment and median age at first marriage. It appears, then, that reducing the differences in social roles between men and women may have affected gender-stereotypical beliefs. Overcoming childhood socialization factors may also be required. Accordingly, Thorne (1993) has stressed the importance of encouraging cross-sex interaction in children. Children's common practice of segregating themselves into same-sex play groups may serve to increase gender stereotyping. She recommends that educators organize small, cooperative, mixed-sex work groups in classrooms to counteract stereotypical beliefs about competence and power dynamics.

Few researchers, however, have explored alternatives for reducing gender-stereotypical beliefs about communication in everyday interactions. It appears that such knowledge may be necessary to enable individuals to succeed in areas that do not conform to gender expectations.

References

Anderson, K. J., & Leaper, C. (1998). Meta-analyses of gender effects on conversational interruption: Who, what, when, where and how. *Sex Roles, 39,* 225–253.

Aries, E. (1996). *Men and women in interaction: Reconsidering the differences.* New York: Oxford University Press.

Bandura, A. (1977). *Social learning theory.* Englewood Cliffs, NJ: Prentice-Hall.

Bandura, A. (1986). *Social foundations of thought and action: A social cognitive theory.* Englewood Cliffs, NJ: Prentice-Hall.

Bradley, P. H. (1981). The folk-linguistics of women's speech: An empirical examination. *Communication Monographs, 48,* 73–90.

Broverman, I. K., Broverman, D., Clarkson, F., Rosenkrantz, P., & Vogel, S. (1972). Sex-role stereotypes: A current appraisal. *Journal of Social Issues, 28,* 59–78.

Brown, P. (1993). Gender, politeness, and confrontation in Tenejapa. In D. Tannen

(Ed.), *Gender and conversational interaction* (pp. 144–162). New York: Oxford University Press.

Cameron, D., McAlindon, F., & O'Leary, K. (1988). Lakoff in context: The social and linguistic functions of tag questions. In J. Coates & D. Cameron (Eds.), *Women in their speech communities: New perspectives on language and sex* (pp. 74–93). New York: Longman.

Carli, L. L. (1989). Gender differences in interaction style and influence. *Journal of Personality and Social Psychology, 56,* 565–576.

Carli, L. L. (1990). Gender, language and influence. *Journal of Personality and Social Psychology, 59,* 941–951.

Crawford, M. (1995). *Talking difference: On gender and language.* Thousand Oaks, CA: Sage.

Crosby, F., & Nyquist, L. (1977). The female register: An empirical study of Lakoff's hypothesis. *Language in Society, 6,* 313–322.

Deaux, K., & Kite, M. E. (1987). Thinking about gender. In B. B. Hess & M. M. Ferree, (Eds.), *Analyzing gender: A handbook of social science research* (pp. 92–117). Newbury Park, CA: Sage.

Deaux, K., & Major, B. (1987). Putting gender into context: An interactive model of gender-related behavior. *Psychological Bulletin, 94,* 369–389.

Eagly, A. H. (1987). *Sex differences in social behavior: A social-role interpretation.* Hillsdale, NJ: Erlbaum.

Eagly, A. H., & Johnson, B. T. (1990). Gender and leadership style: A meta-analysis. *Psychological Bulletin, 108,* 233–256.

Eagly, A. H., & Karau, S. J. (1991). Gender and the emergence of leaders: A meta-analysis. *Psychological Bulletin, 108,* 233–256.

Eagly, A. H., & Steffen, V. J. (1984). Gender stereotypes stem from the distribution of women and men into social roles. *Journal of Personality and Social Psychology, 46,* 735–754.

Erickson, B., Lind, E. A., Johnson, B. C., & O'Barr, W. M. (1978). Speech style and impression formation in a court setting: The effects of "powerful" and "powerless" speech. *Journal of Experimental Social Psychology, 14,* 266–279.

Filardo, E. K. (1996). Gender patterns in African-American and White adolescents' social interactions in same-race, mixed-gender groups. *Journal of Personality and Social Psychology, 71,* 71–82.

Fishman, P. (1980). Conversational insecurity. In H. Giles, P. Robinson, & P. Smith (Eds.), *Language: Social psychological perspectives* (pp. 127–132). Oxford: Pergamon Press. Reprinted in D. Cameron (Ed.). (1990). *The feminist critique of language* (pp. 253–258). London: Routledge.

Gervasio, A. H. (1987). Assertiveness techniques as speech acts. *Clinical Psychology Review, 7,* 105–119.

Gervasio, A. H., & Crawford, M. (1989). Social evaluations of assertiveness: A critique and speech act reformulation. *Psychology of Women Quarterly, 13,* 1–25.

Gleason, J. B. (1987). Sex differences in parent–child interaction. In S. U. Philips, S.

Steele, & C. Tanz (Eds.), *Language, gender, and sex in comparative perspective* (pp. 189–199). Cambridge: Cambridge University Press.

Goodwin, M. H. (1980). Directive-response speech sequences in girls' and boys' task activities. In S. McConnell-Ginet, R. Borker, & N. Furman (Eds.), *Women and language in literature and society* (pp. 157–174). New York: Praeger.

Goodwin, M. H. (2001). Organizing participation in cross-sex jump rope: Situating gender differences within longitudinal studies of activities. *Research on Language and Social Interaction, 34,* 75–106.

Gray, J. (1992). *Men are from Mars, women are from Venus: A practical guide for improving communication and getting what you want from your relationships.* New York: HarperCollins.

Gumperz, J. J., & Cook-Gumperz, J. (1982). Language and the communication of social identity. In J. J. Gumperz (Ed.), *Language and social identity,* (pp. 1–21). Cambridge: Cambridge University Press.

Hall, J. A. (1978). Gender effects in decoding nonverbal cues. *Psychological Bulletin, 85,* 845–857.

Hall, J. A. (1984). *Nonverbal sex differences: Accuracy of communication and expressive style.* Baltimore: Johns Hopkins University Press.

Heilman, M. E. (2001). Description and prescription: How gender stereotypes prevent women's ascent up the organizational ladder. *Journal of Social Issues, 57,* 657–675.

Henley, N. M. (1977). *Body politics: Power, sex, and nonverbal communication.* Englewood Cliffs, NJ: Prentice-Hall.

Henley, N. M., & LaFrance, M. (1984). Gender as culture: Difference and dominance in nonverbal behavior. In A. Wolfgang (Ed.), *Nonverbal behavior: Perspectives, applications, intercultural insights* (pp. 351–371). Lewiston, NY: C. J. Hogrefe.

Hirschman, L. (1973). Female–male differences in conversational interaction. *Language in Society, 23,* 427–442.

Hochschild, A. (1983). *The managed heart: Commercialization of human feeling.* Berkeley: University of California Press.

Holmes, J. (1995). *Women, men and politeness.* New York: Longman.

Holmes-Lonergan, H. A. (2003). Preschool children's collaborative problem-solving interactions: The role of gender, pair type, and task. *Sex Roles, 48,* 505–518.

Jesperson, O. (1922). The woman. In his *Language: Its nature, development and origin* (pp. 237–254). London: Allen & Unwin. Reprinted in D. Cameron (Ed.). (1990). *The feminist critique of language* (pp. 201–220). London: Routledge.

Kramer, C. (1977). Perceptions of female and male speech. *Language and Speech, 20,* 151–161.

LaFrance, M., Hecht, M. A., & Paluck, E. L. (2003). The contingent smile: A meta-analysis of sex differences in smiling. *Psychological Bulletin, 129,* 305–334.

Lakoff, R. (1975). *Language and woman's place.* New York: Harper & Row.

Leaper, C. (1991). Influence and involvement in children's discourse: Age, gender and partner effects. *Child Development, 62,* 797–811.

Leaper, C., Anderson, K. J., & Sanders, P. (1998). Moderators of gender effects on parents' talk to their children: A meta-analysis. *Developmental Psychology, 34,* 3–27.

Leaper, C., & Gleason, G. B. (1996). The relationship of play activity and gender to parent and child sex-typed communication. *International Journal of Behavioral Development, 19,* 689–703.

Ma, R. (1992). The role of unofficial intermediaries in interpersonal conflicts in the Chinese culture. *Communication Quarterly, 40,* 269–278.

Maccoby, E. E. (1988). Gender as a social category. *Developmental Psychology, 24,* 755–765.

Maccoby, E. E. (1990). Gender and relationships: A developmental account. *American Psychologist, 44,* 513–520.

Maccoby, E. E., & Jacklin, C. N. (1987). Gender segregation in childhood. *Advances in child development and behavior, 20,* 239–288.

Maltz, D. N., & Borker, R. A. (1982). A cultural approach to male–female miscommunication. In J. J. Gumperz (Ed.), *Language and social identity* (pp. 195–216). New York: Cambridge University Press.

McMillan, J. R., Clifton, A. K., McGrath, D., & Gale, W. S. (1977). Women's language: Uncertainty or interpersonal sensitivity and emotionality? *Sex Roles, 3,* 545–559.

Miller, P. M., Danaher, D. L., & Forbes, D. (1986). Sex-related strategies for coping with interpersonal conflict in children aged five and seven. *Developmental Psychology, 22,* 543–548.

Mischel, W. (1966). A social-learning view of sex differences in behavior. In E. E. Maccoby (Ed.), *The development of sex differences* (pp. 56–81). Stanford, CA: Stanford University Press.

Mulac, A., Lundell, T. L., & Bradac, J. J. (1986). Male/female language differences and attributional consequences in a public speaking situation: Toward an explanation of the gender-linked language effect. *Communication Monographs, 53,* 115–129.

Mulac, A., Wiemann, J. M., Widenmann, S. J., & Gibson, T. W. (1988). Male/female language differences in same-sex and mixed-sex dyads: The gender-linked language effect. *Communication Monographs, 55,* 315–335.

Nelson, G. L., Batal, A., & Bakary, E. (2002). Directness vs. indirectness: Egyptian Arabic and US English communication style. *International Journal of Intercultural Relations, 26,* 39–57.

Ridgeway, C. L., & Smith-Lovin, L. (1996). Gender and social interaction: Introduction. *Social Psychology Quarterly, 59,* 173–175.

Romaine, S. (1999). *Communicating gender.* Mahwah, NJ: Erlbaum.

Sachs, J. (1987). Preschool boys' and girls' language use in pretend play. In S. U. Philips, S. Steele, & C. Tanz (Eds.), *Language, gender, and sex in comparative perspective* (pp. 178–188). New York: Cambridge University Press.

Sheldon, A. (1993). Pickle fights: Gendered talk in preschool disputes. In D. Tannen (Ed.), *Gender and conversational interaction* (pp. 83–109). New York: Oxford University Press.

Tannen, D. (1990). *You just don't understand: Women and men in conversation.* New York: Morrow.

Tannen, D. (1994). *Gender and discourse.* New York: Oxford University Press.

Taylor, S. E., Klein, L. C., Lewis, B. P., Gruenewald, T. L., Gurung, R.A.R., & Updegraff, J. A. (2000). Biobehavioral responses to stress in females: Tend-and-befriend, not fight-or-flight. *Psychological Review, 107,* 411–429.

Thomson, R., & Murachver, T. (2001). Predicting gender from electronic discourse. *British Journal of Social Psychology, 40,* 193–208.

Thorne, B. (1993). *Gender play: Girls and boys in school.* New Brunswick, NJ: Rutgers University Press.

Twenge, J. M. (2001). Changes in women's assertiveness in response to status and roles: A cross-temporal meta-analysis, 1931–1993. *Journal of Personality and Social Psychology, 81,* 133–145.

Wagner, D. G., & Berger, J. (1998). Gender and interpersonal task behaviors: Status expectation accounts. In J. Berger & M. Zelditch, Jr. (Eds.), *Status, power and legitimacy: Strategies and theories* (pp. 229–261). New Brunswick, NJ: Transaction.

West, C., & Zimmerman, D. H. (1987). Doing gender. *Gender and Society, 1,* 125–151.

Wilson, K., & Gallois, C. (1993). *Assertion and its social context.* Oxford: Pergamon Press.

Zimmerman, D. H., & West, C. (1975). Sex roles, interruptions and silences in conversation. In B. Thorne & N. Henley (Eds.), *Language and sex: Difference and dominance* (pp. 105–129). Rowley, MA: Newbury House.

Chapter 8

Feminist Research Methods: Studying Women and Gender

Maureen C. McHugh and Lisa Cosgrove

> Feminist psychology names a strategic space between feminism and psychology. It is not a stable topic area, but rather identifies a site of contest (over what counts as knowledge, who defines this and how it is arrived at).
>
> Burman, 1998, p. 3

Psychology: Help or Hindrance?

In the last quarter of the twentieth century, women, including feminists, flocked to psychology, hoping this form of science would help us to understand ourselves and others, and they planned to use psychology to help others. Yet many scholars and researchers have questioned just how useful psychology can be. Over three decades ago, Weisstein ([1969] 2004) argued that there was so much bias in the psychological literature that psychology did not contribute anything to our understanding of women. Rather than being tools for liberation, psychological theory, research, and practice have often been used to sustain an unjust status quo. For example, Shields (1975) demonstrated how early psychological theories about the nature of women were used to justify the exclusion of women from educational institutions and positions of influence within society. Feminists have criticized psychology both for not studying the lives and experiences of women, and for the development of sexist research theory and practice (McHugh, Koeske, & Frieze, 1986).

Feminists have adopted varied strategies in relation to correcting the sexist biases of psychology, and in their attempts to "use" psychology as a tool for understanding and addressing gender inequality and the oppression of women. Hubbard (1981) encouraged scientists to challenge existing research by "fighting with science's own tools" (p. 216). The guidelines for nonsexist research (McHugh et al., 1986) similarly endorse sex-fair research as a strategy and a solution. Alternatively, feminists like MacKinnon (1990) challenge the usefulness of psychological research, especially sex-difference research, as a means of women's liberation: "Difference is the velvet glove on the iron fist of dominance. If a concept like difference is a conceptual tool of gender and of inequality, it cannot deconstruct the master's house, because it has built it" (MacKinnon, 1990, p. 213).

Reflecting on the divergent strategies endorsed by Hubbard and MacKinnon, we discuss the controversies of conducting sex-difference research. Specifically, we examine the methods endorsed by feminists and question whether those methods can be used to address, illuminate, or challenge questions about the differences between men and women. We ask whether the current methods and paradigms of psychology, and science more generally, are adequate as tools for the study of women and gender. Can the same tools that have been used to justify the subordinate position of women also be used to deconstruct popular and scientific beliefs in sex differences and to advocate for women and gender equity? In addressing these questions we pay particular attention to postmodernism because we believe it is an approach that allows psychologists to incorporate a politically engaged gender analysis into all aspects of the research process (see Schiebinger, 2003).

The Question of Sex Differences

Since its inception in the 1970s, the study of the psychology of women has involved a series of implicit or explicit comparisons of females with males. If women are not a distinct or "special" group, then is the study of or theorizing about them valid or useful? If women are the same as (or similar to) men, then why allocate a special course or status to them? Although the study of the psychology of women has been the study of sex and gender differences, many feminist psychologists and theorists have eschewed the study of sex and gender differences, pointing out the sociopolitical consequences of this perspective, and challenging the adequacy of our methodology to illuminate the meaning of gender and the experience of women. Further, theorists have challenged the category "woman," especially in its use relative to the category "man."

Therefore, it is important to remember that debates about the existence and significance of sex differences are tied to researchers' philosophical, conceptual, and methodological perspectives. Although some psychologists have abandoned the question of sex differences (e.g., Hare-Mustin & Marecek, 1994; Hollway, 1994), others continue to address the question empirically or theoretically. Some, such as Halpern (1994) have argued that to avoid or ignore the controversies over sex differences leaves the debate to ideological (nonfeminist) alternatives. Unger (1998) has commented that although various psychological and feminist positions on sex-difference research have been presented, there are limited publication outlets for the more radical ideas on sex differences. A growing number of psychologists have challenged the dominant paradigm in psychology by questioning the assumption that gender is best represented as dichotomous and traitlike. However, work is less likely to be published when it challenges rather than supports the status quo assumption of discrete gender categories, behaviors, and/or identities. Similarly, studies on gender differences that confirm the null hypothesis are more likely to be rejected by journal editors than are studies that support the notion of gender differences.

This publication imbalance leaves both the general public and the psychological community with the erroneous impression that we have "pure," objective, scientific data to prove that gender differences "really" exist. One of the main reasons why psychologists have devoted a considerable amount of time and energy to criticizing, revising, and using psychological methods is to correct this erroneous impression. In community and classroom lectures and in their publications, feminist psychologists continue this tradition, taking on Gray (1992), Stossel (Breen et al., 1998), and others who emphasize women's and men's differences rather than their similarities. Despite the diversity of epistemological positions on the question of sex differences, scholars agree that there are distinct features of feminist research.

What Is Feminist Research?

A starting principle of feminist research is that psychology should at minimum be nonsexist. Sexist bias in the conduct and interpretation of research violates the scientific principle of objectivity. Yet, many scholars have identified numerous sexist biases in the existing psychological literature. Traditional psychological research is sexist to the extent that it incorporates stereotypic thinking about women or gender. Sexist bias also refers to theories or research that does not have equal relevance to individuals of both sexes, and in which greater attention or value is given to the life experiences of one sex (McHugh et al., 1986). Research practices and methods that produce, promote, or privilege sex/gender inequalities are unacceptable. Most important, the *interpretation* of research has been criticized as biased against women.

Feminist research is research that not only is nonsexist, but also works actively for the benefit and advancement of women (McHugh et al., 1986) and puts gender at the center of one's inquiry. Specifically, feminist research examines the gendered context of women's lives, exposes gender inequalities, empowers women, advocates for social change, and/or improves the status or material reality of women's lives (McHugh & Cosgrove, 1998, 2002). In addition, feminist psychologists value collaboration and participatory action-oriented research that specifically asks for structural (not just individual) change. This means that there must be a commitment to an explicit political agenda and to a consideration of values and assumptions as integral in every stage of the research process. Later we examine these features of feminist research in more detail.

Critique of Traditional Psychology

Experiment as Context

An important aspect of the scientific method is the laboratory experiment. Many feminist psychologists have been critical of the laboratory experiment as a way to learn about experience and behavior. The experimental approach has been critiqued as sterile and artificial, removed from the social context in which behavior is embedded (Sherif, 1979). Alternatively, we can consider the laboratory experiment as a social context itself, a situation in which the experimenter, historically a male, controls the situation, manipulates the independent variable, observes women as the "objects" of study, and evaluates and interprets their behavior based on his own perspective. From this critical perspective, the traditional psychological experiment is a replication of the power dynamics that operate in other social and institutional settings. Men define and control the context, and observe and evaluate the behavior of women. The interests and concerns of the research subjects are subordinated to the interests of those of the researcher and theorist (Unger, 1983). Feminists have argued that the controlled and artificial research situation may elicit more conventional behavior from participants, may inhibit self-disclosure, and may make the situation "unreal" to the participants (McHugh et al., 1986). Even in field research, experimenters may intentionally or inadvertently select the context in which the hypothesized sex difference is most likely to occur.

Confirmatory Bias

Further, critics have suggested that the experimental situation is likely to be constructed in a way in which the researcher's hypothesis about behavior is likely to be confirmed (see McHugh et al., 1986). Results are apt to be interpreted in ways that explain women's subordinate position in society. For example, Caplan and Caplan (1994) and Kimball (1995) point out that research on gender differences in math performance has been carefully constructed to produce differences. The superior performance of girls on classroom tests and in graded work in the classroom during elementary school is dismissed in light of a few studies that suggest that some boys perform better than some girls on particular standardized math tests. Male superior performance is found only when using large postpuberty samples and standardized tests, and with special gifted samples (Kimball, 1995). When the research paradigm is modified, gender differences are reduced, eliminated, and even reversed.

Androcentric Bias in Psychology

Feminists have pointed out various ways in which science that was purported to be empirical and objective was actually biased and political. McHugh et al. (1986) provide extensive descriptions of sexist practices within psychology. Some biases in the research process result from the accumulated common experiences of men. Male researchers have addressed questions about the male experience, mistaking their questions and experiences as generic human experiences and questions. Critics have analyzed the ways in which existing knowledge is limited or distorted because it was generated from a masculine or androcentric (i.e., centered on males) point of view. Our ideas about achievement motivation, for example, are based on a group of male theorists studying the achievements of men. When their theories and methods were not successful in explaining or predicting women's achievements, women, rather than the theories, were viewed as deficient. Such theories are not only sexist but also racist and class-biased. Bem (2004) argues that it is not the differences between men and women that are a problem, but how such differences are interpreted in an androcentric culture. Other feminists, too, have argued that it is the (over)valuing of men and masculinity that creates and justifies sexism.

Giving Women a Voice

Thus, feminists have challenged the pervasive androcentism evidenced by research, which at best speaks for women and at worst silences them. Indeed, one of the most important contributions made by feminist researchers has been giving voice to women's experiences. Carol Gilligan's *In a Different Voice* (1982) and Belenky et al.'s *Women's Ways of Knowing* (1986) are classic examples. The popularity of these books and this perspective is tied to the hope that women's practices and ways of knowing may be a source of empowerment. Focusing on the silencing and suppression of women in patriarchal culture, the metaphor of voice highlights the existence of an authentic feminine self.

However, the notion of a "women's voice" has been harshly criticized because it is based on the assumption that it is possible to identify "a" universal voice that is true of all women (Cosgrove & McHugh, 2000). That is, this position implies that women not only have something different to say (than men), but that they say it in a different way. This position is problematic because it fails to appreciate the differences among women. It is also problematic because much of the research that suggested that women or girls speak in a different voice or use different ways of knowing focused mainly on white, middle-class girls and women.

Feminist Research

Feminist research is not a single method or set of procedures, nor even a unitary approach to the discovery or creation of knowledge. Feminist researchers use any and all of the methods that traditional androcentric researchers use, although they may use these methods differently. For example, they may ask different questions, or listen more carefully to how women describe their experiences. Pluralism and the conduct of research using multiple approaches and methods are preferred to hegemony. Rather than identifying *the methods* of feminist research, scholars have identified dimensions of feminist research.

Values

In contrast to traditional psychology, feminist psychology has paid special attention to the role of the values/biases/assumptions of the researcher on all aspects of the research process. Selection of topics and questions, choice of methods, recruitment of participants, selection of the audience, and the potential uses of the research results are choices made within a sociohistorical context that ultimately influences what we "know" about a topic or a group of people (see Bleir, 1984; Harding 1986, 1991; Keller, 1985; Kelly, Burton, & Regan, 1994; Sherif, 1979). Feminist research recognizes that as a result of unexamined androcentric biases at both the epistemological and the methodological levels, women's experiences have been marginalized and pathologized. Feminist researchers have explicated their value systems realizing that an unbiased, objective position is not possible.

Reflexivity

In feminist research, a commonly used reflective approach is one in which the researcher provides an "intellectual autobiography" (Stanley & Wise, 1993), tracing her interest in relationship with and approach to the questions and to the research participants. Ussher (1992) for example, traces her interest in women's madness to her mother's "mental illness," thus eliminating the illusion that she is a detached or disinterested knower. The reflexive stance may involve "reflecting upon, critically examining, and exploring analytically the research process in an attempt to demonstrate the assumptions about gender (and, increasingly, race, disability, and other oppressive) relations which are built into a specific project" (Maynard, 1992, p. 16).

Collaboration

Based on critiques of the experimental method, feminist research has emphasized the need for a collaborative (rather than objectifying) focus. Feminist research seeks to establish nonhierarchical relations between researcher and respondent, and to respect the experiences and perspectives of the participants (Worrell & Etaugh, 1994). Feminist psychologists challenge the regulatory practices of traditional research by developing more explicitly collaborative practices (see Marks, 1993). Collaboration necessitates an egalitarian context *from the inception of the research process to the distribution of results.* For example, instead of conducting an outcome assessment of a battered women's shelter based on the preferred outcomes suggested by researchers and shelter workers (e.g., how many women have left their abusive relationships?), Sanger (1998) conducted focus groups with battered women on *their* goals and desired outcomes. As Lather (1991) notes, empowerment *and* empirical rigor are best realized through collaborative and participatory efforts.

Research as Advocacy

Although we believe strongly that feminist research must explicitly address issues of social injustice, the issue of doing research as advocacy is complex because it is impossible to know in advance how best to empower women and other marginalized groups. Indeed, many scholars have argued that researchers tend to position themselves as active emancipators and to see participants as passive receivers of emancipation (see, e.g., Lather, 1991). Conducting and using research for advocacy requires the researcher to engage in critical reflection on his/her epistemic commitments. Taken-for-granted assumptions about the meaning of validity and objectivity in psychological research are called into question. In this way, feminists strive to design studies that not only avoid objectifying participants but also foster a particular kind of interaction. This has been referred to as participatory or action research. Participatory researchers work with communities to develop "knowledge" that can be useful in advocacy and provide the basis for system change. In terms of doing research with and for women, findings must be developed collaboratively and, whenever possible, they should be used to inform public policy.

Challenging Dichotomies

A common theme in feminist research is the challenge of dichotomous thinking. Dichotomous portrayals of men and women result from the dominant research paradigm in psychology (Thorne, 1990). The sexually dimorphic view influences the way questions are raised, the methods of data collection, and the interpretation of data within psychology and other disciplines (Epstein, 1988). For example, McHugh and her colleagues (1986) reported that misinterpretation of statistically significant sex differences frequently occurs in empirical research on sex differences. Even the most statistically significant differences between men and women are not, in reality, dichotomous. Yet authors of scholarly publications (the very ones that are quickly picked up by the popular media) use language that portrays males and females as dichotomous.

Feminist theorists have argued that difference is a problematic and paradoxical way to construct gender. In contemporary society and in psychological theory and research, women are defined and understood in relation to men. Arguments about whether women are like men or unlike men still proceed with men as the standard of comparison (Rhode, 1990). Thus, both the minimalist and the maximalist positions are androcentric and dualistic (Kimball, 1995). Neither position effectively challenges gender inequality, and both obscure the complexity of human behavior. The current terms of the gender-difference debate are deeply wedded to certain methodological and epistemological positions. The ability to challenge the dichotomous construction of gender, and other existing dichotomies such as objective versus subjective, requires feminist researchers to consider carefully the methodological and epistemological bases of research.

Methods, Methodology, and Epistemology

In her argument against the idea of a single feminist method of research, Harding (1986) encourages us to understand the distinctions among methods, methodology, and epistemology. Methods are the concrete techniques for gathering evidence or data, such as experiments, interviews, and surveys. Methodology is the study of methods, the philosophical position on how research should proceed. Epistemology is the most central issue for feminist research, according to Harding (1986), Stanley and Wise (1993), and others. It involves the study of answers to the question How can we know? Epistemology is a framework for specifying what constitutes knowledge and how we know it. An epistemological framework specifies not only what knowledge is and how to recognize it, but also who the knowers are, and by what means someone becomes a knower. Epistemological frameworks also outline the means by which competing knowledge claims are adjudicated (Stanley & Wise, 1993). Harding (1991) outlines three feminist epistemological positions: feminist empiricism, feminist standpoint theory, and social constructionism.

Feminist Empiricists

Feminist empiricists employ the methods of science to study questions about women and gender. Sex-difference research, or research comparing the attitudes, behaviors, and experiences of women with those of men, would be empiricist, some of it feminist. Research designed to measure concepts such as gender roles, sexist attitudes, and loving and liking would be feminist empiricism. Most of the gender-related research reported in mainstream and feminist journals is empirical.

In the feminist empiricist position, social biases are conceptualized as prejudices that are based on false beliefs and hostile attitudes. These prejudices are seen as affecting all aspects of the conceptualization and conduct of research, including which questions are asked. The operation of sexist and androcentric biases is seen as influencing both methods and methodology. However, the operation of such biases is seen as bad science, and good science is seen both as a possibility and as leading to liberation or gender equality. Feminist empiricists attempt to produce a feminist science, a "better" science that more accurately reflects the world than the incomplete and distorted accounts provided by traditional androcentric psychology. Feminist empiricists criticize the system, but only in a corrective or revisionist way.

Deaux (1984) and other feminists have argued that empirical research on sex-related differences has been effectively used to refute the contention that differences between men and women are universal, significant, and stable. Feminist empiricists from Hollingworth (1914) to Eagly (1994) have used the scientific method to try to convince theorists and the general public that stereotypes about women and men are inaccurate and dysfunctional. In published guidelines for the conduct of nonsexist research in psychology, McHugh and her colleagues (1986) addressed how we might continue to conduct research while minimizing the most glaring methodological errors. For example, they recommended that the experimenter test for gender differences and consider whether demonstrated differences reveal gendered aspects of the research situation. They further encouraged researchers to consider how the construction of the experimental context might differentially impact the behavior or responses of male and female participants.

On the other hand, attempting to conduct nonsexist or feminist empiricist research may be viewed as perpetuating mainstream psychology (Burman, 1998). Feminist empiricists have been criticized for "collud(ing) with positivism in retaining a commitment to existing methods and tools of investigation" (Burman, 1998, p. 3). Specialists in the psychology of women also may contribute to maintaining a gender ghetto within psychology. Yet, by privileging gender, feminist empiricists may presume commonality among women (Spelman, 1988) and contribute to our failure to understand "how other marginalized positions enter into experiences of gender" (Burman, 1998, p. 3).

Standpoint Theories

As previously noted, feminists have criticized psychology and science in general as producing knowledge that is distorted or biased because it was generated from a male or androcentric perspective. Our ideas about both achievement and aggression are limited by the tradition of males studying males. Such biases and distortions are difficult for men themselves to recognize. Even women, as part of the gender system, have difficulty recognizing how patriarchy influences our conceptions of what is "natural" (Johnson, 1997). Feminism provides the ability to view a patriarchal system through an alternative or shifted lens. Thus, feminist criticism of science as biased leads to recognition of the importance of perspective or standpoint.

Researchers who advocate the use of traditional scientific method maintain that scientific inquiry should be conducted by a disinterested or detached individual, one who is able to disengage from the assumptions about the nature of reality shared by members of a society. Yet, who is not grounded in the shared perspectives of a culture, thereby incorporating such assumptions about world into his or her research? According to standpoint theory, individuals who are outsiders to a culture or group are more likely to recognize the assumptions of the culture. People from outside the United States have a unique perspective on American experiences. Similarly, outsiders to the dominant group of white, middle-class males have a unique perspective to offer on the experience of living in a patriarchy. Individuals who are not members of the dominant group have an advantage in being able to view reality from an alternative perspective. In feminist standpoint perspective, women's ways of knowing or women's voices are different from and potentially superior to men's ways of knowing.

The idea that women can bring a special perspective to research has been labeled the feminist standpoint theory. According to feminist standpoint theory, knowledge about women and gender that comes from a feminist perspective is more complete and less distorted than knowledge gained from the traditional social science perspective. Feminist research is viewed as superior in that it at least attempts to explicate its gender assumptions.

Like feminist empiricism, the feminist standpoint theory accepts the existence of a true reality and adopts the basic methods of science as a means of knowing that reality. As members of a subordinate group, women can (better) comprehend the reality of domination and subordination. Recognition of a feminist standpoint raises the probability of other standpoints. Fine (1992) concludes that a single woman's or feminist position is not plausible. Collins (1990) and hooks (1989) have argued that as black women they offer a unique perspective on the world, different from that of white women. Similarly, queer theory argues for the unique perspective of members of the gay, lesbian, bisexual, and transgender community. Legitimate claims to alternative perspectives or worldviews challenge the assumption that there is a single reality that can be discovered using scientific methods.

As feminist researchers, we challenge the implicit values in traditional research that render women as Other and conflate difference with deficiency. However, substituting a gynocentric position, which privileges a distinctly feminine voice, way of being, knowing, or solving moral dilemmas, continues to reify the categories "men" and "women." Therefore, in our attempts to correct psychology's androcentric perspective, we must avoid retelling the same story that essentializes masculinity and femininity (Bohan, 1993; Hare-Mustin, 1994). ("Essentialism" here refers to the location of gender and gender differences as originating or residing within men and women.)

The Postmodern Alternative

An alternative approach to traditional psychological research, a postmodern approach, is considered here in terms of how well it avoids the dualistic and essentialist pitfalls of traditional research on gender difference. This approach challenges traditional notions of subjectivity. In doing so, postmodernism allows feminist psychologists interested in questions of gender difference to challenge the current terms of the gender-difference debate. Specifically, scholars who describe their work as informed by a postmodern epistemology critique the dominant paradigm in psychology as rooted in a foundationalist perspective that espouses the belief that the search for "truths" about experience is an achievable and desirable goal of the social sciences. Hence, postmodern scholars critique the following as impossible projects: the attempt to discover universal truths about human behavior, the belief in the grand narratives of science, and the distinctions between subject and object and between facts and values (Burr, 1995; Cosgrove & McHugh, 2002; Lyotard, [1984] 1993). When psychologists work within a postmodern framework, they are more cognizant of, and reflective about, *the construction* of categories and concepts within the field, especially insofar as these constructions are made to seem natural. Postmodernism is a project that reveals the socially constructed nature of reality and the varied interests that are served by particular constructions (Layton, 1998). It is an approach that brings epistemological, methodological, and political issues to the foreground by calling into question the beliefs and practices that allow social scientists to assume the validity of the categories they use. This attitude of "reflective skepticism" (McPeck, as cited in Gray, 1992) provides a formidable challenge to the science/politics dichotomy, a dichotomy that sustains the belief that scientific research is value-free, objective, and, hence, apolitical (Prilleltensky, 1989).

Feminist empiricists believe in the ability of science to provide value-neutral data and objective findings. Feminist standpoint theorists privilege women's ways of behaving and knowing. In contrast, feminist postmodernists call into question the belief in an objective world and are harshly critical of the belief in privileged standpoints. Feminist postmodernism recognizes that science is *never* innocent (Lather, 1991), methodology is inescapably political, and thus epistemological issues are always at stake. Therefore, by taking a postmodern perspective, we believe that if we continue to study differences in men's and women's experience as gender differences (as opposed, for example, to differences in power), we risk essentializing gender. In turn, this promotes a view of women as a homogeneous group and reinforces the very mechanisms of oppression against which we are fighting. It would be more helpful to study gendered experience without assuming that gender is a trait that can be measured. Similarly, the assumption that researchers can uncover a "woman's" voice, standpoint, or way of knowing is also problematized.

Feminist theorists are increasingly rejecting essentialist perspectives on gender, and they are advocating a view of gender as a construction, that is, gender is produced or performed in a series of interactions and activities (Bohan, 1993). In other words, individuals do not "have" gender, they "do" gender (Bohan, 1993; West & Zimmerman; 1987). Butler (1990) theorized that gender identities are not internal essences but external performances. Unfortunately, however, repeated performances in compliance with gender norms (e.g., smiling) or repeated associations with situations (e.g., beauty parlors) and behaviors (e.g., wearing a dress) result in the conceptualization of a set of activities that appear to represent an internal essence of the individual (i.e., femininity).

Femininity is unarguably a construct; it has been constructed differently in different eras and by different segments of the culture. However, if we continue to essentialize femininity as residing within women (and men) and to reify the construct by measuring it, then femininity will continue to be defined and measured in relation to masculinity (see, e.g., Bem, 1993). Understanding femininity as a traitlike attribute that exists in women leads researchers to make universalist claims about women.

Thus, in order for feminist research to move forward in a politically viable and engaged way, we need to challenge these positivist beliefs that continue to pervade feminist research. In this chapter we have argued that positivist assumptions can be evidenced in both quantitative and qualitative methodologies. Feminist psychologists must go beyond a simple call for the integration of quantitative and qualitative methods, and start focusing on conceptual and epistemological issues. Postmodernism can be very useful to feminism because it helps us ferret out positivist assumptions, especially the assumption that researchers have a privileged status—that they are implicitly authorized (through their statistical or qualitative analyses) to uncover truths about women's experiences (Nelson, 1993). In contrast to the belief that narrative or statistical truths can be found, we maintain the impossibility of any method as a guarantor of truth. Postmodernism reveals the ways in which methods construct and produce knowledge; methods produce certain views and marginalize others.

Lessons from Physics

A postmodern epistemological stance is highly congruent with insights coming from the field of quantum physics. In fact, Karen Barad (1995, 1998, 2003), whose work is influenced by insights from Neils Bohr's philosophy–physics, maintains that there are many aspects of quantum theory that are compatible with feminist theory and with postmodernism. Specifically, both Bohr and Barad argue against a Newtonian worldview—a view that that privileges deterministic notions of causality and experience, and assumes that distinctions between observer and observed, between object of measurement and agency of observation, are "true" or real distinctions. In contrast to this Newtonian view, Bohr claimed that Heisenberg's uncertainty principle (what is referred to in the physics community as an inherent discontinuity in any measurement) has far-reaching epistemological and methodological implications. Briefly, the uncertainty principle refers to the fact that position and momentum are *not* inherent attributes of independently existing objects. Rather, position and momentum have meaning only when an apparatus is used to measure them (Barad, 2003, p. 814). That is, according to Barad and Bohr, position and momentum *acquire meaning only in context,* for there is an inseparability from the object (e.g., position) being observed and the agency of observation (e.g., apparatus used to measure position). To oversimplify a bit, this means that *what we measure for determines what we find.* Hence, it is not surprising that often, when researchers measure for gender differences, they "find" them. But these "findings" of gender difference should not be interpreted as "objective," "true," or universal. Such findings are, from a quantum perspective, more accurately understood as context-dependent constructions. Indeed, Heisenberg's uncertainty principle "is an epistemic principle—*it lays down the limits of what we can know* (Murdoch, cited in Barad, 1995, p. 53; emphasis added).

Therefore, taking Heisenberg's finding seriously requires both the "natural" and the "social" scientist to reject the distinction between observer and observed, and knower and known (Barad, 2003; Bohan, 1990; Cosgrove, in press). Also, as Barad emphasized, *taking these ideas seriously does not negate the importance of causality, validity, or even objectivity in research.* Rather, it means asking different kinds of questions and reconceptualizing commonly accepted terms such as "objectivity." For example, theoretical concepts such as objectivity would no longer be seen as ideational, nor would they be seen as universally defined abstract concepts (Barad, 2003). Similarly, validity from this standpoint would no longer be seen as a "commodity that can be purchased with techniques. . . . Rather, validity is, like integrity, character, and quality, to be assessed relative to purpose and circumstances" (Brinberg & McGrath, cited in Brydon-Miller & Tolman, 1997).

Taking Bohr's and Barad's views seriously may help feminist researchers to avoid dichotomous "either/or" thinking by being more reflective about the meaning of the concepts they invoke to justify their findings. That is, within the current confines of the empiricist/standpoint and quantitative/qualitative debates, the researchers' assumptions about validity, causality, and reality are generally not discussed. Researchers tend to frame their questions in a way that assumes that concepts such as validity, causality, and experience are universally defined. The debate centers around questions like "Are qualitative methods valid?" Little attention is paid to the beliefs that ground the use of terms such as "validity." Taken-for-granted definitions of these terms are accepted, and thus concepts such as validity and experience remain undertheorized.

Alternative Approaches to Studying
Women and Gender

In this last section we introduce a number of alternative or innovative approaches to psychological research that identify alternative strategic spaces between feminism and psychology. The approaches described below are quite diverse. However, they are all congruent with the postmodern, post-Newtonian emphasis on the importance of incorporating a politically engaged gender analysis into all aspects (e.g., theories, practices, and policies) of psychological science relations (Schiebinger, 2003). Thus, in analyzing women's accounts, a social constructionist approach demands a sophisticated analysis of power (e.g., analyzing which—and why—certain discourses are dominant). The interview and analysis are less about discovering "truths" and more about identifying dominant and marginalized discourses so that people are better equipped to resist oppressive discourses. For example, a psychologist interested in the experience of motherhood would first recognize that the discourses of motherhood shape and confine one's understanding of oneself as a mother. The analysis of the data on the experience of being a mother would be contextualized in terms of how discursive and material practices work to produce certain identities (e.g., "supermom," mother as the primary agent responsible for her children's emotional well being, etc.) while marginalizing others. For example, identifying and interrogating the ways in which the policy discourses about a particular problem (e.g., homelessness) do or do not reflect the actual needs and experiences of groups affected by the problem (e.g., homeless women) would be one way to incorporate discourse analysis into feminist psychology (Cosgrove, 1999).

Narratives as Research

The use of narratives as research is compatible with a postmodern or social constructionist perspective. Narratives are the stories people tell about their lives. Narrative research focuses on the ways in which individuals choose to tell their stories, in relation to the frameworks or master narratives provided by the culture for organizing and describing life experiences (Rosenwald & Ochberg, 1992; Sarbin, 1986). Master narratives refer to the cultural frameworks that limit and structure the way that stories are told in order to support the status quo and the dominant groups' perspective on reality. Storytelling can be used, however, to disrupt or challenge accepted perceptions and master narratives. Stories are used to communicate experience, but they also can articulate ideology and can move people to action (Romero & Stewart, 1999).

Feminists have argued that a narrative approach can be employed to further feminist goals. Narratives are discussed as an innovative method (Gergen, Chrisler, & LoCicero, 1999) used by feminists to reveal cultural constructions. Recognizing, resisting, or deconstructing the master narratives that have been used to restrict or limit the experiences of women is one feminist form of narrative research (Romero & Stewart, 1999). Other examples of feminist narrative research include Frantz and Stewart's (1994) edited volume of narratives in which they explore the way in which narratives "create" a psychology of women. Josselson (1996) has examined the construction of identity and gender through the narrative.

Romero and Stewart (1999) view the consciousness-raising groups of the feminist movement as a form of storytelling from which women reached new understandings of the relation of their personal stories to cultural institutions and practices. Thus, storytelling can lead to "ideological transformations and to political mobilization" (Romero & Stewart, 1999, p. xii). Storytelling is seen as a way of redressing the exclusion of women's experience and of breaking the silence of women, and as a way of giving women a voice for the expression and analysis of their own experience (Romero & Stewart, 1999). In this spirit, Romero and Stewart provide narratives in which women break the silence, talk back, and reveal the complexity of women's lives. They argue that social transformative work is done through the telling of previously untold stories, and through women's naming and analysis of their own experience.

From a postmodern perspective, life is multifaceted and fragmented, and a postmodern position challenges us to recognize that there are multiple meanings for an event, and especially multiple perspectives on a person's life. Narrative research reveals our desire to provide a unified and coherent story and to gloss over or ignore paradoxes, inconsistencies, and contradictions in women's lives (Cabello, 1999; Franz & Stewart, 1994). The challenge for feminist researchers is to find methods for including and representing dualities and contradictions present in women's lives (Cabello, 1999). Our lives are not lived as linear progress, and we have complex rather than single, unified identities (Harding, 1986). Cabello (1999) describes the methodological challenge of including the incoherence and contradictions in narrative research. She also discusses the tensions between the researcher's interpretation and the subject's active participation in the telling and interpretation of her life story.

Focus Groups

Wilkinson (1999) argues for the use of focus groups as a feminist method, in that focus groups can meet the feminist goal of examining women's behavior in naturalistic social contexts in a way that shifts the power from the researcher to the participants. A focus group might be described as an informal discussion among a group of people that is focused on a specific topic and is either observed or taped by the researcher. Focus groups avoid the artificiality of many psychological methods. They mimic the everyday experience of talking with friends, family, and others in our social networks. The focus group itself may be seen as a social context, and at the same time as a parallel to the social context in which people typically operate.

People establish and maintain relationships, engage in activities, and make decisions through daily interactions with other people. Focus groups may use these pre-existing or naturally occurring groups, or may set up groups of people who know each other (Wilkinson, 1999). For example, Press (1991) studied female friends talking about abortion by having them meet in one woman's home to view and discuss an episode of a popular television show. The focus group can thus avoid artificiality by making naturalistic observations of the process of communication in everyday social interaction (Wilkinson, 1999). More important, the focus group provides the opportunity to observe how people form opinions, influence each other, and generate mean ing in the context of discussion with others (Wilkinson, 1999). For feminists who see the self as relational (e.g., Gilligan), or identity as constructed (e.g., Kitzinger, 1994), the focus group can be an ideal method. In focus groups, the influence of the researcher is minimized as women in the group speak for themselves and voice their own concerns and themes. Focus groups may also provide an opportunity to access the views of individuals who have been underrepresented in traditional methods (Wilkinson, 1999). They may lead to consciousness-raising, or to the articulation of solutions to women's problems (Wilkinson, 1999).

Feminist Phenomenological Approaches

A phenomenological approach can perhaps best be characterized by its commitment to the articulation of individuals' experience through description rather than hypothesis testing. The advantage of a phenomenological perspective is that it does not sacrifice an empirical perspective in order to render itself relevant to human science research. One of the most fundamental tenets of a phenomenological approach is that consciousness (or we could use the term "experience," which is more familiar to contemporary psychologists) is the proper subject matter of psychology. A phenomenological approach represents a paradigm shift; it is in this sense that phenomenology is not simply another methodology that can be used by feminist researchers. The paradigm shift may be described as one that emphasizes the importance of an individual's lived experience as the proper subject matter for psychology; as such, it allows researchers to investigate the descriptive differences in men's and women's experiences *without essentializing gender.* Since it is beyond the scope of this chapter to go into detail regarding method, we recommend Cosgrove (1987), Fischer and Wertz (1979), Giorgi (1985), and Reitz (1999) for detailed descriptions of phenomenological methodology.

Feminism and phenomenology share a commitment to creating a space in which to hear women's stories. Both feminist and phenomenologically grounded research allow for an examination of the ways in which gender (along with race, class, and culture) plays a key role in shaping women's experiences. In addition, both share the commitment to test theory against experience. Indeed, rather than advocate hypothesis testing, a phenomenologically informed psychology suggests instead that theory should be generated from data (i.e., individuals' experiences). Recognizing the limits of laboratory-based research, emphasizing the importance of listening to individuals' experiences (prior to and apart from one's theoretical or ideological biases), and appreciating the possibilities of a descriptive science are critical to both feminist and phenomenological projects. As a growing number of feminist psychologists have noted, relying, epistemologically and methodologically, on quantification and measurement to the exclusion of life-world description makes for a rather hollow science and produces alienated rather than emancipatory knowledge.

Both feminists and phenomenologists define research as "a dialogue between the researcher and the research participant" (Garko, 1999, p. 170). Giorgi (1985) could just as easily have been speaking about feminist psychology when he said the following about phenomenological psychology:

> [A] research situation is conceived of as one in which two humans engage but relate differently to the same situation, and because they relate differently, the meanings experienced by each in the same situation differ, and one of the best ways to find out the respective meanings is by having the participants enter into a dialogue and systematically and rigorously pursue all the implications of the different perspectives on

the same situation . . . a full comprehension should tap into both perspectives (experimenter and subject) as well as their interaction. (p. 78)

The phenomenological approach emphasizes the inevitable unity among self, world, and others, and thus it allows the researcher to hear women's experiences as contextualized within the larger social order. Phenomenology can lead the researcher "back to concrete experience in which sociopolitical meanings . . . are experienced as lived-through phenomena, rather than as mere subjective additions to experience, or conversely, as political structures removed from experience" (Nelson, 1989, p. 227).

Consistent with a feminist research perspective, a phenomenological one demands that we hear, describe, and try to articulate the meaning of women's experiences. The researcher can hear stories that have been marginalized and/or silenced. It is in this sense that a phenomenological approach demands respectful listening (Keen, 1975), and thus objectivity becomes redefined as "fidelity to phenomena" (Garko, 1999, p. 170).

Action Research

In contrast to the traditional valuation of theoretical and pure science over applied science, some feminist psychologists have challenged the dichotomous view of applied versus theoretical research, arguing that theory is political and action has theoretical implications (Hoshmand & O'Byrne 1996; Reinharz, 1992). For example, Hoshmand and O'Byrne view action research as consistent with postmodern and postpositivist revisions of science; action research takes an explicitly contextual focus, and thus action researchers may be less likely to commit the "errors" of essentialism and universalism. In a very real sense, then, we might say that all research is action-oriented, but what varies (and ultimately what matters) is whose agenda is being served. Or, as Rappaport and Stewart (1997) note, "When justice is the goal we must ask, 'who gets to decide what is just?' " (p. 306).

Toward that end, we must not be afraid to challenge theories and research which may essentialize women's problems, and therefore contribute to victim blame and to continuing efforts to change the individual. For example, McHugh and her colleagues (McHugh, 1990, 1993; McHugh, Frieze, & Browne, 1992) critique the psychological literature on battered women as not addressing the questions battered women most want answered, as not providing clear benefit to battered women, and as potentially contributing to a victim-blame perspective. Fine (1992) documents that authors of articles published in *The Psychology of Women Quarterly* "psychologized the structural forces that construct women's lives by offering internal explanations for social conditions, and through the promotion of individualistic change strategies, authors invited women to alter some aspect of self in order to transform social arrangements" (p. 6).

An example of more emancipatory and more beneficial research may be found in Gondolf's work (1985, 1993) evaluating the mandatory arrests of batterers and the effectiveness of interventions with groups of batterers, and in Bowker's (1984) research which examined help-seeking behavior in battered women. Rather than the helpless, passive victims described in interview-based research focusing on personal histories, Bowker's focus allows us to see these women as active help seekers, *resisting the victim role and repeatedly requesting help from a variety of individuals and agencies, and characterizing the social agencies they contacted as not very helpful.* The overarching question in developing action-oriented research is, How can our research be designed and carried out so that *social systems*, and not just individuals, are problematized and asked to change?

Satirical Empiricism

Satirical empiricism was introduced by McHugh and Cosgrove (2002) as a method for exposing biases in psychological research. It is described as an attempt to transcend patriarchal perspectives on gender by using science's own tools in laughter. Satirical empiricism may be described as an empirical method that exposes gender assumptions and reveals the "real" nature of essentialistic and universalist thinking in psychological research; it exposes folly through exaggeration, ridicule, sarcasm, and irony or reversal. As introduced by McHugh and Cosgrove, it involves the application of satire to the research process. Satire here implies both critcism and *corrective purpose.* The exaggeration involved in satire parallels the exaggeration of gender differences inherent in psychological research, and exposes, through reversal or extension, the hidden assumptions in both the minimalist and the maximalist traditions. By employing satirical empiricism it is possible to demonstrate that gendered behavior is determined (or elicited) by context, and it is possible to "deconstruct" (i.e., reveal the hidden assumptions in) existing research projects. For example, as a counterpoint to the numerous psychological positions on women's emotionality, a satirical empiricist might design an experimental context in which adult men (but not women) are brought to tears. It may involve creating a situation in which men are totally frustrated by their own powerlessness in the situation, or one in which they are shamed or embarrassed to the point of tears.

It is not only in the construction (or the selection) of the context that researchers determine their results, but also in the selection of the sample. Considering the emphasis on the samples used to demonstrate gender differences in math (as reviewed above), a satirical empiricist approach might be to use the groups of white, middle-class, precocious teens (from the math studies) as a sample to examine gender differences in aggressive play. Another example of satirical empiricism would be to conduct research on work values using a sample of African American, middle-aged lesbians. Objecting to that sample as not being representative of the general population exposes the (implied) position that if you used a college sample that was predominantly white and whose sexual orientation is not specified, the results could have been applied to nonwhite or nonheterosexual individuals. Discomfort with drawing universal conclusions based on data collected from African American women suggests there is something gendered or racial about the context or the constructs under study. Such research exposes the universalizing tendencies masked by cultural belief systems when the research "subjects" are all white and male. Satirical empiricism could be used to deconstruct the androcentric assumptions that result in the privileging of certain comparison groups over others. For example, one might study the difficulties or pathologies experienced by children raised by stay-at-home working-class mothers without any comparison groups, or as compared with children adopted by professional, affluent lesbians.

On Choice of Methods

The approaches included here are by no means a definitive set of feminist approaches or of innovative approaches. Crawford and Kimmel (1999) argue that some of them, such as discourse analysis, may not even be innovative. The decision on which approaches to include, such as the researcher's decision of which research to conduct, is based on our own experiences, expertise, and interests. Practicing feminist reflexivity, we might offer the explanation that Lisa Cosgrove was trained in the phenomenological method at Duquesne University, where she earned her degree in clinical psychology. Lisa is deeply immersed in critical psychology. Maureen McHugh was trained in social psychology and the feminist empiricist tradition at the University of Pittsburgh. Coming from an Irish American, working-class background, Maureen has been known to be sarcastic. Both of us have moved to postmodern, constructionist positions, though not identical ones. We see our review here, like any research study or line of research, as not reflecting a single reality, feminist research, but rather as representing the multifaceted, complex, contextual, and sometimes fragmented, contradictory, and imperfect phenomenon that is feminist research in the United States in 2004.

Conclusions

> No one—scientist or otherwise—likes to be criticized: the best way to
> change a particular aspect of science is to do it better than those you
> wish to criticize.
>
> Schiebinger, 2003, p. 861

Feminists have a long tradition of challenging the theories, methods, and "truths" traditional psychologists believe to be real, objective, and value-free. In an attempt to transform psychology, feminists have developed many innovative ideas, methods, and critiques. However, changing the science of psychology so that it can better attend to issues of social injustice is neither an easy nor a straightforward task. Transforming psychology means that we must not be afraid of self-critique; we must not shy away from deconstructing feminist psychology (Burman, 1998). We hope that the criticisms outlined in this chapter, and the suggestions we have made for future research, will contribute—albeit in a small way—to doing science better and making psychology more useful.

In this chapter we have offered the challenge of resisting dichotomous thinking and have encouraged the practice of taking multiple perspectives. Thus, it is no longer necessary to decide between a feminist empiricist and a social constructivist position, or to argue over surveys or focus groups as the "right" method. A dialectical approach calls for us to move between methodological and epistemological positions, and to use multiple methods. Decisions about methods are based not on which method will uncover the truth, but on which methods will provide functional "knowledge." Similarly, Cacioppo, Semin, and Berntson (2004) advocate an iterative deployment of scientific realism and scientific instrumentalism as a way to promote more rigorous and useful science.

Like Kimball (1995), we argue for the practice of double visions with regard to feminist theory and research on gender. One might choose a particular position in a certain context, or prefer a given perspective on gender, but practicing double visions means that neither alternative is foreclosed. In the practice of double visions, feminist psychologists would recognize the partialness of any perspective, and respect theoretical diversity. Having a double vision, we resist making a choice and maintain a tension between/among the alternative positions and practices. We encourage the practice of double visions with regard to gender research—to shift between and among varied theoretical, empirical, and methodological positions, without foreclosing or privileging any particular perspective.

References

Barad, K. (1995). A feminist approach to teaching quantum physics. In Sue V. Rosser (Ed.), *Teaching the majority: Breaking the gender barrier in science, mathematics, and engineering* (pp. 43–76). New York: Teachers College Press.

Barad, K. (1998). Getting real: Technoscientific practices and the materialization of reality. *Differences: A Journal of Feminist Culture Studies, 10,* 87–128.

Barad, K. (2003). Posthumanist performativity: Toward an understanding of how matter comes to matter. *Signs, 28,* 801–831.

Belenky, M. F., Clinchy, B. M., Goldberger, N. R., & Tarule, J. M. (1986). *Women's ways of knowing: The development of self, voice, and mind.* New York: Basic Books.

Bem, S. (1993). *The lenses of gender.* New Haven, CT: Yale University Press.

Bem, S. (2004). Transforming the debate on sexual inequality: From biological difference to institutionalized androcentrism. In J. C. Chrisler, C. Golden, & P. Rozee (Eds.), *Lectures on the psychology of women* (pp. 3–15). Boston: McGraw-Hill.

Bleir, R. (1984). *Science and gender: A critique of biology and its theories on women.* New York: Pergamon.

Bohan, J. (1993). Regarding gender: Essentialism, constructionism and feminist psychology. *Psychology of Women Quarterly, 17,* 5–21.

Bowker, L. (1984). Coping with wife abuse: Personal and social networks. In A. R. Roberts (Ed.), *Battered women and their families* (pp. 168–191). New York: Springer.

Breen, J., Gustafson, N., Messina, R. (producers), & Stossel, J. (host/writer). (1998, January 17). *Men, women and the sex difference: Boys and girls are different.* ABC News special. Available from MPI Home Video, Oak Forest, IL.

Brydon-Miller, M., & Tolman, D. L. (1997). Engaging the process of transformation. *Journal of Social Issues, 53,* 803–810.

Burman, E. (1997). Minding the gap: Positivism, psychology, and the politics of qualitative methods. *Journal of Social Issues, 53*(4), 785–801.

Burr, V. (1995). *An introduction to social constructionism.* New York: Routledge.

Butler, J. (1990). *Gender trouble: Feminism and the subversion of identity.* New York: Routledge.

Cabello, R. (1999). Negotiating the life narrative: A dialogue with an African American social worker. *Psychology of Women Quarterly, 23*(2), 309–322.

Cacioppo, J. T., Semin, G. R., & Berntson, G. G. (2004). Realism, instrumentalism, and scientific symbiosis: Psychological theory as search for truth and the discovery of solutions. *American Psychologist, 59*(4), 214–223.

Caplan, P., & Caplan, J. (1994). *Thinking critically about research on sex and gender.* New York: HarperCollins.

Collins, P. H. (1990). *Black feminist thought: Knowledge, consciousness and the politics of empowerment.* Boston: Unwin Hyman.

Cosgrove, L. (1987). *The aftermath of sexual assault: An existential–phenomenological investigation.* Unpublished Ph.D. dissertation, Duquesne University, Pittsburgh, PA.

Cosgrove, L. (1999, March). *Developing social action research for homeless women.* Paper presented to the Association for Women in Psychology, Providence, RI.

Cosgrove, L. (In press). Toward some rapprochement between social construction-ism and phenomenology: Implications for researching women's experiences of emotional distress. *Feminism and Psychology.*

Cosgrove, L., & McHugh, M. (2002). Deconstructing difference: Conceptualizing feminist research from within the postmodern. In L. H. Collins, M. R. Dun-lap, & J. C. Chrisler (Eds.), *Charting a new course for feminist psychology* (pp. 20–36). Westport, CT: Praeger.

Crawford, M., & Kimmel, E. (1999, March). Promoting methodological diversity in feminist research. *Psychology of Women Quarterly, 23*(1), pp. 1–6.

Deaux, K. (1984). From individual differences to social categories: Analysis of a decade's research on gender. *American Psychologist, 39,* 105–116.

Eagly, A. H. (1994). On comparing men and women. *Feminism and Psychology, 4,* 501–506.

Epstein, C. F. (1988). *Deceptive distinctions: Sex, gender, and the social order.* New Haven, CT: Yale University Press.

Fine, M. (1992). *Disruptive voices: The possibilities of feminist research.* Ann Arbor: University of Michigan Press.

Fischer, C. T., & Wertz, F. (1979). Empirical–phenomenological analyses of being criminally victimized. In A. Giorgi, R. Knowles, & D. L. Smith (Eds.), *Existential phenomenological perspectives in psychology: Exploring the breadth of human experience* (pp. 99–112). New York: Plenum.

Franz, C. E., & Stewart, A. J. (Eds.). (1994). *Women creating lives: Identities, re-silience, and resistance.* Boulder, CO: Westview Press.

Garko, M. (1999). Existential phenomenology and feminist research. *Psychology of Women Quarterly, 23,* 170–175.

Gergen, M., Chrisler, J. C., & LoCicero, A. (1999). Innovative methods: Resources for research, publishing and teaching. *Psychology of Women Quarterly, 23*(2), 431–456.

Gilligan, C. (1982). *In a different voice: Psychological theory and women's development.* Cambridge, MA: Harvard University Press.

Giorgi, A. (Ed.). (1985). *Phenomenology and psychological research.* Pittsburgh, PA: Duquesne University Press.

Gondolf, E. W. (1985). *Men who batter: An integrated approach for stopping wife abuse.* Holmes Beach, FL: Learning Publications.

Gondolf, E. W. (1993). Treating the batterer. In M. Hansen & M. Harway (Eds.), *Battering and family therapy: A feminist perspective* (pp. 105–118). Newbury Park, CA: Sage.

Gray, J. (1992). *Men are from Mars, women are from Venus.* New York: HarperCollins.

Halpern, D. (1994). Stereotypes, science, censorship, and the study of sex differences. *Feminism and Psychology, 4,* 523–530.

Harding, S. (1986). *The science question in feminism.* Ithaca, NY: Cornell University Press.

Harding, S. (1991). *Whose science? Whose knowledge?: Thinking from women's lives.* Ithaca, NY: Cornell University Press.

Hare-Mustin, R. (1994). Discourses in the mirrored room: A postmodern analysis of therapy. *Family Process, 33,* 19–35.

Hare-Mustin, R. T., & Marecek, J. (1994). Asking the right questions: Feminist psychology and sex differences. *Feminism and Psychology, 4,* 531–537.

Hollway, W. (1989). *Subjectivity and method in psychology: Gender, meaning, and science.* London: Sage.

hooks, b. (1989). *Talking back: Thinking feminist, thinking black.* Boston: South End Press.

Hoshmand, L., & O'Bryne, K. (1996). Reconsidering action research as a guiding metaphor for professional psychology. *Journal of Community Psychology, 24,* 185–200.

Hubbard, R. (1981). The emperor doesn't wear any clothes: The impact of feminism on biology. In D. Spender (Ed.), *Men's studies modified: The impact of feminism on academic disciplines* (pp. 214–245). Oxford: Pergamon Press.

Johnson, A. G. (1997). *The gender knot: Unraveling our patriarchal legacy.* Philadelphia: Temple University Press.

Josselson, R. (1996). *Revising herself: The story of women's identity from college to midlife.* New York: Oxford University Press.

Keen, E. (1975). *A primer in phenomenological psychology.* New York: Holt, Rinehart and Winston.

Keller, E. F. (1985). *Reflections on gender and science.* New Haven, CT: Yale University.

Kelly, L., Burton, S., & Regan, L. (1994). Researching women's lives or studying women's oppression? Reflections on what constitutes feminist research. In M. Maynard and J. Purvis (Eds.), *Researching women's lives from a feminist perspective* (pp. 22–48). London: Taylor and Francis.

Kimball, M. M. (1995). *Feminist visions of gender similarities and differences.* Binghamton, NY: Haworth.

Kitzinger, C. (1992). The individuated self: A critical analysis of social constructionist writing on individualism. In G. Breakwell (Ed.), *The social psychology of identity and self concept.* London: Academic Press/Surrey University Press.

Kitzinger, C. (1994). Should psychologists study sex differences? *Feminism and Psychology, 4,* 501–546.

Lather, P. (1991). *Getting smart: Feminist research and pedagogy within the postmodern.* New York: Routledge.

Layton, L. (1998). *Who's that girl? Who's that boy? Clinical practice meets postmodern gender theory.* Northvale, NJ: Jason Aronson.

Lyotard, J. F. ([1984] 1993). *The postmodern condition: A report on knowledge* (Geoff Bennington & Brian Massumi, trans). Minneapolis: University of Minnesota Press.

MacKinnon, C. A. (1990). Legal perspectives on sexual difference. In D. L. Rhode

(Ed.), *Theoretical perspectives on sexual difference* (pp. 213–225). New Haven, CT: Yale University Press.

Marks, (1993). Case conference analysis and action research. In E. Burman & I. Parker (Eds.), *Discourse analytic research: Repertoires and readings of texts in action* (pp. 135–154). New York: Routledge.

Maynard, M. (1992). Methods, practice, and epistemology: The debate about feminism and research. In M. Maynard & J. Purvis (Eds.), *Researching women's lives from a feminist perspective* (pp. 10–26). London: Taylor and Francis.

McHugh, M.C. (1990). *Gender issues in psychotherapy: Victim blame/woman blame.* Invited address presented at the annual meeting of the American Psychological Association, Boston.

McHugh, M.C. (1993). Studying battered women and batterers: Feminist perspectives on methodology. In M. Hansen & M. Harway (Eds.), *Battering and family therapy: A feminist perspective* (pp. 54–69). Newbury Park, CA: Sage.

McHugh, M.C., & Cosgrove, L. (1998). Research for women: Feminist methods. In D.M. Ashcraft (Ed.), *Women's work: A survey of scholarship by and about women* (pp. 3–19). Binghamton, NY: Haworth.

McHugh, M.C., & Cosgrove, L. (2002). Gendered subjects in psychology: Satirical and dialectic perspectives. In L.H. Collins, M.R. Dunlap, & J.C. Chrisler (Eds.), *Charting a new course for feminist psychology* (pp. 3–19). Westport, CT: Praeger.

McHugh, M.C., Frieze, I., & Browne, K. (1992). Research on battered women and their assailants. In M. Paludi & F. Denmrk (Eds.). *Psychology of women: A handbook of issues and theories* (pp. 231–276). Westport, CT: Greenwood.

McHugh, M.C., Koeske, R., & Frieze, I. (1986). Issues to consider in conducting nonsexist psychological research: A guide for researchers. *American Psychologist, 41,* 879–890.

Nelson, J.L. (1989). Phenomenology as feminist methodology: Explicating interviews. In K. Carter & C. Spitzack (Eds.), *Doing research on women's communication: Perspectives on theory and method* (pp. 221–241). Norwood, NJ: Ablex.

Nelson, L.H. (1993). A question of evidence. *Hypatia 8,* 174–189.

Press, A.L. (1991). Working class women in a middle class world: The impact of television on modes of reasoning about abortion. *Critical Studies in Mass Communication, 8,* 421–441.

Prilleltensky, I. (1989). Psychology and the status quo. *American Psychologist, 44,* 517–535.

Rappaport, J., & Stewart, E. (1997). A look at critical psychology: Elaborating the questions. In D. Fox & I. Prilleltensky (Eds.), *Critical psychology: An introduction* (pp. 301–317). London: Sage.

Reinharz, S. (1992). *Feminist methods in social research.* New York: Oxford University Press.

Reitz, R.R. (1999). Batterer's experience of being violent: A phenomenological study. *Psychology of Women Quarterly, 23,* 143–165.

Rhode, D. L. (Ed.). (1990). *Theoretical perspectives on sexual difference*. New Haven, CT: Yale University Press.

Romero, M., & Stewart, A. J. (1999). Introduction. In M. Romero & A. J. Stewart (Eds.), *Women's untold stories: Breaking silence, talking back, voicing complexity* (pp. ix–xxi). New York: Routledge.

Rosenwald, G., & Ochberg, R. (Eds.). (1992). *Storied lives: The cultural politics of self-understanding*. New Haven, CT: Yale University Press.

Sanger (1998). Outcome assessments for battered women's shelters. Paper presented at the annual meeting of the Association for Women's Psychology. Baltimore, MD.

Sarbin, T. R. (Ed.). (1986). *Narrative psychology: The storied nature of human conduct*. New York: Praeger.

Schiebinger, L. (2003). Introduction: Feminism inside the sciences. *Signs: Journal of Women in Culture and Society, 28,* pp. 859–866.

Sherif, C. (1979). Bias in psychology. In J. A. Sherman & E. T. Beck (Eds.), *The prism of sex: Essays in the sociology of knowledge* (pp. 93–133). Madison: University of Wisconsin Press.

Shields, S. A. (1975). Functionalism, Darwinism, and the psychology of women: A study in social myth. *American Psychologist, 30,* 739–754.

Spelman, E. V. (1988). *Inessential woman: Problems of exclusion in feminist thought*. Boston: Beacon Press.

Stanley, L., & Wise, S. (1993). *Breaking out again: Feminist ontology and epistemology* (2nd ed.). New York: Routledge.

Thorne, B. (1990). Children and gender: Constructions of difference. In D. L. Rhode (Ed.), *Theoretical perspectives on sexual difference* (pp. 100–113). New Haven, CT: Yale University Press.

Unger, R. K. (1983). Through the looking glass: No wonderland yet! *Psychology of Women Quarterly, 8,* 9–31.

Unger, R. K. (1998). *Resisting gender: Twenty-five years of feminist psychology*. Thousand Oaks, CA: Sage.

Ussher, J. (1992). *Women's madness: Misogyny or mental illness?* Amherst: University of Massachusetts Press.

Weisstein, N. (1969/2004). "Kinder kuche, kirch" as scientific law: Psychology constructs the female. Reprinted in T. A. Roberts (Ed.), *The Lanahan Readings in Psychology of Women*. Boston: New England Free Press.

West, C., & Zimmerman, D. H. (1987). Doing gender. *Gender and Society, 1,* 125–151.

Wilkinson, S. (1999). Focus groups: A feminist method. *Psychology of Women Quarterly, 23*(2), 221–244.

Worrell, J., & Etaugh, C. (Eds.). (1994). Transformations: Reconceptualizing theory and research with women [special issue]. *Psychology of Women Quarterly, 18*(4).

Chapter 9

Social Role Theory of Sex Differences and Similarities: Implications for the Sociopolitical Attitudes of Women and Men

Alice H. Eagly and Abigail A. Mitchell

One of the enduring problems that attract scientists is unraveling the causes of the differences and similarities of women and men.[1] Scientific journals in many fields provide a steady flow of articles addressing these issues. Theories about causes abound, challenging scientists' ability to sort out the contending causal theories. This chapter highlights one particular set of frequently discussed sex differences: differences in attitudes on sociopolitical issues and in voting patterns. Specifically, women, compared with men, have attitudes that are, for example, more socially compassionate, and women are more likely to vote for Democratic candidates.

To produce some order among the many competing explanations of psychological sex differences and similarities, the social role theory of these differences and similarities offers a comprehensive account of why men and women sometimes differ on skills, abilities, attitudes, and behaviors and sometimes are very similar or identical. This theory integrates a wide range of causal influences into a coherent theory, including socialization, gender stereotypes, social roles, and hormonal activation. The distinctive aspect of this theory is its considerable emphasis on the causes and consequences of the differential distribution of men and women into social roles within societies (Eagly, 1987; Eagly, Wood, & Diekman, 2000). In industrialized societies this differential distribution takes the form of women usually occupying the role of primary family caregiver and men the role of primary provider, even though both sexes generally participate in caregiving and providing.

The ultimate causes of the distribution of the sexes into differing social roles lie in physical differences between the sexes: women's reproductive activities and men's greater size, strength, and speed of locomotion. Depending on a society's circumstances, these physical sex differences lead to certain activities being more efficiently accomplished by one sex than the other. Because of the universality of these physical sex differences in humans, every known culture has shown a division of labor by sex (Murdock & Provost, 1973). Nonetheless, the specific behaviors that are typical of each sex vary between societies, depending on the particular contours of each society's division of labor, which in turn reflects its particular socioeconomic, ecological, and cultural niche (Wood & Eagly, 2002). Therefore, as the external situation of the members of a society changes, the roles that women and men occupy change as well. The psychology and behavior of the sexes then accommodate to the requirements of the new social roles.

The social roles that are occupied more by one sex than the other set in motion a range of societal- and individual-level processes, including socialization, the formation of gender roles, expectancy confirmation, and self-regulation, that result in sex-differentiated behavior and psychology. Especially emphasized in social role theory is the formation of gender roles, by which women and men are expected to manifest characteristics that equip them for the activities that are typical of their sex.

In brief, social role theory argues that the psychology of women and men arises from social and individual processes that follow in an ultimate sense from the interaction between physical sex differences and the socioeconomic, ecological, and cultural contexts in which people live. This interaction shapes the social roles of men and women in society, from which other influences follow to affect behavior. This approach has been tested and applied to several domains of behavior, including partner selection preferences (Eagly & Wood, 1999; Eagly, Wood, & Johannesen-Schmidt, 2004) and leadership (Eagly, Johannesen-Schmidt, & Van Engen, 2003; Eagly & Karau, 2002). The purpose of this chapter is to review social role theory and illustrate it by applying it to understand a particular area of sex-differentiated psychology, sociopolitical attitudes and voting behavior. We first review the theory and then consider this application of it.

Origins of Division of Labor and Gender Hierarchy

In its analysis of the ultimate, or distal, causes of sex differences, social role theory argues that the distinctive physical attributes of men and women, in interaction with the contexts provided by particular societies, produce a division of labor by sex and often a gender hierarchy. Illustrating the prevalence of a division of labor, Murdock and Provost (1973) analyzed anthropologists' records of 185 nonindustrial societies and found that the majority of productive activities in each society were performed solely or primarily by one sex rather than by both sexes jointly. For example, smelting ores was exclusively in the province of men and the preparation of food from plant sources was consistently in the province of women. Despite finding this substantial cross-cultural similarity, Murdock and Provost also discovered considerable variability between societies in the specific activities that are sex-typed, reflecting the influence of the socioeconomic, ecological, and cultural forces at work in each society.

Another important pattern is the presence of a gender hierarchy in the majority of societies. With the exception of some egalitarian societies, men have greater power and status than women across societies, although the specific ways in which men exercise power over women vary by culture (e.g., Whyte, 1978). Thus, in many societies women possess fewer resources than men; in some societies less value is placed on women's lives; and often greater restrictions are placed on women's marital and sexual behavior.

The division of labor and gender hierarchy arise from the interaction of physical sex differences and the demands of the cultural, economic, and ecological environments of a society (Wood & Eagly, 2002). Primary in these physical differences are women's reproductive activities, which are particularly influential in favoring a division of labor. Because these activities entail gestation and the performance of critical aspects of child care, they place limitations on the other activities in which women can easily engage. Women's nursing of babies means that they perform infant care roles across societies (Wood & Eagly, 2002). These reproductive activities make it more difficult for women than men to engage in tasks that require speed of locomotion, uninterrupted periods of activity, or travel far from home. Under most circumstances, women's reproductive activities are thus not easily combined with hunting large game, plowing, or warfare. In addition, these reproductive activities make it difficult for women to receive specialized training that requires uninterrupted periods away from the home. Women's reproductive activities have less impact on their roles in societies with low birthrates, less reliance on lactation for feeding infants, and more nonmaternal care of young children. Because all of these conditions are present in postindustrial societies, it is not surprising that the roles of men and women have become more similar there.

Men's greater size, strength, and speed are also determinants of social roles. The average man is more likely than the average woman to efficiently perform tasks that require brief bursts of force, upper-body strength, and speed of locomotion. Such tasks include smelting ores, logging, hunting large game, plowing, and warfare. The distinctively male physical attributes have less impact on social roles to the extent that activities requiring physical prowess are less prevalent in a society, such as an industrialized society, in which a wide range of productive activities are mechanized. In general, the physical attributes of women and men interact with the demands of the local economy, social structure, and ecology to foster a division of labor by sex that is functional and efficient in that environment.

A male–female division of labor does not necessarily result in men gaining power over women. Relatively egalitarian relations between men and women are not infrequently found in decentralized, nonhierarchical foraging societies with very limited technology (Hayden et al., 1986; Salzman, 1999; Sanday, 1981). Yet, patriarchy ensues when the kinds of roles that men typically occupy confer higher status than those occupied by women. In more complex, technologically advanced societies, the physical differences between the sexes have interacted with socioeconomic factors, particularly technology, to produce roles that confer higher status and power on men.

What types of roles confer status and power, and thus produce patriarchy, when occupied more by women than men? Although the specific roles that generate power and status differ by society, such roles typically yield access to resources that can be exchanged in the public economy and provide opportunities for consequential decision-making and the exercise of authority. Also, such roles often require specialized training, which provides trainees with knowledge and skills that make them a valuable resource to others, thereby conferring power on them. For example, becoming a successful blacksmith requires training, and this type of labor creates products that are valuable to a large number of families and may produce goods for trade. As suggested by this example, the activities that produce higher status usually provide goods that can be exchanged in the public economy or general marketplace rather than items that are useful only in the domestic economy (Wood & Eagly, 2002). Roles requiring such activities become common when societies develop technology. In addition, some roles allow a greater span of influence than others, and thereby may confer greater power and status than roles involving a limited span of influence. For example, warrior roles provide opportunities for authority over others in warrior bands and for decision-making that is highly consequential for all members of a society. Warrior roles also bring access to resources in victorious situations.

Why do men dominate most of these roles that confer power and status? Women's reproductive activities make it more difficult for them to participate in specialized training or in activities that take them away from home. This tendency for women's activities to be more likely to be performed in and around the home than those of men limits their span of influence primarily to their families and close neighbors, thereby decreasing the scope of the power and status that they can obtain. Also, men's greater upper-body strength and speed allow them to participate more effectively than women in activities such as warfare and hunting, which have yielded status and power in many societies.

Consistent with this argument, more egalitarian gender relations are found in decentralized societies that lack complex technology, especially in very simple economies in which people derive subsistence from foraging (Hayden et al., 1986; Salzman, 1999; Sanday, 1981). One example of such a gender-equal society is the Vanatinai, a foraging and horticultural society located on a remote island southeast of New Guinea (Lepowsky, 1993). This society is matrilineal, meaning that inheritance is through the female line. Women have considerable access to resources and participate in activities that are economically and ritually important. Residence is bilocal in the sense that families alternate their residences between the hamlets of the wife's and husband's families. The society has no chiefs with formal authority, although both women and men have access to a "big woman" or "big man" role entailing informal influence and authority. Male and female roles overlap considerably, although women have more domestic responsibility and men more responsibility for extensive hunting.

In general, in foraging societies that gain substantial sustenance from gathering, an activity that is usually female-dominated, women contribute important resources. Also, in socioeconomically simple, decentralized societies, there is little opportunity for any individual to gain a large sphere of influence. The existence of some egalitarian societies is consistent with the social role theory argument that it is the roles occupied by men and women that lead to patriarchal gender hierarchies. Moreover, it is consistent with social role theory that many postindustrial societies manifest increasing gender equality in part because women are less restricted by reproductive activity, and in part because almost all status-conferring roles demand primarily intellectual, social, and political skills, not physical prowess.

In summary, sex-typed roles involving a division of labor and gender hierarchy emerge mainly from socioeconomic and ecological factors that interact with the physical sex differences that are inherent in women's reproductive activity and men's size, strength, and speed (Wood & Eagly, 2002). These biosocial interactions provide a framework that can explain cross-cultural similarities and differences in the activities most commonly undertaken by men and women. Although in postindustrial societies, physical sex differences are less consequential, even these societies retain a weak division of labor by sex and aspects of patriarchy. These sex-typed roles in turn promote sex differences in many aspects of social behavior, including the sociopolitical attitudes and voting behavior that we discuss later in this chapter.

Social Construction of Gender by Gender Roles

In social role theory, the contrasting social positions of the sexes produce gender roles, which in turn foster sex differences in behavior. In general, social roles are shared expectations about behavior that apply to people on the basis of their membership in a certain social position or category (e.g., Biddle & Thomas, 1979). At an individual level, roles exist in people's minds as schemata, or abstract knowledge structures, about groups of people. Although schemata may vary between individuals, role schemata are generally held consensually within societies, existing as shared ideologies that are communicated among society members.

Gender roles constitute shared expectations about behavior that apply to people on the basis of their socially identified sex (Eagly, 1987). Because gender roles apply to the general categories of male and female, they are diffuse, or broadly relevant across situations. More specific roles based on factors such as family relationships (e.g., mother, son) and occupation (e.g., nurse, carpenter) are primarily relevant only in a particular context and to some people. Gender roles therefore combine with more specific social roles to structure interaction in a given situation (Ridgeway, 2001). For example, workplace occupational roles, such as a manager, and gender roles may both influence expectations for behavior. Therefore, a female manager and a male manager, although in the same occupational role, are subject to somewhat different expectations (Eagly & Karau, 2002). Male managers, more than female managers, are expected to be self-confident, assertive, firm, and analytical (Heilman et al., 1989).

Evidence supporting the existence of gender roles comes most directly from research on gender stereotypes, which has consistently found that people have differing beliefs about the typical characteristics of men and women (e.g., Diekman & Eagly, 2000; Newport, 2001). An important aspect of these differing expectations consists of women being viewed as more *communal* than men and men as more *agentic* than women. Communal characteristics reflect a caring concern for other people and involve affection, kindness, interpersonal sensitivity, and nurturance. Agentic characteristics, on the other hand, involve assertion, control, and confidence. Gender stereotypes also include beliefs about sex differences in many other aspects of individuals, including physical characteristics, cognitive abilities, skills, and emotional dispositions (Deaux & Lewis, 1984; Diekman & Eagly, 2000).

Another aspect of people's sex-typed expectations about women and men consist of their preferences that men and women behave in certain ways. This consideration highlights the distinction between *descriptive norms* and *injunctive norms,* both of which are part of gender roles (Cialdini & Trost, 1998). Descriptive norms, also known as *descriptive stereotypes,* represent beliefs about men and women. For example, people believe that women, more than men, support socially compassionate government policies (Diekman, Eagly, & Kulesa, 2002). In ambiguous situations, descriptive norms provide guidance concerning what behaviors are likely to be appropriate and effective. When people are in doubt about what to do in a particular situation, they often conform to behaviors they have observed are typical of their sex. In general, behaviors that deviate from descriptive norms can elicit surprise because they are unexpected.

Injunctive norms, also known as *prescriptive stereotypes,* encompass the obligatory aspect of gender roles by including expectations about what men and women should do. Injunctive norms provide information about the behaviors that elicit social approval. Generally, people approve of communal characteristics in women more than in men and agentic characteristics in men more than in women. People view the ideal woman as emphasizing communal characteristics and the ideal man as emphasizing agentic characteristics (e.g., Spence & Helmrich, 1978; Williams & Best, 1990). These norms are often internalized, and thus become part of the self, with women and men manifesting sex-typed ideal selves (Wood et al., 1997). Common attitudes and beliefs about the roles and responsibilities of men and women also include preferences for women holding communally demanding roles such as child caretaker and teacher, and men holding agentically demanding roles such as boss and police officer (e.g., Glick & Fiske, 1996; Spence & Helmreich, 1978). In general, behaviors that deviate from injunctive norms elicit social disapproval and attempts to induce compliance.

Individuals differ to some extent in their endorsement of stereotypical beliefs about typical and appropriate male and female behavior (e.g., Spence & Buckner, 2000). Nevertheless, these beliefs appear to be widely shared by women and men, younger and older adults, and people differing in social class and income. Virtually everyone is at least aware of stereotypical beliefs about the sexes (e.g., Zenmore, Fiske, & Kim, 2000), and gender roles are a very important component of the culture of every society (Best & Thomas, 2004). Although the beliefs that constitute gender roles are often automatically activated, their impact is moderated by various contextual, informational, and motivational variables (e.g., Blair, 2002; Deaux & Major, 1987; Zenmore et al., 2000). As a consequence, many stereotypical sex differences occur in some contexts but not in others.

The Relation of the Social Position of Men and Women to Gender Roles

Sex-typed expectations about psychological attributes emerge from the differing social roles that men and women occupy. People observe men and women engaging in different types of activities and infer the inner dispositions of the sexes from these actions. The tendency for people to infer inner dispositions from behavior in a wide variety of situations is a well-documented principle of social psychology, known as *correspondent inference* or *correspondence bias* (Gilbert, 1998). People observe women engaging in communal, nurturing behaviors such as child care and infer from these behaviors that women possess communal characteristics, failing to take into account the requirements of the domestic role. Similarly, people observe men engaging in assertive, task-oriented activities such as those involved in being a foreman or business executive, and infer from these behaviors that men possess agentic characteristics, failing to take into account the requirements of these roles.

Through the process of correspondent inference, gender stereotypes can emerge in the absence of true dispositional sex differences, as long as the sexes are engaged in different activities. In an experimental test of the idea that stereotypes can emerge without any psychological differences between men and women, Hoffman and Hurst (1990) presented participants with a fictional group that consisted of two occupation categories, city workers and child raisers. Participants were told that the members of the two occupational groups were comparable in their communal and agentic traits. Despite this information, participants assigned role-consistent traits to the members of each group—specifically, agentic traits to the city workers and communal traits to the child raisers. Even explicit instructions to the contrary did not override correspondent inferences from behavior to underlying dispositions.

Processes by Which Gender Roles Influence Behavior, and Their Implications

Once gender roles have been formed on the basis of division of labor by sex and correspondent inference, they can impact behavior through several processes: (1) receiving social penalties for behavior incongruent with one's gender role and rewards for congruent behavior, (2) regulating one's own behavior to be consistent with gender role norms, (3) learning and practicing role-appropriate skills, and (4) recruiting hormones that support role performance. In natural settings, any of these processes might work alone but more typically they would operate together to produce sex-differentiated behavior.

Receiving Social Penalties and Rewards

The argument about social penalties and rewards promoting sex-typed behavior is straightforward: Men and women are often rewarded for engaging in gender-appropriate behavior and punished for gender-inappropriate behavior. Because the injunctive norms associated with gender roles are supported by others in society, individuals who choose to engage in gender-inappropriate behavior often face at least some degree of social disapproval. It is therefore not surprising that research on gender-stereotypical expectations has yielded very clear demonstrations that people behaviorally confirm others' expectancies (see Deaux & LaFrance, 1998; Geis, 1993).

Sanctions for role-inconsistent behaviors can be communicated verbally and nonverbally, often without people being aware that they are communicating disapproval. Sanctions include overt, obvious penalties (e.g., failing to receive a raise in salary) and more subtle penalties (e.g., a disdainful glance). Empirical evidence of these penalties abounds. For example, a review of sixty-one studies found that women who adopted a male-stereotypical assertive and directive leadership style were evaluated more negatively than men with the same style (Eagly, Makhijani, & Klonsky, 1992). Also, men are often penalized for behaving passively and unassertively and expressing negative emotions such as shame, fear, and embarrassment (e.g., Anderson et al., 2001; Costrich et al., 1975).

Although studies of socialization practices from nonindustrial societies suggest that parents use reward and punishment to induce their children's conformity to gender roles (Barry, Bacon, & Child, 1957), research in North American and other Western nations has produced more inconsistent findings, with many studies suggesting that boys and girls are treated relatively equivalently. However, evidence remains that these parents use reward and punishment to encourage gender-typed activities and interests—for example, chores, toys, games, and sports (Lytton & Romney, 1991). Also, and probably more important, parents communicate stereotypical expectations through subtle processes not typically monitored in socialization studies. In particular, parental modeling of behaviors is important (Bussey & Bandura, 2004). To the extent that parents enact traditionally sex-typed role behaviors (for example, mothers as primary caretaker), children learn these behaviors through observation and modeling themselves after their same-sex parent.

The positive consequences of gender-role-consistent behavior are evident in the realm of sociopolitical attitudes and voting behavior. Several studies using fictitious candidates have found that female politicians are viewed as competent in their ability to deal with social compassion issues, such as education, health care, and poverty, but as less competent with issues that have more agentic implications, such as big business, the military, and defense (Leeper, 1990; Mueller, 1986; Rosenwasser & Seale, 1988; Sapiro, 1981–1982). Although stereotypical perceptions of female candidates can be outweighed by individuating information (e.g., information about personality characteristics; Huddy & Terkildsen, 1993), such information is not necessarily available to voters or noticed by them. Gender roles provide an available standard by which voters may judge the political actions and positions of candidates of both sexes (Huddy & Capelos, 2002). The lesser willingness to support female than male candidates for the presidency or vice presidency thus follows in part from people's tendency to see them as less competent than male candidates at handling issues related to war, the economy, and big business (Mueller, 1986). Therefore, a campaign emphasis on political issues that citizens view as incongruent with candidates' gender roles could hurt their ability to win elections, and encourage them to discuss issues and take positions that citizens perceive as gender-congruent.

Regulating One's Own Behavior to Conform to Gender Role Norms

Gender roles foster sex-differentiated behavior through the self-regulation of behavior to conform with gender roles. One such process concerns unfamiliar or uncertain situations in which it is unclear how to behave. Utilizing the descriptive norms relevant to a situation, individuals can guide their own behavior according to how members of their sex generally respond to the situation or to similar situations. In such instances, people do not necessarily have a prior preference for a course of action, and their decision to engage in gender-role-consistent behavior is not a product of contingencies of reward or punishment. For example, if a female voter is unsure which candidate to vote for in an election, she may vote for the candidate who is favored by her female friends and relatives.

Individuals can also internalize others' preferences for their gender so that the injunctive norms related to their gender role become part of their self-concept. This internalization produces a set of personal standards for behavior. To the extent that people live up to such standards, they are happy with themselves and are disappointed to the extent that they fall short of these self-imposed expectations (Wood et al., 1997). This mechanism can have a powerful effect on behavior because the motivation to adhere to the gender role derives from the self rather than from an external source that might be more easily discredited.

Evidence supporting the idea that gender roles influence people's perceptions of themselves derives from studies demonstrating that on average, people tend to view themselves in a gender-stereotypical manner (e.g., Spence & Buckner, 2000; Spence & Helmreich, 1978). Specifically, women, more than men, have self-schemata that focus on their relationships with others who are important to them, especially in close, dyadic relationships (e.g., Cross & Madson, 1997). Men, more than women, have a collective sense of self that focuses on the self as a member of a large group, such as a sports team or a corporation (Baumeister & Sommer, 1997; Gardner & Gabriel, 2004). This sense of self orients men more toward competition and status within and between the larger groups to which they belong. These self-construals are consistent with social role theory's emphasis on the role occupancy of the sexes. Thus, women, more than men, spend their time in social roles that focus on close relationships with individuals, such as family members and close friends. Men, more than women, spend their time in social roles that focus on larger groups of people, such as work groups, sports teams, and military groups, within which many relationships have elements of competition and aggression.

Research supports the idea that internalized gender norms influence how people perceive themselves and their behavior. Wood et al. (1997) investigated the effects of internalized normative beliefs that men ought to be powerful, dominant, and self-assertive, and that women ought to be caring, intimate with others, and emotionally expressive. Participants who had internalized the gender role norms felt good about themselves when their behavior was consistent with the norm for their sex and less good when it was inconsistent. The gender role norms served as self-standards, and fulfilling those standards with gender-role-consistent behavior led people to view themselves as closer to their ideal selves. However, when people fail to live up to gender role norms, they may experience depression and lowered self-esteem (e.g., Crocker & Wolfe, 2001). Therefore, gender roles can influence behavior when these roles become internalized so that women and men treat gender role norms as personal standards by which they evaluate their own behavior.

Learning and Practicing Role-Appropriate Skills

Another mechanism by which gender roles influence behavior takes the form of men and women developing different skills and traits to the extent that they spend considerable time in roles that place a premium on skills and traits that are consistent with gender roles. Because the sexes are differentially distributed into specific roles, they learn and practice different types of skills, develop different attitudes, and orient themselves toward different life goals. Women, more often than men, practice communal behaviors in the domestic role and female-dominated occupational roles, and men, more often than women, practice agentic behaviors in male-dominated occupational roles (Cejka & Eagly, 1999). In preparing for and occupying these roles, both sexes build skills that are congruent with their gender roles. For example, women learn to care for children when they gain practice as girls in child-rearing skills through playing with baby dolls as well as baby-sitting and caring for younger siblings. As young adults, women are thus more prepared for the role of child caretaker, and subsequently gain further expertise to the extent that they occupy the role of primary caretaker of their own children. Men and women thus gain gender-typical skills and interests in their preparatory and actual participation in social roles.

Recruiting Hormones That Support Role Performance

Finally, biological processes, such as hormonal changes, provide another mechanism by which gender roles influence behavior. For instance, studies have shown that men's testosterone levels rise in anticipation of athletic and other competitive events or in response to insults (e.g., Booth et al., 1989; Cohen et al., 1996). Presumably, this response aids them in energizing and directing their physical and cognitive performance. This effect demonstrates how biological processes, such as hormonal levels, can be influenced by and interact with the expectations of the male gender role, such as men being aggressive and competitive. Women also experience role-supportive hormonal changes, particularly increases in cortisol, with the initiation of their parental role in childbirth, which presumably stimulate nurturing behaviors (Corter & Fleming, 1995; Fleming et al., 1997). Although some of these hormonal changes are likely sex-specific, other hormonal changes have been found in both sexes. In particular, men anticipating wives' childbirth experienced hormonal changes parallel to the changes that occurred in mothers (i.e., involving estradiol, cortisol, and prolactin), as well as a drop in testosterone (Berg & Wynne-Edwards, 2001; Storey et al., 2000). Thus, in facilitating role performances, social, psychological, and biological processes mediate the influence of social roles on behavior.

Implications of Analysis for the Accuracy of Gender Stereotypes

Because gender roles are derived from role behavior and in turn foster sex differences, social role theory predicts that gender stereotypes and actual sex differences are similar. Therefore, given that gender stereotypes are consensually shared, people should be relatively accurate in their beliefs about men's and women's behavior. In fact, research comparing social perceivers' perceptions of sex differences against actual differences has found that people are generally accurate (Briton & Hall, 1995; Swim, 1994). Hall and Carter

(1999) produced evidence of this accuracy in their study of sex differences and similarities in seventy-seven traits, abilities, and behaviors. Participants' mean estimates of these differences and similarities correlated 0.70 with actual research findings (as established in meta-analyses). In addition to knowing whether men or women were more likely to posses the trait or perform the behavior, participants understood which differences tended to be larger and which were smaller.

This research on the accuracy of gender stereotypes has focused primarily on traits and behaviors that either are directly observable (e.g., aggressive behavior) or can be easily inferred from behavior (e.g., mathematical ability inferred from test performance). Attitudes on sociopolitical issues are generally not as directly observable, and so provide a more stringent test of the assumption that gender stereotypes are generally accurate. In research on the accuracy of stereotypes about the attitudes of men and women, participants' estimates of women's and men's attitudes were compared with actual attitudinal sex differences, as documented by the General Social Survey, a nationally representative survey (Diekman et al., 2002). Research participants' beliefs about these attitudinal differences and similarities proved to be moderately accurate.

Even though social perceivers are generally accurate about sex differences and similarities, there are systematic biases in their judgments (Ryan, 2002). For example, in estimating sociopolitical attitudes, participants of both sexes tended to underestimate men's support for policies that favored women's interests (Diekman et al., 2002). Furthermore, even though people are generally accurate in predicting average differences between men and women, they are often inaccurate in predicting the behavior of individual men and women. In fact, stereotypes tend to bias perceptions of individuals by producing overly homogeneous perceptions of stereotyped individuals, whereby people categorized together in a group are believed to be similar to each other. In reality, all psychological sex differences take the form of overlapping distributions whereby average men and women differ but a given man can be higher or lower than a given woman. Typically, within-sex variability is relatively large compared with between-sex variability.

Reciprocal Causality

So far in this chapter, the causal chain of social role theory has appeared to flow from physical sex differences within societal contexts to a division of labor, which then leads to the social construction of gender in gender roles and socialization, which in turn foster sex-differentiated behavior (see Figure 9.1). However, the causal chains in social role theory are more complex

Figure 9.1
Causal Chain of Social Role Theory

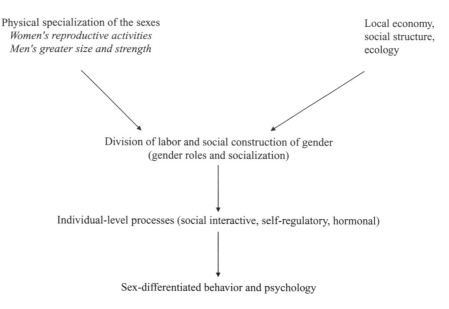

Physical specialization of the sexes
   Women's reproductive activities
   Men's greater size and strength

Local economy,
social structure,
ecology

Division of labor and social construction of gender
(gender roles and socialization)

Individual-level processes (social interactive, self-regulatory, hormonal)

Sex-differentiated behavior and psychology

than this representation, allowing for the various causes of the model to influence each other in reciprocal fashion. Therefore, although causes often proceed in this forward sequence, they may also proceed backward, with gender-stereotypical behavior strengthening gender roles and stereotypes, and channeling men and women into different social roles. For example, women often participate in peace movements and antiwar campaigns (Goldstein, 2001). Observation of these activities suggests that women are less favorable than men toward aggression and violence, and thus strengthens the perception of women as pacifistic and unaggressive. These observations thus support traditional distributions of men and women into social roles, especially the favoring of men in roles, such as soldier and police officer, that require socially approved aggressive behavior.

Sex Differences and Similarities in Sociopolitical Attitudes and Voting Behavior

Social role theory illuminates some of the causes of the sociopolitical attitudes and voting patterns of men and women. In this section, we summarize research on attitudinal sex differences that demonstrates the utility of the theory. From the social role theory perspective, sex-related attitudinal differences emerge both from the direct effects of sex-typed occupational and family roles on individual occupants of these roles and from gender roles, because the characteristics that are required to carry out sex-typical tasks become stereotypical of women and men. For example, the general expectation that women are, and should be, warm and nurturant likely arises from their disproportionate occupancy of caring roles, even though a more specific demand for these qualities applies to individuals (primarily women) who actually occupy such roles. With respect to attitudes, social role theory therefore hypothesizes that gender gaps reflect the gender role influences that apply to individuals, depending on their membership in the social category of men or women, as well as the influences of sex-typed specific family and occupational roles.

Although studies conducted prior to the last quarter of the twentieth century suggested that men and women differ little in their attitudes (see Sapiro, 1983), attitudinal data have shown some gender differentiation in recent decades, with women's greater support for social provision and opposition to violence gaining attention by the 1980s (e.g., Goertzel, 1983; Shapiro & Mahajan, 1986; T. W. Smith, 1984). When women increased their gender consciousness and political activism as the women's movement gained strength in the 1970s (Gurin, 1985; Gurin & Townsend, 1986), they not only became less approving of traditional gender relations (Harris & Firestone, 1998; Twenge, 1997a) but also increased their political knowledge (e.g., Slevin & Aday, 1993) and began to vote in elections at a slightly higher rate than men (Seltzer, Newman, & Leighton, 1997). When people gain expertise concerning sociopolitical issues, they develop mental structures with more coherent and internally consistent attitudes (e.g., Lavine, Thomsen, & Gonzales, 1997). Women's increasing political expertise and involvement apparently have enabled them to develop policy preferences that reflect their distinctive position in society. Presumably, men's attitudes have represented their social position over a much longer span of years, consistent with their historically greater political power and involvement.

In terms of explaining the observed gender gaps in attitudes in the late decades of the twentieth century, the most obvious shift is the increase in women's labor force participation (U.S. Census Bureau, 2002). This change strengthened women's involvement in the public sphere, fostering a more elaborated political ideology and greater political participation. Nonetheless, as we argued earlier in this chapter, men and women tend to occupy different types of occupational roles (Reskin, McBrier, & Kmec, 1999); women, compared with men, are concentrated in jobs that entail less authority (R. A.

Smith, 2002) and that have lower wages (U.S. Bureau of Labor Statistics, 2003). Also, women have continued to have disproportionate responsibility for domestic work in the United States, including child care (Bianchi et al., 2000; Shelton & John, 1996) and other caring responsibilities, such as tending ill or disabled family members (Cancian & Oliker, 2000). In view of these sex differences in social roles, the key to understanding contemporary gender gaps in attitudes is that the political activation of women is accompanied by continuing differentiation of the sexes in many of their roles and responsibilities.

The female dominance of the domestic sphere may cause women's sociopolitical attitudes to reflect the goals inherent in their traditional private-sphere responsibilities—for example, promoting the welfare of children and families. In addition, women's domestic responsibilities and concentration in jobs with lower wages and lesser authority maintain their status disadvantage relative to men. These differences in the social roles occupied by the sexes support attitudinal sex differences (a) in part through the influence of gender roles, which in turn reflect the continuing aggregate differences in the specific roles occupied by men and women, and (b) in part through the influences on individual role occupants of the particular roles occupied by one sex more often than the other.

Analyses of the General Social Survey and a community sample (Eagly, Diekman, Johannesen-Schmidt, & Koenig, 2003) showed that the most substantial gender gaps on sociopolitical issues are the following. Women, more than men, endorse policies that are socially compassionate and traditionally moral. These sex differences in social compassion attitudes include women's greater opposition to racial discrimination in housing, policy brutality, and the death penalty, and their greater support for gun control, government spending for African Americans, and reducing income differences between the rich and poor. The sex differences in traditional morality attitudes include women's greater opposition to extramarital relationships, divorce, suicide, and the legalization of marijuana. In addition, women are more supportive than men of equal rights for women and for gays and lesbians. In analyses of the General Social Survey extending from 1972 to 1998, the attitudinal gender gaps showed temporal constancy.

To clarify the relations between the social roles of women and men and these attitudes, the research examined similarities between gender gaps and gaps associated with other respondent attributes that are associated with social disadvantage (e.g., minority racial or ethnic status) or family responsibility (e.g., parenthood). If disadvantage or family responsibility underlies attitudinal sex differences, such a variable should, like sex, be correlated with higher endorsement of gender-gap attitudes. In general, these patterns held, although social compassion related more consistently to social disadvantage than did moral traditionalism, and moral traditionalism related more consistently to family responsibilities than did social compassion.

These data are consistent with the assumption that the persistence of generally lower status relative to men and their greater domestic responsibilities maintain gender roles, which then influence attitudes by means of self-regulatory influences and the impact of others' expectations. Given some political activation of women and men as social groups, these culturally shared beliefs about gender foster sex-differentiated policy preferences.

In contrast to this account of the influence of roles on attitudes, an overly simple view would be that controlling for sociodemographic differences between the sexes would eliminate attitudinal sex differences because differences in current roles produce the attitudinal differences. Contrary to this logic that men and women who are positioned in the same roles should have the same attitudes, the sex effect in the attitudinal data was diminished only slightly by sociodemographic controls in Eagly, Diekman, Johannesen-Schmidt and Koenig's (2003) analyses. Social role theory thus argues that the differing typical placement of men and women in the social structure produces shared beliefs about women and men. These diffuse, culturally shared gender roles have some general impact on the social identities and attitudes of individual men and women, regardless of their placement in specific occupational and family roles. For example, female gender role expectations may encourage women's support for policies that favor children and education, even among childless women or women whose children are adults. From the perspective of these indirect links between overall role distributions and attitudes by means of culturally shared gender roles, it is not surprising that attitudinal differences persisted in Eagly, Diekman, Johannesen-Schmidt, and Koenig's (2003) analyses, despite controls for sociodemographic variables.

The temporal stability that Eagly, Diekman, Johannesen-Schmidt, and Koenig (2003) observed in attitudinal gender gaps resembles findings on sex-related beliefs and behaviors. Specifically, the tendency of women to describe themselves as more communal (i.e., feminine) than men proved to be relatively constant from 1973 to 1993 when meta-analytically summarized, despite erosion in the tendency for women to describe themselves as less agentic (i.e., masculine) than men (Twenge, 1997b). Similarly, research on the stereotypical traits ascribed to women and men of the past, present, and future showed that social perceivers view the sex difference in feminine, communal qualities as remaining relatively constant over time even though they view the sex difference in masculine, agentic qualities as eroding as women adopt these qualities (Diekman & Eagly, 2000). These changes in agentic, masculine qualities are consistent with the role shifts that have occurred on a large scale—that is, increasing labor force participation of women. In contrast, the absence of change in communal, feminine qualities likely reflects the relative stability of women's greater family responsibility and lower status relative to men, factors that also underlie the observed stability of socially compassionate and traditionally moral attitudes.

Attitudinal gender gaps are consequential, even though they are not large. The consequences that are most readily demonstrated are gender gaps in voting. A greater preference of women than men for Democratic candidates has been apparent in most presidential elections since the early 1970s and in congressional elections since the early 1980s (Seltzer et al., 1997). Analyses of the correlational relations between attitudes and these voting gender gaps in the United States are largely consistent with the claim that attitudinal differences underlie these gaps (e.g., Kaufmann & Petrocik, 1999; Manza & Brooks, 1999; Seltzer et al., 1997). In addition, experimental tests portraying candidates as differing in their issue stances have shown that attitudinal sex differences can account for voting gender gaps (Eagly, Diekman, Schneider, & Kulesa, 2003). These experiments demonstrated an attitudinal gender congeniality effect on voting whereby participants of each sex reported greater likelihood, compared with participants of the other sex, of voting for the candidate who endorsed positions typically favored more by their own sex than by the other sex.

The particular policy attitudes generally implicated as causing voting gender gaps are variants of socially compassionate attitudes (Manza & Brooks, 1999). The impact on voting of women's greater endorsement of traditionally moral policies and policies ensuring equal rights for women and gay and lesbian rights is less clear. In general, moral and rights issues, except for abortion, are not among the issues that the majority of voters consider most important in elections (e.g., Washington Post Poll, 2000), although it is possible that moral considerations can influence perceptions of candidates' character, which in turn influence voting (Kinder, 1998).

Conclusion

This chapter outlined the basic tenets of the social role theory of sex differences and similarities, and described the application of the theory to sex differences in attitudes and voting behavior. We argued that attitudinal gender gaps reflect the differing placement of the sexes in social roles. This differential role occupancy in turn reflects physical sex differences that interact with the cultural, socioeconomic, and ecological environments to create a division of labor by sex. Gender roles emerge from this division of labor through the process of correspondent inference from role behaviors to underlying personal dispositions. These gender roles then influence behavior through causes such as sex-typed expectancies and self-regulation. Illustrating this analysis, the attitudes of women and men differ mainly on issues pertaining to compassion and traditional morality that reflect the female gender role, although their attitudes are very similar in many other domains.

Despite the emphasis of our analysis on sex differences, these differences may be eroding in modern societies in which the roles of women have undergone relatively rapid change. As a consequence, gender roles are under pressure to change, and such changes will likely decrease actual sex differences in the long run, thereby increasing the behavioral flexibility of both men and women.

Note

1. In this chapter, *sex* and *sexes* denote the grouping of people into female and male categories. *Sex differences* and *sex similarities* are used to describe the results of comparing these two groups. *Gender* refers to the meanings that societies and individuals ascribe to these female and male categories. We do not intend to use these terms to give priority to any class of causes that may underlie sex and gender effects.

References

Anderson, C., John, O. P., Keltner, D., & Kring, A. M. (2001). Who attains social status? Effects of personality and physical attractiveness in social groups. *Journal of Personality and Social Psychology, 81,* 116–132.

Barry, H., III, Bacon, M. K., & Child, I. L. (1957). A cross-cultural survey of some sex differences in socialization. *Journal of Abnormal and Social Psychology, 55,* 327–332.

Baumeister, R. F., & Sommer, K. L. (1997). What do men want? Gender differences in two spheres of belongingness: Comment on Cross and Madson (1997). *Psychological Bulletin, 122,* 38–44.

Berg, S. J., & Wynne-Edwards, K. E. (2001). Changes in testosterone, cortisol, and estradiol levels in men becoming fathers. *Mayo Clinic Proceedings, 76,* 582–592.

Best, D. L., & Thomas, J. J. (2004). Cultural diversity and cross-cultural perspectives. In A. H. Eagly, A. Beall, & R. J. Sternberg (eds.), *The psychology of gender* (2nd ed.) (pp. 296–327). New York: Guilford.

Bianchi, S. M., Milkie, M. A., Sayer, L. C., & Robinson, J. P. (2000). Is anyone doing the housework? Trends in the gender division of household labor. *Social Forces, 79,* 191–228.

Biddle, B. J., & E. J. Thomas (Eds.). (1979). *Role theory: Concepts and Research.* Huntington, NY: R. E. Krieger.

Blair, I. V. (2002). *Role theory: Expectancies, identities, and behaviors.* New York: Academic Press.

Booth, A., Shelley, G., Mazur, A., Tharp, G., & Kittok, R. (1989). Testosterone, and winning and losing in human competition. *Hormones and Behavior, 23,* 556–571.

Briton, N. J., & Hall, J. A. (1995). Beliefs about female and male nonverbal communication. *Sex Roles, 32,* 79–90.

Bussey, K., & Bandura, A. (2004). Social cognitive theory of gender development and functioning. In A. H. Eagly, A. Beall, & R. J. Sternberg (Eds.), *The psychology of gender* (2nd ed.) (pp. 92–119). New York: Guilford.

Cancian, F. M., & Oliker, S. J. (2000). *Caring and gender.* Thousand Oaks, CA: Pine Forge Press.

Cejka, M. A., & Eagly, A. H. (1999). Gender-stereotypic images of occupations correspond to the sex segregation of employment. *Personality and Social Psychology Bulletin, 25,* 413–423.

Cialdini, R. B., & Trost, M. R. (1998). Social influence: Social norms, conformity, and compliance. In D. T. Gilbert, S. T. Fiske, & G. Lindzey (Eds.), *The handbook of social psychology* (4th ed.), vol. 2 (151–185). Boston: McGraw-Hill.

Cohen, D., Nisbett, R. E., Bowdle, B. F., & Schwarz, N. (1996). Insult, aggression, and the Southern culture of honor: An "experimental ethnography." *Journal of Personality and Social Psychology, 70,* 945–960.

Corter, C. M., & Fleming, A. S. (1995). Psychobiology of maternal behavior in human beings. In M. H. Bornstein (Ed.), *Handbook of parenting,* vol. 2 (pp. 87–116). Mahwah, NJ: Erlbaum.

Costrich, N., Feinstein, J., Kidder, L., Marecek, J., & Pascale, L. (1975). When stereotypes hurt: Three studies of penalties for sex-role reversals. *Journal of Experimental Social Psychology, 11,* 520–530.

Crocker, J., & Wolfe, C. T. (2001). Contingencies of self-worth. *Psychological Review, 108,* 593–623.

Cross, S. E., & Madson, L. (1997). Models of the self: Self-construals and gender. *Psychological Bulletin, 122,* 5–37.

Deaux, K., & LaFrance, M. (1998). Gender. In D. T. Gilbert, S. T. Fiske, & G. Lindzey (Eds.), *The handbook of social psychology* (4th ed.), vol. 2 (pp. 788–827). Boston: McGraw-Hill.

Deaux, K., & Lewis, L. L. (1984). Structure of gender stereotypes: Interrelationships among components and gender label. *Journal of Personality and Social Psychology, 46,* 991–1004.

Deaux, K., & Major, B. (1987). Putting gender into context: An interactive model of gender-related behavior. *Psychological Review, 94,* 369–389.

Diekman, A. B., & Eagly, A. H. (2000). Stereotypes as dynamic constructs: Women and men of the past, present, and future. *Personality and Social Psychology Bulletin, 26,* 1171–1188.

Diekman, A. B., Eagly, A. H., & Kulesa, P. (2002). Accuracy and bias in stereotypes about the social and political attitudes of women and men. *Journal of Experimental Social Psychology, 38,* 268–282.

Eagly, A. H. (1987). *Sex differences in social behavior: A social-role interpretation.* Hillsdale, NJ: Erlbaum.

Eagly, A. H., Diekman, A. B., Johannesen-Schmidt, M. C., & Koenig, A. M. (2003). *Gender gaps in sociopolitical attitudes: A social psychological analysis.* Unpublished manuscript. Northwestern University, Evanston, IL.

Eagly, A. H., Diekman, A. B., Schneider, M., & Kulesa, P. (2003). Experimental tests of an attitudinal theory of the gender gap in voting. *Personality and Social Psychology Bulletin, 29,* 1245–1258.

Eagly, A. H., Johannesen-Schmidt, M. C., & Van Engen, M. L. (2003). Transformational, transactional, and laissez-faire leadership styles: A meta-analysis comparing women and men. *Psychological Bulletin, 129,* 569–591.

Eagly, A. H., & Karau, S. J. (2002). Role congruity theory of prejudice toward female leaders. *Psychological Review, 109,* 573–598.

Eagly, A. H., Makhijani, M. G., & Klonsky, B. G. (1992). Gender and the evaluation of leaders: A meta-analysis. *Psychological Bulletin, 111,* 3–22.

Eagly, A. H., & Wood, W. (1999). The origins of sex differences in human behavior: Evolved dispositions versus social roles. *American Psychologist, 54,* 408–423.

Eagly, A. H., Wood, W., & Diekman, A. B. (2000). Social role theory of sex differences and similarities: A current appraisal. In T. Eckes & H. M. Trautner (Eds.), *The developmental social psychology of gender* (pp. 123–174). Mahwah, NJ: Erlbaum.

Eagly, A. H., Wood, W., & Johannesen-Schmidt, M. (2004). Social role theory of sex differences and similarities: Implications for the partner preferences of women and men. In A. H. Eagly, A. Beall, & R. J. Sternberg (Eds.), *The psychology of gender* (2nd ed.) (pp. 269–295). New York: Guilford.

Fleming, A. S., Ruble, D., Krieger, H., & Wong, P. Y. (1997). Hormonal and experiential correlates of maternal responsiveness during pregnancy and the puerperium in human mothers. *Hormones and Behavior, 31,* 145–158.

Gardner, W. L., & Gabriel, S. (2004). Gender differences in relational and collective interdependence: Implications for self-views, social behavior, and subjective well-being. In A. H. Eagly, A. Beall, & R. J. Sternberg (Eds.), *The psychology of gender* (2nd ed.) (pp. 169–191). New York: Guilford.

Geis, F. L. (1993). Self-fulfilling prophecies: A social psychological view of gender. In A. E. Beall & R. J. Sternberg (Eds.), *The psychology of gender* (pp. 9–54). New York: Guilford.

Gilbert, D. T. (1998). Ordinary personology. In D. T. Gilbert, S. T. Fiske, & G. Lindzey (Eds.), *The handbook of social psychology* (4th ed.), vol. 2 (pp. 89–150). Boston: McGraw-Hill.

Glick, P., & Fiske, S. T. (1996). The Ambivalent Sexism Inventory: Differentiating hostile and benevolent sexism. *Journal of Personality and Social Psychology, 77,* 642–655.

Goertzel, T. G. (1983). The gender gap: Sex, family income, and political opinions in the early 1980's. *Journal of Political and Military Sociology, 11,* 209–222.

Goldstein, J. S. (2001). *War and gender: How gender shapes the war system and vice versa.* Cambridge: Cambridge University Press.

Gurin, P. (1985). Women's gender consciousness. *Public Opinion Quarterly, 49,* 143–163.

Gurin, P., & Townsend, A. (1986). Properties of gender identity and their implications for gender consciousness. *British Journal of Social Psychology, 25,* 139–148.

Hall, J. A., & Carter, J. D. (1999). Gender-stereotype accuracy as an individual difference. *Journal of Personality and Social Psychology, 77,* 350–359.

Harris, R. J., & Firestone, J. M. (1998). Changes in predictors of gender role ideologies among women: A multivariate analysis. *Sex Roles, 38,* 239–252.

Hayden, B., Deal, M., Cannon, A., & Casey, J. (1986). Ecological determinants of women's status among hunter/gatherers. *Human Evolution, 1,* 449–473.

Heilman, M. E., Block, C. J., Martell, R. F., & Simon, M. C. (1989). Has anything changed? Current characterizations of men, women, and managers. *Journal of Applied Psychology, 74,* 935–942.

Hoffman, C., & Hurst, N. (1990). Gender stereotypes: Perception or rationalization? *Journal of Personality and Social Psychology, 58,* 197–208.

Huddy, L., & Capelos, T. (2002). Gender stereotyping and candidate evaluation: Good news and bad news for women politicians. In V. C. Ottati, R. S. Tindale, J. Edwards, F. B. Bryant, L. Heath, D. C. O'Connell, Y. Suarez-Balcazar, & E. J. Posovac (Eds.), *The social psychology of politics* (pp. 29–53). New York: Kluwer Academic Plenum.

Huddy, L., & Terkildsen, N. (1993). Gender stereotypes and the perception of male and female candidates. *American Journal of Political Science, 37,* 119–147.

Kaufmann, K. M., & Petrocik, J. R. (1999). The changing politics of American men: Understanding the sources of the gender gap. *American Journal of Political Science, 43,* 864–887.

Kinder, D. R. (1998). Opinion and action in the realm of politics. In D. T. Gilbert, S. T. Fiske, & G. Lindzey (Eds.), *The handbook of social psychology* (4th ed.), vol. 2 (pp. 778–867). Boston: McGraw-Hill.

Lavine, H., Thomsen, C. J., & Gonzales, M. H. (1997). A shared consequences model of the development of inter-attitudinal consistency: The influence of values, attitude-relevant thought, and expertise. *Journal of Personality and Social Psychology, 72,* 735–749.

Leeper, M. S. (1990). The impact of prejudice on female candidates: An experimental look at voter inference. *American Politics Quarterly, 19,* 248–261.

Lepowsky, M. (1993). *Fruit of the motherland: Gender in an egalitarian society.* New York: Columbia University Press.

Lytton, H., & Romney, D. M. (1991). Parents' differential socialization of boys and girls: A meta-analysis. *Psychological Bulletin, 109,* 267–296.

Manza, J., & Brooks, C. (1999). *Social cleavages and political change: Voter alignments and U.S. party coalitions.* New York: Oxford University Press.

Mueller, C.M. (1986). Nurturance and mastery: Competing qualifications for women's access to high public office? In G. Moore & G.D. Spitze (Eds.), *Women and politics: Activism, attitudes, and office-holding* (pp. 211–232). Greenwich, CT.: JAI Press.

Murdock, G.P., & Provost, C. (1973). Factors in the division of labor by sex: A cross-cultural analysis. *Ethnology, 12*, 203–225.

Newport, F. (2001, February 21). *Americans see women as emotional and affectionate, men as more aggressive.* [On-line]. Gallup Poll News Service. Available: Retrieved August 18, 2001.

Reskin, B.F., McBrier, D.B., & Kmec, J.A. (1999). The determinants and consequences of workplace sex and race composition. *Annual Review of Sociology, 25*, 335–361.

Ridgeway, C.L. (2001). Gender, status, and leadership. *Journal of Social Issues, 57*, 637–656.

Rosenwasser, S.M., & Seale, J. (1988). Attitudes toward a hypothetical male or female candidate—A research note. *Political Psychology, 9*, 591–598.

Ryan, C.S. (2002). Stereotype accuracy. In W. Stroebe & M. Hewstone (Eds.), *European Review of Social Psychology,* vol. 13 (pp. 75–109). Philadelphia: Psychology Press.

Salzman, P.C. (1999). Is inequality universal? *Current Anthropology, 40*, 31–44.

Sanday, P.R. (1981). *Female power and male dominance: On the origins of sexual inequality.* New York: Cambridge University Press.

Sapiro, V. (1981/1982). If U.S. Senator Baker were a woman: An experimental study of candidate images. *Political Psychology, 3*, 61–83.

Sapiro, V. (1983). *The political integration of women: Roles, socialization, and politics.* Urbana: University of Illinois Press.

Seltzer, R.A., Newman, J., & Leighton, M.V. (1997). *Sex as a political variable: Women as candidates and voters in U.S. elections.* Boulder, CO: Lynne Rienner.

Shapiro, R.Y., & Mahajan, H. (1986). Gender differences in policy preferences: A summary of trends from the 1960s to the 1980s. *Public Opinion Quarterly, 50*, 42–61.

Shelton, B.A., & John, D. (1996). The division of household labor. *Annual Review of Sociology, 22*, 299–322.

Slevin, K.F., & Aday, D.P. (1993). Gender differences in self-evaluations of information about current affairs. *Sex Roles, 29*, 817–828.

Smith, R.A. (2002). Race, gender, and authority in the workplace: Theory and research. *Annual Review of Sociology, 28*, 509–542.

Smith, T.W. (1984). The polls: Gender and attitudes toward violence. *Public Opinion Quarterly, 48*, 384–396.

Spence, J.T., & Buckner, C.E. (2000). Instrumental and expressive traits, trait stereotypes, and sexist attitudes. *Psychology of Women Quarterly, 24*, 44–62.

Spence, J.T., & Helmreich, R. (1978). *Masculinity and femininity: Their psychological dimensions, correlates, and antecedents.* Austin: University of Texas Press.

Storey, A. E., Walsh, C. J., Quinton, R. L., & Wynne-Edwards, K. E. (2000). Hormonal correlates of paternal responsiveness in new and expectant fathers. *Evolution and Human Behavior, 21,* 79–95.

Swim, J. K. (1994). Perceived versus meta-analytic effect sizes: An assessment of the accuracy of gender stereotypes. *Journal of Personality and Social Psychology, 66,* 21–36.

Twenge, J. M. (1997a). Attitudes toward women, 1970–1995: A meta-analysis. *Psychology of Women Quarterly, 21,* 35–51.

Twenge, J. M. (1997b). Changes in masculine and feminine traits over time: A meta-analysis. *Sex Roles, 36,* 305–325.

U.S. Census Bureau. (2002). *Statistical abstract of the United States: 2002.* Washington, DC: U.S. Government Printing Office. [Also on-line.] Retrieved April 8, 2003. Available: http://www.census.gov/prod/2002pubs/01statab/labor.pdf

U.S. Department of Labor, Bureau of Labor Statistics. (2003). *News: July 17, 2003.* [On-line]. Retrieved August 24, 2003. Available: http://www.bls.gov/news.release/pdf/wkyeng.pdf

Washington Post Poll (2000, November 3). *Which one of these issues is most important in your vote for president?* [On-line.] Retrieved April 1, 2004. Available: http://www.washingtonpost.com/wp-srv/politics/polls/polls.htm.z

Whyte, M. K. (1978). *The status of women in preindustrial societies.* Princeton, NJ: Princeton University Press.

Williams, J. E., & Best, D. L. (1990). *Sex and psyche: Gender and self viewed cross-culturally.* Newbury Park, CA: Sage.

Wood, W., Christensen, P. N., Hebl, M. R., & Rothgerber, H. (1997). Conformity to sex-typed norms, affect, and the self-concept. *Journal of Personality and Social Psychology, 73,* 523–535.

Wood, W., & Eagly, A. H. (2002). A cross-cultural analysis of the behavior of women and men: Implications for the origins of sex differences. *Psychological Bulletin, 128,* 699–727.

Zenmore, S. E., Fiske, S. T., & Kim, H.-J. (2000). Gender stereotypes and the dynamics of social interaction. In T. Eckes & H. M. Trautner (Eds.), *The developmental social psychology of gender* (pp. 207–241). Mahwah, NJ: Erlbaum.

Chapter 10

Gender, Justice, and Social Change

William P. Gaeddert

It perhaps goes without saying that issues of justice and fairness (consistent with most social research, these terms will be used interchangeably) matter a great deal to people. Students are concerned about the fairness of the distribution of grades in their classes ("Will there be a curve?"), employees are concerned with the fairness of their pay and compensation packages, divorce laws are written to distribute marital assets fairly, and it's just not at all fair that Chicago Cubs fans have to "wait until next year." These examples encompass a wide range of justice determinations. This chapter will focus on perspectives derived from research on the social psychology of justice in the context of the gender wage gap.

Research and theory on the psychology of justice have been focused by considering two features of social exchange in determining individuals' judgments of the fairness of an allocation decision. The study of distributive justice is focused on people's judgments regarding the outcomes of an allocation process (e.g., Adams, 1965; Tyler, 1994), whereas the study of procedural justice concerns people's judgments about the formal rules and procedures by which allocation decisions are made (e.g., Leventhal, 1980; Tyler, 1994; Blader & Tyler, 2003). There is a substantial body of research regarding gender effects in distributive justice and far less research on gender effects in procedural justice.

Research concerning gender differences in distributive justice was sparked by concerns regarding the distribution of rewards on a societal scale. Observations such as the fact that among the full-time employed, women's pay is approximately 60 percent that of men's (Council of Economic Advisors, 1998), coupled with findings that suggest that women are no less satisfied with their work and pay than men are (Major, 1987), led to a search for causes of these phenomena. It is possible that women perceive themselves to be less entitled than men (Major, 1987) or that they have a more interpersonal orientation than do men, and are therefore less interested in their pay than men are (Kahn et al., 1980), or that they are oriented toward evaluating procedural rather than distributive fairness more than men are (Clay-Warner, 2001; Tata, 2000). Changing societal distributions of outcomes, such as the gender wage gap, has proceeded slowly, although since the passage of the Equal Pay Act, the gap has narrowed appreciably (Council of Economic Advisors, 1998).

Gender Effects on Distributive Justice Decisions

The most influential perspective in the domain of distributive justice has been equity theory (e.g., Adams, 1965; Leventhal, 1980). Equity theory is a cognitively oriented social comparison theory, and is therefore focused by comparisons that people make with others regarding the outcome of an allocation decision. The original formulation has been expanded by considering norms (such as basing allocative decisions on need rather than equity) used in distributive justice decisions (e.g., Deutsch 1985; Sabbagh, Yechezkel, & Resh, 1994), characteristics of inputs (such as status) deemed relevant (Berger, Cohen, & Zelditch, 1977) and characteristics of outcomes (e.g., Foa & Foa, 1980; Sabbagh et al., 1994).

According to equity theory, in order to arrive at a judgment regarding the fairness of the outcome of an allocation decision, an individual compares his or her input/outcome ratio with the input/outcome ratio of another person or group. Inputs can include personal abilities, amount of effort, and/or level of performance, depending upon the circumstances surrounding the distribution of outcomes. Outcomes, again depending upon the situation, can include tangible rewards (such as money or grades) as well as intangible resources such as respect or power (Foa & Foa, 1980; Sabbagh et al., 1994). An allocation decision is considered by an individual to be fair to the degree that differences in inputs are reflected in commensurate differences in outcomes. That is, an equitable (fair) decision provides greater levels of outcome favorability in direct proportion to levels of inputs when compared with the inputs and outcomes of relevant others. Judgments of allocation fairness based on an equity formulation are considered to enhance status differentiation, highlight differences in achievement, and, therefore, to be agentically oriented (Kahn et al., 1980; Kahn & Gaeddert, 1985). Men's allocation decisions typically follow predictions based on equity theory, whereas women's decisions typically diverge from predictions. Much of the research on these gender effects in allocation decisions has taken one of two directions: one focused on allocative norms relevant to distributive justice decisions, the other focused on the social comparison processes inherent in justice decisions.

Gender and Distributive Justice: Allocation Norms

As stated above, use of an equity rule in determining fair distributions of outcomes focuses on differences between people with regard both to their inputs (contributions) and to their outcomes. Although equity theory was originally proposed as a very general theory of fairness in social exchange, other normative expectations regarding the distribution of outcomes have been found to be relevant. These norms include using equality-based standards and need-based standards for making judgments about fairness in outcome distributions (Deutsch, 1985; Kahn et al., 1980). In a review of the extant literature, Kahn et al. (1980) asserted that choosing between an equity norm and an equality norm would be determined by individuals' degree of self-interest in the outcome of the distribution, their degree of control over the allocation decision, and whether interpersonal concerns are highlighted in the situation in which allocation decisions are made.

According to Kahn et al.'s (1980) perspective, self-interest in the distribution refers to whether or not an individual obtains distributed outcomes, or is responsible for making an allocation decision that distributes rewards to others. Control over the distributive decision refers to whether an individual is the sole decision maker, is making an allocation decision as part of a group, or is the recipient of outcomes based on another person's decision-making. When participants in an allocation decision become acquainted prior to interacting during the decision-making, interpersonal concerns are highlighted. Gender effects on allocation decisions are consistently obtained in research when the interpersonal concerns are highlighted (as in allocations among group members) and when self-interest is high (as when an individual makes allocation decisions relevant to self and/or others). Women generally behave as if communal concerns are important, whereas men behave more agentically (see Bakan, 1966). The strong situational effects for the interpersonal nature of allocation settings and degree of control observed in this research call into question the generality of the equity norm as a rule of fairness in distributive justice. Kahn and Gaeddert (1985) described the liberating effects on theory development of taking gender differences seriously, and called for development of theoretical perspectives that take into account gender differences as well as the perspectives of ethnic minorities, people with varying sexual orientations, and other groups whose perspectives have been neglected. Extensive development of such perspectives has yet to be undertaken.

Gender and Distributive Justice: Social Comparison and Entitlement

Focusing on the social comparison aspects of equity theory, Major and colleagues (see Major, 1987, for a review) have produced a substantial body of research regarding gender differences in feelings of entitlement. Feelings of personal entitlement provide individuals with the sense that they deserve positive outcomes from allocation decisions. According to the entitlement perspective, this sense of deservingness underlies cognitions regarding the fairness of an allocation.

Major and colleagues have found that when given the opportunity to set their own wage rates, women pay themselves less than men do (Major et al., 1984), and that women expect to receive lower starting salaries than do men (Major et al., 1984), suggesting that women believe they are entitled to less positive outcomes than men are with respect to pay for work. However, these effects seem to be confined to the domain of work, rather than outcomes in relationships (Major, Bylsma, & Cozzarelli, 1989). These gender differences in evaluations of fairness in allocation may be based on comparisons with others, comparisons with past distributions, or with comparisons of societal values placed on performance in different domains. Thus, from an equity theory perspective, women's most relevant comparison group against whom to balance their sense of deservingness is other women, who are appreciably underpaid relative to men (Major, 1987). Similarly, in comparing expected rates of compensation, women, who have been traditionally underpaid relative to men, would be expected to feel that they deserve less. The finding that these effects occur with respect to work, rather than relationships, suggests that societal valuing of work over relationship outcomes underlies women's sense of deservingness for pay (Major, 1987).

Gender Effects on the Valuing of Procedural Justice

The study of procedural justice refers to issues regarding the formal procedures by which outcomes are distributed (Leventhal, 1980, Thibaut & Walker, 1975; Tyler, 1994). A substantial body of literature supports the conclusion that people care as much about how an allocation decision is reached as they do about the outcomes they receive (see, e.g., Lind & Tyler, 1988). Blader and Tyler (2003) have proposed a four-component model of procedural justice based on a relational model of procedural justice (e.g., Tyler,

1994). In the four-component model, both formal and informal features of procedures are considered on the basis of their value in individuals' decisions about the quality of the allocation decision as well as their judgments about their standing in a group. If, as suggested by the Kahn et al. (1980) perspective on distributive justice, women are more focused on interpersonal concerns than men are, gender differences in concerns for procedural justice can be predicted on the basis of a relational model. For example, heightened interpersonal concerns could predict increased valuing of informal treatment in procedural justice determinations. On the other hand, if men are more interested in status within a group (e.g., Kahn & Gaeddert, 1985; Kahn et al., 1980), a relational model of procedural justice could be used to predict heightened valuing of formal treatment in procedural matters as an indication of one's relative standing in a group.

In contrast to research on distributive justice judgments, gender differences in procedural justice concerns have not been heavily studied. Sweeney and McFarlin (1997) predicted that women's work satisfaction would be more strongly tied to procedural justice concerns than would men's, and that men's satisfaction would be more related to distributive issues than would women's. These predictions are consistent both with an entitlement view of women's evaluations of their outcomes (Major, 1987) and with predictions that could be based on the relational model of procedural justice. Sweeney and McFarlin's (1997) predictions were supported by results of analyses of survey data. Lee and Farh (1999) compared the relationships between perceptions of distributive justice, procedural justice, and organizational outcomes (pay satisfaction, trust in supervisor, and organizational commitment). Although perceptions of both distributive and procedural fairness affected organizational outcomes, gender did not moderate these relationships. Tata (2000) studied men and women business students' predictions of the degree to which they would base pay raise decisions on distributive issues (e.g., amount of experience, effort) and on procedural issues (e.g., correctability, representativeness) when assuming the role of a subordinate or a supervisor. Distributive matters were perceived to be more important when participants assumed the role of a subordinate and by men. Procedural issues were perceived to be more important when participants assumed the role of a supervisor, but contrary to predictions, women did not weigh procedural justice matters more heavily than did men.

Clay-Warner (2001) studied male and female judges' and attorneys' perceptions of procedural injustice in court settings. Behaviors such as overly familiar forms of address and comments about attorneys' physical appearance were taken by Clay-Warner to be indicators of procedural injustice. Her predictions, based on a relational model of procedural justice—that female attorneys perceived more injustice than did female judges, male attorneys, and male judges—were supported by survey data.

In contrast to the large literature and consistent findings regarding gender differences in distributive justice perceptions, the small literature on gender and procedural justice does not yield consistent results. Differences in participants, such as Tata's (2000) use of business students versus Lee and Farh's (1999) use of employed persons, might account for some of the inconsistencies. However, at this point the question of gender effects on perceptions of procedural justice is wide open.

The social psychological literature regarding gender effects on distributive and procedural justice highlights interesting differences (and similarities) between men's and women's justice determinations. This literature does not provide clear prescriptions for change. See, however, Crosby and Franco (2003) for an example of applying traditional social psychological perspectives on justice to real-world concerns related to affirmative action.

Social Change

The gender wage gap, indicated by the fact that full-time-employed women earn on average substantially less than full-time-employed men, has been studied in the United States and as a worldwide phenomenon (e.g., Blau & Kahn, 1999). The gender wage gap (expressed here as the ratio of women's median wages to those of men) has narrowed, from a low of approximately 60 percent during the 1950s (Council of Economic Advisors, 1998) to 76 percent in 2001 (DeNavas-Walt & Cleveland, 2002). There is, however, substantial variation in the gender gap based on demographic characteristics in the United States, with older women (68 percent for women aged sixty-five or older), African–American women (69 percent of white male earnings), and Hispanic women (56 percent of white male earnings) experiencing appreciably wider gaps (U.S. Department of Labor, 2004). In addition, the gender wage gap is substantially narrower in Europe (Blau & Kahn, 1999). Explanations for the wage gap in the United States intersect with both distributive and procedural justice concerns.

A human capital explanation (Blau & Kahn, 1999; Council of Economic Advisors, 1998; Wittig & Lowe, 1989) suggests that the gender wage gap signifies true differences in the valuing of the skills, labor market experience, and educational attainments of men and women. This view, consistent with an equity theory perspective on distributive justice, holds that women's and men's decisions regarding inputs such as educational attainment and labor market participation result in fair (equitable) differences in rates of pay. Careful analyses of the effects of inputs such as labor market experience, however, typically indicate an "unexplained" portion of the gender wage gap of approximately 10 to 12 percent (Blau & Kahn, 1999; Council of Economic Advisors, 1998). Major (1989) argued that many women's tolerance of the gender wage gap is explained by their (lower) sense of entitlement to monetary compensation when comparing inputs and outcomes in making decisions about the fairness of wage distributions.

A number of discrimination hypotheses stand in contrast to the human capital explanation for the gender wage gap by focusing on the "unexplained" portion of the gap as well as characteristics (such as occupational choices) taken into account by the human capital explanation. These sorts of hypotheses indicate differences in the structure of occupations (i.e., occupational segregation; Wittig & Lowe, 1989), overt discrimination in hiring and wage determination (e.g., Wood, Corcoran, & Courant, 1993), and family structure (e.g., Council of Economic Advisors, 1998) as explanations for the gender wage gap. Although not mutually exclusive explanations, the human capital and discrimination hypotheses suggest very different routes to narrowing the gender wage gap. From a human capital perspective, narrowing of the gap will occur naturally as women and men come to make more similar decisions with respect to equitably valued inputs such as educational attainment and labor market participation. A discrimination perspective focused on the effects of occupational segregation, however, suggests a more active approach to narrowing the gender wage gap.

Beginning in 1963 with the passage and signing of the Equal Pay Act, equal pay for the same work was mandated. Although the gender wage gap has narrowed since then, parity with respect to men's and women's median wages has not been achieved. In order to take into account issues of occupational segregation, comparable, rather than equal, work has been suggested as a standard by which to determine equitable pay distributions, because job categories that are female-dominated are typically underpaid relative to job classifications that are male-dominated (e.g., Hegtvedt, 1989; Wittig & Lowe, 1989). Occupational segregation by sex has narrowed in some categories but has not changed in others. For example, job categories such as aircraft pilot and flight engineer, electrician, and carpenter contain less than 5 percent women, whereas job categories such as secretary and registered nurse contain more than 90 percent women (U.S. Department of Labor, 2004). Some (e.g., Preston, 1999) argue that a substantial portion (as much as 89 percent) of the gender wage gap can be attributed to the differential pay scales occasioned by occupational segregation.

Although comparable worth has been the subject of substantial debate, the procedures that form the basis for comparable worth determinations (e.g., job evaluation and establishing wage trend lines) are well understood and accepted practices in management and industrial psychology. Job evaluation is a process by which characteristics of jobs (often termed compensable factors) are determined and then used to compare average pay rates across job categories with levels of compensable factors by constructing wage trend lines. Taking into account demographic characteristics, such as gender, in constructing the wage trend lines creates a comparable worth analysis.

Job evaluation is typically preceded by a job analysis. Using any of a variety of well-known techniques, a job analyst prepares a description of a job in terms of the knowledge, skills, abilities, and other relevant characteristics (such as degree of training) needed to perform a particular job or class of jobs. From a job description, lists of compensable factors can be developed. Compensable factors are characteristics of people (such as amount of education) and characteristics of jobs (such as level of responsibility and amount of physical effort required) that are considered to be valid sources of worth to an organization. As part of the job evaluation process, they are weighted, typically using point values, according to their perceived worth to the organization. The determination of compensable factors, and particularly judgments of their worth to an organization, provide opportunities for biases, such as subtle gender bias in perceived worth of job activities, to affect the outcome of the job evaluation (Hegtvedt, 1989). Beuhring (1989) provided an example of procedures that address this potential for bias and provide for the potential for heightened perceptions of procedural fairness. Her procedure, implemented by examining nearly 1,500 positions in 125 job classifications at the University of Minnesota, relies on employee input in determining compensable factors. Visibly and systematically incorporating employees' perceptions in job evaluation is in contrast to typical job evaluation procedures, in which committees of subject matter experts (i.e., managers, supervisors, professional job analysts) determine compensable factors and their weights (Aamodt, 2004).

Beuhring (1989) developed a job evaluation questionnaire based on input from committees of employees that were carefully formed to represent each of the job classes at the University of Minnesota. For example, job classes that were represented included "clerical and administrative," "data processing and analysis," and "physical operations." Categories of compensable factors, such as "mental effort," "effect of error," and "physical effort," were developed and reviewed by the employee committees. Subsequent administrations and revisions of the questionnaire resulted in a final job evaluation plan and the assignment of points to job classes. These procedures yielded a highly reliable (test–retest reliability of $r = .96$) and valid job evaluation. According to Beuhring (1989), the job evaluation system also resulted in enhanced valuing of job characteristics associated with lower-level and female-dominated jobs than would likely have been the case with using a more traditional system that relied on subject matter experts.

In their simplest form, wage trend lines are scatter plots that position jobs on dimensions that reflect wages and values associated with compensable factors (i.e., job-evaluation point values). These analyses are often used to ensure equitable pay rates within an organization. When separate plots are portrayed—for example, separate lines for men and women—comparable worth assessments are possible. More complex analyses using hierarchical multiple regression can be used to take into account worker characteristics, such as job tenure, in conducting a comparable worth analysis. Using her employee-input-based job evaluation procedures, Beuhring (1989) performed a comparable worth analysis. Separate wage trend lines (regression lines) were constructed for job classes dominated by males, those that were balanced, and those dominated by females. Appreciable underpayment for female-dominated jobs was discovered and, interestingly, the underpayment was greater for job classes deemed more important (based on job evaluation point values). This job evaluation procedure resulted in policy changes and wage structure adjustments. Although some classes received substantial pay adjustments (e.g., child care co-head teacher), Beuhring reported that the overall cost of adjustments was merely 6 percent of the base payroll. The salary adjustments were phased in over six years in order to minimize budgetary problems.

Particularly from the standpoint of a relational model of procedural justice (Blader & Tyler, 2003; Tyler, 1994), the procedure used by Beuhring (1989) would be expected to enhance employees' feelings of fairness in the procedure. The relational model of procedural justice posits that having outcome distributions decided by consistently applied procedural rules that provide a measure of valuation of one's social standing and worth in a group are perceived to be more fair and satisfying than rules that do not provide such valuing. The job evaluation procedures and comparable worth analyses undertaken by Beuhring were public, engaged the participation of a substantial number of directly interested parties, and thereby would have enhanced employees' feelings of worth to the organization as well as their perceptions of the fairness of the procedures. Indeed, Smith and Tyler (1996) showed that even those who are advantaged by unfair procedures are willing to lose this advantage in order to restore justice. Thus, it seems likely that when they are conducted under conditions that heighten perceptions of procedural justice, comparable worth analyses will be well accepted by all employees. Furthermore, the tangible benefits to organizations of procedures that are equitable and are perceived to be fair are substantial. These effects include, but are not limited to, heightened organizational commitment, productivity, and job satisfaction (e.g., Lind & Tyler, 1988; Masterson, 2001).

Some authors (e.g., Crosby & Franco, 2003) have pointed to Rawls's (2001) political philosophy as a useful departure point for supporting and justifying change. His assertion that allocation decisions be made under a "veil of ignorance" may be a useful ideal, but is an impossibility in reality. The "veil of ignorance" concept suggests that allocation decisions (such as the setting of wage scales) be made without knowledge of the identity of the recipients of the goods or outcomes (pay). However, procedural rules that minimize the potential for biases inherent in knowing the recipients of allocation decisions may produce outcomes similar to a veil of ignorance. Job evaluation methods, such as those used by Beuhring (1989), which reduce bias by engaging multiple viewpoints, may well substitute for the veil of ignorance. Based both on the extant literature on the effects of distributive and procedural justice on organizational effectiveness, and on the political philosophy of Rawls, such procedures should be encouraged.

It is possible that women in general are less dissatisfied with inequitable pay than men are (Major, 1989). However, in light of the positive effects of fair wage scales, and the well-established procedures for conducting job evaluations and comparable worth analyses, the persistence of the inequitable distributions of societal resources (such as the gender wage gap) can be understood only in political terms. Although continued research on gender, racial, and ethnic biases is warranted, meaningful solutions are most likely to be based on political action.

References

Aamodt, M. G. (2004). *Applied industrial/organizational psychology* (4th ed.). Belmont, CA: Thomson/Wadsworth.

Adams, J. S. (1965). "Inequity in social exchange." In L. Berkowitz (Ed.), *Advances in experimental social psychology,* vol. 2 (pp. 267–299). New York: Academic Press.

Bakan, D. (1966). *The duality of human existence.* Chicago: Rand McNally.

Berger, J., Cohen, B. P., & Zelditch, M., Jr. (1977). Status characteristics and social interaction. *American Sociological Review, 37,* 241–255.

Beuhring, T. (1989). Incorporating employee values in job evaluation. *Journal of Social Issues, 45,* 169–189.

Blader, S. L., & Tyler, T. R. (2003). A four component model of procedural justice: Defining the meaning of a "fair" process. *Personality and Social Psychology Bulletin, 29,* 747–758.

Blau, F. D., & Kahn, L. M. (1999). Analyzing the gender pay gap. *Quarterly Review of Economics and Finance, 39,* 625–646.

Clay-Warner, J. (2001). Perceiving procedural injustice: The effects of group membership and status. *Social Psychology Quarterly, 64,* 224–238.

Council of Economic Advisors. (1998). Explaining trends in the gender wage gap. [On-line.] Retrieved November 13, 2003. Available: http://clinton4.nara.gov/WH/EOP/CEA/html/gendergap.html

Crosby, F. J., & Franco, J. L. (2003). Connections between the ivory tower and the multicolored world: Linking abstract theories of social justice to the rough and tumble of affirmative action. *Personality and Social Psychology Review, 7,* 362–373.

DeNavas-Walt, C., & Cleveland, R. W. (2002). *Money income in the United States.* Washington, DC: Bureau of the Census.

Deutsch, M. (1985). *Distributive Justice: A social-psychological Perspective.* New Haven, CT: Yale University Press.

Foa, E. B., & Foa, U. G. (1980). Resource theory: Interpersonal behavior as exchange. In K. J. Gergen, M. S. Greenberg, and R. H. Willis (Eds.), *Social exchange: Advances in theory and research* (pp. 77–101). New York: Plenum.

Hegtvedt, K. A. (1989). Fairness conceptualizations and comparable worth. *Journal of Social Issues, 45,* 81–97.

Kahn, A., & Gaeddert, W. (1985). "From theories of equity to theories of justice: The liberating consequences of studying women." In V. E. O'Leary, R. K. Unger, and B. S. Wallston (Eds.), *Women, gender, and social psychology* (pp. 129–148). Hillsdale., NJ: Erlbaum.

Kahn, A., O'Leary, V. E., Krulewitz, J., & Lamm, H. (1980). Equity and equality: Male and female ways to a just end. *Basic and Applied Social Psychology, 1,* 173–197.

Lee, C., & Farh, J. (1999). The effects of gender in organizational justice perception. *Journal of Organizational Behavior, 20,* 133–143.

Leventhal, G. S. (1980). What should be done with equity theory? In K. J. Gergen, M. S. Greenberg, and R. H. Willis (Eds.), *Social exchange: Advances in theory and research* (pp. 27–55). New York: Plenum.

Lind, E. A., & Tyler, T. R. (1988). *The social psychology of procedural justice.* New York: Plenum.

Major, B. (1987). Gender, justice, and the psychology of entitlement. In P. Shaver & C. Hendrick (Eds.), *Review of Personality and Social Psychology,* vol. 7, *Sex and Gender* (pp. 124–148). Beverly Hills, CA: Sage.

Major, B. (1989). Gender differences in comparisons and entitlement: Implications for comparable worth. *Journal of Social Issues, 45,* 99–115.

Major, B., Bylsma, W. H., & Cozzarelli, C. (1989). Gender differences in distributive justice preferences: The impact of domain. *Sex Roles, 21,* 487–497.

Major, B., McFarlin, D. B., & Gagnon, D. (1984). Overworked and underpaid: On the nature of gender differences in personal entitlement. *Journal of Personality and Social Psychology, 47,* 1399–1412.

Major, B., Vanderslice, V., & McFarlin, D. B. (1984). Effects of pay expected on pay received: The confirmatory nature of initial expectations. *Journal of Applied Social Psychology, 14,* 399–412.

Masterson, S. S. (2001). A trickle down model of organizational justice: Relating employees' and customers' perceptions of and reactions to fairness. *Journal of Applied Psychology, 86,* 594–604.

Preston, J. A. (1999). Occupational gender segregation: Trends and explanations. *Quarterly Review of Economics and Finance, 39,* 611–624.

Rawls, J. (2001). *Justice as fairness: A restatement* (E. Kelly, ed.). Cambridge, MA: Harvard University Press.

Sabbagh, C., Yechezkel, D., & Resh, N. (1994). The structure of social justice judgments: A facet approach. *Social Psychology Quarterly, 57,* 244–261.

Smith, H. J., & Tyler, T. R. (1996). Justice and power: When will justice concerns encourage the advantaged to support policies which redistribute economic resources and the disadvantaged to willingly obey the law? *European Journal of Social Psychology, 26,* 171–200.

Sweeney, P. D., & McFarlin, D. B. (1997). Process and outcome: Gender differences in the assessment of justice. *Journal of Organizational Behavior, 18,* 83–98.

Tata, J. (2000). Influence of role and gender on the use of distributive versus procedural justice principles. *Journal of Psychology, 134,* 261–268.

Thibaut, J., & Walker, L. (1975). *Procedural justice: A psychological analysis.* Hillsdale, NJ: Erlbaum.

Tyler, T. R. (1994). Psychological models of the justice motive: Antecedents of distributive and procedural justice. *Journal of Personality and Social Psychology, 67,* 850–863.

U.S. Department of Labor, Women's Bureau. (2004). *Statistics and data.* [On-line.] Accessed January 29, 2004. Available: http://www.dol.gov/wb/stats/main.htm.

Wittig, M. A., & Lowe, R. H. (1989). Comparable worth theory and policy. *Journal of Social Issues, 45,* 1–21.

Wood, R. G., Corcoran, M. E., & Courant, P. (1993). Pay differences among the highly paid: The male–female earnings gap in lawyers' salaries. *Journal of Labor Economics, 11,* 417–441.

Chapter 11

The Role of Shame in Socio- and Subcultural Influences on Disordered Eating

Jean E. Denious, Nancy Felipe Russo,
and Lisa R. Rubin

In their review of the literature, Polivy and Herman (2002) noted that "literally thousands of studies" (p. 191) have examined possible causes of eating disorders (primarily anorexia nervosa and bulimia nervosa), illustrating the compelling and complex nature of these appearance-related disorders. Research has identified myriad factors—from individual to cultural—that appear to increase women's risk for eating pathology. For example, personality characteristics such as neuroticism (Feldman & Eysenck, 1986) and perfectionism (Garner, Olmstead, & Polivy, 1983; Garner et al., 1984), as well as interpersonal factors, including distrust of others (Garner et al., 1983; Garner et al., 1984), early experience of abuse—sexual abuse, in particular—and family dysfunction (Andrews, 1995, 1997; Murray, Waller, & Legg, 2000; Weiner & Thompson, 1997), have all been found to contribute to women's eating disorder risk.

The greatest amount of attention (and criticism), however, has been directed at the broader cultural milieu in which girls and women learn that their bodies are central to their social worth and identity, and that the only acceptable "expression" of oneself is in the form of extreme thinness. Indeed, eating disorders are among the very few psychiatric diagnoses specific to Western culture that have been categorized as *culturebound syndromes* (King, 1993; APA, 1994).

Hence, it is of little surprise that U.S. culture has "become the prime suspect" (Polivy & Herman, 2004, p. 1), with media serving as the most observable and indictable messenger of its values. Both the number of media programs and publications that focus on women's appearance (e.g., fashion and fitness magazines) and the extent of body exposure in television, movies, and magazines have increased since the 1980s (Plous & Neptune, 1997;

Striegel-Moore, Silberstein, & Rodin, 1986). Meanwhile, numerous observational and experimental studies have shown that the influence of media exposure on women's body-related feelings and behaviors can be immediate, cumulative, and more often negative than positive or neutral (see Groesz, Levine, & Murnen, 2002, for a meta-analysis of the literature).

Nonetheless, fundamental questions regarding women's individual risk for disordered eating, and the processes by which these dysfunctional patterns of weight regulation evolve remain unanswered (see Polivy & Herman, 2002). For one, despite the presumably powerful influence of mediated messages regarding body appearance, we know that most women never develop "full-blown" eating disorders, although most feel dissatisfied with their bodies (Polivy & Herman, 1987, 2004; Cash & Henry, 1985) and many evidence some perceptual distortion regarding their own body size (Cullari & Trubilla, 1989; Garner et al., 1984; Thompson & Psaltis, 1988; see also Hsu & Sobkiewicz, 1991). If we are all aware of the cultural mandate to be thin (and the corresponding stigma of overweight) and we are all exposed (albeit to varying degrees) to media images that effectively endorse these values, what makes some of us particularly vulnerable and others of us more resistant and resilient in the face of such demands?

Further, what are the mechanisms by which awareness and internalization of such beauty standards lead to disordered eating? Although the literature is rich with identification of factors contributing to eating disorder risk, relatively little is understood regarding the more proximal (intrapsychic) processes by which these influences compel eating-disordered behaviors (Polivy & Herman, 2002).

We argue that a closer look at the role of shame in girls' and women's relationships to their bodies (a) provides important insight into the proximal mechanisms by which sociocultural factors, such as media exposure and internalization of its appearance standards for women (Stice & Shaw, 1994; Striegel-Moore et al., 1986), encourage eating disorder development; and (b) clarifies the moderating role of subcultures on the relationship of sociocultural beauty norms to women's appearance-related behaviors.

The Relationship of Sociocultural Influences to Body Shame

Striegel-Moore and colleagues (Silberstein, Striegel-Moore, & Rodin, 1987) first identified shame as an important emotion to explore in the context of women's feelings about their bodies. They touched upon compelling similarities in clinical transcripts of women's discussions of their bodies to theoretical descriptions of shame. Their initial observations were strictly descriptive, however, and only more recently have empirical studies examined possible relationships of shame to body image and eating-disorder (ED)-related behaviors. This small but growing body of empirical research demonstrates that body shame plays a significant role in the development of eating-disordered behaviors, including both intensified efforts to control dietary intake such as restrained eating (Fredrickson et al., 1998; Noll & Fredrickson, 1998) and disregulatory behaviors such as binge eating (Andrews, 1997; Burney & Irwin, 2000; Garner et al., 1983, 1984; Sanftner & Crowther, 1998).

In an important conceptual advance, Fredrickson and Roberts (1997) articulated the tenets of objectification theory, presenting a theoretical model explicitly positing a causal link between sociocultural influences and the development of body shame. Objectification theory posits that women in our culture learn to adopt an observer's perspective of self in response to chronic objectification, and that it is this cognitive adaptation that primes women to experience shame with regard to their body appearance.

Objectification is the experience of being treated as if the body were representative of the self. A wide range of social stimuli can be considered objectifying, but a central argument is that "subtle and everyday" (Fredrickson & Roberts, 1997, p. 175) occurrences, such as advertisements that use scantily clad women to sell products and, at a more personal level, comments and behavioral gestures directed toward a person's body appearance, exert a powerful, if insidious, influence on women's psychological and physical health.

Specifically, as women learn the centrality of their body appearance in their social evaluation and opportunities (see Berscheid et al., 1971; Eagly et al., 1991), they develop the capacity and motive to pre-emptively adopt an outside view of self. To the extent that a woman believes others will evaluate her on the basis of body appearance, she may spend a lot of time contemplating her physique, and, once engaged in social interaction or in a public context, she may continue to monitor how she appears to others.

Objectification theory posits that being chronically engaged in this mode hinders one's ability to experience positive emotional states while increasing the conditions that lead to negative feelings, such as shame and anxiety. This makes sense, given that shame is a social, self-conscious emotion. Shame requires being able to imagine another's perspective on the self. Specifically, shame is "the empathic experience of the other's rejection of the self" (Lewis, 1987, p. 18), and to experience it is to feel one has failed or is lacking *as a person* in the eyes of a "critical" other (Emde & Oppenheim, 1995). This other need not be physically present (Barrett, 1995) but, rather, may be vividly and painfully imagined. The "observer" may be a specific person (e.g., parent, partner), but arguably may also be generalized to a social view-point, as long as the putative evaluator is meaningful to the individual. Thus, to experience body shame is to perceive wholesale social rejection due to body appearance. It is important to emphasize that shame necessarily involves global devaluation, and thus, in body shame, the body is the apparent basis of the emotion but not its sole focus (rather, the entire self is).

Because shame implicates the entire self (Lewis, 1987), it is presumably triggered only by perceived shortfalls on dimensions that are highly linked to one's *social* self-concept. Thus, to the extent that an individual believes his or her body appearance is a crucial component of his or her social self, the body becomes a viable basis for shame. The greater importance of appearance for women than for men in social evaluation is sufficient to suggest that women may be more susceptible to shame deriving from body appearance than men, especially given that standards for the ideal female physique and American women's actual physiques have become increasingly discrepant. Moreover, the literal visibility of body appearance as a dimension of evaluation suggests that opportunities for body shame may be greater than opportunities for shame deriving from potentially less visible bases, such as income or intelligence.

The Relationship of Shame to Eating-Disordered Symptomatology

As noted, empirical studies have linked body shame to eating-disordered symptomatology. Body shame predicts both restrained eating (Fredrickson et al., 1998; Noll & Fredrickson, 1998) and severity of eating-disordered symptoms (Burney & Irwin, 2000; Tiggeman & Slater, 2001). Fredrickson et al. (1998) hypothesized that experience of objectification would lead women to restrict their intake of food and that this relationship would be mediated by body shame. The results of their study, in which participants were placed alone in dressing rooms and required to try on swimsuits (as part of a cover story on consumer attitudes), confirmed their hypothesis. After wearing the swimsuits, women, but not men, reported greater body shame and chose to eat lesser amounts of cookies and candy (also part of the consumer cover story) than their control counterparts. Analyses supported the authors' model in which body shame accounted for the relationship of self-objectification to restrained eating.

Tiggemann and Slater (2001) also found support for Fredrickson et al.'s (Fredrickson et al., 1998; Noll & Fredrickson, 1998) model in their study, with body shame mediating the relationship of self-objectification and body surveillance to disordered eating in two separate samples of women (ballet dancers and nondancers).

Burney and Irwin (2000) examined the relationships of shame proneness, eating-related shame, and body shame to the severity of eating-disordered symptoms in a community sample of Australian women. They found that while a propensity to feel shame in general was not significantly related to eating disturbances, the extent to which women expressed shame in relation to their bodies and in response to eating-related situations was significantly associated with attitudes and behaviors indicative of having an eating disorder.

Body shame has also been found to mediate the relationship of childhood physical and sexual abuse to bulimia (Andrews, 1997) and depression (Andrews, 1995). In two studies, Andrews found that body shame accounted for the relationship of early abuse to subsequent eating-disordered symptomatology, including the feelings of worthlessness and hopelessness that characterize depression. She also tested the possibility that body shame may have moderated the consequences of abuse, but this explanation was not supported by the data (Andrews, 1995).

Other studies have examined the extent of shame proneness (i.e., trait shame) in clinical populations. Sanftner and colleagues (Sanftner et al., 1995) found shame proneness to be positively associated with eating-disordered symptoms, including drive for thinness, feelings of ineffectiveness, lack of interoceptive awareness (i.e., awareness of internal bodily states and cues, such as hunger), and difficulties with impulse regulation, echoing earlier research findings by Garner and colleagues (Garner et al., 1983; Garner et al., 1984).

In a later study, Sanftner and Crowther (1998) had women report their state self-esteem and levels of shame at various time points to investigate changes in affect in relation to bingeing episodes. Not only did women who binge report overall higher levels of shame than non-bingeing women, they reported lower levels of state self-esteem and evidenced greater fluctuation on both these measures.

Research has identified negative affect as a precipitant of bingeing episodes (see Heatherton & Polivy, 1992) and as a factor that contributes more generally to the maintenance of eating pathology (see Stice, 2002). So why does the emotion of shame merit special attention? We propose that shame—with its specific relevance to global, *social* devaluation—is uniquely linked to exaggerated, dysfunctional behaviors, such as those exhibited in disordered eating patterns.

Accounting for the Relationship of Shame to Eating-Disordered Behaviors

In the context of self-regulation, negative emotions are often construed as representing negative self-discrepancies (Higgins, 1987), thereby signaling the need for behavioral adjustments that will narrow the distance between one's actual self and desired self. Higgins (1987) specifically proposed that shame results from a discrepancy between one's actual self and another's ideal for oneself, because it involves loss of another's regard. According to this notion, one who experiences body shame fails to meet the appearance standard that an important other wishes or hopes for that person. In the context of body shame, this perspective would seem to suggest that individuals would respond to the emotion by undertaking behaviors that would realign the actual self with the (presumably thinner) desired self.

More recent research calls into question the utility of Higgins's (1987) theory in conceptualizing shame. Tangney and colleagues (1998) tested whether Higgins's discrepancies could reliably predict and differentiate shame from other negative emotions, and found that shame proneness associated positively with both (other-) ideal and (other-) ought discrepancies. Moreover, at the definitional level, Higgins's construal of shame as signaling a loss or lack of something positive seems at odds with theoretical descriptions of the emotion. Shame is characterized as representing a fatal blow to the self. It is not a simple demotion in status, but a pointed and complete failure that is implicated in shame. This sounds more like a negative outcome than the mere absence of a positive outcome.

In fact, research that has considered a larger range of "possible" selves (Carver, Lawrence, & Scheier, 1999; Ferguson, Eyre, & Ashbaker, 2000; Markus & Nurius, 1986; Oyserman & Markus, 1990) suggests that consideration of whom we do *not* want to be is just as meaningful as whom we desire to be in guiding affect and motivation. Although we agree that it may be technically appropriate to characterize shame as signaling a negative self-discrepancy, it may be more informative to consider shame in an alternative light—beyond a mere failure to approximate a desired self, shame may more pointedly signal "achievement" of a feared self. Conceptualizing body shame as a realization of one's "feared" or "dreaded" self (Carver et al., 1999; Markus & Nurius, 1986) may help account for its relationship to ED behaviors.

Shame as Achievement of a Feared Self

Markus and colleagues (Markus & Nurius, 1986; Oyserman & Markus, 1990) state that one's self-concept and goals are characterized largely by representations of possible selves—including "who we *could* become, *would like to* become, and *are afraid of* becoming" (Oyserman & Markus, 1990, p. 112; italics theirs). Our feared selves are entities that we hope never materialize, but that we believe have the potential to develop. The content of feared selves likely differs across individuals, depending on what things are most important to them, and what most threatens access to those things.

In applying this perspective to body appearance concerns and body shame, what can be assumed is that (1) the individual possesses a feared self (in addition to a desired self) that relates to body appearance; and (2) this embodiment is feared precisely because it is associated with socially relevant negative consequences, such as loss of social acceptance, respect, or love. All feared representations of the self that are tied to *social* rejection are potentially implicated in shame, since shame involves failure in the eyes of others.

As discussed earlier, being attractive confers meaningful benefits to women in this culture. However, more pointedly, being "fat" or otherwise physically inadequate incurs significant negative consequences. Overweight women experience considerable stigma in this culture, and obesity has been linked to a number of negative social and economic consequences for women (Hebl & Heatherton, 1998; Rothblum, 1992). Thus, body appearance is likely relevant to representations of both desired and dreaded selves in women. Indeed, an intense fear of fat has been identified as a criterion of diagnosis for both anorexia nervosa and bulimia nervosa (see Garner & Garfinkel, 1988).

Thinking about this "flip side" of body appearance issues—that is, focusing more on appearance fears than on appearance ideals—also helps us to understand why men may indeed care about their appearance and fitness, but do not appear to be as predisposed to body shame or eating disorders. They may possess desired selves that are defined by or include appearance-relevant attributes (e.g., being strong and healthy), but likely do not associate being fat or otherwise physically inadequate with the profound negative social consequences that women do. For men, physical attractiveness is not as strongly implicated in their social self, and therefore it is not intimately linked to social rejection or acceptance, as it may be for women.

Carver et al. (1999) note that proximity to negative system-level reference values (i.e., undesired selves) affects motivation differently than mere discrepancy with positive reference values (i.e., desired selves). Thus, the process of acquiring distance from a feared self may be qualitatively different from the process of acquiring proximity to a desired self or positive reference value. When an individual is perilously close to one's feared self, the desire to move away from it is intense, and more salient than the desire to move toward a corresponding desired self. Avoidance motives are more pressing and urgent than approach motives, since the drive to escape an aversive state of being is stronger than the drive to obtain a pleasant state. Thus, when a negative reference value threatens to materialize, behavioral responses are more extreme than those that might occur when positive reference values are not being achieved.

Overcompensatory Behaviors as a Response to Body Shame

The urgent and impactful nature of avoidance motives helps account for *overcompensation* of appearance-related behaviors following body shame experiences. Body shame signals achievement of or proximity to an appearance-related feared self, and the individual's subsequent actions are extreme because sufficient distance is desired as quickly as possible. The rate of progress perceived to be necessary in moving away from a feared self may be considerable. Carver and Scheier (1990) note that in monitoring our self-regulation, we don't just determine the direction of our progressive efforts, but also have perceptions of the necessary rate of such progress. In the case of body shame, both the amount and the rate of effort perceived to be necessary to remove the threat may be substantial. Thus, moderate behavioral adjustments following body shame, such as choosing to follow a healthier diet, would be insufficient to create the amount of distance needed in a short time. In order to escape one's feared self, a stronger and more extreme response is necessary. Fasting, overexercise, and purging, for example, are more extreme measures which may be perceived by an individual as delivering himself or herself safely far from the feared self, thus making one feel he or she has regained adequate control (which is necessary for successful self-regulation) and reducing perceived vulnerability to subsequent episodes of body shame. One can think of shame as a punishing indicator of failure to keep distance from the feared self. Its affect motivates the individual to do whatever can be done to avoid experiencing this failure again.

Research has construed overcompensatory eating behaviors as a natural consequence of internalizing thin appearance ideals (e.g., Stice, 1994). This perspective would likely understand restrained eating, overexercise, and other extreme forms of weight control to reflect an intense desire to attain the ideal physique—that is, as attempts to approximate a desired self. Although we would agree that all eating-disordered individuals see thinness as an ideal, we suggest that *overcompensatory* behaviors are better explained by avoidance, rather than approach, dynamics. It is the distress of approximating a feared self, rather than failure to reach an ideal self, that pushes weight-regulating behaviors toward the extreme.

Disregulatory Behaviors as a Response to Body Shame

A conceptualization of body shame as indicating achievement of or proximity to one's feared (fat) self explains overcompensatory eating behaviors as a function of strong avoidance motives. However, body shame appears to precipitate disregulation (e.g., bingeing) as well. What accounts for such divergent paths of behavior? How can both overcompensatory and disregulatory eating behaviors be understood as possible outcomes of realizing one's feared self? Carver and Scheier (1990) note that an interruption in self-regulation (for example, an experience of body shame) causes the individual to assess the likely outcomes of attempts to regain control and resume successful regulation.

The result of this assessment is referred to collectively as *outcome expectancies*. In the case of achieving distance from a feared self, these expectancies may include determinations of one's ability to create sufficient distance and consideration of the outcomes of such efforts. Outcome expectancies tend to be dichotomized into favorable and unfavorable assessments (Carver & Scheier, 1990). It is proposed here that the outcome expectancies that follow a given experience of body shame are key to understanding the likelihood that body shame will lead to overcompensation or disregulation of appearance-related behaviors.

Outcome Expectancies

At stake in the shame experience is whether the individual believes he or she has the ability to regain control over the shaming dimension, and thus salvage the social self. Shame makes one feel powerless, and the immediate phenomenology of the emotion illustrates this. However, shame also ostensibly motivates the individual to avoid future transgressions. Thus the individual who has just had a bout of body shame wishes never again to feel that way, and would rationally see the solution as pulling oneself as far away from the feared embodiment as possible. This explains why overcompensatory behaviors aimed at short-term, appreciable changes in one's body are associated with body shame, and we posit that at earlier stages of disordered eating development, overcompensatory behaviors are the dominant response to experiences of body shame. The instinctual response is to achieve distance from the feared self, extremely and quickly. The individual makes strong, exaggerated attempts to regain control over his or her body and sufficiently reduce its inadequacy.

However, what must be kept in mind is that it can be highly difficult to sustain such extreme behaviors and, in the body-shame-prone individual, to sustain the perception of successful self-regulation. Following realization that one is near the feared self, the individual determines whether he or she should renew efforts at appearance regulation (i.e., make efforts to achieve distance from the feared self) or disengage from such attempts. These outcome expectancies are based on "a wide variety of information pertaining to the situation and to internal qualities such as skill, anticipated effort, and available response options," but memory of prior experiences is particularly influential (Carver & Scheier, 1990, p. 21). Over time, as experiences of body shame accrue (and they will inevitably do so), the individual gets the repeated message that he or she has been unable to sustain successful regulation of body appearance. Body shame signals to the individual that he or she has not sufficiently managed his or her body, and after multiple failed attempts at body regulation, he or she may become increasingly less likely to believe that escape from the feared self is possible. Perceptions of ability to reclaim and maintain control over one's appearance decrease, and perceptions of the probable outcome of attempts at regulation become increasingly unfavorable (i.e., the individual believes such efforts are ultimately in vain). When these thought processes lead the body-shamed individual to feel the feared self is an inescapable reality, he or she may temporarily disengage from the goal of escaping the feared self and give up *completely*.

The dichotomous nature of these behavioral outcomes of body shame—overcompensation versus disregulation (i.e., vigorous escape versus total surrender)—fits the cognitive style of women with established eating pathologies. The anorexic, for example, "feels that 'If I am not 85 pounds then I might as well be 200 pounds.' . . . Exceeding her weight limit by even one pound is equal, in her mind, with being totally out of control" (Garner & Garfinkel, 1988, p. 8). This rigid thinking would seem to discourage, or render meaningless, moderate behaviors. Body maintenance is an all-or-nothing enterprise, and modest slip-ups (e.g., gaining a pound; eating one piece of chocolate) are tantamount to total failure. It is possible, then, that upon determining that one cannot achieve sufficient distance from one's feared self, the body-shamed individual may feel that the magnitude of subsequent eating behaviors is of little significance. Disregulation, rather than the absence of restraint, may occur because the individual feels hopelessly consigned to being "fat" or whatever constitutes one's appearance-related fears.

Disengagement from unattainable goals can be adaptive when it breaks the cycle of negative affect, and redirects the individual toward more realizable pursuits. The individual can decide to change his or her principles or reference values (thus making previous goals less important or self-relevant), or replace goals with related but more attainable ones. However, when goals are highly relevant to paramount reference values (e.g., refraining from eating bad foods is highly relevant to maintaining distance from one's feared fat self), psychological disengagement can be difficult to maintain. It requires the individual literally to shake up his or her value system and decide that what was of fundamental importance will no longer be so. Thus, the disregulatory behaviors (which only serve to *increase* proximity to one's feared self) will likely continue to cause distress, and trigger subsequent episodes of body shame.

This pattern may help explain why body shame and eating disturbances have been found to be associated with depression (Andrews, 1995; Attie & Brooks-Gunn, 1992; Stice et al., 2000). The person begins to learn and accept that he or she cannot effect the desired outcomes, despite his or her efforts, but cannot change the system-level reference values. One cannot just decide not to fear being fat. This may be particularly true for socially based reference values, since they are based on others' values and are therefore not under the individual's control to change. The increasing feelings of hopelessness and negative affect relating to one's feared self may generalize over time. "This bind—being unable to let go of something that is unattainable—lies at the heart of exogenous depression" (Carver & Scheier, 1990, p. 29).

Moderators of the Relationship of Sociocultural Factors to Body Shame

To review, body shame occurs when an individual perceives a negative social evaluation of his or her body appearance, and perceives this evaluation to translate to global rejection. Media and other transmitters of sociocultural norms are presumed to increase propensity for body shame—and, subsequently, eating-disordered behaviors—by encouraging women to take an observer's perspective and communicating that attainment of the ideal body appearance is crucial, yet futile.

Shame is ultimately determined by multiple factors, however. For example, examination of the more immediate social environment(s) more precisely determines vulnerability to experiencing body shame and eating disorders.

Protective Social Identities: The Role of Immediate Evaluative Others

Recall that shame is experienced when one feels unworthy in the eyes of important others, and that these others may be generalized societal others or specific others, such as one's partner or parent. Feminist critiques of the cultural emphasis on women's appearance have focused on the powerful influence of societal norms for body appearance, with proposed remedies for combating negative body image involving large-scale societal changes (e.g., featuring more full-figured women in media) and teaching resistance at the individual level (e.g., encouraging girls to "celebrate" their curves). However, family, peers, and romantic others may constitute the most "critical" others in one's life, and their influence on women's perceptions of their bodies has been found to be crucial. A vast literature attests to familial and peer influences as key factors in understanding early development of eating pathology (see Pike & Wilfley, 1996; Rosen, 1996; Thelen, Lawrence, & Powell, 1992).

Indeed, it has been noted that our more immediate social or reference groups may serve to "either amplify or dampen broader sociocultural messages" (Twamley & Davis, 1999, p. 470). To the extent that one's more immediate social environment is comprised of others who are *less* likely to (be perceived to) have unrealistic standards for one's appearance or consider it representative of the self, one should be less likely to experience body shame. This helps explain why certain subgroups of women have been found to have less negative body image and lower incidence of eating disorders than other women.

For example, although recent research has challenged the myth that ethnic minorities are *immune* to developing disordered eating (e.g., Crago, Shisslak, & Estes, 1996; Root, 1990; Silber, 1986), women of color are still perceived as relatively *protected* compared with their Euro-American counterparts.

Generally, results suggest that black women are more satisfied with their bodies than white women (Altabe, 1998; Harris, 1994; Wilfley et al., 1996) and have a lower prevalence of bulimia nervosa (Gray, Ford, & Kelly, 1987) than white women, although rates of obesity are higher among black women (White et al., 1993). Striegel-Moore and Smolak (1996) note that this difference may be partially explained by black girls' reporting less social pressure to be thin, and less appearance-related criticism from family members. King (1993) found this may be interpreted as their perceiving more flexible standards for, and less emphasis on, body appearance among important others, which translates directly to decreased likelihood of body shame.

Research also suggests that Asian American girls and women are more satisfied with their bodies and engage in less eating-disordered behaviors than their white counterparts (Akan & Grilo, 1995; Altabe, 1998; Mintz & Kasubeck, 1999).

It must be noted, however, that more recent studies of eating concerns evoke a less clear picture. There is evidence that black women exhibit comparable levels of binge eating relative to white women (D. E. Smith et al.,

1998), and are more likely to use fasting or to abuse diuretics for weight loss (Emmons, 1992; Striegel-Moore et al., 2000). Further, while it has been suggested that Latinas maintain larger body ideals than white women (Winkleby, Gardner, & Taylor, 1996), studies have found that Latinas experience eating problems at rates equivalent to white girls and women (Fitzgibbon et al., 1998; J. E. Smith & Krejci, 1991).

Future research on body image and eating disorders in ethnic minority women should examine variables relevant to body shame, such as individual women's perceptions of the level of importance of and standards for body appearance among their referent others, and the degree to which these perceptions mirror those regarding broader cultural values. Such factors correspond to elements of psychological acculturation (Marín, 1992).

Research indicates that women who identify as lesbian show lower levels of body dissatisfaction and indicate lower levels of agreement with societal ideals of female beauty (Bergeron & Senn, 1998). What may be crucial in protecting these women from body shame is not just the different appearance values that they themselves may hold, but also the extent to which they are surrounded by other individuals whose appearance values are more flexible. Because shame derives from social rejection, the influence of others' values, in addition to one's own, must be considered. This is why group membership, rather than group-related principles, may be more influential in matters relating to shame.

For example, Twamley and Davis (1999) tested the significance of feminist attitudes as a buffer against eating disturbance and found no effect. This may be attributable to the fact that many women who indicate feminist beliefs may not actually identify as feminists, and thus may not be involved in feminist social groups. Indeed, we also found feminist identity—but not feminist attitudes—to moderate the relationship between body dissatisfaction and self-esteem, demonstrating that even though women who considered themselves feminist did not perceive less distance between their actual and ideal bodies, such discrepancies did not correspond as robustly to perceptions of social worth (Denious et al., 2004).

Moderating Influence of the Importance of the Other

"In order for shame to occur, there must be a relationship between the self and the other in which the self *cares* about the other's evaluation" (Lewis, 1987, p. 18). Research indicates that high importance placed on others may predispose women to eating-related problems (Striegel-Moore, Silberstein, & Rodin, 1993), whereas a preference for disregarding social norms protects women against ED behaviors (Twamley & Davis, 1999). It has been found that bulimic individuals are highly affected by social interactions and are particularly sensitive to the judgments of others (Schupak-Neuberg & Nemeroff, 1993; Steiger et al., 1999; Striegel-Moore et al., 1993). Alternatively, Twamley and Davis (1999) found that nonconformity confers protection against eating disorders by moderating the extent to which awareness of thinness norms leads to internalization of those norms. These findings illustrate the fact that opportunities for shame are, in part, a function of how likely one is to care about another's evaluation.

There may be good reasons for caring about what others think, however. As noted, one promoted avenue of resistance to negative body image is encouraging girls and women to see that the beauty ideals of our culture are rooted in myth, and should therefore be dismissed. But this may be far easier said than done.

For example, a qualitative study of body image in self-identified feminists revealed that many of these women felt unable to ignore societal values of body appearance, despite having principled objections to such sociocultural mandates and making a conscious effort to reject them (Rubin, Nemeroff, & Russo, 2004). Furthermore, a study of lesbian college students revealed that many lesbians experienced conflict in their attempts to accommodate both mainstream and lesbian cultures' appearance ideals (Beren et al., 1997). Indeed, Beren et al.'s characterization of these interacting influences—a struggle to simultaneously accommodate conflicting cultural demands—suggests that both the more generalized other (i.e., mainstream society) and immediate others hold sway in women's perceptions of their social selves. Given the possibility that such individuals may consider themselves bicultural, that is, having "intimate relationships with two or more cultures" (LaFromboise, Coleman, & Gerton, 1993, p. 401), it may be fruitful for future studies to examine acculturation strategies among such women with particular regard to body appearance norms and values.

In sum, it is important to note that subcultural "identities" may moderate, but not completely supplant, broader sociocultural influences. It is unlikely, however, that media and businesses—which have a stake in keeping women unhappy with their bodies and eager to "improve" them—will move to effect positive change in women's appearance-related feelings and behaviors. At the more individual level, insofar as women value connectedness and belonging, it may be difficult for them to learn to reject the expectations others hold for the self. Thus, highlighting the positive influence that certain social identities can confer on women, or even working to establish supportive "subcultures" or peer groups for girls and women, may be the most effective means of fostering resilience in a culture that attaches moral meaning to women's dietary consumption and body appearance.

References

Akan, G. E., & Grilo, C. M. (1995). Sociocultural influences on eating attitudes and behaviors, body image, and psychological functioning: A comparison of African–American, Asian–American, and Caucasian college women. *International Journal of Eating Disorders, 18,* 181–187.

Altabe, M. (1998). Ethnicity and body image: Quantitative and qualitative analysis. *International Journal of Eating Disorders, 23,* 153–159.

American Psychiatric Association. (1994). *Diagnostic and Statistical Manual of Mental Disorders* (4th ed.). Washington, DC: American Psychiatric Association.

Andrews, B. (1995). Bodily shame as a mediator between abusive experiences and depression. *Journal of Abnormal Psychology, 104,* 277–285.

Andrews, B. (1997). Bodily shame in relation to abuse in childhood and bulimia: A preliminary investigation. *British Journal of Clinical Psychology, 36,* 41–49.

Attie, I., & Brooks-Gunn, J. (1992). Developmental issues in the study of eating problems and disorders. In J. H. Crowther, S. E. Hobfall, M. A. Stephens, & D. L. Tennenbaum (Eds.), *The etiology of bulimia nervosa: The individual and familial context* (pp. 35–53). Washington, DC: Hemisphere.

Barrett, K. C. (1995). A functionalist approach to shame and guilt. In J. P. Tangney & K. W. Fischer (Eds.), *Self-conscious emotions: The psychology of shame, guilt, embarrassment, and pride* (pp. 25–63). New York: Guilford.

Beren, S. E., Hayden, H. A., Wilfley, D. E., & Striegel-Moore, R. H. (1997). Body dissatisfaction among lesbian college students: The conflict of straddling mainstream and lesbian cultures. *Psychology of Women Quarterly, 21,* 431–445.

Bergeron, S. M., & Senn, C. Y. (1998). Body image and sociocultural norms: A comparison of heterosexual and lesbian women. *Psychology of Women Quarterly, 22,* 385–401.

Berscheid, E., Dion, K., Walster, E., & Walster, E. (1971). Physical attractiveness and dating choice: A test of the matching hypothesis. *Journal of Experimental Social Psychology, 7,* 173–189.

Burney, J., & Irwin, H. J. (2000). Shame and guilt in women with eating-disorder symptomatology. *Journal of Clinical Psychology, 56,* 51–61.

Carver, C. S., Lawrence, J. W., & Scheier, M. F. (1999). Self-discrepancies and affect: Incorporating the role of feared selves. *Personality and Social Psychology Bulletin, 25,* 783–792.

Carver, C. S., & Scheier, M. F. (1990). Origins and functions of positive and negative affect: A control-process view. *Psychological Review, 97,* 19–35.

Cash, T. F., & Henry, P. E. (1985). Women's body images: The results of a national survey in the U.S.A. *Sex Roles, 33,* 19–28.

Crago, M., Shisslak, C. M., & Estes, L. S. (1996). Eating disturbances among American minority groups: A review. *International Journal of Eating Disorders, 19,* 239–248.

Cullari, S., & Trubilla, R. S. (1989). Body-image distortion in normal-weight college women. *Perceptual and Motor Skills, 68,* 1195–1198.

Denious, J. E., Cunningham, K., Rubin, L. R., & Russo, N. F. (2004). *Feminism identity: A protective factor in body image?* Unpublished manuscript. Arizona State University.

Eagly, A. H., Ashmore, R. D., Makhijani, M. G., & Longo, L. C. (1991). What is beautiful is good, but . . . : A meta-analytic review of research on the physical attractiveness stereotype. *Psychological Bulletin, 110,* 109–128.

Emde, R. M., & Oppenheim, D. (1995). Shame, guilt, and the Oedipal drama: Developmental considerations concerning morality and the referencing of critical others. In J. P. Tangney & K. W. Fischer (Eds.), *Self-conscious emotions: The psychology of shame, guilt, embarrassment, and pride* (pp. 413–436). New York: Guilford.

Emmons, L. (1992). Dieting and purging behavior in black and white high school students. *Journal of the American Dietetic Association, 92,* 306–312.

Feldman, J., & Eysenck, S.B.G. (1986). Addictive personality traits in bulimic patients. *Personality and Individual Differences, 7,* 923–926.

Ferguson, T. J., Eyre, H. L., & Ashbaker, M. (2000). Unwanted identities: A key variable in shame–anger links and gender differences in shame. *Sex Roles, 42,* 133–157.

Fitzgibbon, M. L., Spring, B., Avellone, M. E., Blackman, L. R., Pingitore, R., & Stolley, M. R. (1998). Correlates of binge eating in Hispanic, black, and white women. *International Journal of Eating Disorders, 24,* 43–52.

Fredrickson, B. L., & Roberts, T.-A. (1997). Objectification theory: Towards an understanding of women's lived experiences and mental health risks. *Psychology of Women Quarterly, 21,* 173–206.

Fredrickson, B. L., Roberts, T.-A., Noll, S. M., Quinn, D. M., & Twenge, J. M. (1998). That swimsuit becomes you: Sex differences in self-objectification, restrained eating, and math performance. *Journal of Personality and Social Psychology, 75,* 269–284.

Garner, D. M., & Garfinkel, P. E. (Eds.). (1988). *Diagnostic issues in anorexia nervosa and bulimia nervosa.* New York: Brunner/Mazel.

Garner, D. M., Olmsted, M. P., & Polivy, J. (1983). Development and validation of a multidimensional eating disorder inventory for anorexia nervosa and bulimia. *International Journal of Eating Disorders, 2,* 15–34.

Garner, D. M., Olmsted, M. P., Polivy, J., & Garfinkel, P. E. (1984). Comparison between weight-preoccupied women and anorexia nervosa. *Psychosomatic Medicine, 46,* 255–266.

Gray, J. J., Ford, K., & Kelly, L. M. (1987). The prevalence of bulimia in a black college population. *International Journal of Eating Disorders, 6,* 733–740.

Groesz, L. M., Levine, M. P., & Murnen, S. K. (2002). The effect of experimental presentation of thin media images on body satisfaction: A meta-analytic review. *International Journal of Eating Disorders, 31,* 1–16.

Harris, S. M. (1994). Racial differences in predictors of women's body image attitudes. *Women and Health, 2,* 89–104.

Heatherton, T. F., & Polivy, J. (1992). Chronic dieting and eating disorders: A spiral model. In J. H. Crowther, S. E. Hobfall, M. A. Stephens, & D. L. Tennenbaum (Eds.), *The etiology of bulimia nervosa: The individual and familial context* (pp. 133–155). Washington, DC: Hemisphere.

Hebl, M. R., & Heatherton, T. F. (1998). The stigma of obesity in women: The difference is black and white. *Personality and Social Psychology Bulletin, 24,* 417–426.

Higgins, E. T. (1987). Self-discrepancy: A theory relating self and affect. *Psychological Review, 94,* 319–340.

Hsu, L. G., & Sobkiewicz, T. A. (1991). Body image disturbance: Time to abandon the concept for eating disorders? *International Journal of Eating Disorders, 10,* 15–30.

King, M. B. (1993). Cultural aspects of eating disorders. *International Review of Psychiatry, 5,* 205–216.

LaFromboise, T., Coleman, H.L.K., & Gerton, J. (1993). Psychological impact of biculturalism: Evidence and theory. *Psychological Bulletin, 114,* 395–412.

Lewis, H. B. (Ed.). (1987). *The role of shame in symptom formation.* Hillsdale, NJ: Erlbaum.

Marín, G. (1992). Issues in the measurement of acculturation among Hispanics. In K. Geisinger (Ed.), *Psychological Testing of Hispanics.* Washington, DC: American Psychological Association.

Markus, H. R., & Nurius, P. (1986). Possible selves. *American Psychologist, 41,* 954–969.

Mintz, L. B., & Kasubeck, S. (1999). Body image and disordered eating among Asian American and Caucasian college students: An examination of race and gender differences. *Psychology of Women Quarterly, 23,* 781–796.

Murray, C., Waller, G., & Legg, C. (2000). Family dysfunction and bulimic psychopathology: The mediating role of shame. *International Journal of Eating Disorders, 28,* 84–89.

Noll, S. M., & Fredrickson, B. L. (1998). A mediational model linking self-objectification, body shame, and disordered eating. *Psychology of Women Quarterly, 22,* 623–636.

Oyserman, D., & Markus, H. R. (1990). Possible selves and delinquency. *Journal of Personality and Social Psychology, 59,* 112–125.

Pike, K. M., & Wilfley, D. E. (1996). The changing context of treatment. In L. Smolak, M. P. Levine, & R. Striegel-Moore (Eds.), *The developmental psychopathology of eating disorders: Implications for research, prevention, and treatment* (pp. 365–398). Mahwah, NJ: Erlbaum.

Plous, S., & Neptune, D. (1997). Racial and gender biases in magazine advertising: A content-analytic study. *Psychology of Women Quarterly, 21,* 627–644.

Polivy, J., & Herman, C. P. (1987). Diagnosis and treatment of normal eating. *Journal of Consulting and Clinical Psychology, 55,* 635–644.

Polivy, J., & Herman, C. P. (2002). The causes of eating disorders. *Annual Review of Psychology, 53,* 187–213.

Polivy, J., & Herman, C. P. (2004). Sociocultural idealization of thin female body shapes: An introduction to the special issue on body image and eating disorders. *Journal of Social and Clinical Psychology, 23,* 1–6.

Root, M. (1990). Disordered eating in women of color. *Sex Roles, 22,* 525–536.

Rosen, K. (1996). The principles of developmental psychopathology: Illustration from the study of eating disorders. In L. Smolak, M. P. Levine, & R. Striegel-Moore (Eds.), *The developmental psychopathology of eating disorders: Implications for research, prevention, and treatment* (pp. 1–30). Mahwah, NJ: Erlbaum.

Rothblum, E. D. (1992). The stigma of women's weight: Social and economic realities. *Feminism and Psychology, 2,* 61–73.

Rubin, L. R., Nemeroff, C. J., & Russo, N. F. (2004). Exploring feminist women's body consciousness. *Psychology of Women Quarterly, 28,* 27–37.

Sanftner, J. L., Barlow, D. H., Marschall, D. E., & Tangney, J. P. (1995). The relation of shame and guilt to eating disorder symptomatology. *Journal of Social and Clinical Psychology, 14,* 315–324.

Sanftner, J. L., & Crowther, J. H. (1998). Variability in self-esteem, moods, shame, and guilt in women who binge. *International Journal of Eating Disorders, 23,* 391–397.

Schupak-Neuberg, E., & Nemeroff, C. J. (1993). Disturbances in identity and self-regulation in bulimia nervosa: Implications for a metaphorical perspective of "body as self." *International Journal of Eating Disorders, 13,* 335–347.

Silber, T. J. (1986). Anorexia nervosa in blacks and Hispanics. *International Journal of Eating Disorders, 5,* 121–128.

Silberstein, L. R., Striegel-Moore, R. H., & Rodin, J. (1987). Feeling fat: A woman's shame. In H. B. Lewis (Ed.), *The role of shame in symptom formation* (pp. 89–108). Hillsdale, NJ: Erlbaum.

Smith, D. E., Marcus, M. D., Lewis, C. E., Fitzgibbon, M., & Schreiner, P. (1998). Prevalence of binge eating disorder, obesity, and depression in a biracial cohort of young adults. *Annals of Behavioral Medicine, 20,* 227–232.

Smith, J. E., & Krejci, J. (1991). Minorities join the majority: Eating disturbances among Hispanic and Native American youth. *International Journal of Eating Disorders, 10,* 179–186.

Steiger, H., Gauvin, L., Jabalpurwala, S., Seguin, J. R., & Stotland, S. (1999). Hypersensitivity to social interactions in bulimic syndromes: Relationship to binge eating. *Journal of Consulting and Clinical Psychology, 67,* 765–775.

Stice, E. (1994). Review of the evidence for a sociocultural model of bulimia nervosa and an exploration of the mechanisms of action. *Clinical Psychology Review, 14,* 633–661.

Stice, E. (2002). Risk and maintenance factors for eating pathology: A meta-analytic review. *Psychological Bulletin, 128,* 825–848.

Stice, E., Hayward, C., Cameron, R., Killen, J. D., & Taylor, C. B. (2000). Body image and eating disturbances predict onset of depression in female adolescents: A longitudinal study. *Journal of Abnormal Psychology, 109,* 438–444.

Stice, E., & Shaw, H. E. (1994). Adverse effects of the media portrayed thin-ideal on women and linkages to bulimic symptomatology. *Journal of Social and Clinical Psychology, 13,* 288–308.

Striegel-Moore, R. H., Silberstein, L. R., & Rodin, J. (1986). Toward an understanding of risk factors for bulimia. *American Psychologist, 41,* 246–263.

Striegel-Moore, R. H., Silberstein, L. R., & Rodin, J. (1993). The social self in bulimia nervosa: Public self-consciousness, social anxiety, and perceived fraudulence. *Journal of Abnormal Psychology, 102,* 297–303.

Striegel-Moore, R. H., & Smolak, L. (1996). The role of race in the development of eating disorders. In L. Smolak, M. P. Levine, & R. Striegel-Moore (Eds.), *The developmental psychopathology of eating disorders: Implications for research, prevention, and treatment* (pp. 259–284). Mahwah, NJ: Erlbaum.

Striegel-Moore, R. H., Wilfley, D., Pike, K., Dohm, F., & Fairburn, C. (2000). Recurrent binge-eating in black women. *Archives of Family Medicine, 9,* 83–87.

Tangney, J. P., Neidenthal, P. M., Covert, M. V., & Barlow, D. H. (1998). Are shame and guilt related to distinct self-discrepancies? A test of Higgins's (1987) hypotheses. *Journal of Personality and Social Psychology, 75,* 256–268.

Thelen, M. H., Lawrence, C. M., & Powell, A. L. (1992). Body image, weight control, and eating disorders among children. In J. H. Crowther, S. E. Hobfall, M. A. Stephens, & D. L. Tennenbaum (Eds.), *The etiology of bulimia nervosa: The individual and familial context* (pp. 81–98). Washington, DC: Hemisphere.

Thompson, J. K., & Psaltis, K. (1988). Multiple aspects and correlates of body figure ratings: A replication and extension of Fallon and Rozin (1985). *International Journal of Eating Disorders, 7,* 813–817.

Tiggemann, M., & Slater, A. (2001). A test of objectification theory in former dancers and non-dancers. *Psychology of Women Quarterly, 25,* 57–64.

Twamley, E. W., & Davis, M. C. (1999). The sociocultural model of eating disturbance in young women: The effects of personal attributes and family environment. *Journal of Social and Clinical Psychology, 18,* 467–489.

Weiner, K. E., & Thompson, K. J. (1997). Overt and covert sexual abuse: Relationship to body image and eating disturbance. *International Journal of Eating Disorders, 22,* 273–284.

White, M. A., Kohlmaier, J. R., Varnado-Sullivan, P., & Williamson, D. A. (1993). Racial/ethnic differences in weight concerns: Protective and risk factors for the development of eating disorders and obesity among adolescent females. *Eating and Weight Disorders, 8,* 20–25

Wilfley, D. E., Schreiber, G. B., Pike, K. M., Striegel-Moore, R. H., Wright, D. J., & Rodin, J. (1996). Eating disturbance and body image: A comparison of a community sample of adult black and white women. *International Journal of Eating Disorders, 20,* 377–387.

Winkleby, M., Gardner, C., & Taylor, C. B. (1996). The influence of gender and socioeconomic factors on Hispanic/white differences in body mass index. *Preventive Medicine, 25,* 203–211.

Chapter 12

Development of Sex and Gender: Biochemistry, Physiology, and Experience

Ethel Tobach

Glossary

Biochemical processes   Those carried out by genes, that is, segments of DNA (deoxyribonucleic acid)—that together with RNA (ribonucleic acid) work to produce proteins. Proteins are made of amino acids and are the structural units of all cells, hormones, neurotransmitters, enzymes, and other vital substances.

Development   The history of all the changes—biological (biochemical and physiological) and psychological (psychosocial/societal experience)—that an organism goes through, including all life experiences from the time that the gametes (sex cells) from the mother and father fuse to form the zygote. Development starts with the parents, or ancestors, because of what they bring to the gametes and zygote as a result of their experiences. Their contributions and the conditions under which the zygote develops in the uterus of the mother are the foundations for processes of change, including the exit from the uterus into the world in which the individual lives. In the development of sex for both women and men, the experiences produced by the mother's and father's biochemistry and physiology are significant.

Gender   Relates only to human beings; "women" and "men" will refer to all those who are of an age at which they are presumably physiologically able to copulate (have sexual intercourse), fuse gametes, and produce offspring; this is usually true of people at puberty. Prepubertal individuals (those not yet likely to be able to produce offspring) are designated as girls or boys. Gender is the psychosocial/societal integration of the codes of activity, social relations, and societal status prescribed for individuals on the basis of their presumed sex.

Physiological processes   Those functions and structures resulting from the activities of the biochemical entities as they develop and change, producing the foundations for the various developmental stages in the history of the individual's activities.

Sex reproductive processes   Fusing the genetic material of different organisms (biological term: *conjugation*); sex is defined by the gametes carried by the person.

Social behavior   Face-to-face, contemporaneous activity of people with each other, in the process of living in a society.

Society   That which prescribes the rules for living in groups. The social and societal settings change and are changed by the activity of the individual(s).

The study of sex and gender in this chapter is based on an integrative levels approach. In this approach, the "biological" factors, that is, the biochemical and physiological processes, and the "cultural" factors, that is, the psychosocial/societal processes, are not opposed. The approach takes into consideration the total experience of the individual as a developmental, historical process in which all processes are integrated. It views sex as a part of the individual's development, distinct from, but integrated into, gender development. It resolves the apparent contradiction of biology and psychology, of genes and experience. As biochemical levels and psychosocial/societal levels are always functioning in the life of the individual, all these levels must be studied to understand sex and gender. The processes in the histories of sex and gender are interdependent. Sex is differentiated from gender to elucidate how the similarities and differences between women and men develop, without placing all explanations in biology or culture.

Issues in Sex and Gender Research

Newspapers, magazines, movies, and television are full of talk about sex and gender. We are led to believe that so much is known about genetics that one's sex and gender can be easily changed. We are told genetic engineering makes it possible to order the sex of the baby one wants, as well as the characteristics of that baby. Genomic research and development to describe all the genes (genome) in different species, including people, using sophisticated computerized instruments, produce genetic information quickly. The genomics industry is on the international stock market, and the announcements of discoveries and stock values encourage us to believe what we are told about the science of genomics in the media. All this makes it necessary for people who are interested in sex and gender to be literate in the sciences of genetics and behavior, in the relationship among genes, hormones, sex, and gender. This relationship is complex, and learning about genes, hormones, sex, and gender is challenging.

Sex and Gender Research

The hereditarian or determinist view about the differences between women and men are featured most often in all forms of media and public entertainment, despite the significant representation of the gender socializing or learning theorists in psychology and developmental psychology in particular. The three prevailing approaches to the study of gender may be described as (1) determinist, that is, determined by inherited/genetic/biological factors (ethology, sociobiology, and evolutionary psychology); (2) based on learned/environmental/socializing factors (e.g., the sociocognitive perspective concept of Bussey and Bandura); and (3) "interactionist," that is, seeing both genetic factors and learning or socialization as contributing to gender (behavior geneticists).

The approach to the study of sex and gender in this chapter is based on an integrative levels approach. In this approach, the biological and cultural factors are not apposed. It takes into consideration the total experience of the individual as a developmental, historical process. It views sex as a part of the individual's development, distinct from, but integrated into, gender development. It removes the apparent apposition of biology and psychology, of genes and experience. As biochemical levels and psychosocial/societal levels are always functioning in the life of the individual, all these levels must be studied to understand sex and gender.

Each level requires its own methods and instrumentation. When we ask questions about sex, we are asking about biochemical and physiological processes, and the instruments and methods used would not be the same as those used in answering psychosocial/societal questions about gender. Usually, these levels are not studied at the same time, or by the same investigators, but the inferences reached on the basis of the studies of each level must be integrated to understand the processes that produce sex and gender.

This approach differs from the interactionist approach, which asks, What and how much is inherited, and what and how much is acquired? Several questions are posed by the levels of integration approach: Which biochemical and physiological processes are related to sex? Which psychosocial/societal processes are related to gender? How do biochemical and physiological histories bring about the developmental psychosocial/societal history of the individual? The processes in both histories are interdependent.

Why Should Sex and Gender Be Differentiated?

As the dominant approaches to the study of sex and gender emphasize biological processes, the terms "sex" and "gender" are frequently used interchangeably, and the biological processes are seen as fundamental and inherited. However, heredity is not sufficient to explain the apparent differences and similarities between women and men. Biochemical and physiological processes are necessary to maintain life and the integrity of the individual, however these are not sufficient to explain the behavior of the individual. The psychosocial/societal development of the human individual is also necessary. Neither set of processes by itself is sufficient. Seeing the differences between sex and gender helps us understand how the similarities and differences between women and men develop and involve all the processes of behavior, without placing all explanations in one set or the other.

The experiences of the incubating individual, the mother—beginning with the fusion of the two gametes, formation of the zygote, through the placentation period (incubation)—are always relevant to the activities of the gametes. Changes in her biochemistry as a result of foods, climatic processes (radiation, temperature, toxicity), exposure to infecting organisms, and both physiological and psychological stress are expressed in changes in gene/protein and hormonal function during the development from zygote, to embryo, to fetus. These experiences will re-form the activities of the genes, thus continuously producing new foundations for gender development.

Why Do People Study the Differences between Sexes and Genders?

"Scientific" Method. The strongest stimulus comes from scientific traditions for investigating existing differences or creating differences among individuals or groups to provide clues for understanding a particular phenomenon. By suggesting the sources of differences found, investigators can change the treatment of one group and compare it to the unchanged group (the so-called control group). In looking at sex and gender differences, the proper "control" is difficult to define. As an alternative, qualitative, developmental, long-term studies are being used more frequently. Another technique is to choose two known characteristics that are different in women and men as groups, and then ask whether they are correlated. Correlations do not explain the process responsible for the differences, but they do suggest other possibilities for research.

Evolutionary Theory and Behavior. Darwin's concept of sexual selection (competitive choice of partners for mating) was important in his theory of the evolution of species and of behavior. That concept was further elaborated by three theories: ethology, sociobiology, and evolutionary psychology (sometimes called human sociobiology). The three theories consider the differences between women and men, and between female and male animals, as evidence of the important evolutionary role of sex differences in species survival.

1. Ethology, the study of inherited behavioral patterns to clarify evolutionary relationships of species, sees reproductive behavior as inherited; gender and sex are not differentiated usually.

2. Sociobiology elaborates the evolutionary inheritance of sexual differences by positing that cultural gender patterns follow the same selective processes as genetic, morphological, and functional characteristics: Those gender differences that promote the survival of the species will be maintained and retained in all cultures.

3. Evolutionary psychology integrates sociobiological theory with human genetics and psychology. Cosmides and Tooby posited that the genes that were responsible for human survival early in evolution (2.5 million years ago) are still present in the human genome (all the genes of the human species) and play an important role in cognition, including social cognition (e.g., gender roles). Genes are carried by the nucleus and the mitochondrion (an intracellular organelle that produces most of the sources of energy within all cells and that has its own DNA and RNA). Although the cells of women and men have both structures, the genes in the mitochondrion are usually passed on by the females of the species, whereas the genes in the nucleus are passed on by both females and males. This division of labor suggests to them that the nucleus is the "male" carrier of genes, whereas the mitochondrion is the "female" carrier of genes. Based on a sociobiological tenet that genes are programmed to do anything necessary to assure that they are passed on in the next generation, the "male" genes will do as much as possible to be passed into the next generation, and thus be in conflict with the "female" genes in the mitochondrion. Although the two organelles must work together to maintain the life of the cell, this concept that female/male conflict is inherent has become a popular theory supporting various theories about differences between women and men.

Evolutionary Biology, Biomedicine, and Reproduction. Humans were likely always to be curious about the genital and reproductive differences between women and men, although they did not always understand the relationship between sexual intercourse and reproduction. In the course of human history, differences in reproductive function became an essential consideration in regard to labor, when hands were needed to pursue activities for survival. With sedentation and agricultural societies, women were engaged not only in production of human beings, or reproduction, but also in life-maintaining activities (production). In this era of human history, slavery was prevalent, and women became special commodities. Their gametic sex was the predominant consideration; their gender was secondary insofar as they were seen as good housekeepers, children's caregivers, and so on, but also as able to do heavy labor. As Sojourner Truth said, enslaved women were considered able to do the heavy work that was usually considered men's work; gender differences for "hard" labor disappeared.

The biological Darwinian revolution elaborated the interest in reproduction. Evolutionary biologists discovered varied patterns of reproduction: sexual (when two or more individuals mix their genetic materials) and asexual (when cells reproduce without mixing their genetic material with that of another organism). This stimulated interest in the underlying morphology and physiology that make such diversity possible. The study of the sexual differences between females and males fits in with the early concern with reproduction and production, and stimulated research on problems of fertility and sterility in women and men. Concern about sterility and fertility was always intimately related to the formulation of gender roles in society. Being able to produce heirs has been an important societal concern in all classes throughout history because of the economic value of having hands for labor (which contributed to survival) and for the accumulation of wealth. This history suggests how it is that sex and gender are frequently confounded.

As the development of the genomics industry increased our information about genetic processes, evidence was found that the biochemical processes that were different in women and men played roles in life functions other than reproduction. The biochemistry appeared related to many processes in health and disease. Recently, the National Institutes of Health listed ten studies of the differences between women and men as possibly having a bearing on medical practice: Women progress to AIDS with half the viral load that men require; women's blood alcohol levels are higher than men's when imbibing the same amounts of alcohol; brain mapping shows certain language functions are evidenced in both hemispheres in women while men show the activity in only one hemisphere; men synthesize serotonin at a higher rate than women, suggesting why depression is more frequent in women than in men; pain processes are different in women than in men as they respond differently to antipain medications; women's heart attack symptoms are different than men's; liver transplants donated by a woman are less likely to be successful than donations made by men.

It should be noted that these examples may not have taken into account the psychosocial/societal experiences that play a role in the biochemical and physiological processes described, as suggested by the integrative levels approach. Studies of depression in women have shown that gender-related experiences are a major factor in depression. Women and men may respond differently to stresses in part because of the attitudes physicians have toward women as contrasted with their attitudes toward men when both are being examined for the same problems.

These experiences on the psychosocial/societal level are integrated with the biochemical processes in depression. Human and animal research has demonstrated that levels of serotonin, a neurotransmitter, vary with depression. In addition, estrogen and progesterone, produced by the ovary, and testosterone, produced by the testes, have been found to affect serotonin function. Estrogen and progesterone or testosterone can play a role in the function of serotonin in the development of depression. The relationship between psychosocial/societal experiences and the biochemical processes are complex; they work uniquely in each individual.

This does not mean that differences should not be investigated. Rather, it points to the need for biomedical research to ask how genderized medical experiences may affect physiology, requiring different diagnostic and treatment regimens.

The Processes That Define Sex and Gender

How Sex Gets Defined

Humans (mammals) are a sexually reproducing species, that is, humans carry two gametes (egg and sperm), each of which has half the chromosomes that carry the genes that fuse to form one or more new individuals. The biochemical level of sex definition involves two X chromosomes or an X and a Y chromosome, along with their genes and related proteins; hormonal processes (e.g., the structures and functions of estrogens or androgens); and enzymes. The physiological level involves the systems of cells, tissues, and organs that develop in the individual (e.g., hormonal and neural) and how they function in reproduction. Reproduction is a physiological process. Individuals carrying two Xs are labeled women ("females" in medical practice); those carrying an X and a Y chromosome are labeled men ("males" in medical practice).

Mammals can reproduce by cloning offspring, a process in which introducing appropriate cells from one organism into the nucleus of an appropriate cell in another organism leads to the formation of an embryo. However, this embryo must be incubated in an organism with XX chromosomes, whose hormonal functions will make development, growth, and birth possible. To date, it is not known that humans can be cloned in this fashion. The psychosocial/societal processes whereby this type of reproduction will take place are unknown.

The process whereby the two gametes are usually mixed in humans is complicated and offers many opportunities for unusual combinations of gametes to occur. The psychosocial/societal gender development of individuals carrying such unusual combinations is insufficiently studied and understood.

How Gender Gets Defined

Gender is the psychosocial/societal integration of the codes of activity, dress, social relations, and societal status prescribed for individuals on the basis of their presumed sex.

How Many Sexes? How Many Genders?

The suggestion that there may be more than two sexes (XX and XY) is based on the fact that individuals usually considered women or men as to their gender may have different combinations of X and Y chromosomes. Based on the chromosomes carried, individuals may be categorized variously as intersexes, or as demonstrating syndromes such as Turner's, Klinefelter's, and so on.

A range of secondary sex characteristics (e.g., stature, hairiness, musculature) are so-called quantitative gender-defined traits, related to hormones and sex organs (ovary and testis), although they may also be related to non-sex organs, such as the adrenal glands, which produce hormones affecting these traits. These are modified by the life experiences of the person as well as by hormonal function. Such variations in gender traits raise questions about the easy definition of girl/boy, woman/man. These are issues of gender, not of sex, which is defined by the gametes carried by the person. Individuals elect to define their genders by clothing and by morphological and physiological manipulations in which secondary sex characteristics are changed in order to assume a particular gender (so-called sex-changing procedures).

Individuals who are homophilic (liking same sex as self: gay men, lesbian women, and bisexuals) may be considered genderized; their sex cells are usually either XX or XY carriers.

Psychosocial/Societal Customs of Sex/Gender Definition

In many societies, the genitalia are not displayed. The gender dress is presumed to be concordant with the gametes (e.g., on the visual evidence of a sex characteristic involved in reproduction), such as mammaries. Mammary glands are in evidence in most societies, either conspicuously covered or bare. In men, sex characteristics as represented by the penis and scrotum are not visually evident in most societies. There are some exceptions, such as the wearing of a codpiece (a shell-like covering of the penis and scrotum incorporated into the trousers) in Europe during the Middle Ages or a special cover for the penis (penis gourd; gourds are grown in different shapes for adornment) used today.

The roles that women and men play in the daily life of the group is qualified by the reproductive roles they play: women are producers of the children and their nurturants in early stages of development. However, women and men may engage in food gathering and preparation and in building shelters, according to social/societal prescription.

Developmental Processes Defining Sex

The development of sex definition is founded on preceding biochemical and physiological processes reflecting the developmental history of the woman and man who carried the gametes that fused to create the individual.

Development of Gamete Definition

The history of the individual begins with what the woman and man bring to the egg and sperm (gametes) and the circumstances of the fusion of the egg and sperm. Assuming that the circumstances were usual, voluntary sexual intercourse; that the gametes were fused in the woman's body; that the partners were healthy; that the egg carried a nucleus with twenty-two autosomal (body) chromosomes and one X chromosome (sex chromosome); that the sperm carried twenty-two autosomal chromosomes and either one Y chromosome or one X chromosome (sex chromosome); and that the egg and sperm cells fused, a zygote is formed. Each chromosome usually carries one form of a gene; a gene is an arrangement of four nucleotides (adenine, cytosine, guanine, and thymine), each of which may appear a different number of times in different sequences, on a base of sugar (deoxyribose) and a phosphate (gene = DNA = deoxyribonucleic acid). Different arrangements of the nucleotide sequences are called alleles, and each chromosome carries one of the alleles of each nucleotide sequence. Parts of the DNA arrangement can move and cause relocation of a part of a chromosome to another chromosome or a different area of a chromosome (transposons). These translocations can affect the function of the nucleotides.

In addition, in the nucleus and in the organelles (small structures in the cell), other sequences of nucleotides (adenine, cytosine, guanine, and uracil) with a sugar (ribose) and a phosphate appear; these constitute RNA (ribonucleic acid). During much of the history of the cells of the body, the chromosomes look like a string that is coiled in a mass in each cell. On each of these chromosomes, genes are located in bands.

As the sex cells grow and begin to reproduce, the pairs of chromosomes line up on special filaments (spindles) and begin a process that splits the cell and produces two copies of each of the original pairs of chromosomes, producing four daughter cells, each of which contains one chromosome. In the ovary, the four cells each usually have an X chromosome; in the testis, usually two cells carry X chromosomes and two carry Y chromosomes. This process is called meiosis, and the resulting daughter cells are called haploid cells.

Body cells (somatic, autosomal cells) grow in a similar process, called mitosis, except that when the chromosomes line up, they split and reproduce themselves in a pair of daughter cells, each of which has a pair of chromosomes rather than half a pair.

During meiosis and mitosis, the separation of the chromosomes and their rearrangement usually proceeds as described here; however, their rearrangement is also a matter of circumstances and chance. In these processes of splitting and reassembling in new cells, rearrangements of chromosomes and nucleotides may take place. Chromosomes may lose part of their two arms (one is a short arm, referred to as "p," and one is a long arm, referred to as "q"), which are joined at the center by a structure called a centromere; one part of one arm may get attached to the other arm of the same chromosome or to another chromosome; a part of the chromosome may be lost; some of the nucleotides (genes) on the chromosome may be changed or rearranged (transposons), changing the function of the nucleotide segment; and there may be other changes still to be discovered. These rearrangements and changes may also take place in the X and Y chromosomes. It has been said that the production of a viable, usual individual, given all the possible events, is astounding.

Egg/Sperm Fusion

The two gametes are usually fused, forming the zygote internally in the woman's body. However, in contemporary practice in industrialized societies, the gametes may be fused outside the woman's body; the resulting zygote must be placed in an incubating woman whose hormonal physiology will make development of the resulting zygote possible. This practice is used when sterility of the woman or the man prevents zygote formation in the usual fashion. Sterility or fertility is a function of the biochemical level, involving nucleotide sequences, proteins, and hormones.

The psychosocial/societal processes resulting in the decision to fuse the gametes integrate the biochemical processes with the genders of the woman and man (ancestors). Contemporary societal practices for reproduction in industrialized cultures have been extended to homophilic individuals (gay men or lesbian women) who elect to have children. Foster zygote formation is accomplished by the participation of individuals who carry the appropriate gametes and who can incubate the zygote; sometimes the incubating individual is homophilic, or lesbian.

When the egg and sperm fuse, the zygote may carry one X from the mother and one X or a Y from the father. In the case of the zygote that carries two X chromosomes, the alleles on each chromosome could result in a double dose of the same allele. In evolution, through a process that is incompletely understood, one X chromosome remains active, while the other X chromosome is inactivated through the function of a nucleotide sequence on the active chromosome called Xist, the inactivating gene in the inactivating region of the chromosome (XIC), during early embryonic stages. Research with mice (considered a model for humans) has shown that usually the X chromosome from the sperm is inactivated. However, it has recently been discovered that in humans some of the genes on the so-called inactive X chromosome "escape" inactivation. These may be responsible for some of the X-linked characteristics. When the second X chromosome does not become inactivated during embryogeny, the person may show severe mental retardation.

The structures and functions of the egg are significant, first in making the fusion possible and then for the developmental processes that follow.

The Egg. The egg is a complex cell containing a nucleus with half the body chromosomes and one X chromosome; yolk proteins deposited from maternal blood in the egg; intracellular structures (e.g., ribosomes carrying the RNA necessary for protein synthesis); the mitochondrion, the energy-producing engine that also carries its own DNA and RNA; proteins that facilitate the activity of DNA and RNA, producing other proteins in the egg and developing organism; and molecules that function in differentiating cell types during embryonic development.

The X chromosome is known as the "sex" chromosome. As of September 2000, 581 nucleotide sequences (genes) have been identified on the X chromosome. Only two genes have been identified as responsible for the development of the ovary, that produces estrogen and progesterone, two hormones necessary for reproductive function. Estrogen is active in many other physiological functions. Although most of the research is done with animals, the finding of sites for estrogen activity are important suggestions for further investigation of human estrogen function. There are sites for estrogen activity in the cardiovascular system, liver, immune system, bone, kidney, lung, and thymus. Although it has also been found that estrogen plays an important role in the death of cells, which affects neural function, estradiol (a form of estrogen) plays a role in neuroprotection (e.g., in stroke).

The association of mental dysfunction with the X chromosome (fragile X, other forms of mental retardation) is well supported in human research. There are estrogen receptors in two areas of the brain associated with learning and memory. These areas are also active in cognitive activity and areas in which new neurons are formed throughout life (neurogenesis). Again, it should be noted that almost all of these findings are the result of work with animals, but some human research points to its relevance for human behavior. It is also important to point out that estrogen function occurs in women and men, although there are some differences.

The Sperm. The sperm consists of a nucleus with chromosomes (some sperm contain an X chromosome and some a Y chromosome), a sperm head with an acrosomal vesicle containing enzymes activating the fusion with the egg, a mitochondrion that is thought not to be functional once the sperm and the egg have fused, and fibers (flagellum) important for the motility of the sperm. Actual movement of the sperm into the egg, however, does not take place immediately after intercourse. The movement of the sperm is facilitated by the muscular activity of the uterus and possible chemical stimulation by different cells in the woman's reproductive tract. Complex chemical processes at the egg's membranes facilitate the fusion of sperm and egg. The sperm mitochondrion and flagellum disintegrate after fusion. Most of the mitochondrial genes in the ensuing individual come from the woman.

The Y chromosome is the other "sex" chromosome, and it is decisive in defining the sex of the new individual as either female or male. As of September 2000, forty-seven genes have been identified on the Y chromosome; of these, a nucleotide sequence known as the sex-determining region (SRY gene) is active in producing the testis, which in turn elaborates testosterone, the hormone necessary for reproduction. No matter how many X chromosomes are in the developing organism, if the SRY area is active on the Y chromosome, the primary reproductive system will be that of a male.

Androgen receptors have been found in the frontal cortex of monkeys, an area involved in cognitive function. It is generally believed that there are no diseases or phenotypic characters (individual traits) linked to the Y chromosome, but this is still a question for further investigation.

Embryogeny: Development of Ovary and Testis

Embryogeny occurs during the first two months after fusion. The zygote splits into two cells; each cell (and all later cells that develop) usually has forty-six chromosomes: twenty-two pairs are autosomal chromosomes (body, nonsex cells), and one pair is composed of XX or XY chromosomes. All autosomal cells reproduce mitotically.

After the two-cell stage, in the first few days after fusion, primordial germ cells (sex cells) develop, and by the third week they have moved into an area known as the genital ridge. The cells in the ridge develop into a "bipotential" gonad. Two structures are present in the indifferent gonad: the Mullerian duct is active in forming female reproductive structures, and the Wolffian duct, in forming male reproductive structures. The bipotential gonad may become an ovary or a testis, depending on whether the embryo has an X and a Y chromosome or two X chromosomes.

If only two X chromosomes are present, the gene DAX1, carried on the active X chromosome, participates in the formation of the ovary, which will produce estrogen. Another gene, WNT4a, that is not on either the X or Y chromosome, but on a "body" chromosome (in a somatic cell), is also active in the development of the ovary. The process whereby these genes act is not yet completely understood. It is interesting to note the activity of a gene on a "sex" chromosome and a gene on a "body" chromosome in sex definition.

The participation of nonsex chromosomal material in sex definition is also seen in the activity of the Y chromosome. The sex-determining region (SRY gene) works together with proteins on both the Y chromosome and on autosomal chromosomes, the SOX proteins, to elaborate a testis, which produces two hormones: testosterone and anti-Mullerian duct factor (AMH).

Genes involved in the development of sex definition are also found on other chromosomes: SF1 (in the mouse) on chromosome 9, WT1 on chromosome 11, SOX9 on chromosome 17, and MIS on chromosome 19. The activity of these genes is known for its effects on changing the usual development of sex definition. When the tip of chromosome 9 is deleted, the individual with XY chromosomes develops as a woman rather than as a man. The process responsible for this reversal is not yet known. Conceptualization of the X and Y chromosomes as *the* "sex determinants" is being modified in the light of new information.

If there is no Y chromosome present, the Mullerian duct, under the influence of estrogen, elaborates the internal feminine reproductive system. If a Y chromosome had been present, and produced a testis, an anti-Mullerian hormone, AMH, would have been produced by the testis. AMH would have influenced regression of the Mullerian duct, and the Wolffian duct would elaborate the internal male reproductive system.

The estrogens produced by the ovary, in addition to those that come from the mother through the placenta, work to differentiate the Mullerian duct into female genitalia. They also produce the secondary sex organs (external: labia, clitoris, and mammary gland; internal: vagina, uterus). The development of the clitoris in monkeys responds to testosterone during development. The testosterone produced by the testis is active in developing the secondary male sex characteristics (external: penis, scrotum, which contains the primary sex organ, the testis, and the epididymis; internal: prostate, seminal vesicle).

Fetal Stage

The fetal stage lasts seven months intrauterine. During the period of incubation (placentation of a biochemical link between embryo/fetus and mother) until birth, the individual develops the sensory, motor, endocrine, and neural systems that are usual in the individual to be born. The various structural (muscle, bone, skin), activating (enzymes), and hormonal proteins are produced from the nutriment from the mother in the placental blood and the activity of the nucleotide sequences and the proteins produced by the embryo/fetus. The input of events outside the body of the mother, such as auditory and tactile stimuli, which have been found to affect the incubating fetus, as well as other stimuli, which may affect the mother's biochemistry and physiology through the activity of neurotransmitters, hormones, and other neural changes brought about by these stimuli external to the mother and the fetus, are transmitted through the placenta. These externally derived changes become integrated with the biochemical (nutritional, hormonal, neurotransmitters, steroids, growth factors, adrenal stress responses, etc.) that develop in the mother in the course of the pregnancy. In the usual situation (usual nucleotide configurations, hormonal function of the mother, etc.), the primary sources of possible effects on the development of sex definition come from the nutritional status of the mother, its effect on the developing individual, and the biochemistry of stress responses.

Evolutionary biologists, biomedical researchers, and now psychologists have been interested in the processes that maintain a developing individual within the mother. The developing organism could act as a foreign chemical stimulus to which the mother's antigenic system would usually react. It has been suggested that the chorion (sac holding the embryo) produces substances that block the antigens, so that the mother does not reject the embryo as a foreign cell. How this process comes about is not yet known. However, it is thought that if the developing organism is the same sex as the mother, certain antigens are not formed.

Ray Blanchard and Anthony Bogaert have hypothesized an explanation for the apparent birth-order effect during the fetal stages on the development of a homophilic man. The more male babies precede the birth of an individual, the more likely the individual will be homophilic. This does not affect homophilia in women, as the process is related to H-Y antigens that are linked with the Y chromosome. The H-Y antigens act like anti-Mullerian hormone (AMH), the hormone that suppresses the development of the female reproductive system. According to that hypothesis, if the zygote has a Y chromosome, the mother's antibody response is to suppress the "masculinizing" effect of the H-Y antigen, which acts like AMH. As the body has a "memory" for immunogenic experience, her reaction to the Y-antigen is built up in the mother's repeated response to the developing male fetuses, so that there is no suppression of "feminization" processes. Thus, the likelihood of a homophilic male child being born after a number of male siblings in the same family is increased (birth-order effect in homophilia).

The statistical finding that homophilic men are more likely to have more brothers than sisters may be a "sufficient" finding to suggest a relationship between birth order and homophilia in men, but not a "necessary" explanation. To understand how this happens, the pathway from antigen to behavior would have to be clarified. The integrative levels approach would ask: How is it that not all the brothers born after the same number of siblings become homophilic? Could there be psychosocial/societal processes involved that would have to be integrated with the biochemical/physiological levels? Despite the fact that biological factors have been proposed to "explain" homophilia, primarily in men (androgen "insensitivity"; genes; familiality; hormonal processes), there is insufficient research attention to the integration of all the psychosocial/societal experiences with biochemical/physiological processes in these individuals. In 1991, Sandra Wittelson commented:

> [A]lthough there appears to be some association among early hormonal events, brain anatomy, functional asymmetry and sexual orientation, there is certainly independence among these factors. This likely contributes to the considerable inconsistency in results among converging lines of evidence. The situation is further complicated by the likelihood that the associations and interactions among these factors are different between the sexes.

Among the factors not sufficiently considered is the psychosocial/societal activity as it refigures the developmental history of gender, leading to the unique complexity of each individual's gender. We also do not discuss why we are asking questions about differences between women and men and about homophilia. Wittelson recognized this in saying, "The challenge to society is to accept, respect, and effectively use the neural diversity among human beings."

Birth to Maturity

Although many of the findings resulting from research with humans and animals remain to be verified, they suggest that sex definition may be a process that involves several chromosomes, genes, and proteins, a pattern that has been found for many other expressions of gene function. Broadening the research to include other so-called nonsex chromosomes increases the probability that many experiences that are not usually considered "sexual" play an important role in defining sex and sexual (reproductive) behavior. How experience affects the brain is not yet completely understood, but this is an active area of research.

The usual direction of traditional thought about the relationship between experience and biological factors (such as the organization and activity of the brain) is that the biological factors direct the experience. S. Marc Breedlove considered that perhaps the direction could also go the other way. He found that if one gave male rats copulatory experience, the neurons in the spine that were involved in the activity were changed, whereas if the rat did not have copulatory experience, the neurons did not change. As he says, "It is possible that differences in sexual behaviour cause, rather than are caused by, differences in brain structure." One must be cautious about extrapolating from animal behavior to human behavior, but other research supports the concept that experience is reflected in changes in brain structure and function.

Continuing Complex Biochemical Processes in Sex and Gender Definition

As indicated earlier, the experience of the mother translates through the placenta into the experience of the developing organism she carries. Psychosocial/societal activity begins with birth and goes on through the life of the person. All the experiences that the individual lives through have different effects on the development of gender. Just as we still do not understand all the processes involved in the development of sex definition, we are far from understanding the processes that are involved in gender development. The profound processes of psychosocial/societal activity have the most valence in the development of gender, and many of the biochemical and physiological processes that were begun before birth continue in the person after birth. These continue to be involved in the definition of sex and are integrated into the development of gender.

Receptor Function. When sequences of nucleotides (genes) produce proteins, cells respond to those proteins (e.g., hormones, neurotransmitters, enzymes) when the structure of the proteins fits the molecular configurations in the membranes enclosing the cell, so that the proteins can go through the membrane. The same "fitting" process is necessary once the proteins enter the cell: They must fit some molecule in the cell; there must be molecules in the membrane and in the cell that can receive the proteins, that can perform the receptor function. The receptor process is integral to the expression of nucleotide and protein function in sex definition and other physiological activities.

For example, the evident involvement of androgens in sex definition is complex. Testosterone is changed to estradiol in many cells and tissues (but not in all) and in different systems of the body, including the nervous system, so that it can work.

Receptors for estrogen have been found in the human amygdaloid complex (an area involved in emotional behavior) as well as in the cerebral cortex and hippocampus, both participating in cognitive function. Such receptors have also been found in mouse and rat brains.

Aromatization. The process of change from testosterone to estradiol takes place through the activity of an enzyme (aromatase) and is called aromatization. This takes place during fetal development. It was found that male mouse neurons in the hypothalamus, an important neural area for reproductive activity, show more aromatase activity than female neurons. There may be some proteins that inhibit the aromatization. The increased aromatase activity shows up in late fetal development and is sensitive to the amount of androgen circulating in the area. It is suggested by the investigators that this affects the activity of the estrogens in their nourishment of the brain during sexual differentiation of the brain. The processes relate to sex definition, not to gender definition, as this research was done with mice. It is interesting to consider this finding along with the finding that copulatory activity changes the neurons involved in that activity. Copulatory activity and, in the case of humans, masturbation may increase the level of testosterone produced and circulating, and thus affect the development of the brain's organizational differences between females and males.

Androgen Insensitivity. One set of cells that have testosterone receptors are specialized fatty cells. Testosterone destroys these cells. If these receptors are not functioning, the cells continue to function and grow, producing "breasts" in men who have XYchromosomes. These tissues do not function as mammary glands. These men produce testosterone in the usual fashion. This condition is known as the androgen insensitivity syndrome.

Individuals with the androgen insensitivity syndrome may appear to be women for another reason. The adrenal glands produce androgens that are involved in the development of secondary sex characteristics (hairiness). As these androgens are also not "received," there is no stimulation for secondary sex characteristics. These individuals appear to be women but cannot conceive, because the anti-Mullerian hormone produced by the testis during embryogeny caused the Mullerian duct to regress and internal reproductive organs were not developed. Such individuals may adopt a gender identity defined as a woman. Gametic sex and gender are not necessarily congruous. The psychosocial/societal development of such individuals deserves further study.

Location of a Gene Is Important. Animal research has shown that the DAX1 gene is a complex actor in sex definition. When the DAX1 gene is on both the active and the inactive X chromosomes, the individual produces a female sex identity (XX chromosomes) and ovaries. If the X and Y chromosome are present, but the two copies of the DAX1 gene are on the active X chromosome and the SRY gene is on the Y chromosome, testes are produced but they are undescended and nonfunctional; usually such an individual is identified as having a female sex identity. If there is only one copy of the DAX1 gene on the X chromosome, and SRY on the Y chromosome, the normal testes develop and the sexual identity is male. The exact process whereby this occurs is not yet known. Again, it should be noted that this research was only performed on animals.

Origin of a Gene Is Important. Before fusion is achieved, the pronuclei (as the nuclei are termed at this stage) of the egg and sperm may not be equivalent. Based on research with mice, the female pronucleus and the male pronucleus carry genes that are usually equivalently activated. However, it was found that if a nucleotide sequence changed in the female pronucleus and was not able to produce the protein that encourages growth (growth factor), the offspring grew in the usual manner. If the change was in the male, the offspring did not grow properly and were stunted. The activity of the genes depends on whether it came from the egg or the sperm chromosome. Both pronuclei are important for development.

Unfortunately, the term "imprinting" is also used to describe the behavior of newborn birds that can walk and follow the female bird after hatching. Genomic imprinting results from a different process. If the X chromosome comes from the male, it functions differently than when it comes from the female: This is genomic imprinting. The responsible processes are not yet known.

For example, if the arrangement of a nucleotide sequence (allele) has changed when it is on chromosome 15 in the mother, it will be expressed as Prader Willi syndrome. If on the father's chromosome, it is expressed as the Angelman syndrome. Although both may feature mental retardation, this is not always true for the Prader Willi syndrome people. In addition, the Angelman syndrome is rarely diagnosed earlier than at two years of age; speech is absent, and inappropriate laughter, hyperactivity, and seizures are presented. Life expectancy is of usual length. In the Prader Willi syndrome, dysfunctional characteristics are sometimes seen at birth or during infancy; these are difficulty in sucking, necessitating special feeding techniques; excessive eating, seen at about one year of age; and ensuing obesity, which can be life-threatening. Although the eating pattern can be controlled, other obsessive–compulsive behavior is seen. Both syndromes occur in girls and boys (women and men).

Genomic imprinting is also being reported in other chromosomal-genomic patterns, such as Down's syndrome, Turner's syndrome, and Klinefelter's syndrome. The evidence for some clear genomic imprinting in schizophrenia and bipolar syndrome as defined in *DSM-IV* is inconclusive.

The integrative levels approach may be useful in considering the reports of imprinting in individuals with Turner's syndrome (in which the individual has only one X chromosome, XO), as reported by Skuse and his colleagues. They report that an area on the X chromosome from the father facilitates "social cognition." That area is missing on the maternal X. Turner women experience difficulties in social situations, such as peer ridicule, and generally have low self-esteem. To attribute an apparent lack of social cognitive skills would require us to know how the biochemistry of the X chromosome from the mother differs from that of the X chromosome from the father, and how that difference is expressed in protein function throughout the psychosocial/societal developmental history of the individual. Some research is being carried out on the psychosexual development of "imprinted" individuals.

Unusual Numbers of X and Y Chromosomes. Zygotes may have more than one X or Y. The resulting embryo may carry as many as five X chromosomes and one Y, or may not receive the X from the sperm, and therefore have only one X (XO). These and other unusual assemblies of chromosomes are then reflected in the development of the different physiological systems. The fact that these unusual chromosomal patterns usually concern the X chromosome and affect not only the reproductive and nervous systems but other systems (circulatory, skeletal, dermatological) points to the broad involvement of the X chromosome with many aspects of development. The consequent integration of these unusual chromosomal systems with the nervous system leads to many unique gender developmental histories.

Multiple X chromosomes are more frequently reported in industrialized societies than multiple Y chromosomes, but their frequencies throughout the human species are not known. Individuals with XYY chromosomes were at one time thought to be more likely to be aggressive men who were frequently in trouble with the law in industrialized societies. However, research did not support this inference.

The two more frequently found combinations of unusual numbers of chromosomes are the Turner and Klinefelter individuals. Turner's syndrome appears in 1 out of 5,000 girls born in industrialized societies; Klinefelter's syndrome appears in 1 out of 1,000 boy births. People with these syndromes are clearly genderized, are said to have poor cognitive skills, and are frequently sterile. However, spontaneous menstruation and fertility have been reported in Turner women, although not all pregnancies are carried through.

Although both women with Turner's syndrome and men with Klinefelter's syndrome are considered moderately retarded, research does not always support that contention about Turner women. The gender and cognitive development in individuals with Turner's syndrome is considered functional by some researchers. The presence of only one X chromosome in Turner women has been considered to be especially relevant to their visual–spatial performance, and Turner women do not do as well as Klinefelter men on spatial ability tasks, but they improve with training.

The implications of underdeveloped internal reproductive systems for understanding "gender" and "sexual" definition and self-identity are demonstrated in a consideration of the research with the two syndromes. The psychological aspects of Turner's syndrome function are frequently studied; Klinefelter's syndrome individuals are studied less often. Individuals with either syndrome usually have socialization difficulties, but these are not the same. For example, in Klinefelter's syndrome, the man usually has small testes. Depending on the socialization history of the individual, the small testes may not occasion any concern in family and friends. Such an individual may not be thought to have an XXY chromosome configuration and may have identified himself as a "normal" male. Here the sexual identity (because there is one Y chromosome) and the gender identity are compatible, but the complete gamete picture is not taken into consideration. Sometimes such individuals have a usual sexual behavioral history, but cannot produce offspring (e.g., aspermatogonia, or low sperm count). Physicians have been counseled to check on the sperm levels when an individual has small testes, so that he can be advised "to consider not marrying because of sterility." Modern techniques have made it possible for Klinefelter men to have medical help in obtaining viable sperm (although the count is low) and have the sperm introduced into a woman, producing viable offspring. Sufficient numbers of such children have been born to warrant a call for continued study of them.

In consideration of the social adjustment of Turner women, the attempts to intervene constructively have turned in two directions. In one, supplemental treatment with estrogen is found to somewhat reverse neurocognitive deficits. In the other, concern about the usual short stature of the women as an important factor of psychosocial/societal adjustment has resulted in programs in which growth hormone is provided to the women. Most of the reports published deal with the anatomical and physiological results of the treatment.

In Klinefelter's syndrome, exogenous testosterone has been given to improve the immune system and to study its effect on brain morphology. It is not clear whether the difference in diagnosis, treatment, and study is related to the fact that the two syndromes are expressed in women and men, who usually have different psychosocial/societal experiences in contemporary industrialized societies. In both syndromes, the approach has been to study the development of neuroanatomy and reproductive physiology. Understanding sex and gender definitions in the experiences of individuals with Klinefelter's and Turner's syndromes calls for the integrative levels approach to elucidating the intimate interconnection between biochemical/physiological and psychosocial/societal levels.

Biochemical and Psychosocial/Societal Integration of Sex and Gender Definition. Activities of genes and proteins at one stage of development usually lead to an expected developmental pattern. When some of the genes and proteins are not functional at the usual developmental stage, as a result of changes in their nucleotide sequences or the amino acid configuration in the proteins produced, individuals do not develop the usual sexual structures and functions at the usual time. During the embryological stage, the testis produces testosterone that is converted to 5-alpha-dihydrotestosterone (DHT) by an enzyme. In some males, the nucleotide sequence that codes for that protein (enzyme) is lacking. They develop all the male reproductive internal organs but not the secondary sex characteristics (male urethra, prostate, penis, or scrotum). Accordingly, these infants are considered females and they are genderized as girls until they begin to develop secondary male sex characteristics at puberty. This developmental sequence illustrates that genes, proteins, and hormones act at different developmental stages to define sex and gender. Julianne Imperato-McGinley and her coworkers have found populations of such individuals in the Dominican Republic, Turkey, Papua New Guinea, Ireland, and Brazil. Their reports indicate that when the gamete identity is revealed, the gender identity usually changes, although it is clear that the "men" cannot produce offspring.

Changes in gender may be related to the class of the individual. In the Dominican Republic, those in the upper classes can marry and arrange for offspring to be born to the wives in those marriages and claimed as their children. Middle-class individuals change gender identity in variable social/societal adjustments. Poor people may become prostitutes or unskilled laborers. Today, individuals diagnosed early with this difference in hormonal function can be treated with appropriate medication to affect further development.

Development of Gender

Definition: Psychosocial/Societal Processes Integrate Biochemical and Physiological Experience.

Gender Definition Based on Sex

The neonate is part of a genderizing process that begins at birth with the decision of the caregivers that the visible, identifiable genitalia are sufficient to assign a gender to the child. Usually, this practice is founded on no information about the gametes carried by the child. From that point forward, the ways in which the child is addressed, handled, and dressed are based on that decision. In some cultures, girl babies are fed less than boy babies. The effect of malnutrition on mental growth and development at any stage during the life of the individual is well documented.

Genital Awareness

Usual Development of Gender Definition. The development of external genitalia becomes part of the experience of the neonate, infant, and child; the recognition of the relation between the genitalia and the self may be through self-manipulation or the socialization among caregivers, peers, and the individual. The child integrates self-awareness of bodily changes and the development of secondary sex characteristics with the ensuing societal definitions of acceptable activity, perceptions, and cognitive experience of the differences between girls and boys.

Freudians have seen gender development as evidence of psychosexual development; the vagina is seen as an evidence of penis envy. Sandra Bern and Barbara Lloyd and James Stroyan found that children acquire information about genitalia, and that gender differences are seen in children thirty-six to sixty-five months of age. The effect of the awareness and information about genitalia on the child's gender development is related to the child's understanding of gender differences in terms of desirability and social/economic inferiority or superiority.

Unusual Genitalia and Secondary Sex Characteristics. Differences in genitalia, such as unusual size (e.g., Klinefelter's syndrome), presence of enlarged clitoris, gynecomastia ("breasts") in men, and hairiness in women call attention to the relation between sex and gender. The effects of such awareness have been studied to some extent. Such research requires sensitivity. These individuals should not be considered "subjects" who are "subjected" to being photographed as examples of unusual development of secondary sex and other anatomical characteristics because of biochemical/physiological history, a practice found in many genetic, medical, and reference texts. Such research should be undertaken with the participation of the individuals in developing research questions and methods that address the issues as they affect their lives. Each individual should be considered a national treasure worthy of financial and every other support to make of their lives what they desire.

Puberty as a Psychosocial/Societal Process (Maturity of Reproductive System)

Societies decide the point of maturity of both girls and boys and perform rituals to mark it. These rituals may or may not have a basis in reproductive maturity, although they are more likely to be linked to menarche in girls. In societies in which young girls and boys may be married through financial arrangements at ages before puberty, the consummation of the marriage in order to reproduce is usually based on menarche in the girls and the age of the boys. However, genderization has taken place before the maturity of the reproductive systems. The biology is assumed, the gender is prescribed, and rituals of passage to mature gender roles are customary.

The rituals are frequently tied to age, regardless of concern about reproductive ability, which is assumed. In most societies, such assumed reproductive ability is greeted with approbation and celebration. In contemporary industrialized societies, because of improved nutrition during early stages of development, puberty is reached earlier than in societies with economic problems leading to poor nutrition. In many societies with economic problems, the "sale" of girls and boys for prostitution, regardless of reproductive status, places the emphasis on sexual activities rather than on self-identified gender. The physiological changes in hormonal function resulting in the evidence of secondary sex characteristics is referred to as "hormonal rush" in some societies, emphasizing the sex of the individual rather than the gender, but acceptable behavioral patterns related to reproductive activity are prescribed by society. In some societies, rituals are performed to recognize a new gender status in society, in terms of assuming responsibilities independent of the reproductive activities expected and for the appropriate activity in regard to adults and people of power.

The requirement for women to have children when menarche occurs may change their economic responsibilities, in that they must work and bear children at the same time. The type of labor may be genderized in the light of the reproductive responsibilities. However, the girls are expected to be able to labor at muscularly demanding work as well as the boys in societies in which the economic situation is such that each individual must earn the right to be fed. This results in child labor excesses, further affecting biochemi-

cal/physiological processes (e.g., exposure to toxins) that may affect reproductive function. The stress of hard labor under poor conditions, as well as
the psychosocial/societal stress of such conditions, changes hormonal activity; hormonal dysfunction leading to difficulties in reproduction becomes a
factor in gender status.

In families where elementary and higher education are possible, the type
of profession and jobs to be held are genderized. Women are more likely to
be in the service and "helping" professions (teacher, nurse, physician) than
in the technical physical sciences and engineering. In industrialized countries, the genderization of academic participation and achievement takes
place as early as three years, and affects self-evaluation of academic ability
and performance so that girls are less likely to acknowledge their abilities.
The genderization leads to different access by women and men to appropriate training. It has been found in rats that increased stimulative activity facilitates production of new neurons (neurogenesis), and in birds, learning to
map an area for food induces neurogenesis. Neurogenesis in areas of the brain
that are active in learning has been reported also. Human learning experiences may accelerate neurogenesis, and this may facilitate performance.

Sex and Gender in Nonreproductive (Productive) Societal Activities

Two activities reflect changes in the economic and technical character of
human activity, and with them, changes in the position of women in society:
sports and labor. Both are genderized and rely on biochemical/physiological
(biological) differences between women and men to justify the differences in
participation by women or men.

Sports: Who Does What if It "Takes Brawn"?

In most societies, group and individual games of athletic skill are genderized; boys usually play most of them, but girls do not. In the history of such
activities in industrialized societies, most sports remained traditionally genderized until the era of women's activities for equal rights. Women, particularly upper-class European women, began to engage in the sports that had been
reserved for men. In recent years in many societies, including those that were
originally colonialized and that maintained the European sports traditions
brought to them by the colonists (cricket, rugby, football, soccer, tennis, etc.),
women have become players in some of those games (tennis, basketball, soccer, swimming). As the globalization of communication and sports developed,
many international events increased the financial value of competing in those
games. Even though in most sports women have their own organizations, this

has sharpened the motivation to "equalize" women with men in the competition for attracting audiences and honors, which bring financial rewards.

This has resulted in sophisticated techniques to determine whether women who compete successfully are using steroids, and whether they are gametic women. Any competence that women achieve is attributed to externally administered steroidal hormones to affect musculature, strength, and performance. The reliability of analysis of urine and blood to discover the use of steroids has been challenged. The identification of gender with gametic sex is clearer when genomic techniques are used. Reliance on gametic sex without consideration of accessibility to training to develop psychomotor skills disadvantages women in pursuit of sports achievements. The physiological differences between women and men are products not only of the biochemicals (genes, hormones, etc.) but of the ways in which the expression of those biochemicals developed in the physiological history of the individual. Motor differences between women and men are considered to be independent of training by some, but this is disputable. When groups of women and men are compared on various motor measures, there are significant differences in the scores within groups, so that some women are "equal" to or better than some men. The developmental histories of these women and men are specific to their ability, and a study of how those abilities developed would be informative.

Labor: Who Does What If It "Takes Brains"?

Some Historical Considerations. Historical studies of postsedentation societies show that the prescription for certain types of labor for women and men was frequently a function of the reproductive activity of women. In many contemporary industrialized societies and those in the process of becoming industrialized, given the advances in technical tools and the drive of women for equity in all aspects of life, it is not necessary to define the division of labor by reproductive role. Both women and men can engage in all types of labor, including those requiring mental abilities (computer science, other types of sciences) as well as those requiring psychomotor skills (e.g., construction industries). The jobs that are usually held by men have different, and more desirable, rewards. In industrialized societies, girls and boys learn this lesson early (preschool and primary school children) and understand the genderized nature of the differences in employment of women and men. Much of the research comparing the thinking abilities of women and men may be undertaken to demonstrate a "scientific" basis for the limited accessibility by women to jobs with complex mental tasks.

Spatial Abilities as Mental Competence. Spatial abilities in women and men as indicators of mental competence are intensively studied, possibly because they are considered essential in scientific, mathematical, and engineering labor. As Diane Halpern has stated, the term "spatial abilities" refers to a complex interrelationship of many skills (e.g., spatial perceptual, spatiotemporal, visual identification of an object when orientation is changed [mental rotation], and spatial relations between/among objects). She and other investigators, such as Anne Petersen and Kathyrn Hood, have noted that gender differences are not found on all tests of spatial ability. Many psychosocial/societal processes are involved (e.g., developmental, emotional, method of observing individual differences, effects of training), and these may be responsible for the variability in the findings. Some studies have found that if the time for response is not limited, there is no difference between women and men; that training will improve the performance of girls more than boys (embedded figures, mental rotation) even after the differences between the girls and boys before training are taken into account; that women do better on map-reading tests than men; and that women do better on spatial memory tests than men. However, despite weaknesses in methods and statistical inference interpretations, most behavioral scientists believe that women are poorer in spatial ability than men. Most researchers in the area of spatial ability seek explanations of gender differences in biochemical factors (biological)—genes, hormones, and neurotransmitters—and at physiological levels (neurophysiological and neuroanatomical processes, reaction time).

What Are the Underlying Research Assumptions?

Many of the questions are based on explicit or implicit assumptions: (1) the same biochemical factors (genes, proteins, and hormones) that produce different sexes (gametes) produce different neuroanatomical and neurophysiological characteristics in groups defined by gender; and (2) as behavioral genetic studies find mental ability differences among differently related people (fraternal twins, siblings, parents) with less shared nucleotide configurations, the differences between women and men are based on their having different genes that correlate with gametic sex differences. Behavior geneticists analyze group differences statistically to state how much of the variation in the scores may be attributed to heredity and how much to the environment. At this time, there is no definitive research about the process whereby spatial ability is inherited, which is not in dispute. Studies with mice and rats in which genes are either removed ("knocked" out) or implanted in other individuals of the same species or of other species (transgenic animals) are cited by behavioral geneticists as evidence for a genetically determined difference between women and men in spatial ability. By studying spatial behavior in people with unusual genes, it is hoped that a gene for spatial behavior will be found. The assumption (which needs to be supported by further research) underlying this approach is that if a mutation of a gene (change in nucleotide sequence or function), as in Williams's syndrome, is correlated with a behavioral characteristic, there should be an unchanged gene that will be correlated with that characteristic as it develops usually.

The investigation of genetic processes underlying cognitive behavior is widely carried out with nonhuman animals. In addition to the preceding assumptions of such research, other assumptions are (1) the same biochemical factors (genes, proteins, and hormones) that produce different gametic sexes produce different neuroanatomical, neurophysiological, and behavioral characteristics in female and male animals; (2) genes will be found in animals to correlate with neural structures and functions involved in spatial abilities; (3) as many nucleotide configurations that correlate with female and male animal reproductive behavior are also found on human chromosomes, and the genes must function in humans as they do in nonhuman animals; and (4) the genes that correlate with cognitive ability in animals will be found on human chromosomes and will function similarly in humans.

Research Issues

These assumptions are challenged by the following considerations of the ways in which research may be carried out to test them: (1) humans and animals compared; (2) nucleotide functions in gametic sex and neuroanatomy and neurophysiology; and (3) methods and theory: reductionist and integrative approaches.

Humans and Animals Compared. Animal research can offer significant suggestions for research on human spatial behavior. It offers necessary information about biochemical and neuroanatomical/neurophysiological processes in animals that suggest similar processes in humans. When an inference can be made from animal and human research, it leads to certain generalizations (e.g., social and spatial experience is a central factor in spatial ability performance). However, the differences between animal and human biochemistry and neuroanatomy/neurophysiology, and psychosocial/societal spatial experiences, may be significant. Biochemical and physiological information obtained on the basis of animal research may be necessary, but it is not sufficient to understand the processes involved in human spatial ability or how differences in performance develop.

The psychosocial/spatial experiences of animals are based on their gametic sex (reproductive behavior); animals have no societal experiences, that is, there are no group-decided prescriptions as to the behavior of female mice and rats, in contrast to the behavior of males, as to how they use space or spatial cues. People have psychosocial/spatial experience based on the genderization of their behavior and abilities from early stages of development, from birth through every aspect of their lives through maturity, including the workplace. Spatial experience in rats has been shown to have biochemical/physiological effects and to improve performance; the neurophysiology of people changes as they participate in learning and memory research. However, how the effects of human experience and of rat experience are similar or different has not been studied, as it is not possible to give either species the experience of the other. Yet, based on animal research, one can approach the issues of the role of experience in changing human function on biochemical and physiological levels.

How is spatial ability studied in people and animals? In one technique, animals are placed in a pan of water with a platform just below the level of the water. The animal has to solve the problem of finding the platform to avoid having to swim. It should be noted that both mice and rats will avoid swimming in water, and the test is stressful. In another situation, the animals have to solve the problem of finding food or escape from a complex circular maze. Spatial ability in people is observed in situations in which language and reading/writing are involved. An individual is asked to indicate spatial relationships between objects (rod and frame situation), or to distinguish between drawings of the same object from different orientations, or to find subsections in complex drawings, or to visualize changes in shape resulting from manipulations of objects from two dimensions to three dimensions (mental rotation), or read maps, or to use paper-and-pencil mazes. Some animal species (birds and primates) have been trained to record responses to figures or drawings presented in the ways in which they are presented to humans. Experiments have been done with people in mazes similar to those used by animals. However, the converse is not possible with nonhuman animals; they cannot be given problems as presented to humans without special training. People who have been studied in the non-paper-and-pencil mazes similar to those in which animals are studied have not been studied while solving paper-and-pencil problems.

"What Can We Infer from the Research Results?

First, the data are usually group data. A group is defined by the characteristics chosen by the investigator: strains of mice and rats; girls and boys defined by their location (school, country, etc.); and women and men by their availability for study (e.g., college). The relevance of such findings for other groups needs to be demonstrated before inferences can be made with confidence. Group differences are correlational: The difference is correlated with the groups, but the process responsible for the difference is not demonstrated. Finding differences between groups tells us nothing about the characteristics of any one individual.

Studying a quantifiable characteristic (trait), such as scores on spatial task performance, in groups (populations) raises an issue when those traits are correlated with the supposed existence of particular genes, or neuroanatomy, or neurophysiology. Plant geneticists know that once a genetic or nucleotide configuration is found to be related to a quantifiable trait (height, weight, etc.) and its chromosomal location found, the number of individuals with that trait in a group is affected by the environment in which the individual plant or animal developed. This will result in different frequencies of the occurrence of the particular form of the trait. In other words, if it were possible to rear each group with different experiences, differences between groups might be different. Even though the nucleotide configuration is the same, it expresses itself differently when the organism has different experiences.

Genes for Spatial Ability and "Smartness"

The announcement is widely made in the media that a gene has been found for "spatial ability" or "smartness." Genetic manipulations have created mice with changed or missing nucleotide configurations; these "knockout" mice cannot use their spatial memories in water and radial mazes, nor can they solve problems of spatial relationships. The inference is than made that in the intact mouse or rat, those genes are the "spatial ability" genes. One of the lessons that genomics has taught is that a single gene is rarely found to be responsible for a function or a structure.

It has also been found that when a gene is changed or missing, other genes and proteins are affected, and that these may be related to the change in structure or function found when the gene is changed: other genes and proteins may have also been changed, which may have also been involved in the behavior, structure, or function reported. Recognizing this, the investigators of these "knockout" mice also study reproductive behavior; finding that this is the same as that in mice that have not been deprived of the "smartness" gene, they assume that the gene described is independent of other genes or functions. However, it is not possible to state that other genes were not affected. Further, the investigators observe the rodents in more than one spatial task, and when the performances are the same, they take this as further proof of the relevance of that gene for spatial ability. The repetition of observations that yield the same scores does not demonstrate that the "gene" is the same.

What Is the Role of Estrogen and Testosterone, or of the Gene or Chromosome for Estrogen and Testosterone?

It is clear that doing genomic research with people would be expensive and time-consuming. The creation of a "knockout person" is not possible.

However, there are individuals born with certain chromosomal or genetic variations who perform poorly on spatial tasks. One such population consists of people with Turner's syndrome. Individuals with Turner's syndrome typically show other mental patterns that are unusual, as well as poor training and poor social skills. As people with Turner's syndrome lack one X chromosome, the inference is made that this is related to poor spatial ability. The developmental and experiential history of these people is not part of the analysis of the behavioral performance measured, nor has the necessary nucleotide function been reported yet.

Some of the evidence that testosterone or the Y chromosome is responsible for the difference in spatial abilities between women and men is based on men with Klinefelter's syndrome. Klinefelter men do better on spatial ability tasks than do Turner women.

As testosterone is converted to estradiol in order for it to be active in many cells, tissues, or organs in which it is found, the relationship between genes, hormones, and spatial ability would seem to require some investigation as to the aromatization of the testosterone in Klinefelter men before this complex finding can be understood.

The ubiquity of estrogen receptors in the nervous system and the wealth of protein-producing genes on the X chromosomes are worth investigating in regard to spatial and other cognitive abilities. The recent finding that estrogen is essential for neurogenesis (formation of new neurons and precursors of neurons) also highlights the significance of experience in behavior. The increase in neurogenesis and estradiol activity in significant areas of the brain (frontal cortex, hippocampus) after training or other experiences designed to modify the behavior of the individual also makes consideration of developmental processes important. Investigation of the changes that take place with disease, stroke, or other traumatizing experiences are other traditional means of understanding neuroanatomy and neurophysiological processes behavior.

Methods and Theory: Reductionist and Integrative Approaches

Looking for genes, hormones, and transmitters to explain behavior is a reductionist approach and leads to an insufficient analysis. Such information is useful and is used in the integrative levels approach. The integrative levels approach, however, is dependent on developmental information: How do the gametic and other nucleotides produce the proteins? How do the proteins work with the nucleotides? How do these entities work with others? How does the experience of the person affect the ways in which these nucleotides and proteins express themselves in the structures and functions that are involved in the performance defined as spatial ability? Most of the research done with people does not include studies of the neurophysiological/neuroanatomic foundations of the behavior being observed, nor is the developmental history of the individuals taken into account. By defining groups, it is assumed that the experience of the individuals in the group is sufficiently similar to limit the variability of performance. This is the usual behavioral genetic approach: Any similarities of the individuals in the group are evidence of their shared inheritance; any variability is evidence of environmental factors.

Information about the biochemical/physiological foundations of behavior in and of itself is necessary, but it is not sufficient, to clarify the process of spatial perception or how the differences develop in women and men, however. The information about biochemistry and physiology would have to be integrated with information about the psychosocial/societal developmental history. The significance of using the developmental history is that it resolves the need to choose between the genetic or the experiential process as the pre-eminent one, the ultimate process. It also obviates the need to quantitatively define the genetic and experiential contribution to the behavior; it seeks at all times to understand how the biochemical/physiological and psychosocial/societal processes become integrated in any behavior pattern, function, or structure.

An Integrated Approach to Studying the Development of Gender

If the societal motivation for the research questions is designed to relate to policies and practices so that equity is possible for women and men, the relative valence of all processes is important. To begin to understand the development of gender, questions asked about biochemical/physiological processes need to be answered as well as psychosocial/societal processes: education, training, family, and peer activities. Such research is demanding and challenging, but the demands and the challenges need to be met if the societal goal is to be achieved.

Note

Reprinted from *Encyclopedia of Women and Gender*, E. Tobach (Ed.), "Development of Sex and Gender: Biochemistry, Physiology, and Experience," © 2001, with permission of Elsevier.

Suggested Reading

Alberts, B., Bray, D., Johnson, A., Lewis, J., Raff, M., Roberts, K., & Walter P. (1998). *Essential cell biology.* New York: Garland.

Carson, R. A., & Rothstein, M. A. (Eds.). (1999). *Behavioral genetics: The clash of culture and biology.* Baltimore, MD: Johns Hopkins University Press.

Fausto-Sterling, A. (2000). *Sexing the body.* New York: Basic Books.

Ford, D. H., & Lerner, R. M. (1992). *Developmental systems theory: An integrative approach.* Newbury Park, CA: Sage.

Gilbert, S. F. (1997). *Developmental biology* (5th ed.). Sunderland, MA: Sinauer Associates.

Griffiths, A.J.F., Miller, J. H., Suzuki, D. T., Lewontin, R. C, & Gelbart, W. M. (Eds.). (1993). *An introduction to genetic analysis* (5th ed.). New York: W. H. Freeman.

Halpern, D. F. (1992). *Sex differences in cognitive abilities* (2nd ed.). Hillsdale, NJ: Erlbaum.

Rogers, L. (2000). *Sexing the brain.* London: Phoenix Press.

Smith, E., & Sapp, W. (Eds.). (1997). *Plain talk about the Human Genome Project.* Tuskegee, AL: Tuskegee University.

Chapter 13

Feminism and Psychology

Joan C. Chrisler and Christine A. Smith

Feminism and psychology have a history of mutual influence. For example, sexist theories that were developed and promulgated by psychologists and psychiatrists were among the first targets of feminist activists in the second wave of the women's movement. Classic feminist books such as *The Second Sex* (De Beauvoir, 1952), *Women and Madness* (Chesler, 1972), *The Female Eunuch* (Greer, 1971), *The Dialectic of Sex* (Firestone, 1970), *Sexual Politics* (Millett, 1970), and *Against Our Will* (Brownmiller, 1975) took aim at Sigmund Freud, Erik Erikson, and other male psychologists and psychoanalysts whose theories described the psychology of women in ways that justified, as well as maintained, a power imbalance in favor of men. One might say that sexism in psychology was one of the sparks that ignited the women's liberation movement.

The women's movement, in turn, had an enormous influence on women psychologists and psychology students. Excited by consciousness-raising groups and inspired by feminist political activism, many women psychologists and psychologists-to-be labeled themselves feminists and set out to make changes that would alter the direction of psychological science, practice, and training. It is the influence in this direction from feminism to psychology that will be the focus of this chapter.

What Is Feminism?

Before we examine feminism's influence on psychology, we must first define feminism. A number of definitions of feminist have been put forth (see, e.g., Kramarae & Treichler, 1985). Each, at its core, refers to the belief that women and men should have equal social and political rights, responsibilities, and opportunities. Feminism acknowledges that women have been denied equality in many areas of life, and feminists seek to remove the oppression that has limited women's roles and choices. Feminism and feminists value women and believe that women should be empowered to define themselves and to be the subjects of their own experiences.

Although there are some universal elements to feminism, various feminist viewpoints with divergent ideas do exist. Each offers its own perspective on the sources of women's oppression, the ramifications of oppression, and the solutions necessary to dismantle the system of oppression and inequality. The prominent perspectives most relevant to psychology are discussed below.

Liberal feminists (sometimes referred to as moderate feminists) support changes in social and political institutions (e.g., laws, values, and customs) in order to attain equality between women and men (Crawford & Unger, 2004). In general, psychologists who hold this perspective tend to see differences between women and men as the result of differential social conditioning, reinforcements, and modeling. If they are given similar treatment (e.g., support for career advancement, praise for showing emotions), liberal feminists believe, women and men will behave similarly. Thus, women and men are more alike than different; when differences in behavior, cognition, and personality are found, they are the result of socialization rather than innate biological (e.g., genes, hormones) influences.

In contrast to liberal feminists' emphasis on the similarities of women and men, cultural feminists focus on the differences. They highlight the unique aspects of women. For example, cultural feminists have suggested that women tend to place more value than men do on interpersonal relationships, nurturance, and connections with others (Tavris, 1992). These relational attributes, commonly associated with girls and women, have been devalued historically, and they continue to be so across many cultures. Cultural feminists emphasize the importance of these attributes, see them as strengths and assets, and believe that they should be valued, even celebrated. With this in mind, cultural feminists suggest a move toward a more woman-centered culture, one that is based on the values of caring and connection (Henley et al., 1998).

Liberal feminists espouse working for women's rights within the current social and political structures, whereas radical feminists believe that these very structures are the root of women's oppression, which can be alleviated only by widespread sociopolitical transformations (Rowland & Klein, 1996). Radical feminists believe that women are currently, and have been historically, oppressed by a patriarchal system, and this system is the source of women's interpersonal, economic, and psychological problems (Worrell & Johnson, 2001). Until the patriarchy is eliminated, women will continue to suffer. Thus, an important part of radical feminist beliefs is the importance of empowering women to engage in collective activism to enact social change.

Socialist or Marxist feminism is sometimes included in radical feminism, since it focuses on the economic structures in society. A major component of socialist feminism is the belief that capitalism as an economic system works with patriarchy to oppress women (Jaggar & Rothenberg, 1993). Socialist feminists believe that until our economic system is changed, women will continue to be oppressed by, for example, being funneled into low-paying, dead-end jobs and bearing most of the responsibility for child care, housework, and other unpaid family and community responsibilities. This type of feminism is less represented in feminist psychology because economic restructuring has been considered less directly relevant to psychology's emphasis on behavior and mental processes. However, as feminist psychologists begin to examine such issues as the effects of poverty and social class on women's lives (see, e.g., *Journal of Social Issues,* 57, no. 2), socialist and Marxist feminism may increase in influence.

Women of color feminism (also called womanism) stresses that feminism and gender issues may be experienced differently by women of different cultures and that issues of particular relevance to women of color have often been ignored or given low priority by the mainstream women's movement (Comas-Diaz, 1991). For example, one tenet of feminism has been that men are the source of women's oppression. Yet women of color often report a strong sense of commonality with men of color as a result of their shared oppression based on race and ethnicity. As a result, women of color may resist varieties of feminism that seem to call for them to work against the men in their communities (hooks, 1984). Important influences of womanism on feminist psychology have been the understanding that individuals' experiences are influenced by the intersection of their various identities and the notion that there is likely to be a diversity of psychologies of women rather than one general psychology that can be discovered and described.

Although each feminist perspective has the potential to influence psychological theory, research, and practice, liberal and cultural feminisms have been most prevalent in feminist psychology to date. As psychologists recognize the need to study and serve all people, research on race and ethnicity (as well as sexual orientation, social class, aging, and disability) is increasing. Thus, womanism may come to have a greater impact on the field. Because radical feminism often emphasizes the intersections of oppressions, and it recognizes that race, sexual orientation, and other oppressed categories are socially constructed to support those in power (Hartman, 1981), it, too, may have an increasing impact on psychology.

Psychology as a Male Bastion

The history of psychology is said to have begun in 1879 with the founding of Wilhelm Wundt's laboratory at the University of Leipzig. Prior to that, psychological questions were addressed by philosophers and researchers with training in medicine and other sciences. During the 1890s psychology became recognized as a science in the United States, and colleges and universities began to add formal psychology programs, departments, and laboratories. In 1894 Margaret Floy Washburn became the first woman to receive a doctorate in psychology from a major American university; a few other women were already active in the field (e.g., Christine Ladd-Franklin, Ethel Puffer) after having done their graduate study in Germany or completed the degree requirements without being awarded an official degree (Scarborough & Furumoto, 1987). Some of the early women psychologists (e.g., Mary Whiton Caulkins, Margaret Floy Washburn) obtained faculty positions at women's colleges, where they were able to set up laboratories and conduct research; others made their careers in applied psychology, especially in child development, child welfare, counseling, and educational psychology. Then, as now, women made major contributions to applied psychology. Until recently, women's opportunities to contribute to the development of research and training in psychology were limited.

In the early years of psychology, few Americans attended college, and a small percentage of them were women. Most colleges and universities did not admit women students, or allowed them to study only as nondegree candidates. In 1910 only 3.8 percent of American women aged eighteen to twenty-one attended college; by 1930 the number had increased to only 10.5 percent (Levine, 1995). It was not until after World War II, when the G.I. Bill made it possible, that large numbers of Americans began to attend college, and new academic institutions (including state universities and community colleges) were founded to meet the demand. The postwar economic boom of the 1950s/early 1960s made it possible for more families to send both their daughters and sons to college, and it became much more common for high school girls to plan to attend college. Today, nationwide, women make up the majority of undergraduate students.

Thus, in the formative years of the discipline, when the core subject matter was being delineated and many of the classic studies were conducted, the vast majority of psychology professors and the majority of the psychology students were men. It is not surprising that those men drew on their own interests, problems, and priorities to set the goals and boundaries of the discipline. Androcentric viewpoints were so commonplace as to be considered, if considered at all, as "normal" or "natural." Thus, the male researchers considered men (i.e., male research participants) to be the best example of man (i.e., human beings). Theories constructed on the basis of the experiences of one sex perpetuated psychology's androcentrism. If data were collected to check theories against women's experiences, and women were found to differ from men, the theory was not considered to be deficient. Instead, men's experiences were considered the "rule," and women's the "exception." Furthermore, psychology, then and now, considers experiments to be the gold standard of methodology. A good experimenter attempts to control as many extraneous variables as possible, so that they do not limit the ability to draw conclusions about the effects of the independent variables. Many psychological researchers considered sex, when they considered it at all, to be a "nuisance variable" that ought to be controlled (Crawford & Unger, 2004). Therefore, even as the number of women college students available to participate in psychological research increased, many researchers continued to recruit only male research participants in order to control for possible sex differences. Thus it is fair to say that at least prior to 1970, psychology was a male bastion. Men led the professional associations, edited the journals, planned the curriculum, wrote the textbooks, devised the theories, conducted the research on topics of interest to themselves using data from other men, and trained the future psychologists. As Naomi Weisstein (1971) wrote in her classic critique, psychology had nothing to say about what women like, need, or want because it simply did not know.

The Second Wave Crashes Ashore

In the late 1960s, as liberal (e.g., National Organization for Women) and radical (e.g., Redstockings) feminist organizations formed and began to work actively for women's rights, graduate students and professional women began to examine the role of women in their fields and to become dissatisfied with what they saw. In 1969 a group of women met during the convention of the American Psychological Association (APA) and shared their frustrations with the APA. There were few women speakers on the convention program, and none of them were talking about the psychology of women. The convention did not offer day care, which made it difficult for many women even to think about attending. This group founded the Association for Women in Psychology (AWP), and decided that they would shake up the APA to make room for women and women's issues (Tiefer, 1991; Unger, 1998). At the 1970 convention the AWP members presented the APA leadership with a list of demands (Tiefer, 1991), including the establishment of a standing committee to expose sexism within APA and rectify it. The Task Force on the Status of Women in Psychology (which later evolved into the Committee on Women in Psychology, CWP) began its work in 1970 (Hogan & Sexton, 1991) with studies of the opportunities available to women in APA governance, editorial work, and convention programs. Among CWP's early successes were the 1977 establishment of the Women's Programs Office at APA, which is staffed by several women who work full-time on women's issues, and the founding in 1973 of an APA division on the psychology of women (Division 35, aka the Society for the Psychology of Women). All of these groups (AWP, CWP, Division 35, and the Women's Programs Office) remain active today, and they have been leaders in the advancement of women and feminist psychological research and practice.

The excitement of the early years of the women's liberation movement led to a veritable explosion of research and theory on the psychology of women, as many women psychologists left behind their former areas of expertise in order to build a feminist psychology. Many journal editors were actively hostile to work submitted by feminists because it attacked popular theories or because it seemed more political than scientific. Thus, feminist psychologists founded their own journals to provide a home for work on women and gender. *Sex Roles* (1975), *Psychology of Women Quarterly* (1977), *Women and Therapy* (1982), and *Feminism and Psychology* (1991) have been that feminist home for many years, and they have published much of the most important and paradigm-shifting work on sex and gender. All continue to publish today, even though it has become possible for feminists to publish their work in many, if not most, mainstream journals. Members of the editorial boards of the feminist journals have played a major role in shaping feminist psychology, and have been important mentors to authors who often were marginalized in the academic or clinical setting.

The first textbooks on the psychology of women were published in 1971, and the first undergraduate and graduate courses on the psychology of women and gender were offered in the early 1970s (Unger, 1998). More than half of all U.S. colleges and universities currently offer such courses. Faculty who teach the psychology of women have contributed to the growth and development of the field of women's studies, including conducting research on the effect such courses have on students both personally and politically, and they have also contributed to the development of feminist pedagogy both in and beyond psychology.

Feminist Research: What Is It?

Feminist psychologists began their research programs by testing theories that were based on men's experiences to see whether they also described women's experiences. They also turned their attention to aspects of the psychology of women that had been overlooked or studied only in terms of how women's experiences affected men's lives. There was plenty of work to be done in these areas, and there still is. Feminist psychologists have broken new ground in the study of such previously neglected topics as motherhood, lesbian couples, menstruation and menopause, violence against women, and the impact the pursuit of beauty has on women's self-esteem and self-concept. Feminist psychologists have also filled in gaps in existing research areas, corrected sexist or androcentric ideas about women's behavior, and critiqued the way psychological research has traditionally been carried out.

An important element of the feminist influence on psychology has been the critique of the experimental method. In their classic article, McHugh, Koeske, and Frieze (1986) pointed out that science is not value-free; sexism can enter into the research process at various stages, including design, implementation, and interpretation of results. Traditional empirical methodologies have been criticized by feminists as methods in which the participants and researchers are at a distance from each other, and the researchers interpret the participants' responses in terms of their own (rather than the participants') framework and expectations (Reinharz, 1992). Other criticisms include the assumption of objectivity (Jayaratne, 1983; McHugh et al., 1986), the selection of topics that either have excluded women or have viewed them in stereotypical ways (Jayaratne, 1983; Lykes & Stewart, 1986), and the emphasis on statistical significance, which reduced women's experiences to numbers (Jayaratne & Stewart, 1991).

Although experimental and quantitative methodologies have their place in the study of the psychology of women, many feminist researchers have come to believe that the problems associated with quantitative methods can be best addressed and solved through the use of qualitative research methods (Landrine, Klonoff, & Brown-Collins, 1992; Reinharz, 1992). They have argued that the use of qualitative methods allows participants, especially those from traditionally understudied and marginalized groups, to have a more active voice and even to shape research questions and interpretations of data. The "standpoints" of members of subordinated groups can provide unique perspectives that are unavailable to privileged people, such as researchers (Harding, 1991). For example, the work of Michelle Fine and her colleagues (Fine et al., 2003) with women in prison gave voice to the prisoners' lived experiences because the women themselves were involved in the design and implementation of the study and the interpretation of its results. Furthermore, unlike traditional experimenters, qualitative researchers do not claim that their work is value-free (Jaffee et al., 1999).

In questioning the primacy of traditional research methodology, feminist psychologists have recognized that there are many ways to gain knowledge, and they have utilized a variety of methodologies to study women's experiences. Examples of alternative methods that have been used by feminist psychologists include focus groups, life narratives, and case studies (see *Psychology of Women Quarterly, 23,* for two special issues on feminist methodologies). New quantitative methods, such as meta-analysis (a technique that allows researchers to combine data from many studies and search for patterns and trends), are being used effectively by feminist psychologists to create a broad database of information about women and gender. Meta-analyses have been especially helpful in showing that culturally accepted gender differences are actually nonexistent, present only in certain age groups or under certain circumstances, or have narrowed over time (e.g., Hyde, Fennema, & Lamon, 1990; Hyde & Linn, 1988).

What, then, is feminist research? Cosgrove and McHugh (200) suggested that feminist research is any study whose results improve women's well-being, advocate for women, empower women, or expose the sexism or inequality that women experience. In addition, feminist research should not strip away the context in which the participants act (Frieze, Sales, & Smith, 1991), and feminist researchers should engage in reflexivity (i.e., think about the ways in which their own and their participants' experiences shape the research process; Russell & Bohan, 1999). As Jayaratne and Stewart (1991) pointed out, "An inclusive viewpoint on methods takes the form of promoting the value and appropriate use of both qualitative and quantitative methods as feminist research tools" (p. 91). We believe that the best method to use in any instance is the one that allows the researchers to answer their particular questions; any method can be used in ways that are consistent with the feminist goals discussed above.

Feminist Theories: New and Revised

Feminist influences on psychological research have resulted in the development of new theories as well as revisions of old ones. Feminist psychologists have produced a number of theories that have shaped not only feminist psychology but also the discipline as a whole. One of the earliest theories that continues to influence how gender is studied is Sandra Bem's work on androgyny. Bem (1974) theorized that femininity and masculinity were not opposite ends of a continuum, as most researchers believed at the time; rather, they could exist simultaneously in individuals. She developed a measurable concept of androgyny, which describes people who are high in both stereotypically feminine and masculine characteristics and behavioral tendencies. Later, Bem (1981) conceptualized gender schema theory, in which she suggested that people tend to internalize the gender-based polarizations of a given culture and learn to organize information they acquire on the basis of gender-linked classifications.

Another influential feminist theory is Alice Eagly's (1987) social roles theory of gender differentiation. Eagly proposed that social roles both describe and proscribe human behavior. For example, homemakers are expected to be caring and nurturing, and anyone who takes on that role will be assumed by others to possess those traits. Because much labor in industrialized societies is divided along gender lines, women are much more likely than men to be homemakers, and thus women in general are expected to be more nurturing than men are.

A more recent, and increasingly influential, theory is Fredrickson and Roberts's (1997) objectification theory, which provides a framework for understanding women's feelings about their bodies. Fredrickson and Roberts theorized that women learn to see themselves as the objects of others' gaze. Objectification theory posits that the result of taking the viewpoint of external evaluators is constant monitoring of the body, which "can increase women's opportunities for shame and anxiety, reduce opportunities for peak motivational states, and diminish awareness of internal body states" (p. 173). This theory has been used by researchers interested in women's self-esteem, depression, body dissatisfaction, and disordered eating.

Other feminist theoretical positions in psychology emerged in response to theories that were seen as sexist. For example, in response to psychoanalytic theories, Nancy Chodorow (1978) proposed that, as a result of the fact that women are usually children's primary caregivers, girls and women come to define themselves in connection to others. According to Chodorow, as boys grow up, they separate themselves from their mothers (and, hence, from women in general) and develop a self-concept based on individuation and independence. Conversely, because they see themselves as similar to their mothers, girls never fully separate themselves from their mothers, and as a result, they develop a self-concept based on empathy and caring, and desire to become mothers themselves. Related to Chodorow's ideas is the more recent self-in-relation theory (Jordan et al., 1991) that was developed by feminist therapists and researchers affiliated with the Stone Center at Wellesley College. Self-in-relation theory posits that girls and women are dramatically impacted by the mother–daughter relationship, such that they define them-selves in terms of their connections to others, and much of their personal growth takes place within their relationships.

Carol Gilligan's influential book *In a Different Voice* (1982) is based on her research on gender-related differences in moral development. She challenged Lawrence Kohlberg's (1969) popular theory of moral development, which, she argued, was based on the experiences of boys and men. Gilligan theorized that women's moral decision making was likely to include an ethic of care for others, and she challenged Kohlberg's notion that moral decisions based on an ethic of justice represent the highest level of morality.

Feminist psychologists have also contributed to broad philosophical debates that cross discipline lines in the study of women and gender. We turn now to a brief examination of one of these: social constructionism versus essentialism.

Social Constructionism versus Essentialism

Essentialists believe that a person's sex reflects an unchangeable reality or essence that holds true for individuals across cultures (Rohmann, 1999). Conversely, social constructionists believe that sociocultural realities, such as gender, are constructed by people with a social and cultural context and are the by-products of interactions between a person and her or his environment (Stratton & Hayes, 1993). To illustrate, we use the familiar example of gender differences on the mathematics section of the Scholastic Aptitude Test (SAT): boys' average score is higher than girls', and this has been the case since the test was designed. An essentialist interpretation of these data might point to sex differences in biology (e.g., genetics, hormone levels) that could contribute to the superiority of the boys' performance. An essentialist would probably predict that boys will continue to outperform girls on this test, and attempts to bridge the performance gap will be fruitless because the source of the difference is innate. However, a social constructionist would want to examine the myriad ways that girls and boys receive differential encouragement in math from teachers, parents, and cultural images that promote men's superiority in math and science. A social constructionist might also point out that not all boys performed better than all girls, and ask which girls and boys (not everyone takes the SAT) contributed data to the study. If both girls and boys produce math scores across a range of performance ability, then factors other than biology are likely to be in play. In addition, if assumptions about gender and mathematics were challenged, and both girls and boys were encouraged to excel in math, then these socially constructed differences in math performance could narrow or even disappear.

The social constructionist perspective, which is popular with feminist psychologists, posits that research findings are interpreted in a social situation and influenced by cultural beliefs (Crawford & Marecek, 1989). Thus, social constructionists do not believe in a universal truth or reality that can be ascertained through scientific research (a core assumption held by most psychologists until recently) because the context and the interactions (e.g., power dynamics, researchers' expectations, worldviews) of the researchers and participants may differ, thus producing different results from similar studies.

Much of the debate about essentialism and social constructionism concerns gender differences, as in the SAT example used earlier. Do feminist psychologists believe that there are no innate differences between women and men, that there are no innate qualities particular to women or men, that any differences we perceive are socially constructed? Social constructionists have pointed out that comparisons between women and men are flawed because no "universal woman" or "universal man" exists. Factors such as race, social class, culture, sexual orientation, age, cohort, and other variations result in different experiences within the categories of "woman" and "man," and these experiences shape psychology and behavior. That said, however, there certainly are obvious physical characteristics unique to women and men, such as the fact that only women can menstruate, lactate, and give birth. Yet, there is limited support in a large empirical literature for differences between women and men in their natures, personalities, traits, and abilities (Tavris, 1992), despite the fact that women and men do differ in their life experiences and opportunities. Sandra Bem (1993) concluded that even if women and men do differ psychologically in some aspects, there is much more overlap than difference between them, and any differences are likely to depend on the context in which they are observed or measured. Feminist psychologists recognize that much of the debate about gender differences is rooted in power differentials and attempts to justify the status quo, especially the patriarchy and class and race stratifications.

Rather than utilizing a model of gender that suggests that women (a universal group) have a shared existence that produces similar behavior, social constructionists see individuals as "doing gender" rather than "having" gender that is innate (Hare-Mustin & Marecek, 1990; West & Zimmerman, 1987). Both the researchers and the participants in their studies are doing gender as they work, and each individual does (or performs) gender differently, depending on the situation and the other people in it (Lips, 2003). Gender is not universal, nor are gender differences. To return to our SAT example, there is no universal math performance by girls. Instead, their individual performances depend on the cultural messages and reinforcements or punishments they had received, and the context in which they took the test. To the extent that all the girls who took the SAT were in the United States at the time, they may have received similar messages about girls' lesser math abilities, seen similar images of mathematicians as men, and taken math tests over the years that did not reflect their experiences (Eccles & Jacobs, 1986). To say that girls' performance is the result of innate biological factors negates the many sociocultural factors and situational interactions that impact girls' performance on the SAT, not to mention the performance of the many girls who outscored at least some boys on the test. Because social constructionism is the perspective that recognizes various factors that essentialism overlooks, many feminists believe that a social constructionist approach is the most comprehensive way to study the psychology of women.

Although social constructionist feminists have sought to challenge assumptions of inherent gender differences, other feminists argue that women and men are indeed different. As we stated earlier, cultural (sometimes termed "difference") feminists highlight differences between women and men and focus their attention on qualities they believe are women's unique strengths, such as those that result in the growth and enhancement of relationships. Cultural feminists point to women's positive qualities and urge that they be celebrated rather than devalued or taken for granted. They have suggested that women learn and use knowledge differently than men do (Belenky et al., 1986), make moral decisions using an ethic of care (Gilligan, 1982), and are more interpersonally caring and sensitive than men are (Miller, 1976).

Cultural feminists have produced a wealth of writings, research, and theory in psychology; however, other feminists have criticized their basic assumptions. For example, Janis Bohan (1997) argued that cultural feminism is based on essentialist beliefs about women and men and fails to consider the diversity of women's experiences. Some work by cultural feminists has been criticized for ignoring status differences between women and men. Arguments for a different voice, for example, do not account for status differentials that may impact moral reasoning, learning styles and knowledge use, or relationship orientation (Hare-Mustin & Marecek, 1990; Unger, 1998).

Data to support cultural feminist theory are sparse (see Jaffee & Hyde, 2000, for a notable exception). As Bohan (2002) suggested, there is no clear evidence that gender differences exist in the way postulated by cultural feminism—that is, that women are inherently more empathic and nurturant, or that women and men learn or reason differently. Many, if not most, feminist psychologists argue that when gender differences are found in these attributes and behaviors, it is the construction of gendered experiences, rather than women's and men's essential natures, that results in contextually different responses. In response to such criticisms, Carol Gilligan (1982) has stated that she does not believe that gender differences in moral development are biologically determined, nor does she see the ethic of care as unique to women. Jean Baker Miller (1976) has argued that differences between women and men are the result of power differentials, and the differences people think are characteristic of women are actually characteristic of social subordinates. Cultural feminists argue that regardless of their origins, these gender differences are real and should be seen as strengths of women. Although women are more likely than men to express attributes such as empathy, cooperation, and caring, cultural feminists seek a transformation of society such that both women and men will be free to develop and express these positive attributes (Enns, 1997).

The belief that women possess unique positive traits is appealing because it offers an alternative to the patriarchal devaluation of women's experiences. However, Bernice Lott (1990) pointed out that the assumption of essential gender differences results in the maintenance of the status quo of inequality, and it locates failure to achieve or develop oneself solely within the individual rather than in sociocultural forces. In addition, if the cultural feminist paradigm were to gain ascendance, it would work against feminist goals to create equality because it suggests that the inherent gender differences suit women and men to different roles. Thus, the cultural feminist perspective, although appealing to many women, has been contentious within feminist psychology.

Feminist Therapy: The Personal Is Political

The Women's Liberation Movement affected the practice, as well as the study and organization, of psychology. Phyllis Chesler's *Women and Madness* (1972) was influential in sparking the politicization of the therapy process (Greenspan, 1995; Williams, 1995). In the early 1970s feminist psychotherapists began to refer to themselves as feminist therapists (Brown, 1994) to signal the importance of gender role socialization and power analysis in their work with clients. Consciousness-raising (CR), which originated around 1970 as a feminist political, educational, and organizing strategy, is widely acknowledged as a precursor to feminist therapy. CR was practiced in small, informal groups, and its purpose was to learn about the connections between gender and power through readings and the sharing of personal experiences, and then to become aware of how gender role expectations and political oppression had affected the participants' own lives.

Early important works on feminist therapy include Betsy Williams's *Notes of a Feminist Therapist* (1976) and Miriam Greenspan's *A New Approach to Women and Therapy* (1983). The Feminist Therapy Institute (FTI) was founded in 1982, and its annual meetings provided the opportunity for psychotherapists to work together to develop the theory and practice of feminist therapy. FTI's meetings resulted in many publications that are now considered foundational works, perhaps the most important of which are the *Handbook of Feminist Therapy* (Rosewater & Walker, 1985) and *Feminist Ethics in Psychotherapy* (Lerman & Porter, 1990). Today feminist therapy is widely recognized as a valuable approach to improving the mental health of women.

Feminist therapy is not defined by a set of therapeutic techniques, as most other forms of psychotherapy are. Rather, it should be thought of as psychotherapy that is informed by feminist political theories. What makes therapy feminist is how the therapists think about what they do, what types of "problems" they address, and the underlying feminist theoretical models that inform the therapy practice (Brown, 1994). Most feminist therapists agree on several defining principles: (1) the personal is political; (2) the importance of analyzing the contributions of power and gender to any social situation; (3) the need to bring women's own experiences from the margins to the center (Ballou & West, 2000; Brown, 1994; Worrell & Remer, 1992). CR and empowerment are also important goals of feminist therapy. Unlike other therapies, feminist therapy will not help troubled or angry women to "fit in" to their traditional roles more comfortably and quietly (Ballou & West, 2000). In fact, feminist therapy is considered most successful when it empowers women to "stand out" boldly and confidently in order to meet their own needs and to demand social and political changes that will make it easier for all women to define themselves (Chrisler & Lamont, 2002). It is not uncommon for feminist therapists to recommend political activism (e.g., attending a "take back the night" marching, writing to advertisers to complain about the objectification of women) to their clients as part of the healing process.

Feminist therapists emphasize both the similarity and the diversity among women, and they recognize that gender is not the only dimension that requires a power analysis. They have contributed to the literature on power and class, race, sexual orientation, disability, chronic illness, age, ethnicity, body size, and other political categories; in fact, *Women and Therapy* has devoted special issues to all of those topics. The postmodern notion of positionality is useful in feminist therapy; one must consider the location of an individual in the larger society in order to understand his or her life experiences (Chrisler & Lamont, 2002). Among the frequent foci of feminist therapy are depression, anxiety disorders, eating disorders, body image issues, relationship concerns, role conflicts, and sequelae of physical or sexual abuse.

Backlash: The Rise of Evolutionary Psychology

It is often the case in power struggles that the success of a radical or liberating group is met with a backlash of conservative or traditional activism. This has happened to feminism in general (for examples, see Faludi, 1991) and to feminist psychology in particular. The emergence of evolutionary psychology, a recent theoretical perspective based on evolutionary biology, coincided with the increasing impact of feminism on psychology and other academic disciplines. The assumptions of evolutionary psychology suggest that "humans have evolved specific, specialized, sexually dimorphic and environmentally mediated psychological mechanisms, particularly with respect to sexuality and reproduction" (Studd, 1996, p. 58).

A basic tenet of evolutionary psychology is that women and men have different mating strategies, which are based on the biological realities of differential parental investment in offspring. Because women can give birth only approximately once per year, and because they carry the primary burdens of gestation, birthing, and lactation, they seek out male partners who can provide concrete resources and other support. Men, for whom procreation involves little effort or commitment, seek to "spread their seed" to as many women as possible, especially to young women who are likely to be fertile (Buss, 1995; Symons, 1979). In order to attract a partner of the other sex, men display their resources, and women display their physical attractiveness (Buss, 1989). These reproductive strategies have been used to explain findings that men are more likely than women to emphasize youth and attractiveness in their partners (Buss, 1989; Singh, 1993); women are more likely than men to emphasize a partner's resources (Buss, 1989); and men desire more sexual variety than women do (Baumeister, 2000). The most controversial application of this theory concerns the proposition that men's rape of women is merely a reproductive attempt (Thornhill & Palmer, 2000). For feminist critiques of this position, see Travis (2003).

Critics of evolutionary psychology have pointed out that the theory is untestable; that some of its hypotheses are illogical (Bem, 1993; Gutek & Done, 2001); that it oversimplifies complex behavior (Travis & Yeager, 1991); that it is based on animal models that may not apply to humans (Derry, 1996; Travis & Yeager, 1991); that it negates the influence of the patriarchy and other sociocultural forces (Eagly & Wood, 1999; Hyde & Durik, 2000); that it establishes gender inequality as innate (Eagly & Wood, 1999) that supporters of the theory exaggerate differences between women and men (Eagly & Wood, 1999; Silverstein, 1996); and that other theories provide equally valid explanations of gender differences in sexual and romantic behaviors (Eagly & Wood, 1999; Gowatry, 2001; Hyde, 1996). The feminist anthropologist Sandra Hrdy (1999) also has opposed many of the tenets of evolutionary psychology, For example, she noted that because women are more likely to produce offspring, and thus carry on the family's genetic lineage, parents should favor daughters over sons as a better genetic "investment."

Many feminist psychologists see evolutionary psychology as a move backward from the advances of feminism. Unlike feminists, who have challenged the findings and interpretations of the gender difference research, evolutionary psychologists appear to suggest that gender differences are innate and cannot be changed. Furthermore, most explanations founded on the principles of evolutionary psychology do not describe women as active agents, and they tend to reinforce existing power hierarchies. The ease with which psychology textbook writers have accepted evolutionary psychology and even, in some cases, made it a focus of their texts, has many feminists deeply concerned that evolutionary psychology may have a negative impact on the movement toward gender equality, both in psychology and more generally.

Conclusion: Where We Are Today

Since the 1960s feminist activism has resulted in major changes in the field of psychology: in science, practice, publication, organizational leadership, and the teaching and training of psychologists. Despite backlash attempts, psychology has opened up to women and feminist psychology to such an extent that the field has changed enormously. In addition to the innovations described above, feminist psychologists have produced guidelines for nonsexist language which are now part of the influential and widely used style manual of the American Psychological Association. Pressure from feminist psychologists contributed to the adoption of blind review of manuscripts as a standard practice and the use of the word "participants" (rather than the older term "subjects") to describe people who contribute data to psychological research.

Today women make up approximately 70 percent of all psychology majors and graduate students, and the psychology of women and gender is a popular field of study. Division 35 is now one of the largest, most active, and most respected divisions of the APA, and feminist theory and research have led to the recent founding of Division 51, Psychology of Men and Masculinity, to further research on how gender affects men's lives. Women have held leadership roles throughout the APA on divisions, boards, and committees, and feminist psychologists have convinced the APA leadership to take many progressive stands on public policy issues. However, only ten women have ever been elected president of the APA. In conclusion, there is plenty of work yet to be done by feminist psychologists to further the cause of gender equality, but we do that work from a position of strength that our foremothers could only imagine.

References

Ballou, M., & West, C. (2000). Feminist therapy approaches. In M. Biaggio & M. Hersen (Eds.), *Issues in the psychology of women* (pp. 273–297). New York: Kluwer Academic Plenum.

Baumeister, R. (2000). Gender differences in erotic plasticity: The female sex drive is socially flexible and responsive. *American Psychologist, 126,* 347–374.

Belenky, M. F., Clinchy, B. M., Goldberger, N. J., & Tarule, J. M. (1986). *Women's ways of knowing: The development of self, voice, and mind.* New York: Basic Books.

Bem, S. L. (1974). The measurement of psychological androgyny. *Journal of Consulting and Clinical Psychology, 42,* 155–162.

Bem, S. L. (1981). Gender schema theory: A cognitive account of sex typing. *Psychological Review, 88,* 354–364.

Bem, S. L. (1993). *The lenses of gender.* New Haven, CT: Yale University Press.

Bohan, J. S. (1997). Regarding gender: Essentialism, constructionism, and feminist psychology. *Psychology of Women Quarterly, 17,* 5–21.

Bohan, J. S. (2002). Sex differences and/in the self: Classic themes, feminist variations, postmodern challenges. *Psychology of Women's Quarterly, 26,* 74–88.

Brown, L. S. (1994). *Subversive dialogues: Theory in feminist therapy.* New York: Basic Books.

Brownmiller, S. (1975). *Against our will: Men, women, and rape.* New York: Simon and Schuster.

Buss, D. M. (1989). Sex differences in mate preferences: Evolutionary hypotheses tested in 37 cultures. *Behavioral and Brain Sciences, 12,* 1–14.

Buss, D. M. (1995). Psychological sex differences: Origins through sexual selection. *American Psychologist, 50,* 164–168.

Chesler, P. (1972). *Women and madness.* Garden City, NY: Doubleday.

Chodorow, N. (1978). *The reproduction of mothering: Psychoanalysis and the sociology of gender.* Berkeley: University of California Press.

Chrisler, J. C., & Lamont, J. M. (2002). Can exercise contribute to the goals of feminist therapy? *Women & Therapy, 25(2),* 9–22.

Comas-Diaz, L. (1991). Feminism and diversity in psychology: The case of women of color. *Psychology of Women Quarterly, 15,* 597–610.

Cosgrove, L., & McHugh, M. C. (2000). Speaking for ourselves: Feminist methods and community Psychology. *American Journal of Community Psychology, 28,* 815–838.

Crawford, M., & Maracek, J. (1989). Psychology reconstructs the female: 1968–1988. *Psychology of Women Quarterly, 13,* 147–165.

Crawford, M., & Unger, R. (2004). *Women and gender: A feminist psychology* (4th ed.). Boston: McGraw-Hill.

De Beauvoir, S. (1952). *The second sex* (H. M. Parshley, ed. and trans.). New York: Knopf.

Derry, P. S. (1996). Buss and sexual selection: The issue of culture. *American Psychologist, 51,* 159–160.

Eagly, A. H. (1987). *Sex differences in social behavior: A social-role interpretation.* Hillsdale, NJ: Erlbaum.

Eagly, A. H., & Wood, W. (1999). The origins of sex differences in human behavior: Evolved dispositions versus social roles. *American Psychologist, 54,* 408–423.

Eccles, J. S., & Jacobs, J. E. (1986). Social forces shape math attitudes and performance. *Signs, 11,* 367–389.

Enns, C. Z. (1997). *Feminist theories and feminist psychotherapies.* New York: Haworth.

Faludi, S. (1991). *Backlash: The undeclared war against American women.* New York: Crown.

Fine, M., Torre, M. E., Boudin, K., Bowen, I., Clark, J., Hylton, D., Martinez, M. M., Roberts, R. A., Smart, P., & Upegiu, D. (2003). Participatory action research: From within and beyond prison bars. In P. M. Camic, J. E. Rhodes, & L. Yardley (Eds.), *Qualitative research in psychology: Expanding perspectives in methodology and design* (pp. 173–198). Washington, DC: American Psychological Association.

Firestone, S. (1970*). The dialectic of sex: The case for feminist revolution.* New York: Morrow.

Fredrickson, B. L., & Roberts, T.-A. (1997). Objectification theory: Towards an understanding of women's lived experience and mental health risks. *Psychology of Women Quarterly, 21,* 173–206.

Frieze, I. H., Sales, E., & Smith, C. A. (1991). Considering the social context of gender research: The impact on college students. *Psychology of Women Quarterly, 17,* 371–392.

Gilligan, C. (1982). *In a different voice: Psychological theory and women's development.* Cambridge, MA: Harvard University Press.

Gowatry, P. A. (2001). Women, psychology, and evolution. In R. K. Unger (Ed.), *Handbook of the psychology of women and gender* (pp. 53–65). New York: Wiley.

Greenspan, M. (1983). *A new approach to women and therapy.* New York: McGraw-Hill.

Greenspan, M. (1995). On being a feminist and a psychotherapist. In P. Chesler, E. D.

Rothblum, & E. Cole (Eds.), *Feminist foremothers in women's studies, psychology, and mental health* (pp. 229–241). New York: Haworth.

Greer, G. (1971). *The female eunuch.* New York: McGraw-Hill.

Gutek, B. A., & Done, R. S. (2001). Sexual harassment. In R. K. Unger (Ed.), *Handbook of the psychology of women and gender* (pp. 367–377). New York: Wiley.

Harding, S. (1991). *Whose science, whose knowledge? Thinking from women's lives.* Ithaca, NY: Cornell University Press.

Hare-Mustin, R. T., & Marecek, J. (1990). Gender and the meaning of difference: Postmodernism and psychology. In R. T. Hare-Mustin & J. Marecek (Eds.), *Making a difference: Psychology and the construction of gender* (pp. 22–64). New Haven, CT: Yale University Press.

Hartman, H. (1981). The unhappy marriage of Marxism and feminism: Toward a more progressive union. In D. B. Grusky (Ed.), *Social stratification: Class, race, and gender in sociological perspective* (pp. 570–576). Boulder, CO: Westview.

Henley, N. M., Meng, K., O'Brien, D., McCarthy, W. J., & Sockloskie, R. J. (1998). Developing a scale to measure the diversity of feminist attitudes. *Psychology of Women Quarterly, 22,* 317–348.

Hogan, J. D., & Sexton, V. S. (1991). Women and the American Psychological Association. *Psychology of Women Quarterly, 15,* 623–634.

hooks, b. (1984). *Feminist theory: From margin to center.* Boston: South End Press.

Hrdy, S. B. (1999). *Mother nature: A history of mothers, infants, and natural selection.* New York: Pantheon.

Hyde, J., Fennema, E., & Lamon, S. J. (1990). Gender differences in mathematics performance: A meta-analysis. *Psychological Bulletin, 107,* 139–155.

Hyde, J. S. (1996). Where are the gender differences? Where are the gender similarities? In D. M. Buss & N. M. Malamuth (Eds.), *Sex, power, and conflict: Evolutionary and feminist perspectives* (pp. 107–118). New York: Oxford University Press.

Hyde, J. S., & Durik, A. M. (2000). Gender differences in erotic plasticity: Evolutionary or social forces? Comment on Baumeister (2000). *Psychological Bulletin, 126,* 375–379.

Hyde, J. S., & Linn, M. C. (1988). Gender differences in verbal ability: A meta-analysis. *Psychological Bulletin, 105,* 53–69.

Jaffee, S. R., & Hyde, J. S. (2000) differences in moral orientation: A meta-analysis. *Psychological Bulletin, 126,* 703–726.

Jaffee, S., Kling, K. C., Plant, E. A., Sloan, M., & Hyde, J. S. (1999). The view from down here: Feminist graduate students consider innovative methodologies. *Psychology of Women Quarterly, 23,* 423–430.

Jaggar, A. M., & Rothenberg, P. S. (1993). *Feminist frameworks* (3rd ed.). New York: McGraw-Hill.

Jayaratne, T. E. (1983). The value of quantitative methodology for feminist research.

In G. Bowles & R. D. Klein (Eds.), *Theories of women's studies* (pp. 140–161). Boston: Routledge & Kegan Paul.

Jayaratne, T. E., & Stewart, A. J. (1991). Qualitative and quantitative methods in social sciences: Current feminist issues and practical strategies. In M. M. Fonow & J. A. Cook (Eds.), *Beyond methodology: Feminist scholarship as lived research* (pp. 85–106). Bloomington: Indiana University Press.

Jordan, J. V., Kaplan, A. G., Miller, J. B., Stiver, I. P., & Surrey, J. L. (Eds.). (1991). *Women's growth in connection: Writings from the Stone Center*. New York: Guilford.

Kohlberg, L. (1969). Stage and sequence: The cognitive-developmental approach to socialization. In D. A. Goslin (Ed.), *Handbook of socialization theory and research* (pp. 347–480). Chicago: Rand McNally.

Kramarae, C., & Treichler, P. A. (1985). *A feminist dictionary*. London: Pandora Press.

Landrine, H., Klonoff, E. A., Brown-Collins, A. (1992). Cultural diversity and methodology in feminist psychology: Critique, proposal, empirical example. *Psychology of Women Quarterly, 16,* 145–163.

Lerman, H., & Porter, N. (Eds.). (1990). *Feminist ethics in psychotherapy*. New York: Springer.

Levine, S. (1995). *Degrees of equality*. Philadelphia: Temple University Press.

Lips, H. M. (2003). *A new psychology of women: Gender, culture, and ethnicity* (2nd ed.). Boston: McGraw-Hill.

Lott, B. (1990). Dual natures or learned behavior: The challenge of feminist psychology. In R. T. Hare-Mustin & J. Marecek (Eds.), *Making a difference: Psychology and the construction of gender* (pp. 65–101). New Haven, CT: Yale University Press.

Lykes, M. B., & Stewart, A. J. (1986). Evaluating the feminist challenge to research in personality and social psychology: 1963–1983. *Psychology of Women Quarterly, 10,* 393–412.

McHugh, M. C., Koeske, R. D., & Frieze, I. H. (1986). Issues to consider in conducting nonsexist psychological research. *American Psychologist, 41,* 879–890.

Miller, J. B. (1976). *Toward a new psychology of women*. Boston: Beacon Press.

Millet, K. (1970). *Sexual politics*. Garden City, NY: Doubleday.

Reinharz, S. (1992). *Feminist methods in social research*. New York: Oxford University Press.

Rohmann, C. (1999). *A world of ideas: A dictionary of important theories, concepts, beliefs, and thinkers*. New York: Ballantine Books.

Rosewater, L. B., & Walker, L.E.A. (Eds.). (1985). *Handbook of feminist therapy*. New York: Springer.

Rowland, R., & Klein, R. (1996). Radical feminism: History, politics, and action. In D. Bell & R. Klein (Eds.). *Radically speaking: Feminism reclaimed* (pp. 77–86). North Melbourne, Australia: Spinifex.

Russell, G. M., & Bohan, J. S. (1999). Hearing voices: The uses of research and the politics of change. *Psychology of Women Quarterly, 23,* 403–418.

Sanger, B. (1998). Outcome assessments for battered women's shelters. Paper presented at the annual meeting of the Association for Women's Psychology. Baltimore, MD.

Scarborough, E., & Furumoto, L. (1987). *Untold lives: The first generation of American women psychologists.* New York: Columbia University Press.

Silverstein, L. B. (1996). Evolutionary psychology and the search for sex differences. *American Psychologist, 51,* 160–161.

Singh, D. (1993). Adaptive significance of female physical attractiveness: Role of waist-to-hip ratio. *Journal of Personality and Social Psychology, 65,* 293–307.

Stratton, P., & Hayes, N. (1993). *A student's dictionary of psychology* (2nd ed.). New York: E. Arnold.

Studd, M. V. (1996). Sexual harassment. In D. M. Buss & N. M. Malamuth (Eds.), *Sex, power, and conflict: Evolutionary and feminist perspectives* (pp. 54–89). New York: Oxford University Press.

Symons, D. (1979). *The evolution of human sexuality.* New York: Oxford University Press.

Tavris, C. (1992). *The mismeasure of woman.* New York: Simon and Schuster.

Thornhill, R., & Palmer, C. T. (2000). *A natural history of rape: Biological bases of sexual coercion.* Cambridge, MA: MIT Press.

Tiefer, L. (1991). A brief history of the Association for Women in Psychology: 1969–1991. *Psychology of Women Quarterly, 15,* 635–649.

Travis, C. B. (Ed.). (2003). *Evolution, gender, and rape.* Cambridge, MA: MIT Press.

Travis, C. B., & Yeager, C. P. (1991). Sexual selection, parental investment, and sexism. *Journal of Social Issues, 47,* 117–129.

Unger, R. K. (1998). *Resisting gender: Twenty-five years of feminist psychology.* Thousand Oaks, CA: Sage.

Weisstein, N. (1971). Psychology constructs the female. In V. Gornick & B. K. Moran (Eds.), *Woman in sexist society* (pp. 207–224). New York: Basic Books.

West, C., & Zimmerman, D. H. (1987). Doing gender. *Gender and Society, 1,* 125–151.

Williams, E. F. (1976). *Notes of a feminist therapist.* New York: Praeger.

Williams, E. F. (1995). An unlikely radical. In P. Chesler, E. D. Rothblum, & E. Cole (Eds.), *Feminist foremothers in women's studies, psychology, and mental health* (pp. 531–541). New York: Haworth.

Worrell, J., & Johnson, D. (2001). Therapy with women: Feminist frameworks. In R. K. Unger (Ed.), *Handbook of the psychology of women and gender* (pp. 317–329) New York: Wiley.

Worrell, J., & Remer, P. (1992). *Feminist perspectives in therapy: An empowerment model for women.* New York: Wiley.

Index

About the Editor and the Contributors

JOHN BALDWIN received his Ph.D. from Arizona State University in 1994. Currently he is an associate professor in the Communications Department at Illinois State University. His main areas of focus include the communication of intolerance (e.g., racism, sexism) and the role of culture and group identity in relationships. He has published essays in major intercultural communication readers. In addition, he has published several journal articles on the concepts of race, gender, and communication, focusing especially on the social construction of race and gender in Brazil and other nations of Latin America. He promotes multidisciplinary and multimethod studies and essays in order to understand better complex social issues and derive better social solutions.

SUSAN BASOW is the Charles A. Dana professor of psychology at Lafayette College. A licensed clinical psychologist, she focuses her teaching and writing on gender issues. She is the author of the textbook *Gender: Stereotypes and Roles,* now in its third edition (1992), as well as chapters on gender and education, body image, gender identity development, and gender influences in adolescent development. Prof. Basow has conducted numerous research studies on gender issues in students' attitudes toward and evaluations of female and male faculty as well as on other topics, such as homophobia and women's body image. A fellow of the American Psychological Association in three divisions (Society for the Psychology of Women; Society for the Psychological Study of Lesbian, Gay, and Bisexual Issues; Society for the Psychological Study of Social Issues), Prof. Basow currently is secretary of Division 35, the Society for the Psychology of Women.

ALYSON BURNS-GLOVER is professor of psychology at Pacific University, Forest Grove, Oregon. She earned her B.A. at California State University, Long Beach, in research psychology, and her M.A. and Ph.D. in social/personality psychology at the University of California, Davis. Her research focuses on social identity theory, minority student academic achievement, and specifically the health and well-being of Native and local Hawaiians.

DONNA CASTAÑEDA is an associate professor in the Psychology Department at San Diego State University, Imperial Valley campus. She completed her BA in psychology at the University of Washington and her M.A. and Ph.D. in social psychology at the University of California, Davis. Her research focuses on gender, ethnicity, and their relationship to physical and mental health. Specifically, her research investigates the impact of close relationship factors in HIV sexual risk behavior, particularly among Latinas/os. A second area of interest is the role of structural factors, or aspects of service delivery systems, in the provision of health services to Latina/o communities. She is presently engaged in cross-national research examining the HIV/AIDS prevention needs of Mexican women living and working at the U.S.–Mexico border.

JOAN C. CHRISLER is professor of psychology at Connecticut College. She is president of the Connecticut Conference of the American Association of University Professors and has served as president of the New England Psychological Association. She has published extensively on the psychology of women and gender, and is especially known for her work on women's health, menstruation, weight, and body image. She is editor of *Sex Roles: A Journal of Research* and of several books, including *From Menarche to Menopause: The Female Body in Feminist Therapy* (2004) and *Lectures on the Psychology of Women* (3rd ed., 2004).

LISA COSGROVE is a clinical and research psychologist and an assistant professor in the Department of Counseling and School Psychology at the University of Massachusetts, Boston. She has published numerous articles and book chapters on critical psychology, research methods, feminist therapy, and theoretical and philosophical issues related to clinical practice. Dr. Cosgrove is co-editor, with Dr. Paula Caplan, of the book *Bias in Psychiatric Diagnosis* (forthcoming). Her research has been supported through grants from NIMH (to the Murray Center, Radcliffe Institute, Harvard University) and from the University of Massachusetts. She was a fellow at the William Jointer Center for the Study of War and Social Consequences (2002–2003) and has conducted research on the intergenerational impact of war-related PTSD.

DARLENE C. DEFOUR is associate professor of psychology at Hunter College of the City University of New York. She received her undergraduate degree from Fisk University and her doctorate in psychology from the University of Illinois at Urbana-Champaign. She has served on the board of directors of the Association of Black Psychologists. Dr. DeFour has studied the impact of social networks and mentors on the career development of black graduate students and professionals. She has published on the intersection of race and gender. In addition, Dr. DeFour is concerned with the influence of violence in the lives of women of color. She is also interested in the intersection of gender and ethnic identity.

JEAN E. DENIOUS received her doctorate in social psychology from Arizona State University in 2004. She is currently teaching in the Department of Psychology and in the Women's Studies Program at Arizona State University. Her research and teaching interests are in gender and health, with emphases on body image and related regulatory processes and on social, psychological, and political contexts of reproductive health issues.

EROS R. DESOUZA was born in Rio de Janeiro, Brazil, and immigrated, as a teenager, to the United States in 1980. He received his Ph.D. in community psychology from the University of Missouri, Kansas City, in 1990. During the summer of 1992, he was a fellow at Center for Advanced Study in the Behavioral Sciences, Stanford University, and in 1999 became a State Farm Insurance fellow for incorporating technology into instruction. He is currently an associate professor in the Psychology Department at Illinois State University. He has numerous publications on gender issues and sexuality in prestigious journals. Presently, his main research focus is on the study of sexual harassment from a psychological, legal, and cross-cultural perspective.

ALICE H. EAGLY is a professor of psychology at Northwestern University. Earlier she served on the faculties of Purdue University; University of Massachusetts, Amherst; and Michigan State University. She earned her doctoral degree in social psychology from the University of Michigan and her bachelor's degree from Harvard University. As a gender researcher, she has carried out primary research and meta-analyses of research literature. Dr. Eagly is the author of *Sex Differences in Social Behavior: A Social Role Interpretation* and of numerous journal articles, chapters, notes, and reviews. She has served as president of the Midwestern Psychological Association, president of the Society of Personality and Social Psychology, chair of the Executive Committee of the Society of Experimental Social Psychology, and chair of the Board of Scientific Affairs of the American Psychological Association. She has received awards that include the Distinguished Scientist Award of the Society for Experimental Social Psychology, the Donald Campbell Award for Distinguished Contribution to Social Psychology, the Gordon Allport Award of the Society for the Psychological Study of Social Issues, and a citation as Distinguished Leader for Women in Psychology from the American Psychological Association.

WILLIAM P. GAEDDERT is a professor in the Psychology Department at the State University of New York, Plattsburgh. He has been at Plattsburgh since receiving his Ph.D. from Iowa State University in 1981. Trained as a social psychologist, and having research interests in gender and equity, he also teaches research methods and statistics at both graduate and undergraduate levels.

JENNIFER L. HARRIS is a graduate student in social psychology at Yale University. She received her M.B.A. from the Wharton School at the University of Pennsylvania and spent eighteen years as a business executive, first at American Express and then with her own marketing consulting firm. During her business career, she had the opportunity to observe the consequences of beliefs about gender and communication in the workplace. She is currently studying the socialization influences of the media, in particular the effects of food advertising on children's eating behaviors and preferences.

SÍLVIA H. KOLLER received her Ph.D. from the Pontifícia Universidade Católica do Rio Grande do Sul, Brazil, in 1994. Currently, she is a professor in the Psychology Department at the Federal University of Rio Grande do Sul in Pôrto Alegre. Her research focuses primarily on developmental applied psychology, especially positive psychology; street children; and resilience, vulnerability, and prosocial moral development. She chairs the Center for Psychological Studies on Street Children in Pôrto Alegre, and was president of the Brazilian Society of Developmental Psychology. She is editor in chief of the *Interamerican Journal of Psychology,* and was editor of the *Brazilian Journal of Psychology: Reflection and Criticism* and associate editor of *Child Development Abstracts and Bibliography.* She is a member of the SRCD International Affairs Council, an ad hoc representative of Latin America at the Executive Committee of ISSBD, and a member of the Scientific Committee of the ISSBD Biennial Meeting (Belgium).

MARIANNE LAFRANCE is professor of psychology and professor of women's and gender studies at Yale University. Her research centers primarily on questions of how gender and power are signaled and reinforced by subtle verbal and nonverbal cues.

PAULA LUNDBERG-LOVE is a professor of psychology at the University of Texas, Tyler. Her undergraduate degree was in chemistry, and her doctorate was in experimental psychology with an emphasis in physiological psychology. After a three-year postdoctoral fellowship in nutrition and behavior in the Department of Preventive Medicine at Washington University School of Medicine in St. Louis, she assumed her academic position at the University of Texas, Tyler, where she teaches classes in psychopharmacology, neuropharmacology, physiological psychology, sexual victimization, and family violence. Subsequent to her academic appointment, Dr. Lundberg-Love pursued postgraduate clinical training and is a licensed professional counselor. She is a member of Tyler Counseling and Assessment Center, where she provides therapeutic services for victims of sexual assault, child sexual abuse, and domestic violence. She has conducted a long-term research study on women who were victims of childhood incestuous abuse, constructed a therapeutic program for their recovery, and documented its impact upon their recovery. She is the author of many presentations and publications, and is co-editor of a book on sexual victimization. As a result of her training in psychopharmacology and child maltreatment, her expertise has been sought as a consultant in various death penalty appellate cases in the state of Texas. She is the current holder of the Ben R. Fisch endowed professorship for humanitarian affairs.

SHELLY MARMION is an associate professor of psychology at the University of Texas, Tyler. After earning a doctorate in experimental psychology from Texas Tech University, she taught for several years at Mississippi State University, where she helped to develop both the Gerontology Council and the women's studies program, while teaching psychology and working as a senior researcher at the MSU Social Science Research Center and the MSU Rehabilitation Research and Training Center for the Blind and Visually Impaired. She currently teaches classes in sex roles, client diversity, cognition, and statistics. The recipient of teaching awards, she has served as a statistics and design consultant for several government agencies and nonprofit organizations, and is the author of many presentations and publications on a variety of topics.

MAUREEN C. MCHUGH is a social psychologist and a gender specialist. A professor of psychology at Indiana University of Pennsylvania, she has been teaching psychology of women since 1975. She served as coordinator for the Association for Women in Psychology (AWP) from 2000 to 2003. For her contributions to feminist psychology she received the Christine Ladd Franklin Award of the AWP. She has presented and published in the areas of feminist research, sex differences, and violence against women. Her scholarship is included in many psychology of women anthologies and in a special issue of *Sex Roles* on sex role attitude measures that she edited with Irene Frieze, which received a Distinguished Publication Award. She is currently working with Irene Frieze on a collection of papers on female use of violence in intimate relationships, and with Lisa Cosgrove on a text on feminist methods.

ABIGAIL A. MITCHELL is a graduate student in social psychology at Northwestern University who is working with Alice Eagly. She received an M.S. from Northwestern University and a B.A. from Kenyon College. Her research interests include the psychology of gender and, more specifically, people's attitudes toward the feminist movement.

MAUREEN NALLY is a doctoral student in clinical psychology at Fairleigh Dickinson University. She received her B.A. degree from Fairleigh Dickinson University.

MARTHA NARVAZ received her master's degree from the University of São Paulo, Brazil, in 2000. She is currently specializing in family therapy at the Federal University of Rio Grande do Sul in Pôrto Alegre. Her research focuses primarily on gender issues, especially child sexual abuse and violence against women. She is an active member of feminist and children's rights movements in Brazil.

RUDY NYDEGGER received a B.A. and M.A. in psychology from Wichita State University, and his Ph.D. in clinical psychology from Washington University in St. Louis. Dr. Nydegger did an internship in clinical psychology at Cochran VA Hospital in St. Louis, and held a postdoctoral fellowship in child and adolescent clinical psychology at Baylor College of Medicine and a fellowship in gerontology from NIH. He has been on the faculties of Rice University and Baylor Medical School. Currently, Dr. Nydegger is a professor of psychology at Union College and a professor of management at the School of Management in the Graduate College of Union University. He is past president of the New York State Psychological Association, and currently chief of psychology at Ellis Hospital. In addition to his teaching and research, Dr. Nydegger has a clinical practice and does organizational consulting. He is married, has five children, and enjoys sports and outdoor activities with his family.

CARMEN A. PALUDI, JR., has been a senior scientific adviser for the El-dyne Division of the Titan Corporation. He holds advanced degrees in electrical, electronics, and computer engineering from Clarkson University and Syracuse University. He also has conducted postgraduate studies at the University of Massachusetts and Kennedy Western University. He has held positions in government, industry, academia, and private consulting, including senior engineer at the Air Force Laboratory in Rome, New York; senior principal engineer at Sanders Associates; member of the technical staff at the MITRE Corporation; senior communications engineer with Maden Tech Consulting; chief scientist of Integrated Device Sciences; adjunct faculty member at New Hampshire Technical College; and instructor at the Advanced Electronics Technology Center, University of Massachusetts. In addition to his technical expertise, Mr. Paludi brings nearly twenty-six years of technical and program management experience to human resource management and its related fields. He provides guidance and direction on risk management and on out-of-the-box thought processes for complex systems and scenarios so that developed policies and procedures can be executed. He has been the motivating force behind integrating technology into the development of Web-based training services that Michele Paludi and Associates provide. Mr. Paludi is the author of more than twenty technical journal articles, and of numerous presentations to national and international conferences, panels, and technical meetings.

MICHELE A. PALUDI is the author/editor of twenty-one college textbooks, and more than 130 scholarly articles and conference presentations on psychology of women, gender, and sexual harassment and victimization. Her book *Ivory Power: Sexual Harassment on Campus* (1990) received the 1992 Myers Center Award for Outstanding Book on Human Rights in the United States. Dr. Paludi served as chair of the U.S. Department of Education's Subpanel on the Prevention of Violence, Sexual Harassment, and Alcohol and Other Drug Problems in Higher Education. She was one of six scholars in the United States to be selected for this subpanel. She also was a consultant to and a member of Governor Mario Cuomo's Task Force on Sexual Harassment. Dr. Paludi serves as an expert witness for court proceedings and administrative hearings on sexual harassment. She has had extensive experience in conducting training programs and investigations of sexual harassment and other equal employment opportunity issues for businesses and educational institutions. In addition, Dr. Paludi has held faculty positions at Franklin & Marshall College, Kent State University, Hunter College, and Union College.

LISA R. RUBIN is a doctoral candidate in clinical psychology at Arizona State University. She is currently completing her clinical internship at the Payne Whitney Clinic of the New York-Presbyterian Hospital-Weill Cornell Medical Center in New York City. Her research and clinical interests are in culture and women's health, with particular emphases on eating disorders, body image, and reproductive health concerns, as well as feminist identity development and qualitative research methods.

NANCY FELIPE RUSSO is Regents professor of psychology and women's studies at Arizona State University (ASU). Before joining ASU, she was founder and director of the American Psychological Association's (APA) Women's Programs Office, where she served as staff liaison to the APA's Committee on Women in Psychology. A past president of the Society for the Psychology of Women and former editor of the *Psychology of Women Quarterly,* Prof. Russo is author or editor of more than 200 publications related to the psychology of women and women's issues. She has been recognized by the APA's Board of Ethnic Minority Affairs for contributions to ethnic minority issues, and was the recipient of the APA's 1995 Award for Distinguished Contributions to Psychology in the Public Interest. In 2003 she received the Distinguished International Psychologist Award of the APA's Division of International Psychology.

JANET SIGAL is a professor of psychology at Fairleigh Dickinson University. She received her Ph.D. in social psychology from Northwestern University. She has published articles and has given numerous conference presentations related to gender issues, including studies on sexual harassment, sexual abuse, and battered women. Dr. Sigal has conducted research on sexual harassment in nine countries.

CHRISTINE A. SMITH received her Ph.D. in social psychology, with a concentration in women's studies, from the University of Pittsburgh. She is an assistant professor of psychology at Antioch College in Yellow Springs, Ohio, where she teaches courses on the psychology of women, as well as courses addressing race and social class. Her current research interests include feminist identity, fat stigma, and self-presentation in personal advertisements.

ETHEL TOBACH received her doctorate in comparative and physiological psychology from New York University in 1957. Her research in comparative psychology at the American Museum of Natural History has focused on emotional/social behavior in various species (sea cucumbers, sea hares, mealworms, fish, several rodent species, and orangutans). She was a founding member of the Association for Women in Psychology and of Division 35 of the American Psychological Association. She was the founding co-editor of the Genes and Gender series devoted to exposing the social damage caused by genetic determinism as evidenced in racism and sexism. She received the Kurt Lewin Award from the Society for the Psychological Study of Social Issues (see *Journal of Social Issues,* 1994) and the American Psychological Foundation's Gold Medal Award for Life Achievement in Psychology in the Public Interest. She is the president of the Society for the Study of Peace, Conflict, and Violence (Division 48 of the American Psychological Association).